THE FRAMEWORK FOR SUCCESS IN POSTSECONDARY WRITING

Writing Program Administration
Series Editors: Susan H. McLeod and Margot Soven

The Writing Program Administration series provides a venue for scholarly monographs and projects that are research- or theory-based and that provide insights into important issues in the field. We encourage submissions that examine the work of writing program administration, broadly defined (e.g., not just administration of first-year composition programs). Possible topics include but are not limited to 1) historical studies of writing program administration or administrators (archival work is particularly encouraged); 2) studies evaluating the relevance of theories developed in other fields (e.g., management, sustainability, organizational theory); 3) studies of particular personnel issues (e.g., unionization, use of adjunct faculty); 4) research on developing and articulating curricula; 5) studies of assessment and accountability issues for WPAs; and 6) examinations of the politics of writing program administration work at the community college.

Books in the Series

The Framework for Success in Postsecondary Writing: Scholarship and Applications edited by Nicholas N. Behm, Sherry Rankins-Robertson, and Duane Roen (2017)

Labored: The State(ment) and Future of Work in Composition edited by Randall McClure, Dayna V. Goldstein, and Michael A. Pemberton (2017)

A Critical Look at Institutional Mission: A Guide for Writing Program Administrators edited by Joseph Janangelo (2016)

A Rhetoric for Writing Program Administrators edited by Rita Malenczyk, 2nd ed. (2016). First ed., 2013.

Ecologies of Writing Programs: Program Profiles in Context edited by Mary Jo Reiff, Anis Bawarshi, Michelle Ballif, & Christian Weisser (2015)

Writing Program Administration and the Community College by Heather Ostman (2013)

The WPA Outcomes Statement—A Decade Later, edited by Nicholas N. Behm, Gregory R. Glau, Deborah H. Holdstein, Duane Roen, & Edward M. White (2012). *Winner of the CWPA Best Book Award*

Writing Program Administration at Small Liberal Arts Colleges by Jill M. Gladstein and Dara Rossman Regaignon (2012)

GenAdmin: Theorizing WPA Identities in the 21st Century by Colin Charlton, Jonikka Charlton, Tarez Samra Graban, Kathleen J. Ryan, and Amy Ferdinandt Stolley (2012). *Winner of the CWPA Best Book Award*

THE FRAMEWORK FOR SUCCESS IN POSTSECONDARY WRITING

SCHOLARSHIP AND APPLICATIONS

Edited by Nicholas N. Behm,
Sherry Rankins-Robertson, and Duane Roen

Parlor Press
Anderson, South Carolina
www.parlorpress.com

Parlor Press LLC, Anderson, South Carolina, USA
© 2017 by Parlor Press
All rights reserved.
Printed in the United States of America on acid-free paper.

S A N: 2 5 4 - 8 8 7 9

Library of Congress Cataloging-in-Publication Data on File

1 2 3 4 5

978-1-60235-929-1 (paperback); 978-1-60235-930-7 (hardcover); 978-1-60235-931-4 (PDF); 978-1-60235-932-1 (ePub); 978-1-60235-933-8 (iBook); 978-1-60235-934-5 (Kindle)

Writing Program Administration
Series Editors: Susan H. McLeod and Margot Soven

Cover image: "Vulcan's Delight" ©2017 by Gregory Glau. Used by permission.
Copyeditor: Jared Jameson.
Cover design: David Blakesley

Parlor Press, LLC is an independent publisher of scholarly and trade titles in print and multimedia formats. This book is available in paper, cloth and eBook formats from Parlor Press on the World Wide Web at http://www.parlorpress.com or through online and brick-and-mortar bookstores. For submission information or to find out about Parlor Press publications, write to Parlor Press, 3015 Brackenberry Drive, Anderson, South Carolina, 29621, or email editor@parlorpress.com.

Contents

ACKNOWLEDGMENTS *vii*
FOREWORD: THEN AND NOW, REFLECTIONS ON
   THE *FRAMEWORK* SIX YEARS OUT *ix*
      Peggy O'Neill, Linda Adler-Kassner, Cathy Fleischer,
      and Anne-Marie Hall

INTRODUCTION *xxi*
      Nicholas Behm, Sherry Rankins-Robertson, and Duane Roen

Scholarship

1 FRAMING THE *FRAMEWORK* 3
      Kristine Johnson

2 FIGURING PROGRAMMATIC AGENCY: THE *FRAMEWORK*
AS CRITICAL REARTICULATORY PRACTICE IN
WRITING PROGRAM ADMINISTRATION 21
      Amy C. Kimme Hea, Jenna Pack Sheffield, and Kenneth C. Walker

3 A PLACE FOR READING IN THE *FRAMEWORK FOR SUCCESS
IN POSTSECONDARY WRITING*: RECONTEXTUALIZING
THE HABITS OF MIND 38
      Ellen C. Carillo

4 ENHANCING THE *FRAMEWORK FOR SUCCESS*: ADDING
EXPERIENCES IN CRITICAL READING 54
      Alice S. Horning

5 STEPS TO COLLEGIATE SUCCESS IN SECOND
LANGUAGE WRITING 69
      Andrea Feldman

6 A WRITING PROGRAM'S TEACHERS SPEAK: METACOGNITION AND
THE *FRAMEWORK FOR SUCCESS IN POSTSECONDARY WRITING* 85
      Dawn S. Opel

7 MESSY BUT MEANINGFUL: USING THE HABITS OF MIND TO
UNDERSTAND EXTRACURRICULAR LEARNING 102
      Faith Kurtyka

8 EXPERIENCE, VALUES, AND HABITUS: TWELFTH GRADERS
AND THE *FRAMEWORK*'S HABITS OF MIND 118
      Rebecca Powell

Applications

9 The *Framework for Success* as Rhetorical Common Denominator 136
  Peter H. Khost

10 The *Framework for Success* Goes Online: Integration of the *Framework* into Online Writing Courses 154
  Beth Brunk-Chavez

11 Using the *Framework* to Develop a Common Core State Standards-Aligned Curriculum for First-Year Composition 169
  Lauren S. Ingraham

12 Applications of the *Framework for Success in Postsecondary Writing* at the University of Mississippi: Shaping the Praxis of Writing Instruction 187
  Alice Johnston Myatt and Ellen Shelton

13 Metacognitive Persistence and Cultural Knowledge: Application of the *Framework* with Preservice Teachers for Writing Instruction in Secondary Schools 204
  Rodrigo Joseph Rodríguez

14 Using the Eight Habits of Mind to Foster Critical Sustained Reflections: Active Teaching and Learning 222
  Angela Clark-Oates

15 A *Framework*-Based "No-Text/Two-Text" Honors Composition Course 237
  Martha A. Townsend

16 Bridging High School and College Writing: Using the *Framework* to Shape Basic Writing Curricula 257
  Lori Ostergaard, Dana Driscoll, Cathy Rorai, and Amanda Laudig

Afterword 283
  Andrea A. Lunsford
Contributors 285
Index 293

Acknowledgments

The editors would like to thank David Blakesley for supporting this collection. As always, it has been a pleasure to work with David and the other amazing people who make Parlor Press an invaluable publisher within the discipline of rhetoric and composition. The editors are also very grateful for the contributors, who invested considerable time and effort in sharing their research and experiences with us and the discipline as part of this volume. We greatly appreciate their patience with us and with the process of shepherding this project to completion. Lastly, this volume would not have been possible if not for the diligent work of those who collaborated to bring the *Framework for Success in Postsecondary Writing* into being. We especially thank Peggy O'Neill, Linda Adler-Kassner, Cathy Fleischer, and Anne-Marie Hall for drafting the *Framework* and for writing the Foreword to this volume. We also thank Andrea Lunsford for graciously writing an Afterword to this volume.

Nicholas Behm expresses appreciation to Sherry and Duane for their hard work, collegiality, and friendship. Nick also wishes to thank his wonderful colleagues at Elmhurst College for their encouragement and humor during these dreadful times of austerity. Most importantly, Nick wishes to express his deep and enduring appreciation for his family: Angie, Mason, Addison, and Ethan, whose love and support make all things possible.

Sherry Rankins-Robertson is grateful for the love and support of her family, particularly Neely and Madeline for their constant encouragement. Sherry is thankful for her colleagues at University of Arkansas at Little Rock. Nick Behm has been a trusted colleague for more than a decade, and Sherry is fortunate to call him her friend. Through the mentorship of Duane Roen, Sherry was introduced to the *Framework for Success*. Duane has championed her through difficult years of administration and the not-so-difficult dairy queries. Sherry holds deep gratitude to her academic family, who continues to provide support and growth at work and in life.

Duane Roen thanks Nick and Sherry for their commitment to this project. Duane also thanks his colleagues at Arizona State University, who work so diligently to serve students. He further thanks the thousands of students and their families who have patiently listened to him talk about habits of mind at dozens of orientation sessions and commencement ceremonies. Above all, Duane thanks his family—Maureen, Nick, Hanna, Brendan, Nicole, Ryan, Keevin, and Liam—for putting life into perspective. He especially thanks his father, Harley, for many decades of support.

Foreword: Then and Now, Reflections on the Framework Six Years Out

Peggy O'Neill, Linda Adler-Kassner, Cathy Fleischer, and Anne-Marie Hall

Reflecting on the enormous reach of the idea of "community of practice" in a 2010 essay, Etienne Wenger writes that he and his colleague Jean Lave "could not have predicted the career the concept would have" ("Communities" 187). While we certainly would never claim that the *Framework* has had the reach of an idea as important as "communities of practice," when the four of us gathered in a windowless conference room at the Sheraton Hotel in Philadelphia just prior to the 2010 Council of Writing Program Administrators (CWPA) annual conference, we never imagined that the document that we compiled—one based on the work of twenty-two members on three separate task forces, each associated with one of the sponsoring organizations and reviewed by hundreds of K–12 and two- and four-year college teachers—would take on the life that it has. At that time, we were focused on a job that we (and the members of the task forces) perceived as associated with what was, as Kristine Johnson and Peter Khost note separately in their chapters in this volume, a very specific exigency, the creation of the then not-yet-finalized Common Core State Standards (CCSS).

The year before, a group of us—which is to say college-level writing instructors, English educators, and high school teachers, all with strong affinity for and to the National Council of Teachers of English (NCTE), the Conference on College Composition and Communication (CCCC), and/or the National Writing Project (NWP)—recognized that, as the now NWP director Elyse Eidman-Aadahl put it in a hallway conversation at CCCC, "If they're going to insist on college readiness, we'd better be the ones defining what that means." Working very quickly, between that year's meeting of the Conference on College Composition and Communication in March and that gathering in the conference room in a steamy Philadelphia July, each group's task force looked, first separately and then together, at the issue of what students needed in order to be truly prepared for success in college-level writing courses. We reached out to hundreds of members within our respective groups by circulating surveys and initiating discussions with teachers. As we collaboratively and painstakingly reviewed that input, searching for themes and commonalities, we found agreement in terms of what we came to call "habits of mind" and the "writing, reading, and critical analysis experiences" necessary to foster those habits. We then created a draft document and began to circulate it among K–12 teachers and two- and four-year college faculty who provided extensive feedback on everything from language to framing. At the end of the process, we produced *The Framework for Success in Postsecondary Writing*, along with an extensive annotated bibliography and the beginning of a database of curricular examples (still located at wpacouncil.org/framework). This *Framework* reflected our desire to represent college readiness in writing in a way that was quite different from the CCSS: in our case, as an organic statement of principles and ideas from the educators closest to the heart of the matter, classroom teachers.

While the *Framework* was developed in response to a particular exigency, we also hoped that it would provide fodder for those seeking to disrupt a powerful narrative led by policymakers responsible for finalizing and implementing the Common Core. This narrative, reflected in documents from *A Nation at Risk* to *A Test of Leadership* (i.e., "The Spellings Report") and bundled into what has come to be known as the "college and career readiness agenda," says that schools are failing to prepare students for the twenty-first century because administrators and, especially, teachers are out of touch with what is required for success in the global economy. In the story of the Common Core, this narrative is coupled with one about the achievement gap between students—rich and poor, Caucasian and non-Caucasian, and district-to-district. To level the playing field for all students and ensure that all would be equally prepared for the rigors of twenty-first century study and work, states would sign on to implement the CCSS.

Another narrative about the CCSS reads quite differently and positions it and its resulting reforms as merely the latest in a long line of efforts to remake public education in the United States, often at the expense of teacher practice and/or expertise. In this narrative, what appear to be "common sense" changes in educational policies to some are seen by others—including teachers and teacher educators—as initiatives that dismiss teacher expertise, stifle creativity, and rely on simplistic representations of reading and writing. To bring this alternative narrative to the public, many educators and educational organizations responded to the CCSS in social media, news media, and in professional venues; the *Framework* is but one response from writing teachers. It was a strategic document intended to add research and heft to the debate, give voice to teachers as advocates for change, and remind others that the teaching and learning of writing and English Language Arts more broadly are activities situated within and across disciplines. By focusing on habits of mind rather than discrete outcomes, the *Framework* suggests that college and career readiness in writing depends on broader understandings of those activities. And because we positioned it as a border-crossing kind of document, based in ideas that came from educators at multiple levels, we hoped that it would lead to important conversations about ideas that are too often taken for granted, particularly what knowledge, competencies, and experiences are needed for success in college writing.

We were conscious, then, of positioning the *Framework* within and against the tide of purported reform represented by the CCSS. At the same time, we also wanted to align it with other proactive efforts to define the terms of successful writing instruction, especially at the postsecondary level. Among the most influential of these documents was the "WPA Outcomes Statement For First-Year Composition" (WPA OS). That document, too, was developed from the ground up by writing instructors talking together within their programs and across institutions. Over a period of years, their ideas were developed into a document, now revised three times, that has been adapted or adopted by hundreds of writing programs nationwide. Both the WPA OS and the *Framework* evoke Etienne Wenger-Trayner's ideas about "plug and play." "Social theories," he writes, "do not compete in terms of being true or false; they compete in terms of the usefulness of their perspective in enabling certain types of accounts about the human world: they are created for different purposes, from different perspectives, and . . . with different languages" ("The Practice" 108). For such theories to connect to one another, in the way that "plug and play" works with technologies, users must consider possible connections:

mutually enriching foci or perspectives; common "stance[s]" (or what we might consider shared principles and commitments); and/or "relationships" between the precisely defined language used across theories ("The Practice" 111). Wenger-Trayner's ideas help us to understand the development of ideas, principles, and/or stances—like the habits of mind or the description of instructional practices that can foster those habits in the *Framework*—as contributions to that "usefulness of . . . perspective."

In the years since the *Framework* and supporting materials were completed, we've heard praise and critique from K–12 and postsecondary teachers as they have moved the *Framework* from a collection of ideas into a living artifact. We have worked with teachers at conferences and workshops, in graduate classes, and in professional development sessions and have been encouraged by their responses to and uses for the *Framework*. We have also used it, and seen it used, as a basis for multiple professional development and outreach activities. In a three-day disciplinary literacies workshop, for instance, K–12 teachers and college faculty were invited to consider the habits of mind outlined in the *Framework* through their disciplinary lenses, picking one that spoke to their interests and understandings and working together to develop writing pedagogies that would move students from the secondary level to college. In the state of Maine, the *Framework* has been part of discussions among the state's department of education and college writing faculty for a number of years. As we write, the American Council of Research Libraries (ACRL) has invoked it as one component among many that will play a role in a workshop about information literacy standards. Each of these illustrates the ways in which the *Framework* seems to have become its own form of plug-and-play—serving as a starting point to consider principles and commitments, a way to connect ideas across sites of practice, and a structure for thinking about teaching and learning. Across these uses, just as Wenger-Trayner ("Communities") suggests the value of mutually enriching foci or perspectives of theories, we see the importance of these cross-level and cross-disciplinary conversations—expanded versions of the same discussions that were integral to the creation of and use of this document. The *Framework* also reminds us of that impulse to reform schools and classroom practices to create the future we want for our students.

As we have considered the chapters in this collection alongside discussions, workshops, and conference sessions, we see these uses within a sort of Venn diagram with four, intersecting themes, all of which are linked to the *Framework*'s plug-and-play functions (see below). Three were clearly considered in the *Framework*'s creation: *communication*—sharing of information within programs and across programs, disciplines, and institutions; *collaboration*—actively working to create something with others such as a new curriculum or course; and *advocacy*—suggesting and pushing for a certain view of writing, resources, or policies. The fourth theme is *research*—using it as the inspiration to design a study or in the analysis of results from a study. This last category was not consciously considered in drafting the *Framework*, yet it seems to be one of the most fruitful since it provides feedback for the other three—and perhaps, as with the WPA OS, for future interpretations, uses, and versions of the *Framework*. As with all taxonomies, we realize these categories leak and overlap, but they help us make connections across the collection, linking what the *Framework* identifies as its purposes (advocacy, communication, and collaboration) with the disciplinary-defining activity of research.

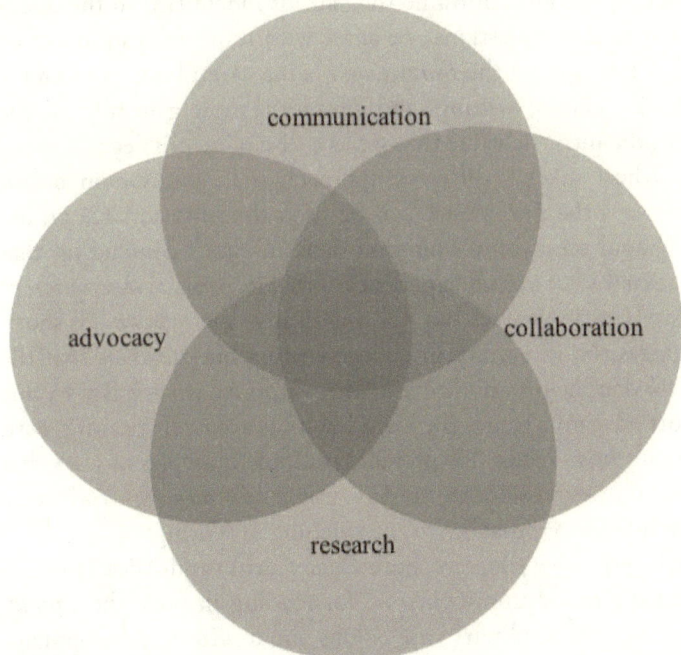

Figure 1. Venn Diagram Representing Uses of the *Framework*

Clearly, given the exigency for the *Framework*, we consciously identified advocacy (i.e., having a statement to use with others outside the field like administrators) as one of its key purposes. This purpose is clearly reflected in responses we have seen in secondary and college settings as well as in several of the contributions included in this collection. In the opening chapter, Kristine Johnson acknowledges ways the *Framework* functions as "evidence" in a range of conversations among teachers, administrators, policymakers, and employers. She then explores the language of the *Framework* via framing theory and encourages us to analyze both the language and the structure of the *Framework* to understand how it both accepts and reinforces a commercial frame, which aligns more readily with the CCSS, yet it also draws on the growth frame, which aligns with our disciplinary values. Johnson focuses on language such as "success" and "within college and beyond" as evidence of the commercial frame, yet she may be too eager to give up that language. We wonder: Can't success also be aligned with growth and intrinsic values? Does "beyond" necessarily link to commercial frames—what about civic, or personal "beyonds"? While Johnson's analysis is persuasive, perhaps part of the reframing is to see success within the growth frame that she also identified in the document. Despite these questions, we agree with Johnson's caution to be mindful of how we use the *Framework*, being careful not to reinforce the extrinsic value of writing (and education more generally) at the expense of the intrinsic value that we as a discipline privilege.

Peter Khost takes a different approach than Johnson in examining the ways the *Framework* can be used for advocacy. He argues that we should see it as a "common denominator," contending that the *Framework*'s habits and experiences provide a partial *description* of college-level writing values but not a definitive *prescription*. In short, he recognizes the variability in college-writing but also sees that the *Framework* does help to both mark with authority what it is we value and exhort educators to use the eight habits as a way of speaking with others about those values. He provides multiple examples of ways that he has—and by extension, we could—use the *Framework* to advocate for research-based approaches to the teaching of writing.

In their respective chapters, both Ellen Carillo and Alice Horning advocate for a more prominent role for reading in both the *Framework* and in our disciplinary discussions about writing development. Carillo emphasizes the research that links reading and writing as she demonstrates how reading can enhance the habits of mind. She reminds teachers in secondary and post-secondary institutions that student success in literacy demands focusing on more than just writing. Horning documents what some perceive to be problems students have in reading through reports and scholarship and calls for an additional section to the *Framework* that focuses on reading and its role in developing writing. These critiques, while not the kind of advocacy we originally imagined, illustrate the ways in which colleagues have added to the *Framework*'s foundation, providing important points of additional discussion as it circulates among writing studies teacher-researchers and beyond.

While we initially saw advocacy as aligned more with activism and communication with those outside of the field, the *Framework* was also intentionally constructed to facilitate discussions about literacy education and successful writing within and across four-year institutions, two-year schools, and secondary schools, much as we have seen in the kinds of work mentioned above: cross disciplinary discussions across grade levels and between organizations like the ACRL and subject areas. The value of collaboration in engaging everyone in a more active learning environment is supported by both research and practical experience. In our complex world, collective work promotes problem solving in college, career, and civic life.

Thus, the second key focus in many of these chapters is collaboration and communication: the *Framework* offers a way to talk about education in language that is relevant and hopeful and that brings diverse groups of people together, encouraging bridges both vertical and horizontal and spanning disciplines, grade levels, and contexts. Amy Kimme Hea, Jenna Pack Sheffield, and Kenneth Walker, for instance, describe how they have used the *Framework* as a starting point among faculty within and beyond the University of Arizona writing program to change a culture of "crisis-driven pragmatism" into a more theoretically informed "institutional praxis." They argue that the *Framework* makes writing's theories and ideologies explicit while enabling faculty to bring their own principles and purposes to it. They literally mapped the *Framework*, along with the WPA OS, onto the goals and student learning outcomes (SLOs) for their writing program, looking at where there were omissions or gaps among the three documents. This process enabled them to revise and strengthen their courses' goals and SLOs.

In the end, the *Framework* taught them to see significance between national conversations and everyday practices.

Others describe using the *Framework* to collaborate across institutions. For example, Lauren Ingraham worked with peers from other Tennessee institutions to align first-year composition curriculum with the CCSS for grades 11–12, thus building on what knowledge and skills high school students have if they are going to be considered, within the current terms of the discussion, "college and career ready." From collaborating on curricular guidelines and outcomes, they were charged with developing appropriate professional development opportunities for educators across the state so that they could learn to teach the new curriculum effectively. Alice Myatt and Ellen Shelton found the *Framework* useful in creating a common language for colleagues across an institution in talking about student success. Andrea Feldman brought the *Framework* to the world of English Language Learners and teachers, looking at habits of mind and experiences with literacy that are particularly useful for ELL. Angela Clark-Oates uses the *Framework* as a tool in helping teachers develop reflective and active teaching practices, noting that the habits of mind encourage inquiry and discovery by enlarging our teaching spaces. She fostered these eight habits of mind by embedding "well-defined opportunities" for the teachers to become more intentional in their writing, to claim agency for writing as an intellectual space within a collaborative classroom.

While the chapters in this collection include examples of how the *Framework* promotes communication and collaboration about the teaching of writing, many of them also focus on research: either by exploring the research-based approaches reflected in the *Framework* or by using the *Framework* as the basis of various kinds of research studies (traditional research, action-research, or teacher-research). Khost's chapter, which is primarily about advocacy, also argues that we can use documents such as the *Framework* to support our positions by adding evidence that is "replicable, aggregable, and data-supported" as Richard Haswell advocates (201). Khost notes that he is conducting empirical studies in postsecondary writing classrooms and secondary schools about student habits of mind.

Drawing on a study of two high schools in the Southwest, Rebecca Powell addresses a point raised in an earlier critique by Kristine Hansen, that the *Framework* prescribes actual ways of being in the world, a step beyond merely prescribing curriculum. This prescription, then, which attends to experiences and habits of mind, is also a description of successful students in postsecondary writing that in turn encourages production of that successful student. Her research provides a reminder about what we are up against—students strongly influenced by standards-based school systems, an increasingly digital world, and local contexts for writing that are more particular than general. Based on her research, she calls for a shift of emphasis in the *Framework* and how we use it—from a focus on individual students to the environments in which students circulate.

Like many of the teacher groups whose work we've noted above, contributors to this volume also use the *Framework* as a lens for understanding learning beyond the writing classroom. In her research study, Faith Kurtyka extends the habits of mind to the extracurricular, sororities in particular, showing how the *Framework* can both "name and interpret extracurricular learning experiences." In the process, she links extracurricular learning of students—typically the purview of student affairs professionals—to what composition scholars know and offers a vision of habits of mind that is deeper, broader, and socially interconnected in multiple contexts. Using the *Framework* as a guiding document, Rodrigo Joseph Rodríguez investigated how preservice teachers in a methods course reveal their deepest writing beliefs when they converse about habits of mind. Also revealed are their linguistic and cultural knowledges that will ultimately affect how they approach the teaching writing. Based on the six case studies he reports, Rodríguez concludes that teacher educators can use the *Framework* to build assignments and pedagogy that models habits of mind in ways that are culturally relevant, thus gaining what he calls rhetorical awareness for the twenty-first century. Both of these research studies not only help us to see the *Framework* in ways we had never imagined, but they also contribute information that can be useful in advocacy.

While Rodríguez used the *Framework* in his research focused on preservice teachers, Dawn Opel used it with writing program instructors. She describes using the *Framework* as a document to facilitate metacognitive analyses of the narratives of writing program teachers across disciplines, pedagogical models, and practices. Teachers in her study were trained with this document to identify particular habits of mind and experiences with writing, reading, and critical analysis that fostered the development of those particular habits. They could then choose to focus their energies in their own classrooms on these particular habits of mind. Naming and even mapping one's own classroom experiences helped teachers create classroom environments more personally suited to their own development as writers.

Other contributors focus more on the classroom and the curriculum, investigating how the *Framework* can be used in specific situations. Studying their basic writing curriculum through the lens of the *Framework*, Lori Ostergaard and her colleagues used it to reshape their basic writing program. Essentially they used the *Framework* as a roadmap, one that enacted positive change in the basic writing course by integrating habits of mind into the writing classroom and eventually improving student performance in more advanced composition classes. They also share the results of a rigorous assessment of the redesigned course and admit to the difficulty in assessing student achievement of the habits of mind. The point, in our view, is not to assess the students in terms of the habits of mind (see Khost, this volume) but rather to provide the opportunities for students to foster these habits so they can achieve the learning goals.

In their respective chapters, Beth Brunk-Chavez and Marty Townsend also consider curriculum design with the *Framework*: Brunk-Chavez links it to the needs of online writing students and teachers, and Townsend details a first-year composition course she designed and taught over several years that used the *Framework* as one of its primary texts.

Involved since the *Framework*'s inception, one of the greatest pleasures we saw was how quickly educators embraced it, especially the habits of mind described in the first part of the document. Surely this speaks to the strong social desire on the part of educators to find a way of talking about more than just standards or outcomes. This edited collection speaks to the vitality of the document and the desire to engage in these discussions. The positive feedback and uses of the *Framework* are exciting, but it is also important to consider the critiques, especially if the document is to remain useful and relevant as contexts shift and disciplinary knowledge grows. Jacqueline Rhodes and Jonathan Alexander call the *Framework* "laudable" in meeting the goals of a "citizenry preparing its children for a tough and uncertain economic future" (484). However, Rhodes and Alexander also suggest that what is missing is a "*critique* of that future." They call on all of us to develop an "imagination to envision alternatives" to that future (484). This edited collection, we believe, is a start in that direction.

Works Cited

Council of Writing Program Administrators. "WPA Outcomes Statement For First-Year Composition." CWPA, 2014. PDF File.

Council of Writing Program Administrators, National Council of Teachers of English, and National Writing Project. *Framework for Success in Postsecondary Writing.* CWPA, NCTE, and NWP, 2011. PDF File.

Hansen, Kristine. "The *Framework for Success in Postsecondary Writing*: Better than Competition, Still Not All We Need." *Symposium: On the Framework for Success in Postsecondary Writing.* Spec. issue of *College English* 74.6 (2012): 540–43. Print.

Haswell, Richard. "NCTE/CCCC's Recent War on Scholarship." *Written Communication* 22.2 (2005): 198–223. Print.

Rhodes, Jacqueline and Jonathan Alexander. "Reimagining the Social Turn: New Work from the Field." *College English* 76.6 (2014): 481–87. Print.

United States. Dept. of Education. *A Nation at Risk: The Imperative for Education Reform.* Washington, DC: US Department of Education, 1995. PDF file.

—. *A Test of Leadership: Charting the Future of U.S. Higher Education.* Washington, DC: US Department of Education, 2006. PDF file.

Wenger, Etienne. "Communities of Practice and Social Learning Systems: The Career of a Concept." *Social Learning Systems and Communities of Practice.* Ed. Chris Blackmore. London: The Open University, 2010. 179–98. Print.

Wenger-Traynor, Etienne. "The Practice of Theory: Confessions of a Social Learning Theorist. *Reframing Educational Research: Resisting the 'What Works' Agenda.* Ed. Valerie Farnsworth and Yvette Solomon. London: Routledge, 2013. 105–18. Print.

Introduction

Nicholas Behm, Sherry Rankins-Robertson, and Duane Roen

The seeds for this volume were planted the moment the Common Core State Standards Initiative (CCSSI) was launched in 2009. When the National Governors Association Center for Best Practices and the Council of Chief State School Officers began working on what would become the Common Core State Standards (CCSS), a wave of support grew for the program. There was a problem with the process, though. Although the "Myths vs. Facts" page on the CCSSI website indicates that the "myth" is that "[n]o teachers were involved in writing the standards" and that the "fact," according to the site, is that "[t]he Common Core drafting process relied on teachers and standards experts from across the country," the process did not involve professional organizations such as the National Council of Teachers of English (NCTE), the National Writing Project (NWP), the Conference on College Composition and Communication (CCCC), or the Council of Writing Program Administrators (CWPA)—even though several of these organizations requested to be engaged in the process. Because professional literacy organizations were largely ignored during the development of the Common Core, NCTE, CWPA, and the NWP formed a task force to determine possibilities for representing the experiences and perspectives of K–16 literacy educators (O'Neill et al.).

As Angela Clark-Oates, Sherry Rankins-Robertson, Erica Ivy, Nicholas Behm, and Duane Roen discuss in "Moving Beyond the Common Core to Develop Rhetorically Based and Contextually Sensitive Assessment Practices,"

> Initially, the authors of CCSS divided the standards into two categories: College and Career Readiness Anchor Standards

and K–12 Standards . . . the momentum for these standards was decades in the making, fostered by a public (and policy) narrative of failing schools and ill-prepared college freshmen. This narrative and its subsequent manifestations, historically, have had little influence over the postsecondary curriculum and assessment up until now, making this call to define college readiness from a K–12 vantage point and address K–16 alignment issues unique.

Clark-Oates et al. argue for a stronger relationship between national organizations and constituencies that govern K–12 programs, K–16 alignment, and curricular focuses for college and university expectations. The *Framework for Success in Postsecondary Writing* can help cultivate such relationships, informing the development of learning outcomes for college preparation programs, developmental education programs, and first-year experience or college seminar courses (specifically with the habits of mind); additionally, the *Framework* can be the guide for a teaching philosophy, for metacognitive writing, or for workshops on critical thinking. To bridge the educational gap, higher education administrators and faculty members must not only develop partnerships with high schools through exposure to documents like the *Framework*, but also colleges and universities must reconsider the sole need for students to be "college-ready" and begin thinking about how to become "student-ready." This is not an either/or issue, but more so an *and* issue where students must have exposure to college environments *and* expectations.

The *Framework* can be a compelling document for facilitating collaboration among secondary and postsecondary constituents particularly because the CCSS has been subjected to much skepticism and even rejection from people at both ends of the political spectrum. For example, the current Arizona Secretary of Education, Diane Douglas, a Tea Party Republican, ran for election in 2014 on a platform that included strong opposition to the CCSS. As reporter Karen Davis Barr noted, Douglas's campaign website included the following statement: "Why am I running for superintendent of public instruction? Quite simply, to stop the Common Core Standards in Arizona and return control over your children's education to you through your locally elected boards." Douglas did not oppose the CCSS on intellectual grounds; rather, she considered it a federal mandate, which of course it never has been.

We find ourselves in a kairotic moment, then, in which we can thrust the *Framework* directly into public discussion and advocate for it as a useful antidote to the CCSS (Purdy and McClure; Sullivan). In his contribution to the Symposium on the *Framework for Success in Postsecondary Writing*, Bruce McComiskey suggests that the *Framework* "will never" possess sufficient clout and authority to displace the CCSS (538). If the discipline positions the *Framework* as a document that competes against CCSS, he claims, "it will struggle to achieve its purpose" (538) of influencing policy conversations regarding career and college readiness and communicating the habits of mind and experiences with writing, reading, and critical analysis that students should cultivate prior to entering credit-bearing college-level writing courses. However, the socio-political tide is changing dramatically, possibly enabling the discipline to assert authority over writing instruction and to insert our expertise into policy conversations. It's our time to "reassert the importance of teachers' judgment in education," as Kristine Hansen notes (542).

One of our goals in assembling this collection is to do just that by illustrating the widespread applications of the *Framework*, especially the eight habits of mind, in helping students be successful not only in postsecondary writing courses but also in four arenas of life: academic, professional, civic, and personal. As Duane Roen, Gregory Glau, and Barry Maid suggest in *The McGraw-Hill Guide: Writing for College/Writing for Life*, postsecondary education, particularly first-year composition courses, need to prepare students to be successful in these four arenas of life because students usually complete their formal education relatively early in life, but they will write in the professional, civic, and personal arenas for many more decades.

To offer one example of how the *Framework* applies in settings outside of undergraduate education, we point to Nicholas Behm and Duane Roen's essay in which they illustrate how the habits of mind can help faculty become more productive writers. Another example of the *Framework*'s applicability is when Duane Roen discusses the eight habits of mind with incoming first-year college students and their families, welcoming them to his institution in the orientation sessions scheduled throughout the spring and summer before students register for fall classes. He explains each of the eight habits of mind, and describes how students can apply those habits to be more successful in college. For instance, he stresses how curiosity is vital for prompting students to ask why, how, and what questions about the world and their communities. He notes how students' postsecondary educational experience will require them to exercise openness when collaborating with classmates from different and distant locales and when engaging course material that will introduce them to new ways of seeing the world, solving problems, and accomplishing goals. He emphasizes how students must take responsibility for their success in college, in their careers, and in their personal lives, which includes being persistent when faced with challenges and engaging sincerely and vigorously with course materials and assignments. The habits of mind of creativity, flexibility, engagement, and metacognition are emphasized in extensive detail as well.

Recognition of the *Framework* has grown quickly—as evidenced by nearly 411,000 results in a May 2016 Google search on the document. Further, the *Framework* has influenced academic programs across the country. For example, in an August 2015 thread on the WPA Listserv, several faculty members noted how they and their colleagues use the habits of mind. For instance, Bradley Smith, a faculty member at Governors State University, noted, "Our bridge program also uses the Framework as part of its curriculum. Our program focuses most specifically on responsibility, flexibility, and metacognition." In that same thread, Stephanie Wade says, "We just started a new summer bridge program at Unity College. The director of this program, a teacher of science education, decided to use the Habits of Mind from the *Framework for Success in Post-Secondary Writing* as part of our curriculum. So far, students have selected several habits to practice over the four-week program." Will Hochman added, "My two cents in one run-on thought is that HOM (Habits of Mind) is the best part of the framework because the rest of the stuff is easy to point out, and the writers in each of our students need to learn about their own psychological make-ups to form the kind of relationship to the act of writing that can sustain their lives." Clearly, as the chapters in this volume demonstrate, the *Framework* is gaining traction across institutions, significantly influencing composition curricula and teaching practices, and providing a key alternative narrative of college and career readiness.

Overview of Collection

Responding to the attention that the *Framework* has enjoyed thus far, this volume consists of sixteen chapters that theorize, critique, and suggest ways in which programs can apply the *Framework* to improve teaching and learning. These chapters appear within two admittedly overlapping areas: scholarship and applications. The scholarship section begins with Kristine Johnson's concern that the *Framework* may offer an inconsistent framing of education. Johnson argues that on one hand the *Framework* speaks to and reinforces a commercial framing of education, one that conceptualizes an educational experience as a compilation of educational products that credentialize students as part of the process of career readiness. On the other hand, Johnson notes that the *Framework* also frames education as self-formation, a frame that privileges how students grow and develop as they learn; overcome challenges; and negotiate different languages, perspectives, and experiences. Johnson sees both of these frames at work in the *Framework*, and she admonishes readers that they must be aware of what frames they are invoking when advocating for writing programs and of the ways in which those frames may compromise programmatic and disciplinary values.

In "Figuring Programmatic Agency: The *Framework* as Critical Rearticulatory Practice in Writing Program Administration," Amy C. Kimme Hea, Jenna Pack Sheffield, and Kenneth C. Walker conceptualize the *Framework* as a discursively contested, theoretically layered document. Critically reflecting on their own institutional context at the University of Arizona and their use of dynamic criteria mapping, they apply articulation theory to argue that the *Framework* can be used strategically as a resource in rearticulating programmatic practices, like assessment, and documents, like mission statements, and in fostering a theoretically informed writing program administrator praxis that can facilitate significant programmatic and institutional changes.

In her chapter, Ellen Carillo emphasizes the interrelation of reading and writing, encouraging readers to consider the ways in which the *Framework*'s habits of mind could help students improve their reading and writing competencies. Faulting the *Framework* for insufficiently discussing how writing and reading are interconnected, Carillo urges the discipline to reconceptualize each of the habits of mind with a focus on reading. Doing so, she argues, would provide a richer, more comprehensive discussion of literacy development.

Similarly, Alice Horning gently critiques the *Framework* for what she sees as an impoverished discussion of the skills and habits of mind necessary to read effectively. This lack of attention to reading, Horning claims, not only deprives writing instructors of pedagogical practices that could help them improve their students' facility with reading but also downplays how reading and writing are interrelated. Horning agitates for an additional section to the *Framework* that would identify specific strategies for enhancing students' critical reading competency and information literacy, like writing twenty-five word summaries and synthesizing multiple sources through the rhetorical moves of comparing, contrasting, and critiquing source material. Revising the *Framework* to account for these suggestions would not only enhance the *Framework*'s discussion of critical reading, but also, Horning implies, provide a stronger support structure for the liberal education lauded by many experts in higher education.

In "Steps to Collegiate Success in Second-Language Writing," Andrea Feldman reports on a research study of how native speakers of English respond to and evaluate the writing of English language learners. Based on the results of this study, Feldman argues that the *Framework* serves as a positive resource for teaching English language learners, particularly in helping them cultivate and apply rhetorical knowledge and critical thinking.

In "A Writing Program's Teachers Speak: Metacognition and the *Framework for Success in Postsecondary Writing*," Dawn S. Opel presents her study of how integrating the *Framework*, particularly the habits of mind, in institutional training may affect how instructors who teach in a large university writing program may perceive the document's influence on their pedagogical practices and materials. Based on her interviews of TAs, part-time faculty, and full-time faculty, she argues that the *Framework* serves as a frame that writing instructors find useful in describing their praxis, articulating what they value in students' writing, and analyzing the experiences that they facilitate in their classes. Ultimately, she suggests that one of the *Framework*'s most significant contributions to the discipline, particularly if it plays an integral role in teacher training, may be how it can be applied to encourage critical reflection of teaching practices across institutional and programmatic settings.

Applying the habits of mind as an analytical framework and demonstrating how the *Framework* possesses relevance outside of writing courses, Faith Kurtyka, in "Messy But Meaningful: Using the Habits of Mind to Understand Extracurricular Learning," reports on her study of narratives of learning provided by social sorority alumnae. Based on this research, Kurtyka discusses how the habits of mind enrich extracurricular experiences, particularly in how they provide an interpretive frame with which sorority alumnae may construct meaning out of their learning experiences. In expanding the scope of the *Framework* and the habits of mind to include extracurricular learning experiences, Kurtyka challenges a common misperception of sorority life as unintellectual, which likely prevents those faculty who hold it from conceptualizing extracurricular activities as dynamic and complex learning experiences that play an integral role in students' intellectual and identity formation. For instance, Kurtyka insightfully shows how students who hold leadership positions in sororities frequently apply several habits of mind, like engagement, persistence, and responsibility, in rich and interesting ways.

In doing so, Kurtyka not only shows how we can apply the habits of mind to achieve a deeper conception of the social nature of learning, but also provides a bridge between the disciplines of rhetoric and composition and student affairs. The habits of mind, then, could serve as a generative tool for facilitating productive interdisciplinary collaboration.

Invoking the theoretical framework of Pierre Bourdieu and reporting on her study of two high schools in the Southwest, Rebecca Powell explores the tension between assumptions about students that may underlie the *Framework*'s habits of mind and actual students who enter writing classes embodying a habitus that has been molded by and reflects their negotiation of numerous social forces, including the fact that they have been socialized in an education system privileging standardized tests and in an era of heretofore unprecedented textual production. For Powell, the *Framework* describes the ideal student, one who has benefited from a supportive family structure, well-funded school system, and largely homogeneous community—the ideal habitus. She suggests, then, that the *Framework* focuses too narrowly on students, implying that individual students can cultivate habits of mind by simply applying diligence, dedication, and discipline. She argues the *Framework* neglects to consider the larger socio-historical circumstances that significantly affect students' literacy development and educational experiences. Ultimately, Powell argues that the

Framework must go beyond a simple itemization of the habits of mind to describe specific ways in which families, schools, and communities can develop enriching writing experiences and cultivate the habits of mind collectively.

The second section of the collection offers chapters that delineate practical applications of the *Framework*, showing how instructors and programs have applied the document, particularly the habits of mind, to improve teaching and learning. For instance, in "The *Framework for Success* as Rhetorical Common Denominator," Peter H. Khost suggests rhetoric and composition must reach consensus regarding a policy on and definition of college readiness, and he proposes the discipline rally around the *Framework*, positioning it as a rhetorical common denominator that WPAs and writing instructors can invoke to make composition pedagogy and theory visible to various stakeholders. Underlying Khost's advocacy of the *Framework* is the implication that WPAs and rhetoric and composition scholars have been largely unsuccessful in intervening in public policy debates regarding college readiness. Persuading politicians that the work of the discipline is meaningful and agitating for the discipline's authority to determine what it means to be prepared for writing and other literate practices in higher education and beyond requires that we engage public audiences concertedly and in as many venues as possible. As a shared point of reference, the *Framework*, Khost suggests, can provide a foundation for such advocacy, and he provides specific suggestions for how WPAs and writing instructors can promote the *Framework* in discussions and forums of public policy regarding college readiness.

Beth Brunk-Chavez, in "The *Framework for Success* Goes Online: Integration of the *Framework* into Online Writing Courses," discusses how she integrated the habits of mind into online courses to improve the persistence of online students, a topic of particular relevance given that many students now take at least a few classes online during their postsecondary educational experience. The chapter provides practical strategies that instructors can implement to help online learners cultivate each habit of mind. Integrating the *Framework* into online writing courses and implementing these strategies, as Brunk-Chavez stresses, can facilitate rewarding learning experiences for students.

Discussing her application of the *Framework* in "Using the *Framework* to Develop a Common Core State Standards-Aligned Curriculum for First-Year Composition," Lauren S. Ingraham narrates a fascinating negotiation of politics and competing interests as she was charged to design curriculum for first-year composition that articulated with Tennessee's Common Core State Standards curriculum for grades 11–12. Cognizant of the risks and challenges concomitant with such an endeavor, Ingraham frames this curriculum work not only as a positive opportunity to collaborate with educators from across Tennessee but also to promote the *Framework* as representing the scholarship and best practices of rhetoric and composition, furtively working to contest the supremacy of CCSS in her state and gently correcting colleagues' modes-driven approach to the teaching of writing. The chapter provides a detailed example of embedding the *Framework* and its habits of mind into curriculum for first-year composition.

Similarly demonstrating how the *Framework* can be used to cultivate consensus and potentially conciliate competing interests, Alice Johnston Myatt and Ellen Shelton discuss how they applied the *Framework* to improve teaching and learning at the University of Mississippi, using it to inform the institution's quality enhancement plan and to initiate an annual writing symposia. They argue that one of the *Framework*'s greatest strengths is its applicability to writing courses and professional development opportunities and how it can serve as a common language to facilitate collaboration among colleagues within a writing program and across an institution.

In "Metacognitive Persistence and Cultural Knowledge: Application of the *Framework* with Preservice Teachers for Writing Instruction," Rodrigo Joseph Rodríguez discusses his case-study of six preservice teachers as they completed his teacher preparation course at the University of Texas-El Paso. He makes connections between the *Framework* and preservice teachers' thoughts about writing and writing pedagogy, and he suggests that the habits of mind can help preservice teachers cultivate a culturally responsive teaching practice.

In "Using the Eight Habits of Mind to Foster Systematic Reflections: Active Teaching and Learning," Angela Clark-Oates outlines the importance of cultivating the practice of critical sustained reflection, and she positions the habits of mind within the *Framework* as a heuristic for facilitating critical reflection. She notes that though the *Framework* was developed to support student learning, it can also be applied to enrich practices of faculty development, particularly practices that relate directly to improving teaching and learning.

Applying the *Framework* to enrich her own teaching practices for an honors first-year composition course, Martha A. Townsend, in "A *Framework*-based 'No-Text/Two-Text' Honors Composition Course," shares how she uses the *Framework* in combination with a nonfiction text to help her honors students achieve the outcomes outlined in the "WPA Outcomes Statement For First-Year Composition" (WPA OS). Elaborating on both quantitative and qualitative data culled from her courses over five years, Townsend narrates how she came to devise the "No-Text/Two-Text" approach to facilitating honors first-year composition, details how she integrates the *Framework* into the course, and describes how she nudges students to engage it as a text. She also reflects on the challenges and potential positive outcomes of this approach.

Similarly, Lori Ostergaard, Dana Driscoll, Cathy Rorai, and Amanda Laudig share how they applied the *Framework* to redesign the curriculum for basic writing at Oakland University to emphasize the habits of mind, rhetorical knowledge, critical thinking, and writing processes. While narrating the process of that redesign and describing positive outcomes, they also reflect on the challenges and potential pitfalls of attempting to assess how effectively students cultivate and exercise the habits of mind. They conclude by noting that the *Framework* can significantly enrich basic writing curricula, though they caution readers regarding the challenges of assessing the habits of mind.

Ultimately, the chapters within this volume evidence the *Framework* as a living disciplinary document that possesses wide applicability and utility across educational institutions and academic disciplines. These chapters attempt to both contribute to and advance the disciplinary conversation regarding the *Framework*, highlighting current lacunas in the document but also describing the ways in which the document, particularly the habits of mind, can be applied to improve student writing and teaching and learning within composition courses. Furthermore, we also encourage readers to use the *Framework* and the chapters within this collection to serve as public intellectuals, as discussed in "The Case for Academics as Public Intellectuals" (Behm, Rankins-Robertson, and Roen). When parents want to know how they can foster characteristics for life-skills and workplace success for college-readiness, talk to them about cultivating the habits of mind. Use the anecdotes and scholarship of this volume to provide examples to your university administration of how to build programs that bring college faculty into high schools and high school students onto college campuses for academic engagement. When authors in the general public write books or reports about the lack of critical thinking in students who graduate college, use this volume to argue for the mindset needed to be a critical thinker opposed to deferring to the hundreds of pages of curricular mandates imposed by legislators and assessed by consortia that default to the same kinds of tests that keep students out of higher education in the first place. We intend that this volume serves as an informative scholarly resource for current and future writing program administrators, writing teachers, AP teachers, high school administrators, and scholars within rhetoric and composition as they develop and shape curricula and programs. Just as important, though, we sincerely hope that the chapters within this volume motivate readers to counteract and complicate the reductive and problematic conceptualizations of writing that are privileged by politicians, testing companies, and uninformed administrators.

Works Cited

Barr, Karen Davis. "Diane Douglas: 'No Common Core'—But Not Saying Much More." *Raising Arizona Kids*. November 2014. Web. 1 August 2015.

Behm, Nicholas, and Duane Roen. "Applications: A Practical Guide for Employing Habits of Mind to Foster Effective Writing Practices." *Contingent Faculty Publishing in Community*. Ed. Letizia Guglielmo and Lynee Lewis Gaillet. New York: Palgrave, 2015. 117–33. Print.

Behm, Nicholas, Sherry Rankins-Robertson, and Duane Roen. "The Case for Academics as Public Intellectuals." *Academe* 100.1 (January–February 2014): 13–18. Print.

Clark-Oates, Angela, Sherry Rankins-Robertson, Erica Ivy, Nicholas Behm, and Duane Roen. "Moving Beyond the Common Core to Develop Rhetorically Based and Contextually Sensitive Assessment Practices." *The Journal of Writing Assessment* 8.1 (2015): n. pag. Web. 15 January 2016.

Common Core State Standards Initiative. Council of Chief State School Officers and the National Governors Association Center for Best Practices, 2009. Web. 1 August 2015.

Council of Writing Program Administrators. "WPA Outcomes Statement for First-Year Composition." CWPA, 2014. PDF File.

Council of Writing Program Administrators, National Council of Teachers of English, and National Writing Project. *Framework for Success in Postsecondary Writing*. CWPA, NCTE, and NWP, 2011. PDF File.

Hansen, Kristine. "The *Framework for Success in Postsecondary Writing*: Better than Competition, Still Not All We Need." *Symposium: On the Framework for Success in Postsecondary Writing*. Spec. of *College English* 74.6 (2012): 540–43. Print.

Hochman, Will. "Habits of Mind + Summer Bridge." WPA-L, 7 Aug 2015. Listerv Post.

McComiskey, Bruce. "Bridging the Divide: The (Puzzling) *Framework* and the Transition from K-12 to College Writing Instruction." *Symposium: On the Framework for Success in Postsecondary Writing*. Spec. issue of *College English* 74.6 (2012): 537–39. Print.

O'Neill, Peggy, Linda Adler-Kassner, Cathy Fleischer, and Anne-Marie Hall. "Creating the *Framework for Success in Postsecondary Writing*." Symposium: On the *Framework for Success in Postsecondary Writing*. Spec. of *College English* 74.6 (2012): 520–33. Print.

Purdy, James P., and Randall McClure, eds. *The Next Digital Scholar: A Fresh Approach to the Common Core State Standards in Research and Writing*. Medford, NJ: Information Today, 2014. Print.

Roen, Duane, Gregory Glau, and Barry Maid. *The McGraw-Hill Guide: Writing for College/Writing for Life*. 3rd ed. New York: McGraw-Hill, 2013. Print.

Smith, Bradley. "Habits of Mind + Summer Bridge." WPA-L, 7 Aug 2015. Listerv Post.

Sullivan, Patrick. *A New Writing Classroom: Listening, Motivation, and Habits of Mind*. Logan, UT: Utah State UP, 2014. Print.

Wade, Stephanie. "Habits of Mind + Summer Bridge." WPA-L, 6 Aug 2015. Listerv Post.

The Framework for Success in
Postsecondary Writing

1 Framing the *Framework*

Kristine Johnson

American educational policy has long addressed career and college readiness in some form, but today these themes are nearly synonymous with American educational policy. In 2010, states began to adopt the Common Core State Standards, which were introduced to parents and the public as rigorous, evidence-based standards aligned with the expectations of employers and post-secondary institutions. Focused on "college and career readiness," the standards aim to prepare "all students for success in our global economy and society" ("About the Standards"). Although the English Language Arts standards give writing a more prominent role than previous accountability movements such as No Child Left Behind, postsecondary writing teachers and scholars were largely not involved in developing them. Members of the *Framework* task force note that composition scholars may find "terms in these standards that are familiar—*purpose, audience,* and *context* are mentioned frequently—but the narrow band in which these concepts are to be developed does not reflect research-based current practices in postsecondary writing instruction" (O'Neill et al. 522). When the Council of Writing Program Administrators, the National Council of Teachers of English, and the National Writing Project published the *Framework for Success in Postsecondary Writing*, one of their aims was clear: to bring expertise from rhetoric and composition into exigent policy conversations about writing (520–22).

As this volume demonstrates, the *Framework* has been tremendously generative, prompting new curricula, assignments, and professional development activities. It has given our discipline fresh ways to promote aims such as curiosity and engagement, and it calls us to reinvigorate historical and liberal frames for teaching writing (Johnson 525–27). As

Peter Khost similarly claims in chapter 9 and as Peggy O'Neill, Linda Adler-Kassner, Cathy Fleischer, and Anne-Marie Hall reiterate in the Foreword to this volume, we must also recognize that the *Framework* was written to speak beyond our disciplinary community and to help writing teachers publicize what we believe about writing, teaching, and learning. My focus in this chapter is how the *Framework* functions as evidence in conversations with other teachers and administrators, policymakers, and employers. The document does not explicitly name its theoretical, political, and ideological allegiances, and I examine how it frames education in ways that reinforce or resist particular theories of education or political agendas. I argue that writing teachers and program administrators must be conscious not only of what educational frame they evoke when using the *Framework* but also of the implications of that frame. Our discipline faces significant challenges when we evoke multiple, opposing frames simultaneously—when we tell stories about writing and writers that we do not intend to tell.

Framing and Disciplinary Activism

The Common Core State Standards frame American education as the institution responsible for making students economically successful. According to the standards themselves and their promotional materials, students "gain" knowledge in school that they will trade for success in "entry-level careers, introductory academic college courses, and workforce training programs" ("About the Standards"). As nearly any discussion about the Common Core demonstrates, the economy functions in American educational discourse as a dominant conceptual frame—a powerful and unconscious way that language structures reality. Charles Fillmore, the linguist who established frame semantics, explains that framing goes beyond simple awareness of context; it recognizes that "people have in memory an inventory of schemata for structuring, classifying, and interpreting experiences" (25). In these schemata, words are connected to frames, such that hearing or reading one word "in an appropriate context activates . . . the particular frame—activation of that frame, by turn, enhancing access to the other linguistic material that is associated with the same frame" (25). Discussions about the Common Core, for example, often use the phrase *the global economy*, which activates a commercial frame, classifies education as an economic activity, and helps people access related words, such as *consumer* and *currency*.

Because conceptual frames are both powerful and pervasive, George Lakoff defines reframing as activism. Frames structure "what we perceive, how we get around in the world, and how we relate to other people" (*Metaphors* 3), and evoking an alternate frame can transform relationships and reality. In *Don't Think of an Elephant!*, Lakoff urges progressives not to use the same words as conservative pundits because any utterance evokes a frame: "When we negate a frame, we evoke the frame. . . . This gives us a basic principle of framing, for when you are arguing against the other side: Do not use their language. Their language picks out a frame—and it won't be the frame you want" (3). Lakoff argues that simply using words or phrases such as *tax relief* or *partial-birth abortion* effectively forfeits progressive arguments because these words activate the conservative frame. Speaking in new words that evoke new frames, however, represents a fruitful way to intervene in public discourse and engender political change.

Writing program administrators have recognized the activist potential of (re)framing. Linda Adler-Kassner and Peggy O'Neill encourage writing teachers and administrators to reframe writing assessment by speaking about writing in fresh language—specifically language not associated with accountability and standardization—that evokes our disciplinary values. They echo Lakoff and contend that negating the dominant accountability frame (such as saying that good writing cannot be measured) simply activates and reinforces that frame by using the language of measurement. In *The Activist WPA*, Adler-Kassner urges writing program administrators to tell stories that disrupt the dominant frame of "students can't write" (2). By telling from a wholly distinct frame about what students and teachers *can* do, writing program administrators empower themselves to do justice to students and the discipline. The *Framework* clearly has activist roots (O'Neill et al. 520–22), and it reframes writing as habits of mind and experiences rather than as standards. I am interested in how the *Framework* interacts with two prominent frames for American higher education: does it accept the frame, accept the frame by negating it, or evoke a new frame? It is my hope that answers to this question will guide our discipline as we use the *Framework* to justify, defend, and change practices at our own institutions and beyond.

Education as Industry

Many Americans understand education through a commercial frame, where each element of the educational experience—students and parents, institutions, standards, and degrees—has a clear commercial role. Institutions are businesses, and as businesses, they exist to provide consumers (students) with services (credentials that can be exchanged for success in the global economy). As consumers, prospective college students should consult the College Scorecard from the Department of Education, which provides information about "college affordability and value," among the most important considerations in a commercial frame (College Affordability). According to the commercial frame, students and parents are consumers of educational products rather than beneficiaries of a public good. Scholars describe the commercial conceptual frame in various ways, but two of its components are important in the context of the *Framework*: it operates under the logic of the free market and it assigns education exchange value.

First, the commercial frame operates under the logic of the free market, which dictates how institutions should function: educational institutions are businesses that sell services, compete for status and reputation, and function best without external regulation. In his work on writing assessment, Chris Gallagher associates market logic with neoliberalism, "the dominant ideological force . . . a form of cultural politics and a set of economic principles, policies, and practices devoted to handing over as much of social life as possible to private interests" (453). Neoliberals argue that, rather than being externally regulated, educational institutions should self-regulate through accountability and competition. In this way, accountability tools such as college scorecards ultimately function as the "lever that will force U.S. higher education to recognize itself for, and start behaving as, what it is: both a competitor in a global market and itself a market in which individual institutions compete" (Gallagher 455). Proving that their commodities are valuable—and also affordable—incentivizes institutions to perform better and produce more.

As institutions compete against one another in the free market, stratification emerges. Annual school rankings demonstrate how stratification is central to the way Americans understand education: property values escalate in school districts labeled blue ribbon, and colleges ranked in the *Princeton Review* use this designation to attract high-performing students. While many rankings are produced in ways our discipline finds problematic, particularly when standardized tests privilege certain groups or ways of knowing, others are based simply on reputation. Status-conscious differences exist among institutions at every level, and reputation for quality often carries more weight than valid, meaningful evidence of quality. Stratification further exists within institutions as students and programs are ranked and differentiated. David Labaree, a sociological historian of American education, contends that "consumers demand a stratified structure of opportunities within each institution, which offers each child the chance to become clearly distinguished from his or her fellow students" (29). Students at all levels are placed into ability-based tracks, ranked according to grades and test scores, and awarded differentiated diplomas (29). Stratified education may market itself as good for society as a whole, yet it is especially good for self-interested individuals.[1]

Stratification and competition coalesce to frame American education as a meritocracy. A meritocratic ideology "captures in idealized form the entrepreneurial traits and values rewarded by a capitalist economy and projects them onto social life in general . . . where success or failure is determined solely by individual merit" (Labaree 33). Competition among institutions and stratification within them offers students and parents the opportunity to distinguish themselves from one another—and to do so at the expense of one another because education is "an arena for zero-sum competition" (32). The same logic that drives entrepreneurs to distinguish themselves from the competition drives students and parents to use the educational system to get ahead or stay ahead. Although the idea that American education is a meritocracy initially appears to be democratic and even egalitarian, Labaree would argue that families from the upper-middle class have far more to gain and far less to lose than their less advantaged peers (33).

Second, the commercial frame assigns education exchange value, which defines the purpose of education. Free-market logic requires goods or services to be exchanged; in the commercial frame, colleges sell educational credentials, which become commodities with exchange value. Exchange value in the free market is based on an abstraction, where goods acquire value not for the actual things they do but for what they can buy. Labaree argues that the capitalist market "abstracts social products from their original context and particular function, reifies this abstraction by converting it to a general commodity, and makes it comparable to all other commodities by assigning it a monetary value" (45). He explains that educating for exchange value is analogous to farming for the market; while growing one lucrative crop cannot feed the community, it can be exchanged to buy food for the community (45). Arguments that emphasize success outside the educational experience frame education as a commodity, solidifying its exchange value and abstracting the value of education beyond student learning.

Education has both intrinsic and extrinsic ends, but the commercial frame focuses almost exclusively on extrinsic ends and then abstracts and commodifies them. Intrinsic ends including the pursuit of knowledge, preparation for citizenship, and personal development exist in American education, but they are secondary to one extrinsic end: a job that provides "financial security, social power, and cultural prestige" (Labaree 31). What happens during the educational process—the curriculum, the relationship between teachers and students, and the intellectual and personal development—is less significant than the end result because the credential is ultimately abstracted from the process.

A common complaint about American college students is that they are overly utilitarian, focused on degrees (the extrinsic) rather than learning (the intrinsic). In the last decade, *My Freshman Year* by Rebekah Nathan, *Our Underachieving Colleges* by Derek Bok, and other scholarly and journalistic pieces have presented college students as utilitarian and anti-intellectual. Labaree argues, however, that student intellectual disengagement suggests not a widespread attitude problem but the power of the commercial frame. Disengaged, utilitarian students behave exactly as the commercial frame requires: "By working the system in order to gain the greatest individual benefit from the smallest investment of time and effort, students are only behaving like savvy consumers, who naturally want to obtain the most valuable commodity at the cheapest price" (Labaree 253). The commercial frame may further encourage students to select professors who assign high grades (valuable commodities) for the smallest amount of effort (the cheapest price), consulting ratemyprofessor.com in the same way that homeowners research plumbers and electricians on crowd-sourced websites.

The *Framework for Success in Postsecondary Writing* entered an educational landscape dominated by the commercial frame, and it certainly interacts with the frame. In their article on the *Framework*, O'Neill et al. offer this perspective: "If the goal is to make certain that all students are prepared to succeed in college and career, then, at least in terms of writing, it's imperative that the Standards and the assessments promote the experiences and habits of mind outlined in the *Framework*" (524). O'Neill and other *Framework* authors raise an important question with implications for conceptual framing: if the goal of the Common Core is college and career readiness, then what is the goal of the *Framework*? Does the *Framework* promote college and career readiness by supplementing the Common Core, or does it promote something entirely different? Bruce McComiskey argues that the "*Framework* is too similar to the CCSS to make anyone (let alone state boards and system administrators) become wary of the CCSS. However, if the *Framework* is viewed as additional support for the CCSS . . . it should have some impact on secondary education and the preparation of high school students for the rigors of college writing" (538). Although McComiskey is concerned about the Common Core primarily because he anticipates inauthentic assessment, he suggests that the *Framework* may actually endorse the Common Core and its commercial perspective on education.

Analyzing the language and structure of the *Framework* reveals the ways in which it accepts and reinforces the commercial frame. The document first assigns writing extrinsic value before it addresses intrinsic value. In the opening sentences of the introduction, the *Framework* evokes the commercial frame before making any other claims about writing: "The ability to write well is basic to student success in college and beyond. Students can become better writers when they have multiple opportunities to write in classes across the curriculum throughout their education—from elementary school through university" (2). Writing ability exists for the purpose of success, and when readers encounter the next, research-based claim about how writers develop, the commercial frame has already been activated. Writing has already been defined as extrinsically and commercially valuable, a skill students will ultimately exchange for something greater. When the *Framework* appeals to "college and beyond" (4), it reinforces the idea that writing ability should be pursued for its value. Writing courses will produce success in more advanced college courses—at higher levels of educational stratification that correlate with higher levels of economic achievement—and in the global economy.

By relying on the word *success* at critical points, the *Framework* further reinforces the commercial frame and the extrinsic value of writing. *Success* appears in the title of the document, acting—at least in grammatical terms—as the object of the *Framework*: the action of the *Framework* is directed toward success. The word also appears seven times in the first three pages (often next to the words *crucial* or *necessary*), generating exigence for the document in the same way the Common Core

State Standards generate exigence by appealing to the competitive global economy. According to the *Framework*, writing courses and the habits of mind they foster are important because they enable success: habits of mind "will support students' success in a variety of fields and disciplines" (1), and "students who come to college writing with these habits of mind . . . will be well positioned to meet the writing challenges in the full spectrum of academic courses and later in their careers" (2). Focusing on success and assigning writing extrinsic value constructs a strong conceptual frame in which writing and education are commodities, abstracted from the educational experience and pursued for future exchange value.

Writing teachers and scholars may also interpret the *Framework* as resisting the commercial frame because it forwards habits of mind in addition to skills and outcomes. Habits of mind are "ways of approaching learning that are both intellectual and practical and that will support students' success in a variety of fields and disciplines" (*Framework* 1), and they evoke a conceptual frame focused on personal and intellectual development. Yet the *Framework* introduces habits of mind as ingredients for success. When habits of mind are first named, the commercial frame has already been activated by the words *success* and *career*, and readers may conceptualize habits of mind within that frame. According to commercial frame logic, writing is a commodity with exchange value, and habits of mind are another commodity that enables students to be even more successful. And when writing teachers and scholars claim habits of mind as the province of our work, we assign our discipline exchange value and promote a commodity we are uniquely qualified to offer.

Education as Formation

Americans may also view education through a growth frame, especially when they focus on the liberal arts and humanities. Concerns about student intellectual disengagement often originate in the growth frame, which understands college as "an aid to reflection, a place and process whereby young people take stock of their talents and passions and begin to sort out their lives in a way that is true to themselves and responsible to others" (Delbanco 15–16). According to the growth frame, education is formation for citizenship. Students enter school to question and debate; reflect and contemplate; develop virtues and values; and master areas of knowledge they will use in their personal, professional, and public lives. Institutions are communities where students undergo the formation process and develop particular values; faculty members are guides who initiate students into the academic community and the citizenry. The primary purpose of education is forming citizens, and although the skills and virtues developed in the formation process exist to be *used*, they do not exist to be exchanged.[2] In religious formation processes, for example, a period of study and reflection precedes initiation into the full life of the community and its work in the world; in the same way, the growth frame defines education as a process of personal and intellectual development that results in democratic participation. The growth frame may also be defined in various ways, but two of its components align with the *Framework* and distinguish it from the commercial frame: it focuses on intellectual formation and assigns education use value in democratic life.

First, according to the growth frame, education forms the intellect by placing students on a quest and grounding them in virtue. This quest may be collaborative, contemplative, and even contentious, but its purpose is always personal, moral, ethical, and intellectual. In *College: What It Is, Was, and Should Be*, Andrew Delbanco frames education as intellectual formation and writes almost exclusively from the growth frame. He argues that college students are primarily "looking for something to care about" (24) and seeking answers to the question of "just what it is that's worth wanting" (13). Answering this question is the end of education and the beginning of a fulfilling life. Anthony Kronman writes in *The End of Education* that contemporary liberal education is ornamental at best and absent at worst because colleges do not save students "from the debilitating frenzy [of credentialing] that precludes contemplation and deep thinking" (34). College should be "a time to survey, with as open a mind as one can manage, the horizons of the stirring and mysterious venture in which . . . every human being is fatefully engaged" (40). While the intellectual quest does not end at college graduation—indeed lifelong learning is highly valued—higher education is a critical first step.

Because institutions guide students on their intellectual quest and cultivate particular virtues, they hold moral authority. The issue of moral authority perhaps highlights the dominance of the commercial frame because scholars of American education agree that contemporary institutions no longer hold moral authority. Labaree argues that primary and secondary schools reward achievement and acceptable behavior more than civic virtue (43), and Richard Arum and Josipa Roksa note that higher education has turned away from its historical purpose of acting *in loco parentis* (127). Advocates of the growth frame believe that a return—in some form—to moral authority will reinvigorate higher education, saving it from morally absent credentialing. Kronman identifies respectfulness and tolerance as habits that colleges should cultivate, in part by "creating an environment in which students are required to interact with others quite unlike themselves—often for the first time in their lives—and to develop the attitudes of open-mindedness and toleration that this demands" (38). Institutions may not agree to promote specific biblical or Enlightenment values, Delbanco notes, but he suggests that college students are "not yet fully formed as social beings, and may still be deterred from sheer self-interest toward a life of enlarged sympathy and civic responsibility" (44). Labaree similarly proposes that education should foster "devotion to the political community and a willingness to subordinate private interests to the public interest" (43). These scholars privilege values such as toleration, openness, and public participation, highlighting one way in which the growth frame is ideologically more liberal than the commercial frame. The growth frame promotes precisely the values absent in the commercial frame; it hopes to form citizens rather than winners, learners rather than achievers.

Second, the growth frame assigns education use value. The formation process begins with an individual undertaking an intrinsically valuable intellectual quest, and those who defend the value of the liberal arts, for example, refuse to assign exchange value to this quest. But because the end of intellectual formation is democratic participation, education holds significant use value. Use value recognizes that the knowledge and virtues developed in the educational experience fulfill actual human needs; education does not need to be commodified and exchanged because it is already valuable for what it does. To return to the farming analogy from Labaree, intellectual formation for the purpose of citizenship is farming to feed the community because it produces something that directly serves the public good.

Student learning is critical in the growth frame because democracies require a wide range of "capacities and resources" for citizens to put into practice (Labaree 45). Colleges and universities often emphasize retention and persistence because the commercial frame encourages them to sell credentials, even if students learn very little (Arum and Roksa 135–36). The growth frame promotes student learning because vibrant democracies cannot be built on only exchange value. Arguing from the growth frame, Delbanco contends that colleges must be a place for "learning in the broad and deep meaning of the word" (24). He implicitly places rhetorical education at the core of democratic life, noting that "the best chance we have to maintain a functioning democracy is a citizenry that can tell the difference between demagoguery and responsible arguments" (29). Although the language of citizenship is almost entirely absent from the Common Core State Standards, the authors of *A Nation at Risk* argued in 1983 that education is "essential to a free, democratic society and to the fostering of a common culture" (National Commission). Just as promoting specific values is contentious and potentially exclusionary, it is problematic to prescribe a common culture: which philosophical, political, or literary tradition should prevail? How should cultural advancement be encouraged? These appeals to a common culture suggest that neoliberal thought also exists in the growth frame, but the frame nonetheless promotes intellectual, cultural, and societal engagement over private enterprise.

The *Framework for Success in Postsecondary Writing* forwards *education as formation* as an alternative to *education as industry*. Several elements of the growth frame are commonplace in rhetoric and composition, which is perhaps most evident in our disciplinary conviction that students learn to write by writing. A full analysis of the growth frame in rhetoric and composition is beyond the scope of this chapter; however, I will note that our scholarship promotes the idea that writing courses exist both for students to make sense of themselves and the world and for students to become critical, capable citizens, a point that Martha Townsend similarly stresses in chapter 15 of this volume. In his discussion of rhetoric, composition, and writing instruction, James Berlin clearly evokes the growth frame: "Writing courses prepare students for citizenship in a democracy, for assuming political responsibilities, whether as leaders or simply active participants. Writing courses also enable students to learn something about themselves, about the often-unstated assumption on which their lives are built" (189). Berlin argues that writing courses prepare students for the future, but he assigns writing use value rather than exchange value. Writing exists to be used, not only in political life but also as students learn about themselves and the world. Because the act of writing is itself useful and valuable, it does not need to acquire value by being abstracted and commodified.

When the *Framework* endorses authentic rhetorical situations and focuses on intellectual development, it resists the commercial frame and evokes the growth frame. The last paragraph of the introduction, a caution against current trends in American education, emphasizes both intellectual development and assigns writing use value:

> At its essence, the Framework suggests that writing activities and assignments should be designed with genuine audiences and purposes . . . in order to foster flexibility and rhetorical versatility. Standardized writing curricula or assessment instruments that emphasize formulaic writing for nonauthentic audiences will not reinforce the habits of mind and the experiences necessary for success as students encounter the writing demands of postsecondary education. (3)

Although this passage ends with another commercial appeal to success, the claim that writing assignments should be rhetorically authentic is warranted on use value. Authenticity is important not because it increases exchange value but because it fosters flexibility and versatility in the practice of writing itself. If students and citizens use writing to do things in the world, then it cannot be reduced to a formula or a standardized score. The *Framework* speaks from the growth frame when it argues for authenticity and versatility, publicizing use value and intellectual engagement against a commercial frame.

I have argued that the *Framework* establishes rhetorical exigence with the commercial frame, but its focus on habits of mind also evokes the growth frame. Habits of mind first address personal and intellectual development: metacognition is the "ability to reflect on one's own thinking" and is fostered through reflection; creativity is the "ability to use novel approaches for generating, investigating, and representing ideas" and is fostered through exploration; and persistence is the intellectual commitment to "grapple with challenging ideas, texts, processes, or projects" (*Framework* 4–5). Other habits of mind in the *Framework* address students and their relationship with the world, affirming the virtues of openness and civic responsibility promoted in the growth frame: openness is the "willingness to consider new ways of being and thinking in the world" and is fostered through interaction; curiosity is the "desire to know more about the world" and is fostered through inquiry; and responsibility, the most clearly civic habit of mind, is "the ability to take ownership of one's actions and understand the consequences of those actions for oneself and others" (4–5). By focusing on habits of mind and the experiences that foster them, the document conceptualizes education as an intellectual quest with use value in society. Writing teachers and scholars may use the *Framework* to articulate all the things we believe about writing, especially the idea that writing holds intrinsic value and use value—and that its value is not primarily as a commodity that enables students to become economic actors.

Arguing with the *Framework*

The *Framework for Success in Postsecondary Writing* regularly functions as evidence in public and institutional arguments. To conclude this chapter, I want to encourage writing teachers, scholars, and program administrators to consider conceptual framing as they make arguments about curricula, course requirements, and the purpose of writing programs. Although my argument that the *Framework* evokes the commercial frame may be challenged, the document nonetheless interacts with this frame by appealing to success and positioning writing as an educational commodity. And although the growth frame may not neatly align with every concept in the *Framework*, it is manifested in both the document and in our disciplinary identity. When writing teachers and scholars use the *Framework* as evidence, I believe we should consider framing in two ways: we must be conscious of not only what frame we are evoking but also the implications of that frame. Our writing courses, writing programs, and rhetoric and composition ultimately face limitations when we speak from multiple frames simultaneously.

Evoking the commercial frame has attractive, positive implications when writing program administrators want to build institutional status. When colleges and universities focus on degree value and/or affordability, for example, programs are wise to provide students with skills that enable persistence in college and success after college—by demonstrating that their outcomes are worth the cost. In this context, writing program administrators may argue that their courses equip students with habits of mind that, in the words of the *Framework*, position them "to meet the writing challenges in the full spectrum of academic courses and later in their careers" (2). They may frame habits of mind as additional differentiators of success. And when institutions revise general education requirements, writing program administrators may defend writing requirements by rehearsing a version of this argument: although engineering programs produce excellent, highly marketable technical experts, technical skills are worth far more—and are even more marketable—paired with writing and critical thinking skills. This commercial argument may also appeal to survey data that identifies writing/communication ability as the most important quality of a successful employee, a move that clearly frames writing ability as a commodity people own, exchange, and sell.

Certainly writing courses foster habits of mind that may enable persistence and success, and certainly these courses have use value and exchange value for students in technical and professional programs. We must question, however, how appeals to success and employability frame writing: is writing valuable for its ability to meet particular needs or for its exchange value in the market? Writing program administrators—and indeed our discipline—reject the idea that writing courses are merely service courses, but promoting writing with the commercial frame defines writing as a basic skill in service of extrinsic ends. Arguments appealing to employability may also undermine writing about writing approaches, which are grounded in the idea that theoretical and practical knowledge about writing has intrinsic and use value (Wardle and Downs). The *Framework* offers opportunities to argue from the commercial frame, and we must understand the consequences of taking those opportunities. When writing teachers, scholars, and administrators appeal to persistence and success, are we speaking from our own values and promoting all the things writing does? When we argue that writing makes technical experts more successful, are we commodifying writing by placing it in service to extrinsic ends? The commercial frame narrows the province of writing to things that can be commodified, abstracted, and exchanged—to those things with exchange value beyond the educational experience.

Alternately, the growth frame may have positive implications when writing program administrators promote the liberal arts or articulate the content of writing courses. Another argument writing program administrators commonly rehearse is this: when people across the university blame writing programs for poor student writing, assuming that the program should teach only basic skills, writing teachers, scholars, and program administrators argue that writing courses teach more than grammatical correctness and rudimentary organizational strategies, that writing is about thinking and context and flexibility. Now we may also use the *Framework* to argue that writing is also about fostering habits of mind. Writing courses may include technical skills such as usage and organization, we might argue, but they have always been connected to personal, intellectual, and civic development. When students learn to write, they have the opportunity to develop persistence, engagement, and curiosity—virtues they will bring to their personal, professional, and public lives.

Appealing to the growth frame affirms our disciplinary values, but it creates at least two challenges: first, it risks irrelevance against a powerful commercial frame, and second, it claims responsibility for outcomes that one program or discipline cannot reasonably accomplish. The commercial frame is pervasive in American education, and writing courses indeed teach skills that hold exchange value—skills many associate with basic professionalism and appropriately credentialed workers. For example, the "WPA Outcomes Statement for First-Year Composition" suggests that students should "develop knowledge of linguistic structures, including grammar, punctuation, and spelling." If writing programs reject these aims, which seem to have exchange value, they risk irrelevance. Writing programs that distance themselves from the primary concerns of many students and institutions risk losing the opportunity to teach and publicize all the things that writing is and does. Perhaps more troubling is the idea that writing programs should claim responsibility for forming citizens and fostering habits of mind. Kristine Hansen rightly argues that students develop habits of mind in a variety of contexts and that these habits may not correlate with writing skills (541). If writing programs claim responsibility for intellectual formation, they put themselves in the difficult position of teaching and assessing not only an expanding set of outcomes but also personal, moral, and intellectual qualities. Writing programs may ultimately be more credible and viable when they articulate the specific ways they foster student intellectual development and demonstrate some degree of effectiveness.

Conceptual framing highlights the reality that arguments are bound by words and the frames they evoke. Using words such as *investment* and *accountability* overpowers the growth frame; speaking about *intellectual growth* and *civic engagement* exposes the limits of the commercial frame. If speakers attempt to evoke two frames simultaneously, Lakoff argues, they will inevitably privilege one because "there are no neutral concepts and no neutral language for expressing political positions within a moral context" (*Moral Politics* 385). In his political work, Lakoff urges progressives to speak from their values at all times, but he also encourages them to find the places where "progressive values [are] already there (perhaps only passively) in your interlocutors" (*Elephant* 113). While conceptual frames may be quite impenetrable, people often hold contradictory values, and there is rhetorical power in appealing to latent or passive values that are actually incongruous with the commercial frame.

The *Framework* itself evokes multiple frames, and I believe writing teachers and program administrators should not use the commercial frame at the expense of the growth frame. The growth frame—at least as I have described it in this chapter—may not fully express every disciplinary value, but it is nonetheless a compelling alternative to the commercial frame. If our words and arguments evoke the commercial frame, we cannot be surprised if writing becomes understood as only a skill or a commodity. And if we do not consistently speak from our disciplinary values, we cannot be surprised if they are overshadowed in our institutions and the public. The *Framework* articulates our values as habits of mind and experiences that form writers and citizens, and it can give us words to speak those values as we tell the story of our programs, our students, and our disciplinary work.

Notes

1. Linda Adler-Kassner argues that the Common Core is "framed by the idea that as a public good, school should cultivate a citizenry that can fill necessary market roles *and* a citizenry that can compete against one another to create and fill . . . jobs" ("Liberal Learning" 442). She views the Common Core through the lens of social efficiency: the idea that education is a public good that prepares citizens to participate in the market (Labaree 18). It is my belief that social mobility is eclipsing other educational goals, including social efficiency; social mobility views education as a private good that prepares individuals to be competitive in the market (18). Both social efficiency and social mobility are motivated by the economic market rather than "citizenship training, equal treatment, and equal access" (Labaree 19). While the distinction between education as a private good or a public good is significant, I am most concerned with this shift toward economic, extrinsic ends.

2. Understanding education as formation has religious connotations. These themes of awakening and conversation are present in the way that Plato conceptualized his academy and in the history of American universities. For example, Harvard was founded with religious aims, and its leaders explained in 1643 that the college exists to "advance learning and perpetuate it to posterity; dreading to leave an illiterate ministry to the churches, when our present ministers shall lie in the dust" (qtd. in Delbanco 11).

Works Cited

"About the Standards." *Common Core State Standards Initiative*. National Governors Association and Council of Chief State School Officers, 2011. Web. 31 July 2014.

Adler-Kassner, Linda. "Liberal Learning, Professional Training, and Disciplinarity in the Age of Education 'Reform': Remodeling General Education." *College English* 76.5 (2014): 436–57. Print.

—. *The Activist WPA: Changing Stories about Writing and Writers*. Logan: Utah State UP, 2008. Print.

Adler-Kassner, Linda, and Peggy O'Neill. *Reframing Writing Assessment to Improve Teaching and Learning*. Logan: Utah State UP, 2010. Print.

Arum, Richard, and Josipa Roksa. *Academically Adrift: Limited Learning on College Campuses*. Chicago: U of Chicago P, 2010. Print.

Berlin, James A. *Rhetoric and Reality: Writing Instruction in American Colleges, 1900–1985*. Carbondale: Southern Illinois UP, 1987. Print.

Bok, Derek. *Our Underachieving Colleges: A Candid Look at How Much Students Learn and Why They Should Be Learning More*. Princeton: Princeton University Press, 2006. Print.

College Affordability and Transparency Center. *College Scorecard*. United States Department of Education, 2014. Web. 31 July 2014.

Council of Writing Program Administrators. "WPA Outcomes Statement for First-Year Composition." CWPA, 2014. PDF File.

Council of Writing Program Administrators, National Council of Teachers of English, and National Writing Project. *Framework for Success in Postsecondary Writing*. CWPA, NCTE, and NWP, 2011. PDF File.

Delbanco, Andrew. *College: What It Is, Was, and Should Be*. Princeton: Princeton UP, 2012. Print.

Fillmore, Charles J. "Frame Semantics and the Nature of Language." *Annals of the New York Academy of Sciences* 280 (1976): 20–32. Print.

Gallagher, Chris W. "Being There: (Re)Making the Assessment Scene." *College Composition and Communication* 62.3 (2011): 450–76. Print.

Hansen, Kristine. "The *Framework for Success in Postsecondary Writing*: Better than the Competition, Still Not All We Need." *Symposium: On the Framework for Success in Postsecondary Writing*. Spec. issue of *College English* 74.6 (2012): 540–43. Print.

Johnson, Kristine. "Beyond Standards: Disciplinary and National Perspectives on Habits of Mind." *College Composition and Communication* 64.3 (2013): 517–41. Print.

Kronman, Anthony. *The End of Education: Why Our Colleges and Universities Have Given Up on the Meaning of Life*. New Haven: Yale UP, 2007. Print.

Labaree, David. *How to Succeed in School Without Really Learning: The Credentials Race in American Education*. New Haven: Yale UP, 1999. Print.

Lakoff, George. *Moral Politics*. 2nd ed. Chicago: U of Chicago P, 2002. Print.

—. *Don't Think of an Elephant! Know Your Values and Frame the Debate*. White River Junction, VT: Chelsea Green, 2004. Print.

Lakoff, George, and Mark Johnson. *Metaphors We Live By*. Chicago: U of Chicago P, 1980. Print.

McComiskey, Bruce. "Bridging the Divide: The (Puzzling) Framework and the Transition from K–12 to College Writing Instruction." *Symposium: On the Framework for Success in Postsecondary Writing*. Spec. issue of *College English* 74.6 (2012): 537–40. Print.

Nathan, Rebekah. *My Freshman Year: What a Professor Learned by Becoming a Student*. Ithaca: Cornell UP, 2005. Print.

National Commission on Excellence in Education. *A Nation at Risk: The Imperative for Educational Reform*. United States Department of Education, 1983. PDF file.

O'Neill, Peggy, Linda Adler-Kassner, Cathy Fleischer, and Anne-Marie Hall. "Creating the *Framework for Success in Postsecondary Writing*." *Symposium: On the Framework for Success in Postsecondary Writing*. Spec. issue of *College English* 74.6 (2012): 520–24. Print.

Wardle, Elizabeth, and Doug Downs. "Looking into Writing-about-Writing Classrooms." *First—Year Composition: From Theory to Practice*. Ed. Deborah Coxwell-Teague and Ronald F. Lunsford. Anderson, SC: Parlor Press, 2014. 276–319. Print.

2 Figuring Programmatic Agency: The *Framework* as Critical Rearticulatory Practice in Writing Program Administration

Amy C. Kimme Hea, Jenna Pack Sheffield, and Kenneth C. Walker

Writing program administration scholarship is rife with stories about power, particularly the ways in which writing program administrators (WPAs) might theorize their roles in inequitable power relations. These narratives offer theoretical grounding and practical advice in hopes that administrators are well equipped with tactics and strategies for engaging in the challenges that make up their everyday working lives. Much of this scholarship might be broadly conceived of as a survival guide for WPAs on how to approach complex relationships with other administrators, teachers, staff, parents, and legislators, and even how to question their own complicity in inequitable practices and structures. In this body of research, WPAs find a rich site of disparate experiences and local contexts, which call for understanding power relations through a greater belief in one's own power (White), administrative praxis that seeks non-hierarchical power relations (Gunner; Handa and McGee), and administrative development that cultivates leadership (Phelps). WPA researchers have argued for paying more attention to the affective dimensions of the work (Micciche), making visible the power structures within the academy and forging strategic relationships among various stakeholders (McGee), and even redefining the value of writing program administration and the teaching of writing to fight against—rather than enable—their debasement (Horner). While survival may seem too strong a claim, we understand that many WPA documents, statements, and research calls have rightly sought to protect—if not rescue—the WPA, the writing program, or writing teachers and students from threats—often external ones—to the program and its members. This is certainly true of the *Framework for Success in Postsecondary Writing*. As its authors explain, one of its central goals was to include teacher voices against national conversations that often dismiss and debase those voices and involve teachers in discussions on the articulation between K–12 and postsecondary education (O'Neill et al. 520–21; See Foreword).

Despite longstanding considerations of power and WPA efforts to conceptualize power relations, many responses to the *Framework* have dominantly focused on its *discourse*—particularly what is or is not included or how it was or was not written (P. Sullivan; Summerfield and Anderson)—at the potential expense of critical reflection about the *Framework* and its role in rearticulating the *practices* of WPAs and writing programs. For our own part, we take seriously the discursive and material aspects of the *Framework* as a contested—yet potentially reflective—resource for teachers and administrators and contend that the *Framework* offers a platform to transform crisis-driven pragmatism into theoretically informed institutional praxis. Using our own local context of the University of Arizona writing program (UA program), we argue for the deployment of the *Framework*, not as part of the narrative arc of program survival, but rather as a tool to rearticulate dominant institutional assessment practices (Behm and Miller; Huot; Porter et al.) and to reveal and reimagine a writing program's mission. To get at the both/and aspects of the *Framework* as a means to provide content as well as impetus for program rearticulation, we argue for its role as a critical tool to foster local and national dialogues about student learning and to promote reflection on our roles as composition teachers and administrators (DeLuca; Rice).

Before turning to the *Framework* itself as a critical rearticulatory tool, we first offer a brief explanation of articulation theory and its critical potentials and then describe our local context to situate our discussion of the *Framework*. Then, we explain our own use of the *Framework* as part of a series of mapping and assessment activities that allowed our program to deploy the *Framework*'s content while simultaneously engaging it as a tool to interrogate power relations, enact programmatic agency, reflect on local outcomes and goals, and rearticulate our own program's commitments.[1] Thus, our story provides insight into the material transformations of writing programs as facilitated by the enactment of the *Framework* as a tool for critical praxis.

ARTICULATION THEORY

Articulation has been deployed widely by technical communication and computers and composition scholars to interrogate the power relations of hypertext, the World Wide Web, and new media composition (Johnson-Eilola; Kimme Hea). Cultural studies scholar, co-founder of the Birmingham Centre for Cultural Studies, and proponent of articulation theory, Stuart Hall argued for the examination of dominant cultural narratives and their ideologies as a means to understand, intervene in, and disrupt inequitable power relations. This cultural intervention is intended to disrupt the normative forces that arise—from the non-necessary relation of dominant narratives, practices, and structures—and to allow for political change. In his own words, Hall suggests that "[a] theory of articulation is both a way of understanding how ideological elements come, under certain conditions, to cohere together within a discourse, and a way of asking how they do or do not become articulated, at specific conjunctures, to certain political subjects" (141–42). Because, however, these relations of power are constructed, dynamic, not inherent, and not universal, narratives can be disrupted, changed, and complicated to perform "rearticulation" in an attempt to shift power, create new practices, and inform new structures that seek equity, not normativity. Hall and other scholars of articulation are quick to assert, however, that the work of articulation is continuous because culture is not static. In feminist and technoscience scholar Donna Haraway's work, she argues that materiality, not just ideology and figuration, nor just articulation, frames these political projects in partial, impermanent, but potentially more socially just ways (52).

Articulation seeks, then, to make visible the connections between discourses and practices to call for material and equitable change without reducing such change to determinism or essentialism. In other words, articulation theory is deployed by its practitioners knowing that change is not bound to linear progress or necessarily achievable as a single act of resolution, and thus, while articulation theory is aptly suited to explore the *Framework* at the level of its content, certainly, it can also serve as a means to critically inform program practices. Because, as noted in our introduction, WPAs are already attuned to power relations—as much of our work involves issues of labor and day-to-day interactions with teachers and students—we understand the *Framework* as an important document that can be deployed for rearticulatory projects related to constructions of writing assessment, WPA agency, and the relations among teachers and students. This chapter provides the context of our own program's use of the *Framework* as such an articulatory resource, one that extended into not only the shaping of other program documents but also into the very practices of the program itself. Thus, our examination of the *Framework* can act to enliven it as both a discourse (its language and content) and as a critical practice (as a *political* document that provides space for dialogue on fundamental assumptions about writing).

Local Context: The University of Arizona Writing Program

Our own local site is the University of Arizona (UA), a land-grant institution serving more than 40,000 undergraduate students each year. The Carnegie system classifies the University of Arizona as an R1 (Doctoral Universities: Highest Research Activity), and it is the state's first and oldest university, dating back to 1885. With more than 5,000 undergraduates enrolled in writing courses each semester, the UA program offers twelve different writing courses, including first-year (developmental, honors, L2); advanced; business and technical writing courses, and the share of its collective labor is dedicated to supporting the university's first-year composition requirement. Each semester, it offers as many as 250 sections of writing (with enrollments of 22–25 students), and the courses are taught by a dedicated cohort of mainly graduate students and lecturers. Since 2005, however, the UA program has faced budget cuts of over one million dollars while at the same time undergraduate enrollments have consistently increased each year by 4% (with the exception of 2008 when enrollments were flat). The UA program has a strong campus presence with many partnerships, including summer bridge programs, an L2 writing bridge program, residence hall and writing center collaborations, and outreach and service-learning initiatives, among others. The UA program has a positive reputation for its contributions to undergraduate student learning, and it is often lauded for its attention to developing graduate student teachers. The program is certainly not without its challenges in terms of support—both financial and political. At its core, however, the UA program has historical and intellectual connections to the whole of the university and community; its WPAs sit on a range of university-wide committees, and the current director was part of the university's faculty leadership initiative.

Framework as Rearticulatory

Every seven years, UA departments must participate in the university's required academic program review (APR)—not to be confused with the *annual performance* review, which also will be discussed. To distinguish, the APR review is an extensive self-study of the entire department, culminating in a report for an external review board made up of national scholars in all four fields of English studies that are represented in our department (English as a second language, rhetoric and composition, creative writing, and literature). The APR self-study is reviewed and assessed by that board and recommendations are made to the university provost and president as to future directions for the department. In 2011, the Department of English, where the UA program is housed, was slated for review. Just one year before the APR, the UA program director and associate director had set out their own vision for the writing program through the development of a three-year strategic plan that included the launching of a five-year longitudinal study of student writers. This strategic plan sought to foster opportunities for more research-focused activities within the program, such as the longitudinal study, and it also expressed ways in which the UA program might contribute to the university's promotion of even more systematic program assessment at the institution. The strategic plan also developed lines of argument to fund two tenure-track positions for the permanent leadership of the program's director and associate director WPA positions. In addition to gaining the support to consistently staff the director positions with tenure-track faculty lines, the strategic plan also helped to secure further funding from the Department of English to hire two research assistants from the local pool of graduate students in the Rhetoric, Composition, and Teaching of English (RCTE) program, and one of the first tasks of the research assistants was to work on analyzing and interpreting data for the writing program's report for the department's seven-year APR.

To make the research involved in preparing for the APR professionally relevant and useful beyond the APR itself, the research team conceptualized the APR not as a discreet and local act, but as a reflective practice connected to broader happenings in its own program—such as the strategic plan and its implementation—as well as writing programs and departments across the country where pressures to assess are ever increasing. In a *WPA: Writing Program Administration* article, John Oddo and Jamie Parmelee argue that "administrators should recognize the centrality of textual objects which delineate the goals and objectives of a Writing Program" because instructors turn to these documents to learn about a curriculum and frame their teaching (80). Recognizing the importance of textual objects, we decided to use the recently produced *Framework* as a site of comparative inquiry to tactically map revisions to student learning outcomes (SLOs) for the APR. This comparative work allowed us to revise the goals and outcomes of our program and make visible the set of relations already in place, or needing to be in place, to enact these visions. Thus, the activity of mapping the program goals and outcomes between the *Framework* and our local program's existing SLOs allowed us to envision our program in new ways, to literally *see* areas where discourses and practices could come to serve our community in important ways. This process informed our mission to establish critical spaces of dialogue and opened the program to understand new sites of struggle. In this way, we value the *Framework* not simply for its content, but for its potential to provide a platform to theorize the relational work and material lives of members of our program, and we value articulation theory as a way to understand how the *Framework* helped us theorize our program's commitments and power relations and even take actions to design new practices. In the sections that follow, we offer four ways in which we used the *Framework* as a rearticulatory tool in our program: (1) as an approach to reflect on local outcomes and goals; (2) as a tool to interrogate power relations; (3) as a method for enacting programmatic agency; and (4) as a process for rearticulating the program's commitments and practices. While we treat these key moments as separate, they are perhaps better understood as imbricated sites of struggle that continue to shape our experiences as WPAs.

Framework as Approach to Reflecting on Local Outcomes and Goals

On a practical level, the APR provided for us the exigency to examine our own student learning outcomes and goals, and the *Framework* provided a tool for reflecting on these key learning objectives and articulating them in new ways. To do so, we designed a mapping process to compare the UA program's local SLOs to the outcomes listed in the *Framework* and the Council of Writing Program Administrators' "WPA Outcomes Statement for First-Year Composition" (WPA OS). We turn briefly to the process we used in hopes that it can be useful to others.

To begin this comparative work, we took the program's current SLOs and listed the outcomes by course, using a numerical code for each outcome. Then, we assigned a numerical code for each of the *Framework*'s outcomes. To elaborate, the *Framework* contains five major sections—Developing Rhetorical Knowledge, Developing Critical Thinking, Developing Flexible Writing Processes, Developing Knowledge of Conventions, and Composing in Multiple Environments. Under each section are bulleted outcomes that show ways teachers can provide guidance to students in each of these categories.

Developing Rhetorical Knowledge
- learn and practice key rhetorical concepts such as audience, purpose, context, and genre . . . ;
- write and analyze a variety of types of texts to identify
  - the audiences and purposes for which they are intended . . .
  - the audiences and purposes for which they are intended . . .

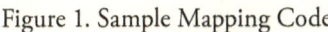

Developing Rhetorical Knowledge (1)
- **1.1** learn and practice key rhetorical concepts such as audience, purpose, context, and genre . . . ;
- **1.2** write and analyze a variety of types of texts to identify
  - **1.2a** the audiences and purposes for which they are intended . . .
  - **1.2b** the audiences and purposes for which they are intended . . .

Figure 1. Sample Mapping Code

Thus, "Developing Rhetorical Knowledge," the first section, was numbered "1," "Developing Critical Thinking" was numbered "2," and so on, and each bullet point became 1.1, 1.2, and so forth. Because we wanted to map to national frameworks committed to writing, we also followed the same process with the WPA OS. Using these codes, we designed an excel spreadsheet with columns for the *Framework* and WPA OS next to each UA SLO, and for each UA SLO, we input the code of any of the *Framework* or WPA OS outcomes that were similar to the UA's outcomes. For example, the UA SLO that students should "analyze texts through close reading" corresponded with the *Framework*'s outcome that students should "read and analyze print and multimodal texts composed in various styles, tones, and levels of formality" (9). At the same time, while both outcomes corresponded in their emphasis on textual analysis, the comparison of these two outcomes revealed gaps in our own outcome, as it did not specifically emphasize the analysis of multimodal texts or stress analyzing texts composed in a variety of styles or formality. A column was added to the spreadsheet to track these differences for later analysis. Additionally, we tracked codes from the WPA OS and *Framework* that did not map onto our own student learning outcomes, and these revealed potential spaces for improvement in our own practices.

This mapping process provided a visual reference to show how our SLOs were aligned with national frameworks. The process enabled us to make visible the consistencies, contradictions, gaps, and overlaps between these national documents and the outcomes in our own program. Some of the connections that were revealed through this process included reassurance that our own SLOs aligned well with the national frameworks when it came to rhetorical knowledge, analysis, and research, but some gaps included recognition that our outcomes were often worded to position students as readers even more than as writers. Further, we noted that we only framed collaboration in terms of writing workshops and realized we should broaden our representation of collaboration to be more than only peer review. We also found a general lack of emphasis on multimodal composing and the use of digital technology in our outcomes, and we recognized that we could better emphasize the evaluation of sources for credibility, quality, and bias. It was not until we worked through this careful comparison of our own goals to those of the national documents, however, that we were best able to see how we needed to rearticulate our own goals.

This activity also allowed us to see gaps in the *Framework*'s content when compared to our local learning outcomes. Other than in the habits of mind section, the *Framework* currently does not reference *reflection*, which is an important component in many of our SLOs, nor does it recommend that students analyze literacy practices or identify concepts and functions of story. While the latter may be more local and contextual to our own program, the lack of emphasis on reflection was a noticeable gap in the *Framework* that aligned with the research interests underway in our longitudinal study of student writers on metacognition and affect. We viewed this gap as one area where our ongoing research to understand student writing development over time might contribute to knowledge in writing studies research.

Thus, while the *Framework* is offered as a national document that describes the "rhetorical and twenty-first-century skills as well as habits of mind and experiences that are critical for college success," we maintain that it is much more (1). As Angela Clark-Oates discusses in chapter 14 of this volume, it also provides a critical space for reflection on local outcomes and goals. As articulation theory recognizes, narratives can be disrupted, changed, and complicated to perform rearticulation in an attempt to shift power and create new practices. Hence, as Lori Ostergaard, Dana Driscoll, Cathy Rorai, and Amanda Laudig demonstrate in chapter 16 of this volume, the *Framework* can be used to disrupt a program's prevailing narratives and lead to new practices through a process of articulating the program's goals against the collective standards of a primary professional organization, such as the Council of Writing Program Administrators. When embedded in institutional requirements like a program review (academic or annual), the document has potential to open up critical spaces for dialogue and reflection in ways that speak to how programs can interrogate power, enact programmatic agency, and potentially rearticulate a program's commitments and practices.

Framework as Tool to Interrogate Power Relations

Articulation theory posits that power is drawn into relations and that those relations can therefore be disrupted and changed, and this disruption must arise from analysis and engagement. As noted, the APR is a good example of a power-laden situation, but so, too, are annual program reviews. Each year, the annual program review interpolates WPAs into institutional ideologies of progress that too often become simply another task to accomplish rather than a site of critical struggle and exploration. To manifest this transformation, however, the writing program directors and research assistants saw an opportunity to integrate our longitudinal study design to offer a quantitative and statistically significant programmatic assessment of student writers as an access point into institutional conversations about assessment that were occurring at our own institution. In other words, drawing on our own strategic plan and the academic program review mapping of SLOs to the *Framework*, we saw the annual program review reconstituted as a critical moment to assert the program's mission and values. Because we determined that the five-year longitudinal study of student writers might also serve as the first-year baseline local assessment data, the APR at the department level was our opportunity to envision the writing program as a site for knowledge production, not just service, and then, the annual review provided opportunities to demonstrate results-based data that helped to solidify our contributions and our need for resources to support local and national writing research.

One specific example of local and national writing goals coming together out of the *Framework* as an articulatory practice was the decision to make the use of evidence by student writers one measure in a multi-trait rubric to evaluate three hundred samples of student writing from week one of the fall semester (first-semester composition) to the last week of the spring semester (second-semester composition) for the same cohort of students. We learned in our quantitative evaluation of first-year student writers that evidence was the only primary trait we measured that did not increase significantly over time. The correlation of both the *Framework* mapping process and this quantitative assessment finding made the importance of teaching evidence more visible to the program directors than ever before, and this gap was subsequently accounted for by an open call for instructors to contribute sections about teaching evidence in our custom textbook and conversations on the teaching of evidence throughout our teacher practica, as we discuss more below when detailing programmatic changes. So, one aspect of our critical practice interrogated institutional power through a required assessment process that is related to a much larger process of rearticulation of student writers and their development through a mixed-methods five-year longitudinal study.

Yet, to take on a critical stance, we also had to interrogate power relations at the level of everyday practices. Articulation theory holds the examination of prevailing cultural narratives and their ideologies as a way to disrupt unequal power relations, and in examining the *Framework* on both micro- and macro-levels, we were able to use this mapping process, one that re-examined not only goals and outcomes but also the relations in place to enact those goals, to fundamentally reconceive of the purpose and practices of various committees and meetings. After the mapping and local assessment work, it became clear that long-standing program committees, such as the committee of course directors, did not adequately reflect, or address, concerns of teachers and students. The committee of course directors had been comprised of faculty members of the UA program and their primary responsibilities (although never put into writing) included determining curriculum, guiding teachers, and evaluating graduate student applications to teach courses, such as honors, that were under their direction. This faculty-only committee was instead re-envisioned as the curriculum and assessment committee with those same course directors, but also with wide representation of graduate students, adjuncts, and other writing program and department committee representatives such as elected members from the difference and inequality committee and the English Graduate Union, among others. This committee even solicited for inclusion of an undergraduate student representative, but our student government contact at UA was not able to secure an undergraduate representative in the committee's inaugural year. This committee now works collectively to shape curriculum, determine teacher development practices, and re-envision teacher selection to ensure that the courses represent both current research and thoughtful input by all of our teachers (and hopefully soon, even students). This shift also provided the opportunity to revisit the mapping project discussed in this chapter to add to the mapping the outcomes of our peer institutions (identified by the Arizona Board of Regents), the revised WPA OS, and LEAD Value Rubrics for Written Communication and Critical Thinking. In other words, inspired by the integrative nature of the *Framework* as a tool for rearticulation, the mapping process opened up a space of inquiry where conversations around curriculum and assessment could be articulated from all the committee members to reveal the values and commitments of the program in ways that had been otherwise invisible. Other UA program committees that same year completed extensive needs analyses to help shape the next strategic plan in process for our program, making the struggles and concerns of different constituencies the foundation for the program's plan.

Just as the *Framework* is embedded in sets of power relations that it seeks to engage and reframe, as WPAs we were able to use the *Framework* as one way to allow others to further map the program's practices and make them visible. Our post-APR mapping process allowed us to integrate even more voices and representation from our program's constituencies in ways that Bob Broad speaks of in his dynamic criteria mapping (DCM) where instructors participate in open discussions of their ideas and judgments about writing to establish key elements that can be part of assessments. Thus, the *Framework* became a tool for multiple points of observation (and change) where the WPA was figured as a conduit of multiple circuits of everyday practice that flows to and through the position, not simply from it. Thus, again, the *Framework* as a rearticulatory tool enabled us to move the program dynamically through a more distributed set of power relations.

Framework as Site for Enacting Programmatic Agency

The questions that were opened and gaps that were revealed through the mapping process led to movements in the UA program that enabled us to assert programmatic agency at the levels of university administration and national contribution. Because power is not assumed to be absolute, but rather constituted through discourses and practices, rearticulating our program's mission and relationships to its members could be enacted, if not ever fully achieved, through the strategic plan, the academic program and annual program reviews, needs assessments, and the mapping process of the *Framework*. These practices provided us the means to engage in a broader visioning of the program, especially in relationship to research as foundational to administration (Rose and Weiser). On one hand, our programmatic assessment for the academic program review could have been a successful end point—at the end of the year, our program was one in four across our campus that received exemplary status from our local Office of Instruction and Assessment (OIA). But the suturing labor between research and administration reminded us this was only a beginning. The recognition our assessment process garnered us further established our relationships with upper administration as key players in the push for campus-wide outcomes-based assessment, but because this outcomes-based assessment was only one part of a larger vision of a five-year longitudinal research project, we also viewed these relations as sites where we might use our qualitative research on and with student writers, particularly as they entered general education and upper division courses, in order to bring depth and complexity to the interpretations coming out of institutional assessment. Assessment scholars, like Broad, continue to remind us that good assessment practices are rooted in qualitative research, and our embedded assessments were no different. The *Framework* became one site embedded in a host of others that allowed us to enact a measure of programmatic agency by rearticulating the normativity found in outcomes-based assessment with the arguably more equitable practices of qualitative research and its ability to deepen institutional understandings of student writers' lives.

Resituating the work of the writing program as research through the APR and other key documents provided opportunities to enact research and assessment practices with research assistants, and it profoundly shifted the UA program to be more like a research lab—a place where local institutional assessments and national research come together. When our program gained national recognition by receiving the College Composition and Communication Conference's Research Initiative Award and the Council of Writing Program Administrators Research Award, our assessment office and vice provost of instruction were some of the first to hear about it. Linking together research with administration, in short, has given us more credibility with our local assessment leaders. Like our own local committee work, these committees are where rearticulatory practice comes into effect by allowing us to maintain a set of relations within the more flexible subject position of researcher, one whose primary roles are to engage in inquiry and to make visible the iterative nature of learning to compose.

While these moments of programmatic agency might seem far removed from the mapping process, we view the mapping activity as a means of opening conversation and spurring many changes. Yet, as Ernesto Laclau and Chantal Mouffe assert, fixed ultimate meanings are impossible and we must recognize the openness of the social (95–96). In this vein, we understand that these changes will require continual reflection, conversation, and additional revision across program stakeholders and practices. In linking the *Framework* to broader visions of a research-driven writing program, we found it to be a critical tool to open conversations about our own practices, and it was in the generative potentials of this process that we found our use of the *Framework* to be a means of enacting programmatic agency. Thus, while the document in and of itself is important, the *Framework* might also be viewed not simply as a document to use, but as a figural space for writing programs to inhabit, to interrogate power, and to rearticulate a WPA's subject position as researcher within the broader dialogues seeking to empower teachers and students.

CONCLUSION: *FRAMEWORK* AS TOOL TO REARTICULATE COMMITMENTS AND PRACTICES

As James Porter et al. claim in their important article about institutional critique, "sometimes individuals (writing teachers, researchers, writers, students, citizens) can rewrite institutions through rhetorical action" (613). For them, such change relied on a method that opened up institutional sites for reflection, resistance, revision, and productive action. For us, rhetorical action was enacted through our use of the *Framework* mapping to compare and rewrite our SLOs, which, we believe, led to other important institutional changes at the level of our program's commitments and practices. We were able to conduct the practical work of revising our goals and outcomes and call for additional sections and chapters related to these new outcomes in our in-house publication, *The Student's Guide to First-Year Writing*. This *Framework* mapping helped us revamp a number of pilots of our first-year writing courses by linking our existing strengths in literary and public writing to goals we realized were absent from earlier iterations of the student learning outcomes. We also standardized best practices for technology use in FYW based on our realization that our SLOs were missing some of the important technology outcomes explicated in the *Framework*. Lastly, this process allowed us to recognize the importance of SLOs in general, which sparked the development of program SLOs for our graduate-level composition practicum being required of all graduate student teachers entering our program.

More than these practical maneuvers, the *Framework* allowed us to conceive of these local acts as only one part of a larger vision to transform administration into nationally recognized research on student writers. By treating the *Framework* as a space for critical work, the UA program was able to partially fulfill its strategic goal of transforming into a more research-centered place for the study of writing across our campus. Our program's revised outcomes were embedded in a quantitative assessment in the first year of our longitudinal study. Our commitment to empower teachers and students by bringing them into the research process and by distributing curricular research activities into newly designed committees with new representatives on them, opened up spaces to listen, to learn, and to create mutuality (as well as disruption).

In their response to the *Framework*, Judith Summerfield and Philip M. Anderson critique the document for its atheoretical disposition, its obfuscation of a larger purpose, and its lost sense of scholarly history (545). But as we have tried to argue here, the *Framework*'s discursive positioning allows other scholars to fill these gaps through a local figuring of the document as a site to open inquiry into local and national research. It is important to view the *Framework* as a place to make our theories and ideologies explicit and to bring our purposes to it. For us, the *Framework* initiated a series of practices that ultimately allowed our program to use the *Framework*'s content dynamically while simultaneously deploying it as a tool to enact programmatic agency, reflect on local outcomes and goals, and rearticulate our program's commitments and practices. The *Framework* teaches us something about the national significance of our everyday practices. It figures relations for transformation made possible through its discursive constructions and reflective platform. For our program, the *Framework* was a tool to transform a crisis-driven pragmatism into theoretically informed institutional practices, and we maintain that it can therefore be a tool to rearticulate dominant institutional assessment practices and to reimagine a program's mission and praxis.

Note

1. We use mapping here to describe a process akin to postmodern mapping (Peeples; Porter and Sullivan, "Working"; Sullivan and Porter, "Remapping" and *Opening Spaces*), which Peeples asserts as a method that "enables WPAs to investigate their own positioning in institutions as well as to investigate and analyze a variety of relationships among various institutional spaces within and outside the writing program" (154). Our mapping included several activities, but the major one was the articulation of our program's student learning outcomes to other national outcomes statements, including the *Framework*.

Works Cited

Behm, Nicholas, and Keith D. Miller. "Challenging the Frameworks of Color-Blind Racism: Why We Need a Fourth Wave of Writing Assessment Scholarship." *Race and Writing Assessment*. Ed. Asao B. Inoue and Mya Poe. New York: Peter Lang Publishing, 2012. 127–38. Print.

Broad, Bob. *What We Really Value: Beyond Rubrics in Teaching and Assessing Writing*. Logan: Utah State UP, 2003. Print.

Council of Writing Program Administrators. "WPA Outcomes Statement For First-Year Composition." CWPA, 2014. PDF File.

Council of Writing Program Administrators, National Council of Teachers of English, and National Writing Project. *Framework for Success in Postsecondary Writing*. CWPA, NCTE, and NWP, 2011. PDF File.

DeLuca, Kevin Michael. "Articulation Theory: A Discursive Grounding for Rhetorical Practice." *Philosophy and Rhetoric* 32.4 (1999): 334–48. Print.

Gunner, Jeanne. "Decentering the WPA." *WPA: Writing Program Administration* 18.1–2 (1994): 8–15. Print.

Handa, Carolyn, and Sharon J. McGee. "Introduction." *Discord & Direction: The Postmodern Writing Program Administrator*. Logan: Utah State UP, 2005. 1–17. Print.

Hall, Stuart. "On Postmodernism and Articulation: An Interview with Stuart Hall." *Stuart Hall: Critical Dialogues in Cultural Studies*. Ed. David Morley and Kuan-Hsing Chen. New York: Routledge, 1996. 131–50. Print.

Haraway, Donna. "Interview with Donna Haraway." *Chasing Technoscience— Matrix for Reality*. Ed. Don Ihde and Evan Selinger. Bloomington: Indiana UP, 2003. Print.

Horner, Bruce. "Redefining Work and Value for Writing Program Administration." *JAC* 27.1 & 2 (2007): 164–82. Print.

Huot, Brian. *Rearticulating Writing Assessment for Teaching and Learning*. Logan: Utah State UP, 2002. Print.

Johnson-Eilola, Johndan. *Datacloud: Toward a Theory of New Online Work*. Cresskill, NJ: Hampton P, 2005. Print.

Kimme Hea, Amy C. "Riding the Wave: Articulating a Critical Methodology for Web Research Practices." *Digital Writing Research: Technologies, Methodologies, and Ethical Issues*. Ed. Heidi McKee and Dànielle Devoss. Cresskill, NJ: Hampton P, 2007. 269–86. Print.

Laclau, Ernesto, and Chantal Mouffe. *Hegemony and Socialist Strategy: Towards a Radical Democratic Politics*. London: Verso, 1985. Print.

McGee, Sharon J. "Overcoming Disappointment: Constructing Writing Program Identity through Postmodern Mapping." *Discord & Direction: The Postmodern Writing Program Administrator*. Logan: Utah State UP, 2005. 59–71. Print.

Micciche, Laura. "More Than a Feeling: Disappointment and WPA Work." *College English* 64.4 (2002): 432–58. Print.

Oddo, John, and Jamie Parmelee. "Competing Interpretations of 'Textual Objects' in an Activity System: A Study of the Requirements Document in the Writing Program." *WPA: Writing Program Administration* 31.3 (2008): 63–88. Print.

O'Neill, Peggy, Linda Adler-Kassner, Cathy Fleischer, and Anne-Marie Hall. "Creating the *Framework for Success in Postsecondary Writing*." *Symposium: On the Framework for Success in Postsecondary Writing*. Spec. issue of *College English* 7.6 (2012): 520–33. Print.

Peeples, Tim. "'Seeing' the WPA With/Through Postmodern Mapping." Rose and Weiser 153—67. Print.

Peer Institutions for the University of Arizona. University of Arizona, University Relations, 2015. Web. 1 July 2015.

Phelps, Louise Wetherbee. "Turtles All the Way Down: Educating Academic Leaders." *The Writing Program Administrator's Resource: A Guide to Reflective Institutional Change and Practice*. Ed. Stuart C. Brown, Theresa Enos, and Catherine Chaput. Mahwah, NJ: Lawrence Erlbaum, 2002. 3–39. Print.

Porter, James E., Patricia A. Sullivan, Stuart Blythe, Jeffrey Grabill, and Libby Miles. "Institutional Critique: A Rhetorical Methodology for Change." *College Composition and Communication* 51.4 (2000): 610–42. Print.

Porter, James E., and Patricia A. Sullivan. "Working across Methodological Interfaces: The Study of Computers and Writing in the Workplace." *Electronic Literacies in the Workplace: Technologies of Writing*. Ed. Patricia A. Sullivan and Jennie Dautermann. Urbana, IL: NCTE/Computers and Composition, 1996: 294–322. Print.

Rice, Jeff. "Conservative Writing Program Administrators (WPAs)." *The Writing Program Interrupted: Making Space for Critical Discourse*. Ed. Donna Strickland and Jeanne Gunner. Portsmouth: Boynton/Cook, 2009: 1–13. Print.

Rodriguez, Caitlin, Jerry Lee, and Gina Szabady, eds. *A Student's Guide to First-Year Writing*. 33rd ed. Plymouth, MI: Hayden McNeil, 2012. Print.

Rose, Shirley K, and Irwin Weiser, eds. *The Writing Program Administrator as Researcher*. Portsmouth: Heinemann, 1999. Print.

Sullivan, Patrick. "Essential Habits of Mind for College Readiness." *Symposium: On the Framework for Success in Postsecondary Writing*. Spec. issue of *College English* 74.6 (2012): 547–51. Print.

Sullivan, Patricia A., and James E. Porter. "Remapping Curricular Geography: Professional Writing in/and English." *Journal of Business and Technical Communication* 7 (1993): 389–422. Print.

—. *Opening Spaces: Writing Technologies and Critical Research Practices*. Norwood, NJ: Ablex/Computers and Composition, 1997. Print.

Summerfield, Judith, and Philip M. Anderson. "A Framework Adrift." *Symposium: On the Framework for Success in Postsecondary Writing*. Spec. issue of *College English* 74.6 (2012): 544–47. Print.

White, Edward M. "Use It or Lose It: Power and the WPA." *WPA: Writing Program Administration* 15.1–2 (1991): 3–12. Print.

3 A Place for Reading in the *Framework for Success in Postsecondary Writing*: Recontextualizing the Habits of Mind

Ellen C. Carillo

Although the *Framework for Success in Postsecondary Writing* has been largely lauded as an insightful and productive response to the Common Core State Standards, its list of eight habits of mind, described as "ways of approaching learning" that are "essential for success in college writing" have been the source of some debate (1). The complete list of these habits is as follows: curiosity, openness, engagement, creativity, persistence, responsibility, flexibility, and metacognition. Patrick Sullivan has argued for the value of the list, noting that he appreciates its focus on these "qualities" rather than on target test scores or some other criteria (547). On the other hand, the list has been criticized as an "arbitrary" and "incomplete" version of Arthur L. Costa and Bena Kallick's "16 Habits of Mind," which also includes "'listening to others—with understanding or empathy,' 'responding with wonderment and awe,' and 'finding humor,' among others" (Summerfield and Anderson 545). I do not fall on either side of this debate, but rather call for the reconsideration of the habits of mind within a different context from that within which it is currently fixed. In the introduction to the list, the habits of mind are described as "essential to success in college writing" (1). Similar to what Alice Horning writes elsewhere in this volume, I argue that these habits also contribute to success in college reading and, furthermore, that thinking about them within this context offers productive ways for high school and college instructors to think alongside each other about reading expectations and, by extension, reading-writing connections. Even though Horning and I both argue for greater attention to reading in college classrooms, I focus primarily on how each of the habits of mind allows writing instructors to enhance reading instruction and facilitate learning in college, and I suggest relatively minor additions in content to how the *Framework* could more effectively articulate the integral connection between cultivating habits of mind and proficiency with college-level reading.

As composition scholars in the 1980s and early 1990s (e.g., Bartholomae; Berthoff, *Forming*; Flower; Petrosky; and Salvatori) and some still today (e.g., Bunn; Salvatori and Donahue; Horning; and Keller) continue to argue, "Reading, responding, and composing are aspects of understanding, and theories that attempt to account for them outside of their interactions with each other run the serious risk of building reductive models of human understanding" (Petrosky 20). Expanding the context within which we consider this list so that it includes both reading and writing allows for a more comprehensive approach to teaching literacy practices and enables instructors to underscore the connections between reading and writing for the benefit of student learning.

Although the second section of the *Framework* does include reading assignments that foster the habits of mind, the *Framework* misses an opportunity to frame how its habits of mind can simultaneously prepare students for success in college reading, which would offer a less compartmentalized approach to postsecondary literacy education. As Mariolina Salvatori notes, "To foreground and to teach—rather than just to understand—that interconnectedness [between reading and writing] is a highly constructed, unnatural and obtrusive activity" (187). In other words, students do not learn to write simply by reading. Instead, it is the instructor's job to deliberately and consistently "foreground and teach" the connections between reading and writing. Thus, I move through all eight habits of mind to demonstrate what might be gained if we were to consider how each has the potential to contribute not just to success in college writing, but to success in college reading, writing's counterpart in the construction of meaning. In so doing, I also hope to bring to light some of the important, but largely neglected scholarship on reading that has emerged from composition studies over the years.

Curiosity and Openness

I pair the first two habits of mind because they are connected by their emphasis on agency in the world—namely through the acts of "desire" and "willingness." Curiosity is defined as the "desire to know more about the world" while openness is described as the "willingness to consider new ways of being and thinking in the world" (4). Particularly if one conceptualizes writing as an act of inquiry, these habits certainly contribute to successful writing. Successful readers must be curious and open. In her book *Turns of Thought*, compositionist Donna Qualley explains the importance of readers "approach[ing] a text with the conscious intention of engaging in genuine dialogue with its ideas, a dialogue that may put the reader at risk. . . . Reading that puts the reader at risk involves learning, the modification (or risk of modification) of what's in our head as a result of our encounters with a text" (61–62). After reminding us that reading in this way might feel risky and even uncomfortable, Qualley goes on to explore the importance of openness: "The reader's judgments must remain tentative, open to the possibility of elaboration, modification, or revision through further dialogue and ongoing reflection on the text and/or others' reactions to the text" (62). While Qualley describes these as "stances" rather than habits of mind, the "conscious" curiosity along with the emphasis on the reader's openness to the text, to herself, and to others' renderings of the text are crucial to stemming students' "rush to closure," which "abbreviates thinking and curtails further inquiry" (Qualley 23). Like the authors of the *Framework*, Qualley (following Freire) has her sights set not just on teaching students how to engage with texts within an academic setting, but also showing students how "the word, the world, and the self are always in continual dialectical play" (5).

So how does one go about fostering curiosity and openness when it comes to reading? The place most scholars go when talking about engaging students in reading is to text selection. We have all heard the common rallying cry for the inclusion of texts that students can relate to so that they will "automatically" be engaged and open to them. But that route is problematic because it assumes that students are a homogenous entity and that what appeals to one student will appeal to all. Moreover, if one's goal is to help students learn through the act of reading in the ways that Qualley describes, choosing texts students can relate to (even if one could) undermines this goal precisely because it puts students in contact with texts with which they (supposedly) already agree and relate.

Although text selection is not totally immaterial, focusing more on helping students develop reading habits that encourage curiosity and openness is potentially a more productive route.

One way to facilitate students' openness is to encourage them to become aware of that which threatens to foreclose that very openness. Social-constructivism (e.g., the work of Kenneth Bruffee; Patricia Bizzell; and Anne Gere) offers the foundation for this approach. When reading a text, students can spend time reflecting on their own assumptions, ideas, and beliefs about the subject or topic the text tackles. They can push themselves to better understand where their assumptions, ideas, and beliefs come from (e.g., their parents, their religion, their previous schooling) to reveal their constructed-ness. This work—whether done in journals, class discussion, or small group work—allows students to recognize the institutions and other factors that have contributed to their belief systems. When students do this work together, they also begin to see that their peers have been influenced differently by the same world, and they become curious about this. As the *Framework* notes, making all of this visible can help students recognize that there are multiple ways of "being and thinking in the world" (4). This potentially opens them up to considering texts (and the belief and value systems therein) as well as other people in ways they have not done so before.

To expand the categories of curiosity and openness to include attention to reading, I would add language that suggests that reading itself offers students opportunities to imagine and put themselves in the position of others, whether characters in fictional texts, real people in nonfiction texts, or even the author of a text. More specifically, I would call attention to how reading can be used to foster openness by revising the first bullet point in the section on Openness as follows: "Openness is fostered when writers are encouraged to *read in order to* examine their own perspectives to find connections with the perspectives of others." Although a slight change, this revision underscores a particular reading practice and how reading in this way has the potential to open students up to voices, ideas, and experiences different from their own. As Robert J. Scholes notes, this is a much-needed reading practice since students often assimilate a text's position to their own or refuse to think about a position that differs from theirs (169). In fact, Scholes ties this myopic reading practice to a larger "cultural problem": "After 11 September 2001 we have begun to learn, perhaps, that this deficiency is serious." He goes on to describe English teachers' responsibility to help our students develop textual practices "in which strength comes, paradoxically, from subordinating one's own thoughts temporarily to the views and values of another person" (167–68). To disregard that reading is a textual practice as important as writing, as does the current *Framework*, means a missed opportunity to underscore what might be at stake if we do not encourage our students to be more open.

Engagement and Persistence

I am pairing engagement and persistence because both habits describe the importance of commitment. On the list of eight habits of mind, engagement is defined as "a sense of investment and involvement in learning" (4) while persistence is described as "the ability to sustain interest in and attention to short- and long-term projects" (5). When it comes to reading, engagement and persistence are particularly important because students can easily become frustrated when they encounter a text that poses various difficulties for them whether these result from the content, structure, tone, vocabulary, or any number of other elements. Mariolina Salvatori and Patricia Donahue build the reading/writing pedagogy described in their textbook *The Elements (and Pleasures) of Difficulty* around the very idea of engaging with difficulty, which they contend is crucial in one's academic career and beyond: "Readers who engage, rather than avoid, a text's difficulties can deepen their understanding of what they read and how they read. If they move away from those difficulties or opt for somebody solving them for them, chances are that they will never know the cause of those difficulties, and the means to control them" (3). One way to help students understand the causes of the difficulties they encounter when they read is to ask them to keep a dialectical or double-entry notebook, first introduced by Ann E. Berthoff and then revised into a triple-entry notebook assignment by Mariolina Salvatori. Berthoff's "double-entry" notebook makes visible the dialectal nature of reading and writing. On one side of the page students put "reading notes, direct quotations, observational notes, fragments, lists" while the other side records "notes about those notes," including "summaries, formulations, questions and queries and mumbles, editorial revisions, [and] comments on comments" (Berthoff, "How We Construe" 85). "The facing pages," Berthoff notes, "are in dialogue with one another" and this method "assures that whatever is learned about reading is something learned about writing" (85–86). This notebook, thus, foregrounds the connections between reading and writing and can enrich student learning as students experience the relationship between these two practices of meaning-making. Moreover, the metacognitive aspect of this assignment, with its "comments on comments" and its constant self-monitoring dovetails nicely with the eighth habit of mind, "metacognition," discussed below.

In addition to the dialectical notebook, Salvatori uses what she calls "the difficulty paper." In their difficulty papers, students spend a page or two dwelling on and unpacking a difficulty they are encountering in the text to work through it. As mentioned above, the difficulty may be a result of the content, vocabulary, tone, structure or something else. Both the dialectical notebook and the difficulty paper help students realize that "understanding can emerge through an encounter with difficulty, and experiences of reading and writing will be enriched and enhanced if difficulty is addressed rather than ignored" (Salvatori and Donahue xxiv). Both Berthoff's and Salvatori and Donahue's approaches are informed by their belief in the "theoretical and practical appropriateness of using reading as a means of teaching writing" (Salvatori 182) and they remind us that reading is a valuable tool that can be mobilized to support the teaching of writing. Moreover, these assignments help students to not only understand the sources of their difficulty and provide tools to work through them, but also demonstrate to students that "all processes involve false starts, getting off the track, getting on again" (Berthoff, *The Making of Meaning* 126). Berthoff continues, "We must persuade [students] that these are not *mistakes*" (126). If understood as mistakes, students' levels of engagement can wane, but if presented as opportunities for real learning students see these as rich moments that—if afforded additional attention—can reap the reward of better understanding.

While the importance of difficulty to engagement and persistence is addressed in the *Framework*'s description of persistence, its description of engagement might be revised to describe how reading can foster these learning experiences that allow students to construct knowledge, whether that knowledge is about "mistakes" they've made or about the subject they are studying. Currently, two of the three bullet points that describe engagement largely position students as passive: "Engagement is fostered when writers are encouraged to find meaning new to them or build on existing meanings as a result of new connections; and act upon the new knowledge they have discovered" (4). I would revise this language to indicate reading as a practice (like writing) that allows students not to "find" new meaning or "discover new knowledge," but to compose and create meaning and knowledge. In this way, reading becomes a way of engaging students as active participants in their educations, and as writing's counterpart in the construction of meaning, reading becomes a foundational component of engagement. Ultimately, this revision diminishes the text's status as that which contains a stable meaning and puts students back in the equation by addressing the importance of their engagement in these processes.

CREATIVITY

Writing—much more so than reading—is thought of as a creative enterprise, but a look back to the reader-response movement in the 1970s reminds us how and why reading must also be thought of as a creative enterprise. We are reminded how this theory continues to infuse the work in English studies today even if it is not readily visible. The reader response movement—a challenge to the New Critical approach to reading—sought to de-center the place of the text in reading and to highlight the role of the reader in the meaning-making process. Reader-response critics, including Louise Rosenblatt whose work finally garnered attention in the 1970s during this movement, led "in American educational circles to the development of new teaching practices in which literature was no longer seen as a body of privileged texts whose meanings students must 'understand correctly'" (McCormick 37). The pedagogy that grew out of this shift turned "readers-as-consumers into readers-as-producers of their own readings of texts" (Comley 130–1). Patricia Harkin points out that this conception of reading is "assumed in every aspect of our work" (413). Harkin explains further,

> Many people have never known a time in the academy when it has not been normal to accept this proposition without demur. But since it was not always thus, it is important . . . for older folks to remember and younger folks to imagine how amazing it was to hear it for the first time. Readers make meaning: readers—and not only authors—engage in an active process of production-in-use in which texts of all kinds—stories, poems, plays, buildings, films, TV ads, clothes, body piercings—are received by their audiences not as a repository of stable meaning but as an invitation to make it. (413)

Drawing attention to the legacy of the reader response movement—which has now become normalized—helps students understand that texts come to mean through an active, creative process, namely through the "transaction"—to use Rosenblatt's term—between text and reader. To talk about reading as a creative process with students also has the potential to correct some misconceptions about interpretation, namely that "language is a muffin tin; that we *have* meanings, a kind of batter we then pour into molds" (Berthoff, *The Making* 25). Instead, we need to draw our students' attention to how meanings are constructed and how language is "an instrument, a means of seeing and articulating relationships" (25). One way to do this in the classroom is to use class discussion to cull various interpretations of a given text or even passages from a text—either published interpretations or those offered by students—and reflect on the validity of these *multiple* interpretations, as well as how and why those emerged from the specific source or person.

With this activity in mind, I suggest revising the final bullet-point in the *Framework*'s section on creativity to emphasize the importance of reading by replacing the word "evaluate" with "read." Thus, that final point would read as follows: "[Creativity is fostered when writers are encouraged to] read for the effects or consequences of their creative choices." This revision locates reading as an encompassing and complex task, one that has more possibilities than a strictly evaluative approach. Students might consider the choices a writer makes for any number of reasons, and reading (rather than evaluating) allows them to do so. In other words, using the term "evaluate" instead of read, as does the *Framework* currently, limits how and why one would consider the "effects or consequences" of their writerly choices. Moreover, I would add that students should not only be reading their own work in this way, but published works, too. This approach has the potential to help students understand how all writers make choices as part of the writing process and how these choices affect how readers construct different meanings.

Responsibility

The *Framework* defines "responsibility," the sixth habit of mind, as "the ability to take ownership of one's actions and understand the consequences of those actions for oneself and others" (5). Responsibility is described further as the writers' ability to "recognize their own role in learning; act on the understanding that learning is shared among the writer and others—students, instructors, and the institution, as well as those engaged in the questions and/or fields in which the writer is interested;" and the writers' ability to "engage and incorporate the ideas of others, giving credit to those ideas by using appropriate attribution" (5). This habit of mind has clear implications for the teaching of writing, but before students can "engage," "incorporate," and "give credit to" the ideas of others in their writing while simultaneously recognizing "their own role in learning" it is crucial that they can make sense of the sources they encounter and the voices therein. A recent study of students' writing and reading habits suggests that they are not competent in this area. This study, "The Citation Project," which is "a multi-institution research project responding to educators' concerns about plagiarism and the teaching of writing," found that students write from sentences not from sources, relying on paraphrasing, copying, citing, and patchwriting rather than summary. In fact, none of the papers in the research sample used in the pilot study described by Rebecca Moore Howard, Tricia Serviss, and Tanya K. Rodrigue in "Writing from Sources, Writing from Sentences" actually uses summary. In Sandra Jamieson and Rebecca Moore Howard's follow-up study of students' writing from sixteen US colleges and universities, only six percent of students' citations were to summary, summary that usually focused on a very limited amount of text. These findings raise questions about "whether students understand the sources they are citing in their researched writing" (Howard, Serviss, and Rodrigue 189). As Howard, Serviss, and Rodrigue explain, "The absence of summary, coupled with the exclusive engagement of text on the sentence level, means that readers have no assurance that the students *did* read and understand" (186). This raises important issues related to responsibility for as Howard, Serviss, and Rodrigue point out, students are "always in danger of plagiarizing": "When one has only the option of copying or paraphrasing, one can easily paraphrase too lightly, producing a patchwritten sentence too close to the language of the original" (187). Expanding the context within which we think about teaching "responsibility" in our writing courses would allow us to foreground the reading-writing connections, which are especially important when working with secondary sources and the issues of academic integrity this work necessarily raises.

Despite how the very act of incorporating ideas of others into one's work foregrounds the relationship between reading and writing, the *Framework*'s section on responsibility does not mention reading. It seems that the word "engage" stands in for reading in the final bullet point that describes responsibility as being fostered when writers are encouraged to "engage and incorporate the ideas of others, giving credit to those ideas by using appropriate attribution" (5). To "engage and incorporate ideas," students need to first read and understand them, which is not a given, according to the research study described above. As such, it seems important to insert the word "reading," either as a substitute for "engage" or in addition to it. Although seemingly minute, this addition would remind instructors that they cannot assume that students can readily and adeptly comprehend the sources they are using. In fact, "America's Skills Challenge: Millennials and the Future," published this year by Educational Testing Services (ETS), found that "one half (50%) of America's millennials," defined as those born after 1980 who were 16–34 years of age in 2012, "failed to reach level 3 in literacy" (11). Level 3 in the literacy component of this study tests how well respondents "identify, interpret, or evaluate one or more pieces of information, and often require varying levels of inference" (48). Level 3, as the study notes, "is considered the minimum standard for literacy" (11), and only 50% of American millennials met this minimum benchmark, highlighting the difficulty young adults have working with "pieces of information" or what we might call sources. The inclusion of the term "reading" in this section would underscore how foundational reading is to research writing and to the responsibilities associated with accurate and appropriate attribution.

FLEXIBILITY

The *Framework for Success in Postsecondary Writing* defines flexibility as "the ability to adapt to situations, expectations, or demands" (5). When it comes to reading as a form of thinking, this might mean "thinking the thoughts of another, inhabiting somebody else's mind—temporarily adopting somebody else's argument" (Salvatori and Donahue 3). This exercise has important implications that go beyond the classroom and beyond developing sophisticated readers. As Salvatori and Donahue describe, "Learning to read in ways that nurture flexibility of mind can be good preparation for encountering and working through difficult life situations" (3). Giving students opportunities to temporarily adopt the personas and values of the characters in pieces of literature they read or the arguments put forth by scholars in the nonfiction texts they read helps students better understand these values. This prepares them for working with a range of people in their future workplaces and, more generally, simply getting along in the world. Peter Elbow's "believing game" offers overt and deliberate exercise in this activity as it encourages students (and, more generally, people) to remain flexible and tentative in their ideas and interpretations (of literature and beyond) and avoid the temptation of "always trying to achieve closure" (171). Elbow describes the value in "keeping something energetically open" (180) and "breaking out of solipsism" (182), two goals of the believing game. He explains, "Continual practice in trying to have other perceptions and experiences helps people break out of their 'sets' and preoccupations—helps them be less rigid, less prey to conventional, knee-jerk, or idiosyncratic responses" (171). As suggested by this passage, Elbow imagines clear connections between flexibility and openness, the second habit of mind on the list. If flexibility (and openness) are addressed as a means to fostering success in student reading and not just writing, students can become more comfortable with working against their "impulse for answers" (176). Still, Elbow reminds us that "fighting the itch for closure" is a process, "a long, slow discipline involving growth and increased flexibility" (176).

It also makes sense to think about the importance of flexibility in reading in light of the different types of texts (e.g., multimodal, digital) students encounter on a daily basis. In *Chasing Literacy*, Daniel Keller looks at what he calls "faster literacies," and how twenty-first century literacy practices, and particularly reading practices, are informed by online and digital environments. Ultimately, he argues for "developing methods of oscillating between faster and slower forms of reading and between hyper and deep ranges of attention" (153), as well as reinforcing and encouraging ways of "shuttling between digital and print texts" (154). In other words, as students encounter a range of texts (e.g., printed, digital, or multimodal) on a daily basis, flexibility becomes that much more important. Students need to be able to quickly adapt to the different expectations that these texts place on them and, as Keller's book accounts, instructors need the tools to help foster students' abilities to do so.

Although my own research on the importance of attending to reading in first-year writing courses does not look specifically at multimodal reading practices, I have developed assignments that encourage students to become aware of their different reading practices in an effort to help them recognize the importance of flexibility when it comes to reading. In my own classes, asking students to keep reading journals wherein they test out and reflect on different reading approaches (e.g., annotating, rhetorical reading, reading for the main point, and skimming) as they read the assigned texts helps them become more active readers, but also more flexible readers. With this toolkit—this repertoire of approaches at their disposal—students tend to be more flexible and willing to try out different approaches rather than sticking with one that isn't as productive as another. Often, students are surprised that I even address—let alone encourage—skimming as one of these approaches. Although instructors are responsible for fostering reading practices that students don't engage in on a daily basis (like skimming), I also feel responsible for giving students *a range* of tools for engaging with texts. Sometimes skimming is the most productive and appropriate practice within a given context.

To indicate how important flexibility is within the context of reading, I would add a fourth bullet-point to the section on flexibility that reads as follows: "[Flexibility is fostered when writers are encouraged to] develop a range of reading strategies and the ability to make productive decisions about which strategies to employ across contexts." This addition overtly connects the flexibility necessary to be a deliberate and successful writer with that necessary to be a deliberate and successful reader no matter the context. Moreover, helping students cultivate a repertoire of reading approaches and giving them practice reading a range of texts that demands their calling on these approaches fosters a degree of adaptability in them that is likely to serve them well as they move across courses and contexts within and beyond academia.

METACOGNITION

The *Framework* defines metacognition as "the ability to reflect on one's own thinking as well as on the individual and cultural processes used to structure knowledge" (5). Defining metacognition similarly, I have written extensively about the importance of metacognition as a means to cultivating productive reading habits and to transferring these habits across contexts. Metacognition is crucial to "positive transfer" wherein "learning in one context improves performance in another context" (Perkins and Salomon). As I detail in *Securing A Place for Reading in Composition: The Importance of Teaching for Transfer*, one way to help students develop their metacognitive abilities within the context of reading is to expose students to texts, as well as accompanying reading and writing assignments that make different demands on them. Asking students to compare their experiences rhetorically reading (however an instructor defines that) and close reading (again, however an instructor defines that) texts, for example, gives students access to multiple approaches. More importantly, it gives them opportunities to develop knowledge about each approach individually, their relationship to that approach, as well as knowledge about that approach in comparison to others. This helps students develop the metacognitive skills useful for moving among reading approaches in deliberate ways since knowledge is less likely to transfer from one context to the next unless students are constructing this knowledge within a metacognitive framework wherein students "reflect on [their] own thinking" (*Framework* 5). I have found that promoting metacognition and flexibility go hand-in-hand and any assignment that asks students to reflect on how and why they read—and construct meaning—as they do, such as the reading journal assignment and dialectical notebook assignments described above, can support this important work.

Helping students develop their metacognitive abilities when it comes to reading also encourages them to assume ownership of their learning, a habit of mind described under "Responsibility." As Richard E. Mayer and Merlin C. Wittrock describe in "Problem-Solving Transfer," "schools are not able to teach students everything they will need to know, but rather must equip students with the ability to transfer. . . . Transfer is a pervasive characteristic of human cognition: New learning is always dependent on previous learning" (49). If students are taught to develop their metacognitive abilities around the practice of reading and not just writing, there is potential for students to also develop their abilities to transfer what they learn about reading in postsecondary settings and beyond. Engaging students in activities that help them become aware of and reflect on their own reading practices can foster the sort of success—as it relates to reading—that the *Framework* is looking to foster in terms of writing.

To signal the importance of metacognition as it relates to reading, I would add a bullet point to the metacognition section that clearly connects the processes of reading and writing through the act of reflection, as do the assignments and activities described above. The addition would read as follows: "[Metacognition is fostered when writers are encouraged to] reflect on their reading practices and make deliberate choices about the reading strategies they will employ when encountered with a range of texts in a variety of contexts." This addition suggests that competent readers—and not just writers—need to cultivate an awareness of their practices and be prepared to recognize how contexts necessarily impact these practices. Few have written about the importance of metacognition to reading, but what Kathleen Blake Yancey has said about the importance of reflection to writing is equally important to reading, writing's counterpart in the construction of meaning: "As [students] learn, they witness their own learning: they show us [teachers] how they learn. Reflection makes possible a new kind of learning as well as a new kind of teaching" (8). In other words, reflecting on one's reading gives the reader access to that process, and by doing so helps her understand how she reads; it teaches her about herself as a reader. That reflection also grants the teacher access to that reader's way of learning, which would be otherwise invisible. Rendering this learning visible creates opportunities for both student and teacher to work together on what has now been brought to light.

CONCLUSION

Ultimately, considering the habits of mind listed in the *Framework* within the context of reading reminds secondary and post-secondary instructors that focusing on the act of writing alone is not enough since students will be expected not just to write in multiple disciplines and contexts but to read in them, as well. Certainly it is not news that reading and writing are connected practices, but, unfortunately, too often reading—writing's counterpart in the construction of meaning—remains an ancillary issue in the field's scholarship when it deserves as much attention as writing. For, as Alice Horning and others have pointed out, issues that are often considered as problems in student writing are in many cases related to reading issues students are having. In the late 1980s, scholars studied this phenomenon, and Horning conducted case studies of basic writing students, concluding that "specific syntactic and semantic difficulties in writing are related to reading problems in syntax and comprehension" (36). This phenomenon affects those beyond basic writing students, though, as the recent research from the Citation Project, discussed above, suggests. Ultimately, to recontextualize the habits of mind in this way and to consider how they might contribute to students' success in reading connects reading and writing in important ways that are absent from this section of the *Framework*. Equally important, this recontextualization enriches the *Framework*'s limited discussion of reading and underscores the idea that reading is as integral to composition as writing.

Works Cited

Bartholomae, David. "The Argument of Reading." *Writing on the Margins: Essays on Composition and Teaching.* New York: Bedford/St. Martin's: 1996, 244–54. Print.

Berthoff, Ann E. *Forming/Thinking/Writing.* Montclair, NJ: Boynton/Cook, 1981. Print.

—. "How We Construe is How We Construct." Comppile.org: 1982. 84–86. PDF File.

—. *The Making of Meaning: Metaphors, Models, and Maxims for Writing Teachers.* Montclair, NJ: Boynton/Cook, 1981. Print.

Bizzell, Patricia, ed. *Academic Discourse and Critical Consciousness.* Pittsburgh: University of Pittsburgh Press, 1992. Print.

Bruffee, Kenneth A. "Collaborative Learning and the 'Conversion of Mankind.'" *College English* 46 (1984): 635–52. Print.

Bunn, Michael. "Motivation and Connection: Teaching Reading (and Writing) in the Composition Classroom." *College Composition and Communication* 64 (2013): 496–516. Print.

Carillo, Ellen C. *Securing a Place for Reading in Composition: The Importance of Teaching for Transfer.* Logan: Utah State UP, 2014. Print.

Comley, Nancy. "A Release from Weak Specifications: Liberating the Student Reader." *Writing and Reading Differently.* Ed. Douglas Atkins and Michael Johnson. Lawrence: UP of Kansas, 1985: 129–38. Print.

Costa, Arthur L and Bena Kallick, eds. *Learning and Leading with Habits of Mind.* Alexandria: Association for Supervision and Curriculum Development, 2008. Print.

Council of Writing Program Administrators, National Council of Teachers of English, and National Writing Project. *Framework for Success in Postsecondary Writing.* CWPA, NCTE, and NWP, 2011. PDF File.

Elbow, Peter. *Writing Without Teachers.* New York: Oxford UP, 1998. Print.

Flower, Linda. "The Construction of Purpose in Writing and Reading." *College English* 50 (1988): 528–50. Print.

Freire, Paulo. *Pedagogy of the Oppressed.* Trans. Myra Ramos. New York: Continuum, 1993. Print.

Gere, Anne. *Writing Groups: History, Theory and Implications.* Carbondale: Southern Illinois UP, 1987. Print.

Goodman, Madeline J., Anita M. Sands, and Richard J. Coley. "America's Skills Challenge: Millennials and the Future." Princeton, NJ: Educational Testing Service, 2015. PDF File.

Harkin, Patricia. "The Reception of Reader-Response Theory." *College Composition and Communication* 56.3 (2005): 410–25. Print.

Horning, Alice. "The Trouble With Writing is the Trouble With Reading." *Journal of Basic Writing* 6.1 (1987): 36–47. Print.

Howard, Rebecca Moore, Tricia Serviss, and Tanya K. Rodrigue. "Writing from Sources, Writing from Sentences." *Writing and Pedagogy* 2.2 (2010): 177–92. Print.

Jamieson, Sandra, and Rebecca Moore Howard. "Sentence-Mining: Uncovering the Amount of Reading and Reading Comprehension in College Writers' Researched Writing." *The New Digital Scholar: Exploring and Enriching the Research and Writing Practices of Nextgen Students*. Ed. Randall McClure and James P. Purdy. Medford, NJ: Information Today, 2013. 109–32. Print.

—. *The Citation Project*. 12 June 2014. Web. 6 June 2016.

Keller, Daniel. *Chasing Literacy: Reading and Writing in the Age of Acceleration*. Logan: Utah State UP, 2014. Print.

Mayer, Richard E., and Merlin C. Wittrock. "Problem-Solving Transfer." *Handbook of Educational Psychology*. Ed. David C. Berliner and Robert C. Calfee. New York: Macmillan Library Reference, 1996: 47–62. Print.

McCormick, Kathleen. *The Culture of Reading / The Teaching of English*. Manchester, England: Manchester UP, 1994. Print.

Perkins, David, and Gavriel Salomon. "Transfer of Learning." *International Encyclopedia of Education*. Web. 10 March 2015.

Petrosky, Anthony. "From Story to Essay: From Reading to Writing." *College Composition and Communication* 33 (1982): 19–37. Print.

Qualley, Donna. *Turns of Thought*. Portsmouth, NH: Boynton/Cook, 1997. Print.

Rosenblatt, Louise. "The Literary Experience." *Literature as Exploration*. 4th ed. New York: MLA, 1983. 25–53. Print.

Salvatori, Mariolina Rizzi. "'The Argument of Reading' in the Teaching of Composition." *Argument Revisited; Argument Redefined*. Ed. Barbara Emmel, Paula Resch and Deborah Tenney. New York: Sage, 1996: 181–97. Print.

Salvatori, Mariolina Rizzi and Patricia Donahue. *The Elements (and Pleasures) of Difficulty*. New York: Longman, 2005. Print.

Scholes, Robert J. "The Transition to College Reading." *Pedagogy* 2.2 (2002): 165–72. Print.

Sullivan, Patrick. "Essential Habits of Mind for College Readiness." *Symposium: On the Framework for Success in Postsecondary Writing*. Spec. issue of *College English* 74.6 (2012): 547–51. Print.

Summerfield, Judith, and Philip M. Anderson. "A Framework Adrift." *Symposium: On the Framework for Success in Postsecondary Writing*. Spec. issue of *College English* 74.6 (2012): 544–47. Print.

Yancey, Kathleen Blake. *Reflection in the Writing Classroom*. Logan: Utah State UP, 1998. Print.

4 Enhancing the *Framework for Success:* Adding Experiences in Critical Reading

Alice S. Horning

> Creative work, in whatever field, depends upon commitment, the energy of participation and the ability to become absorbed in works of literature, art and science. That type of absorption is becoming an endangered species of cultural life, as our non-stop, increasingly fractured technological existence wears down our receptive capacities. . . . Liberal learning depends on absorption in compelling work. It is a way to open ourselves to the various forms of life in which we might actively participate. When we learn to read or look or listen intensively, we are, at least temporarily, overcoming our own blindness by trying to understand an experience from another's point of view. We are not just developing techniques of problem solving; we are learning to activate potential, and often to instigate new possibilities. (Roth 5)

A framework is defined in the dictionary as a skeletal structure intended to provide support or enclosure (Random House), and the *Framework for Success in Postsecondary Writing* certainly does that for writing. Much like Ellen Carillo notes elsewhere in this volume, I argue that the *Framework* outlines key skills that are integral to effective reading. However, unlike Carillo, I argue that the *Framework*'s current discussion of the experiences students need to have to become effective readers is not presented in enough detail to provide a basis for instruction or to provide the support structure for the liberal education described by Michael Roth who is president of Wesleyan University and author of *Beyond the University: Why Liberal Education Matters*. Therefore, I suggest that the *Framework* should be revised to add significantly to the reading experiences with extended prose texts that can lead to the kind of education Roth describes, and later in the chapter, I provide specific content with which the *Framework* ought to be revised. In fact, whereas Carillo outlines minor revisions to the *Framework*'s discussion of the habits of mind, I suggest the addition of an entirely new section that speaks to developing critical reading abilities. The need for additional experiences with critical reading is clear when recent reports of students' weak reading performance are examined in detail (ACT, *Reading;* Fields). The need for these revisions is also clear when the implications of effective reading for writing are revealed through the learning mechanism of implicit learning; implicit learning also plays a key role in the transfer of learning essential to the comprehensive liberal education Roth describes and to long-term learning.

The *Framework* lists eight habits of mind needed for success in postsecondary writing: curiosity, openness, engagement, creativity, persistence, responsibility, flexibility and metacognition. These habits, as described in the document, are clear and make sense for the development of students' writing abilities; given students' need for more effective and efficient reading, engagement, persistence, and metacognition are especially important. They contribute to the deep involvement advocated by Roth and others. The *Framework* also builds on the Council of Writing Program Administrators' "WPA Outcomes Statement for First-Year Composition" (WPA OS), seeking to support the goals articulated in the WPA OS. It is important to note that the WPA OS does include a section on Reading and Critical Thinking. That section does advocate reading development for students. But, in the *Framework*, the experiences designed to cultivate the habits of mind fall short in terms of explicit discussion of critical reading and related skills. The main reason for the shortfall is the lack of focus on developing reading abilities that support the habits. To some extent, this lack of focus is consistent with general inattention to reading in the field until quite recently; some journal special issues, books, and a Role of Reading in Composition Special Interest Group at CCCC have begun to address reading in greater depth. For a high-profile document like the *Framework*, expanded explicit attention to reading could be useful. In its recommendation of experiences for students, the document mentions reading in the Rhetorical Knowledge, Critical Thinking, and Multiple Environments sections, but chiefly in passing. In light of the challenges students face with reading, the *Framework* will be more effective if it presents specific experiences focused on reading that will lead students to develop their skills, and to learn strategies for analysis, synthesis, evaluation and application of their reading to their writing.

THE READING PROBLEM

Over the past few years, the number of reports and studies that reveal students' difficulties with reading has been growing steadily. Beginning with a major quantitative study released by ACT (*Reading*) in 2006 and a second one by the Pew organization that same year, study after study has shown that half or more of students entering or graduating from college have problems with reading. Whether quantitative or qualitative, virtually all of these studies produce the same results. The ACT report examined 563,000 students' performance on the Reading section of the ACT, a paper-and-pencil, timed multiple-choice test where students read four passages and answer ten questions on each. ACT found that 51% of students earned a score of 21 or better (scale is 0–36) and were successful in college, where success is defined as a 2.0 GPA and returning for a second year of study. ACT tracked three cohorts of students who had taken the test for three years, looking at their grades in college and their persistence.

There are a number of questions to be raised about these findings: the test itself, a standardized multiple choice-test on four short passages of text, may not capture students' abilities; it does not examine students' skills with online texts or extended texts at all; it does not allow for what students might be able to do without a time limit; finally, a 2.0 GPA and returning for the second year of study is a fairly low definition of "success." Raise the definition of success to college graduation, as do William Bowen, Matthew Chingos, and Michael McPherson in their highly regarded 2011 study, or to a 2.5 or 3.0 GPA taken together with an ACT Reading score of 21, as indicated in a recent American Institutes for Research study of post-secondary success, and it seems likely that a much larger number of students are not able to read complex texts well enough to succeed in college. On the other hand, it does examine the performance of a very large number of students with a direct test of reading comprehension. Results from more recent ACT studies (*The Condition*), reported in 2013, show a decline in the number of students who earn ACT's benchmark score, now set at 22, to 44%. The Pew study of students graduating from college, also released in 2006, shows a similar poor performance on an untimed test using an instrument developed for a study of adult literacy in the population at large. In the Pew study, the instrument used was the same one used in a national survey of adult literacy commissioned by Congress. It presents participants with tasks requiring both prose and document literacy, including both comprehension and inference from prose passages and the ability to read tables, maps, charts, and other kinds materials. The Pew study drew a representative sample of graduating seniors from colleges and universities across the country.

A third quantitative study comes from the National Assessment of Educational Progress (NAEP), the national test, sometimes called the "Nation's Report Card" (US Department of Education). In 2013, NAEP did a study of "academic preparedness" for college and job training of 47,000 students drawn from a population of more than three million (Fields). The report points out that NAEP is the only representative national sample of twelfth graders, but it also correlates its results to those on the SAT, which entails a self-selected sample. It is a timed, multiple-choice test, but it asks students to read both imaginative and informational texts and to demonstrate their ability to analyze, synthesize, evaluate, and use the material in various ways. The 2013 results show that 38% of students were proficient in reading (Fields 8). NAEP defines the genres of texts it asks students to read this way:

> The NAEP reading framework specifies the use of both literary and informational texts. Literary texts include three types at each grade: fiction, literary nonfiction, and poetry. Informational texts include three broad categories: exposition; argumentation and persuasive text; and procedural text and documents. (NAEP)

And NAEP defines proficiency with these various text types as follows:

> Twelfth-grade students performing at the *Proficient* level should be able to locate and integrate information using sophisticated analyses of the meaning and form of the text. These students should be able to provide specific text support for inferences,

interpretative statements, and comparisons within and across texts. (NAEP)

Although the same questions can be raised about the NAEP results as about the ACT findings and those of other standardized tests, when large numbers of students are tested in different ways and the same results appear, they warrant attention.

The validity of all standardized tests has been questioned repeatedly, particularly in light of increasing concern over the impact of testing in K–12 schools (Ravitch, *Death* and *Reign*). However, more recent work and qualitative studies produce similar outcomes with regard to students' reading abilities and difficulties. In Project Information Literacy, a study done by scholars at the School of Information at the University of Washington in Seattle, the focus was on first-year students' information literacy skills. The study looked at library resources in high schools and colleges, interviewed thirty-five first-year college students, and conducted a national survey of two thousand first-year students. The results show that beginning students, by their own report, had trouble finding, reading, analyzing, and evaluating source materials from the library, actually or virtually (Head 3–4). Project SAILS, a test of information literacy developed by librarians and faculty at Kent State University and based on the Association of College and Research Librarians' Information Literacy Standards for Higher Education (ACRL), shows that 51% of students can formulate an appropriate search strategy, find relevant and useful sources, read and analyze them effectively, and use them in an ethical and accurate way for their own purposes (Project SAILS). So, a forced-choice test supports the students' self-reported challenges with information literacy skills.

A different kind of qualitative study is the on-going work of the Citation Project, headed by Sandra Jamieson and Rebecca Moore Howard. The study examines approximately two thousand references drawn from a representative sample of first-year writing collected from sixteen colleges and universities across the country. In reviewing students' use of sources, Jamieson and Howard's results show these findings: only 6% use substantive summary, 46% cite from the first page of a source, 70% cite from the first two pages of a source, and a majority of sources are cited only once (Jamieson and Howard). According to Jamieson, these results surely reflect students' reading problems, including an unwillingness to read and understand full documents and to engage in conversation with sources. Drawing on the data from the Citation Project, she writes: "it is not possible to say conclusively that the students are comprehending the sources they read—or even that they are reading them at all" (Jamieson). Jamieson goes on to conclude that

> students are less likely to be able to understand the larger concepts in the texts they read, or to be able to assess how an argument unfolds, how sources are in dialogue with each other, or how the author uses an accumulation of references and sources to further a position of his or her own, or support, challenge, or revise a position or interpretation presented by another scholar. . . . However, rhetorical analysis of the *ways* these first-year students interact with their source material suggests that they lack the critical reading and thinking skills necessary to engage with the ideas of others and write papers reflecting that engagement in any discipline.

Because of her close analysis of the data presented by the Citation Project, Jamieson offers a unique perspective on students' reading problems; her analysis shows that students really do have a reading problem, one that warrants explicit attention in the *Framework* document.

Finally, the Citation Project findings are not really surprising given another, smaller, qualitative study done by David Jolliffe with his colleague Allison Harl at University of Arkansas. Reported in *College English* in 2008, this study paid about twenty students at Arkansas to keep logs of their reading activities for about two weeks and to write in response to prompts about two items they read each day. The resulting data showed weaknesses in students' abilities in these same areas: analysis, synthesis, evaluation, and application.

These gloomy results matter for the *Framework* because they point out students' reading difficulties, which are directly connected to their writing difficulties. The *Framework* does recognize the importance of reading and its relevance to writing. The connection is especially clear in the Critical Thinking Experiences section, where teachers are encouraged to provide experiences that will lead students to

- read texts from multiple points of view (e.g., sympathetic to a writer's position and critical of it) and in ways that are appropriate to the academic discipline or other contexts where the texts are being used;

- write about texts for multiple purposes including (but not limited to) interpretation, synthesis, response, summary, critique, and analysis. (7)

Here again, however, given what the research shows, a stronger explicit emphasis on developing reading skills would be more helpful.

Yet, another study supports this claim. Reading and writing are intimately connected, both because research shows that reading enhances students' cognitive development (Bazerman, Simon, and Pieng), and because reading sets the stage for the process of implicit learning discussed below. Bazerman, et al. conducted a small qualitative study with graduate students in a teacher education program. By coding references to materials read in four pieces of writing generated by six students in this program, they examined cognitive and intellectual development. The materials gathered in the study included an observation report on students in classes the graduate students were observing, a seminar paper, a teaching portfolio, and the master's thesis each student prepared over the twelve months of the program. The coding categories included both content and intertextual references showing how the students saw their readings as related to one another and to their own ideas. They also coded the use students made of their sources including quoting, paraphrasing, summarizing, and mentioning (Bazerman et al. 259).

Results showed that students used the sources consistently for their content. In addition, the sentences that included references to source materials had "higher-level thought" (262)—that is, reflected deeper thinking about content and relationships. Moreover, through the course of the year, students' use of sources changed, moving away from direct quotations and toward paraphrase and summary, indicating more focused understanding of the source material. A further finding is that the writing samples changed so that there were more "extensive discussions involving ideas from sources" (268)—that is, more intertextual events, handling sources the way many experts do (see studies by Bazerman; Hillesund; and Horning). Finally, different types of writing tasks elicited different kinds of discussion in the students' papers, possibly a variation related to the different types of writing the students were asked to do, rather than a reflection of their intellectual development (Bazerman, et al. 269). Thinking about these findings as a deeper analysis of what students might do with sources if they read them thoroughly and the positive impact of reading on their thinking and writing, Bazerman, et al.'s results contrast markedly with those of the Citation Project discussed earlier. These findings show that reading can make a positive difference to students' education and cognitive development as well as their performance as writers. More explicit focus on reading in the *Framework* would move in this direction.

IMPLICIT LEARNING

As Bazerman, et al.'s study shows, reading builds students' abilities in higher order thinking. But, reading is crucial to learning for another reason altogether. Reading, and especially the ability to read sustained nonfiction prose (that is, full-length journal articles, books, research reports, and other kinds of informational text), sets the stage for the learning process psychologists call implicit learning, best defined by British experimental psychologist Dianne Berry as follows:

> The term "implicit learning" is typically used to characterize those situations where a person learns about the structure of a fairly complex stimulus environment, without necessarily intending to do so, and in such a way that the resulting knowledge is difficult to express. (Berry 1)

Reading provides precisely this situation: students learn about academic writing, formal writing, proper voice and so on without specific attention to these features and without being able to describe what they have learned. The "stuff" of what is learned in this way through reading comprises a second key benefit of it. Through implicit learning, students can develop an appropriate sense of formal written language and academic voice. This sense opens the door to effective writing in college courses and beyond them in the professional world of work after graduation. The *Framework* acknowledges this approach in the sections discussing rhetorical knowledge (6), critical thinking (7), and composing in multiple environments (10), all of which encourage reading activities. Beyond the mention of critical or analytical reading, a whole section of the experiences in the *Framework* on reading as proposed below would sharpen the focus of the document on students' reading needs.

The importance of implicit learning for reading and especially for fluent reading has been discussed in detail by psycholinguist and second language acquisition scholar William Grabe ("Fluency"). Grabe notes that the essential skills of reading, like vocabulary, grammatical processing, and basic comprehension, develop through implicit learning. But, he points out some additional features of the implicit learning gained through reading that help to explain why it plays such an essential role in the goal of helping students write well. He writes that

> Many researchers and teacher trainers have misunderstood the importance of implicit learning that is central for both reading fluency and reading comprehension. Implicit learning is gradual, initially very fragile, and strongly based in repetition of form and process over a long period of time. This is why the connection between fluency skills and implicit learning clearly points to the pedagogical importance of extensive reading, reading rate practice, and text rereading and recycling as learning activities for reading development. (Grabe, "Fluency")

Thus, as Grabe says, a lot of experience with reading and focused work on it is essential to help students develop the basic skills needed to read sources and assigned material effectively and efficiently.

This point is important enough to warrant some additional explication. An appropriate analogy might come from beginning to learn to play a musical instrument. One can learn to read music by studying the staff and how the notes correspond to the keys of the piano or the positioning of the fingers on the strings of a violin. If the note values and time signature are clear, even a beginner can work out how to play the notes. But, it is much easier to make even beginning efforts sound like music if the beginner knows what the piece is supposed to sound like from recordings, sample playing by a teacher, attendance at a live performance, or some other resource. Knowing what the piece is supposed to sound like provides the implicit learning situation that can help a beginner play a piece accurately. In a similar way, expecting students to produce formal academic writing with which they have little or no experience presents a difficult learning challenge. If they have input through reading, the implicit learning mechanism sets the stage for novice writers to produce appropriate prose. Implicit learning of formal academic and/or professional writing can only happen through reading, and reading of a particular kind: absorption in and attention to intensive reading of extended formal prose. The *Framework* document should include experiences that lead to this kind of intensive reading.

A New Section for the *Framework*

A bit of summary of the discussion up to this point is in order before moving on to the activities that need to be added to the *Framework*. Michael Roth (*Beyond* and "Young") makes the case for liberal education by suggesting that students must have intensive experiences fostered by commitment and engagement. Naturally, interest and motivation are crucial to these experiences. Reading, though, offers just this kind of opportunity, allowing readers to experience the world at large or a specific situation or problem from the perspective of others. And, contemporary students clearly lack this experience. Their reading problems are amply demonstrated by the range of quantitative and qualitative measures and analyses discussed earlier. Expanded experience with reading not only may begin to ameliorate these problems but also sets the stage for implicit learning of the kind of formal, academic writing needed for success in postsecondary education and beyond. To achieve both of these goals, improving students' reading and their writing, specific experiences with reading are needed. The following section might be usefully added to the document, following the format of the other experiences. Unlike the *Framework* document, for each idea explanation and resources are provided here; although, in a revised document, they might not be needed. In this proposed section, the same format used in the present document is followed.

Developing Critical Reading and Information Literacy Abilities

Critical reading entails approaching full-length scholarly journal articles, books, extended online prose documents, research reports, and other similar materials in order to support and develop specific skills essential to good writing. Careful reading and analysis builds abilities in perceiving and comprehending text structure, in seeing how a text relates to and interacts with other texts on the topic or in the discipline, and in noticing the particular language of the text, including specialized vocabulary, phrasing, and fundamental concepts. For example, a research study in science or social science might follow the typical format of such reports, including a statement of problem, literature review, methodology, results, and discussion. Later reports may replicate the study; such material is important to the development of knowledge and insights. Finally, a study may use concepts like *statistical significance* or *independent variables* with which readers may need to familiarize themselves in order to grasp the implications of the report. Teachers can help writers develop critical reading and information literacy abilities by providing opportunities and guidance for students to

- *Read Extended Nonfiction Prose to Follow Extended Argument*: The kinds of reading intended here include those mentioned above: full-length journal articles, research reports, books, and other fully developed texts in which writers present and develop arguments and ideas. Teachers should be assigning work of this kind and helping students learn to do it efficiently and effectively. In part, this skill develops through practice. In part, it develops through guided experience. Scaffolding this kind of work with reading guides (as suggested by Herber) is one approach; teaching students to use graphic organizers (as suggested by Grabe, *Reading*) is another. The focal point here is that students must be required to work with extended nonfiction prose.

- *Work with 25-Word Summaries to Develop Analytical Skill*: In their work with extended arguments, students need experience reading for the key ideas presented in a text. Peter Doolittle and Tom Sherman offer a useful strategy in their work with 25-word summaries. Their research shows that asking students to read extended texts and capture their essence in a 25-word summary is a deceptively simple approach that can help students become speedier and more focused readers. The claim here is not that reducing every text to 25 words provides complete skill in reading. Instead, Doolittle and Sherman's technique offers another kind of experience designed to enhance students' ability to analyze and capture the content of an extended text.

- *Synthesize and Interrelate Multiple Sources through Comparison, Contrast, Integration, and Other Strategies*: The classic research paper assignment calls for students to assemble an array of different types of sources to support their ideas. Here again, deep, rhetorical reading is essential to successful writing. As Cynthia Haller demonstrates in her case studies with three students, effective arguments in writing arise when students can read rhetorically. Doing so means not only analyzing and understanding the content of an article, demonstrated perhaps by capturing its essence in a 25-word summary, but also relating the text at hand to other texts on the topic. Being able to see similarities in ideas and lines of reasoning, noticing differences and disagreements and integrating these all into detailed support for the writer's own ideas is an essential aspect of successful writing.

- *Evaluate for Authority, Accuracy, Currency, Relevancy, Bias, and Appropriateness*: Information literacy skills have increased in importance as the shift to digital modes continues to unfold. Anticipating these on-going changes, the Association for College and Research Libraries, the professional organization of librarians who work with students in college (a sub-group of the American Library Association), has developed a set of *Information Literacy Competency Standards for Higher Education*, originally proposed in 2000 (ACRL, *Information*) lately revised into its own new *Framework* document (ACRL, *Framework*). The new "threshold concepts" describe the key skills that every student should have or be developing while in college. In particular, students should be able to evaluate online materials for these criteria: authority, accuracy, currency, relevancy, bias, and appropriateness. Obviously, these evaluative criteria can be usefully applied to any kind of material anyone might be reading for any purpose. Students need specific experiences applying these criteria so that they become habits of mind whenever they are doing research of any kind. That they do not currently do so is amply demonstrated by librarian Frances Harris in *I Found It on the Internet*, issued in a second edition in 2011 and also by the findings of Project Information Literacy mentioned earlier (Head). Specific exercises to develop skills in evaluating materials in print or online are readily available in Joanna Burkhardt, Mary MacDonald, and Andre Rathemacher's book, *Teaching Information Literacy*, which is tied to the ACRL *Framework*. These experiences can help students build essential evaluative skills.

- *Design Specific and Conscious Plans for Use:* Expert writers go much beyond Google searching to find sources for use in their own work. Once they have appropriate sources, expert writers make clear plans for how and where to use them in support of their own ideas. Articulating conscious plans for the use of sources draws on the foregoing experiences in analysis, synthesis, and evaluation. Effective readers do all of those things, and when they are confident of their understanding of the materials they have read, they can make specific plans to use them in their own work. Here again, practice is essential to success, but it is practice in making explicit plans and executing them in written work. Students can be asked to formulate plans for the use of sources before they begin drafting, perhaps as part of work on annotated bibliographies or in other aspects of pre-writing. Or, as they are reading sources, they can be encouraged to consider how each text might be useful to the paper or other document or website or visual material they are developing. The goal here is that the use of sources should not be a random concoction of materials found on the Internet through Google searching, the kind of work that leads to the findings of the Citation Project mentioned earlier. Instead, students' experiences should lead them to appropriate source materials that they are able to read and then use deliberately and ethically to support their other findings and their own ideas.

Conclusion

The addition of these experiences to the *Framework* can help students develop their reading and writing abilities. The *Framework* offers useful approaches in both its habits of mind and its experiences. However, it should be clear that reading needs a much stronger focus than it has in the current document. The growing collection of studies of students' reading makes clear their difficulties in analyzing, synthesizing, evaluating, and using what they read effectively. Research from librarians shows that these difficulties appear not only when students read traditional printed texts but also, and perhaps more importantly, when they look at material they find online. The *Framework* could be much more helpful if it recommended a wider and deeper array of reading experiences, chiefly because reading sets up the situation where implicit learning can take place. Students who read thoroughly and carefully, who see the relationships among texts, who can evaluate everything they read, are students who will have the experiences that allow them to learn what good writing sounds like implicitly, using what they have read when they write. They will come to an understanding of text structure, of the context of texts, and of the language of a field or topic without conscious effort or awareness. These kinds of expertise are more likely, then, to appear in their own texts. Ultimately, effective reading and effective writing are the keys to the liberal learning we seek to provide in the university and beyond it, so these relatively small revisions to the *Framework* are essential to student success.

Works Cited

ACT. *Reading Between the Lines: What the ACT Reveals about College Readiness in Reading*. Iowa City, IA: ACT, 1 March 2006. Web. 3 July 2014.

ACT. *The Condition of College and Career Readiness-National Report*. Iowa City, IA: ACT, 2013. Web. 3 July 2014.

American Institutes for Research. *Predictors of Postsecondary Success*. Washington, DC: AIR, Nov. 2013. Web. 1 May 2015.

Association of College and Research Libraries. *Framework for Information Literacy for Higher Education*. Chicago, IL: ACRL, 1 Nov. 2014. Web. 1 April 2015.

Association of College and Research Libraries. *Information Literacy Competency Standards for Higher Education*. Chicago, IL: ACRL. 2008. Web 3 July 2014.

Bazerman, Charles. *Shaping Written Knowledge: The Genre and Activity of the Experimental Article in Science*. Fort Collins, CO: WAC Clearinghouse, n.d. Web. 3 July 2014.

Bazerman, Charles, Kelly Simon, and Patrick Pieng. "Writing About Reading to Advance Thinking: A Study in Situated Cognitive Development." *Writing as a Learning Activity*. Ed. Perry Klein, Pietro Boscolo, Lori C. Kirkpatrick, and Carmen Gelati. Leiden: Brill, 2014. 249–76. Print.

Berry, Dianne C. "Introduction." *How Implicit is Implicit Learning?* Ed. Dianne C. Berry. Oxford, England: Oxford UP, 1997. 1–12. Print.

Bowen, William G., Matthew M. Chingos, and Michael S. McPherson. *Crossing the Finish Line: Completing College at America's Public Universities*. Princeton, NJ: Princeton UP, 2011. Print.

Burkhardt, Joanna M., Mary C. MacDonald and Andre J. Rathemacher. *Teaching Information Literacy:50 Standards-Based Exercises for College Students*. 2nd ed. Chicago: American Library Association, 2010. Web. 7 July 2014.

Council of Writing Program Administrators. "WPA Outcomes Statement For First-Year Composition." CWPA, 2014. PDF File.

Council of Writing Program Administrators, National Council of Teachers of English, and National Writing Project. *Framework for Success in Postsecondary Writing*. CWPA, NCTE, and NWP, 2011. PDF File.

Doolitte, Peter E., and Tom Sherman. *25 Word Summaries*. Blackburg, VA: Virginia Tech Center for Instructional Development and Educational Research (CIDER), 2013. Web. 1 June 2014.

Fields, Ray. *Validity Argument for NAEP Reporting on 12th Grade Academic Preparedness for College*. Washington, DC: National Assessment Governing Board, 2013. 1 Nov. 2013. Web. 7 July 2014.

"Framework." *Random House Dictionary of the English Language*. New York: Random House. Print.

Grabe, William. "Fluency in Reading—Thirty-Five Years Later." *Reading in a Foreign Language* 22.1 (2010): 71–83. Web. 13 April 2015.

—. *Reading in a Second Language*. Cambridge: Cambridge UP, 2009. Print.

Haller, Cynthia R. "Toward Rhetorical Source Use: Three Student Journeys." *WPA: Writing Program Administration* 34.1 (2010): 33–59. Print.

Harris, Frances J. *I Found It on the Internet: Coming of Age Online*. 2nd ed. Chicago: American Library Association, 2011. Print.

Head, Alison.J. *Learning the Ropes: How Freshmen Conduct Course Research Once They Enter College*. Seattle, WA: University of Washington. 5 Dec. 2013. Web. 1 July 2014.

Herber, Harold L. *Teaching Reading in Content Areas*. 2nd ed. Englewood Cliffs: Prentice-Hall, 1978. Print.

Hillesund, Terje. "Digital Reading Spaces: How Expert Readers Handle Books the Web and Electronic Paper." *First Monday* 15.4 (2010): n. pag Web. 1 July 2014.

Horning, Alice S. *Reading, Writing and Digitizing: Understanding Literacy in the Electronic Age*. Newcastle-upon-Tyne, England: Cambridge Scholars P, 2012. Print.

Jamieson, Sandra. "Reading and Engaging Sources: What Students' Use of Sources Reveals about Advanced Writing Skills." *Across the Disciplines* 10.4 (Dec. 2013): n. pag. Web. 14 April 2015.

Jamieson, Sandra, and Rebecca Moore Howard. *The Citation Project*. 12 June 2014. Web. 7 July 2014.

Jolliffe, David A., and Alison Harl. "Texts of Our Institutional Lives: Studying the Reading Transition: From High School to College: What Are Our Students Reading and Why?" *College English* 70.6 (2008): 599–617. Print.

National Assessment of Educational Progress. "The NAEP Reading Achievement Levels by Grade." 23 December 2011. Web. 13 April 2015.

Pew Charitable Trusts. *The National Survey of America's College Students*. 10 Dec. 2006. Web. 1 July 2014.

Project SAILS. *Standardized Assessment of Information Literacy Skills*. Kent State University, 2000–2009. 10 Dec. 2009. Web. 1 July 2014.

Ravitch, Diane. *The Death and Life of the Great American School System: How Testing and Choice Are Undermining Education*. New York: Basic Books, 2010. Print.

—. *Reign of Error: The Hoax of the Privatization Movement and the Danger to America's Public Schools*. New York: Vintage/Random House, 2014. Print.

Roth, Michael S. *Beyond the University: Why Liberal Education Matters*. New Haven: Yale UP, 2014. Print.

—. "Young Minds in Critical Condition." *New York Times*, 11 May 2014, Sunday Review p. 5. Print.

United States. Dept. of Education. Institute of Education Sciences. National Center for Education Statistics, National Assessment of Educational Progress (NAEP), various years, 1992–2013 Mathematics and Reading Assessments. 14 May 2014. Web. 7 July 2014.

5 Steps to Collegiate Success in Second Language Writing

Andrea Feldman

English Language Learning (ELL) students are among the nation's fastest-growing group of students (Park; Thompson). In fact, according to the latest census data, the United States will become a majority minority nation by 2042. By mid-century, nearly one in three Americans will be a second-language speaker (US Census). In university writing courses, this increased diversity means potential opportunities for increased awareness, a broadening of perspective, and improvement in content areas with new ways of approaching problems. However, traditional course solutions may not be adequate for the influx of second-language learners. Although these solutions are institution-specific, they tend to be one-dimensional and isolated (Matsuda; Matsuda and Silva). As Paul Matsuda correctly points out, many of the approaches used to handle increasing numbers of ELL students have their own challenges. These possibilities include mainstreaming students, isolated ELL sections, and controlled enrollment within cross-cultural composition classrooms. According to Matsuda, the optimal solution is the cross-cultural composition class, which would contain both ELL and native-speaking students (NSS) in equal proportions. In each of these scenarios, the ways in which NSS assess their ELL peers' writing are crucial for success.

Moreover, as international students prepare for university studies, they face numerous obstacles. Among them are native speakers' perceptions of the academic readiness of those international students based on their writing. What might be considered problematic or bothersome to NSS about ELL writing could interfere with these assessments. The research study discussed in this chapter responds to this question of how

NSS judge their ELL peers' writing in an academic setting where peer review is common. Specifically, this chapter focuses on research conducted at the University of Colorado at Boulder on international students' writing as they prepare to enter university. The research includes interviews with college-level writing instructors, a study of pre-collegiate international student writing, and a survey of first-year native-speaking students. However, to understand and evaluate academic preparedness of our students at the University of Colorado at Boulder, my colleagues and I turned to the *Framework for Success in Postsecondary Writing*. This research leverages the *Framework* to address international student issues: How might second-language writing teachers align their pedagogy with the *Framework*? Which of the habits of mind and experiences with writing, reading and critical analysis might present problems for ELL students? Although the *Framework* did not explicitly address non-native speakers and some readers of the *Framework* may question its applicability to second-language learners, it has considerable utility in helping us prepare native- and non-native speakers alike for the twenty-first century multicultural classroom, a point that Rodrigo Joseph Rodríguez similarly argues in chapter 13 of this volume.

As we search for multi-faceted teaching and learning techniques in these more discursively diverse classrooms, the *Framework* can provide us with scaffolding to measure students' success. Moreover, if we can use the *Framework* to identify where ELL students' potential strengths and weaknesses lie, we can adjust our approaches accordingly. This chapter discusses *Framework* components judged by ELL instructors as measures of success, and focuses on peer review as an area where ELL students and NSS can benefit from this scaffolding. The chapter first outlines the design of the study, including aspects of the *Framework* that might be helpful or problematic for ELL students, the methodology, and the types of writing included. Second, the chapter reports the results, which suggest that, consistent with the *Framework*, NSS are not as bothered by ELL students "writing with an accent" (Silva) as they are by lack of intelligibility or bias.

The purpose of my research design was to gauge how native-speaking first-year writing students assess non-native speaking first-year writing students' writing. In many of our first-year courses, we assign peer-review activities, and often assume that students are familiar with this practice from their high school years. However, as international and multilingual students enter the university in greater numbers, the landscape is changing in multiple ways, and peer review is no exception.

This study addresses the following questions: What rhetorical and structural properties of ELL writing impede or enhance understanding? How can the *Framework* inform the assumptions underlying the assessments made by native-speaking students? To understand this further, I conducted a pre-survey of how faculty view international student writing.

Design of Study

Using the *Framework* in collaboration with Second-Language Writing (SLW) instructors, I designed a series of surveys to investigate and identify strategies for integrating international students into first-year university writing classes.[1] I analyzed how native English speakers conceive of international student writing, based on samples among three different genres: descriptive, argumentative, and inquiry essays.

To analyze how native English speakers (both students and faculty) view international student writing, SLW faculty and I first conducted a pre-survey, in which we interviewed instructors from both university and college-preparatory ELL programs to determine areas of concern. For instance, we asked the following questions: How do you approach surface errors in ELL student writing? Do you correct a lot, a little, none? Other questions addressed broader areas that echo the *Framework*, such as habits of mind, rhetorical knowledge, critical thinking, flexible writing processes, knowledge of conventions, and composing in multiple environments. For example, we asked questions like the following: How do you discuss audience awareness? Do you teach different genres or mainly academic writing? The second step was to collect samples of international student writing among three different genres (description, argument, and inquiry). Instructors at three institutions collected these samples based on the type of writing college-ready SLW students are familiar with. To earn acceptance into American universities, international students prepare for and take the Test of English as a Foreign Language (TOEFL) and/or International English Language Testing System test (IELTS). These tests require students to write descriptive, argumentative, and inquiry essays.

Based on the pre-survey, I created a survey which SLW faculty administered to native-speaking, first-year writing students at CU Boulder and to upper-division students who are studying cultural differences in writing styles. Beyond the expected findings of surface errors interfering with readability, I also found that emotional appeal, bias, and misuse of counter-argument identified students as non-native writers. These qualities have a close bearing on the habits of mind necessary for post-secondary success. While incorporating pathos into writing is a key to success according to the *Framework* (especially drawing on the students' multiple original experiences), bias or lack of flexibility with regard to audience is detrimental.

Methodology

To begin, and in conjunction with other faculty members, I designed a series of questions that were tested by faculty at CU Boulder's International English Center (pre-college program) and by first-year writing instructors in the Program for Writing and Rhetoric (PWR) in order to determine areas of concern. As mentioned above, this pre-survey was intended to help with the construction of the writing survey questions. I expected that to some extent surface errors might impede understanding and signal a non-native speaking writer; however, I was especially interested in exploring the rhetorical practices that extend well beyond surface error.

Based on the pre-survey, I created the survey itself. With regard to the *Framework*, I asked which of the habits of mind might present problems for ELL students. First, pertaining to curiosity, I asked questions to assess whether the student went beyond identifying the rhetorical situation and grounding of her writing to question the contexts and activities of her text. A second habit, openness, applies widely to all students. Yet, as we incorporate different genres, disciplines, and documents into ELL education, I looked for how open students are to different writing practices. I investigated whether the student was able to make connections from her own knowledge, experience, and traditions and align them with expected academic conventions. For engagement, I asked whether student writers are interested in issues in their fields and in contributing new knowledge to their fields. For the criterion of creativity, I asked the question: how original was the thinking? I attempted to separate this notion from the linguistic expression of the ideas. For persistence, I looked for evidence of revision and review because this skill requires repeated effort, concern for detail, and time. With regard to responsibility as an ethical consideration, I looked for how citations were used (or not used) when appropriate, and whether bias influenced the writing. Another important and relevant habit of mind is flexibility. Although students are often asked to write on unfamiliar topics, I asked how the student might have been able to transfer knowledge from one platform to another, employing different strategies in the writing. Looking for metacognition, I examined whether there was evidence of reflection in the writing, and awareness of the writer's and reader's roles.

Although these habits are somewhat abstract and hard to measure, I developed a survey of twenty questions (see Appendix for the survey questions) that my colleagues administered to first-year native-speaking students at the University of Colorado. I included spaces for comments to combine quantitative and qualitative results.

Samples/Stimuli

The second step was to collect samples of international student writing at three different levels of first-year incoming freshmen: Level 1—students already attending university; Level 2—students considered college-ready; and Level 3—students conditionally accepted to a college program (it was assumed that the students who were considered college-ready were at a higher level than the students who were doing remedial work through a conditional acceptance program for college). Each instructor collected approximately twenty samples. The papers were collected at three institutions: The University of Colorado at Boulder first-year SLW class, the International English Center (IEC) at CU Boulder (college-preparatory class), and the English Language Services (ELS) Center at Front Range Community College (pre-collegiate class). From the samples, I asked writing faculty at each of these institutions to select their best college-ready paper. Further, these papers were selected from ELL students who were enrolled in or selected to attend an American university within two to six months.

Twenty pre-collegiate international students at the IEC, a division of Continuing Education at CU Boulder, and at the ELS Center signed a consent form stating that they voluntarily agreed to participate, and no names were attached to the stimuli. As a control, twenty freshman first-year writing ELL students at CU also signed the same consent form.

The stimuli were coded to identify the level of the student. The stimuli were randomly distributed to the subjects, each of whom read three papers in one hour.

Participants

Twenty-six undergraduate CU students participated in the survey. All participants completed informed consent forms prior to taking the survey, as required by the Institutional Review Board. Some of the participants were first-year undergraduate writing students, and others were upper-division students who were studying cultural differences in writing styles. All were native speakers of English. Specifically, we administered the survey to thirteen first-year writing students at CU Boulder and to thirteen upper-division, multi-cultural rhetoric students. The students read the sample papers and answered the survey questions regarding how they prioritize and understand the international student writings.

Because the students were members of a class I was teaching, another instructor administered the survey. The students were offered the opportunity to participate in the research; however, those who did not wish to participate had instead the regular peer review activity that is a typical feature of the class. In a 75-minute class students usually review three full-length papers. As in the peer-review activity, the students read three sample papers and answered the survey questions regarding how they prioritize and understand the student writings. The three sample papers were chosen by the three programs mentioned above (PWR, IEC, and ELS) as their best representative college-ready paper.

The survey results were tabulated using CU-Qualtrics survey software. While many of the questions were multiple choice and could be quantified, some of the questions were qualitative. The qualitative comments were examined for consistencies. Realizing that the numbers of subjects were few, I expected the findings to be tentative and mainly descriptive rather than statistically significant.

WRITING SAMPLES AND CULTURAL ASSUMPTIONS

Before discussing the survey results, I need to provide some background on the writings and classroom activities, including cultural assumptions of the classes surveyed. Paper 1, titled, "The 1997 Asian Financial Crisis: An Investigation into the Economic Impacts on South Korea and its Policy Responses," claimed that South Korea's efforts to handle the economic crisis were largely effective. This paper was written by an ELL student in a mainstream first-year writing class in the PWR at CU-Boulder, in which the students were asked to incorporate personal or primary-source material into their papers. Paper 2, titled "The Causes of

Moving to Big Cities," addressed urban migration in China and claimed that jobs and education are the main reasons for people moving to large cities in China. This paper was written in an advanced level writing class at the ELS language center, where students were also asked to incorporate personal experience into their papers. Paper 3, titled "How Globalization Affects World Cultures," claims that globalization threatens cultural identity and creates a homogenous society lacking diversity. This paper was written in an advanced-level 2 class at the IEC as a research and evidence-based paper. Like many students (non-native and native speakers alike), the student-authors of these samples adopt flexible modes of organization, tone, style, and idea development. However, for the international students, vocabulary and idiomatic expressions can be challenging. Some of the sample papers surveyed included a sprinkling of words from other languages for rhetorical effect. The native-speaking students from the US did not have much difficulty understanding the gist of the international student writing. Yet, when asked to identify whether the student was a second-language writer, the main area that stood out was the ability to achieve intelligibility. Although the peer reviewers commented on non-native use of idioms, misuse of vocabulary and grammatical structure, the most common problematic areas were straight from Western-style argumentation, including issues of bias, emotional appeal, and handling of counter-argument, all of which relate to the *Framework*. Interestingly, some students commented that, although they identified the paper as non-native, the language was not a problem. For instance, one student mentioned in response to Paper 1, "The author is clearly totally fluent, whether English is their second language or not." On the other hand, with regard to the weaker paper (Paper 2) another student commented, "However, this sounds as if it was put into a translator." Paper 2 was riddled with lexical and syntactical errors, and the students found it very confusing and hard to follow. As the *Framework* suggests, conventions (or intelligibility, in this case) are certainly important for success, beyond which rhetorical issues (audience awareness, sensitivity to bias) and creativity (incorporating original experience) influence the assessment of the writing.

Results

Between seven and nine subjects responded to each of the three papers. Seven out of eight students believed that Paper 1 (written by a currently enrolled international student at CU Boulder) was a native speaker of

English. This contrasts with eight out of nine students who believed Paper 2 (written by an ELS student) was non-native; versus three out of seven who thought Paper 3 (written by an IEC student) was non-native. The differences show that the sample papers represented three different levels of English proficiency, with Paper 1 ranking the highest, Paper 2 the lowest, and Paper 3 in the middle.

Although grammatical conventions were one indication of non-native writing ability and Paper 3 was identified as lacking in grammaticality, the student comments suggest that students, nonetheless, very much appreciated the writing and were likely to review the paper favorably. For example, one student commented, "I thought this was very interesting and relevant to many things. It was very interesting the way he laid things out." And another student commented, "Enjoyable. Thought-provoking." However, other students were mixed on their reviews of Paper 3, saying, "I understood the thesis and the argument stayed consistent, but the overall flow was stilted and transitions could've been handled better."

These reviews suggest that other considerations, beyond the linguistic conventions, affect peer review, as they do papers written by native speakers. In fact, more than 50% of the readers did not see emotional appeal (pathos) in the argument of Paper 1. (7 out of 8 responders either did not see emotion or were uncertain if they saw emotion in Paper 1.)

However, we see a difference in the usage of emotional appeal in Papers 2 and 3; 5 out of 9 of the readers thought Paper 2 used emotional appeal and 3 out of 7 identified Paper 3 as emotional. Some of the written comments explain the findings. For instance, regarding Paper 2, one student commented, "Ask someone with a stronger grasp on or more experience with English to help with the grammar, basically. Aside from that, the paper is very much based around opinion and personal sentiment rather than research or anything citable, so the author's bias is a serious question." By contrast, though Paper 1 was seen as near-native in writing, a student reviewer wrote, "Add more personal opinion or voice. Add more examples and things people can relate to." And another student: "I would suggest strengthening their points with emotional appeal if possible. They could also improve sentence structure." With regard to Paper 3, students noticed that the writer was a non-native speaker, but appreciated the use of pathos; as one student said, "The passion behind the issue leads me to believe this is someone with a distinct culture outside of the homogenized West. There are also a few grammatical errors and left out words that lead to this conclusion as well."

In general, the use of emotional appeal appears to be seen as a positive by the student reviewers, but it must be tempered by evidence and a lack of bias. These competing demands on ELL students make striking a balance difficult to handle; they might think of emotional engagement in isolated terms when in fact the rhetorical exigencies are complex. The relationships of pathos, logos, and ethos draw on the *Framework*'s habits of mind, specifically, openness, flexibility, and metacognition. The *Framework* suggests that successful students will be open to new academic conventions, be flexible and adapt strategies from prior experiences to their new settings, and be metacognitively aware of the differences in approaches in strategy and organization. ELL students need to temper their emotional engagement with a metacognitive awareness of its strategic value or liability.

In all three papers, students attempted to use and refute a counter-argument. How this was perceived by native-speaking first-year writing students varied, however. That is, although each of the writers attempted to address and refute counter-arguments, participants' perceptions were equally divided between whether the counter-argument was refuted. However, for Paper 2, 6 out of 9 respondents believed a counter-argument was not refuted, and the remaining three respondents felt a counter-argument was not applicable to the assignment. This is the one question on which the ELL student writers were consistently identified as lacking. This outcome, or lack of an effective counter-argument, may be more distracting than the grammatical differences in peer assessment of international student writing. The *Framework*'s habits of mind ask students to place themselves in another's shoes by being open to new perspectives. I would suggest that several of the *Framework*'s attributes, namely curiosity, openness, responsibility (as required by the assignment), flexibility, and creativity directly contribute to constructing key counter-arguments and rebuttals. Less directly, engagement, metacognition, and persistence contribute, assuming that the student wrote multiple drafts, received student and teacher feedback, and made the effort to complete this part of the assignment.

Finally, both overuse of emotion and lack of counter-argument contribute to a sense of bias in the writing. As predicted, the samples considered less native-like were thought to be unfairly biased, according to norms of Western academic writing. Paper 1 was considered unbiased, and no respondents felt the paper was biased in any way, in spite of mixed responses on counter-argument and emotional appeal. One student commented, "I aspire to write of this caliber," among many other positive comments. Although many students recognized surface and structural errors, the fairness and apparent persuasiveness of an unfamiliar cultural topic appealed to the audience. Paper 2 was considered completely biased, which may have resulted in the overall consensus that the paper was not academically ready. One overall comment sums up the consensus: "I thought overall that Paper 2 was a very poorly written paper." Further, "This form of writing was incredibly informal and not appropriate for an academic text. It had no support from outside sources, and was poorly written with improper grammar." Although the student reviewers did not express that bias was a factor in their written comments and evaluations, they agreed that the weaker papers were biased to a great extent. Paper 3 was considered somewhat biased with 5 out of 7 respondents articulating that assessment. 2 out of 7 respondents felt that the paper lacked bias. The notion of bias as a consideration of formal academic writing was apparent in the students' comments: "The lack of supported argument kind of annoys me, honestly. The essay is all over the place, and seems to be trying to convince me that globalization is bad, but it doesn't seem to be making any effort to explain WHY it's bad beyond the author's feelings and largely unexplicated opinions."

Conclusion

The *Framework* provides us with tools that students can acquire to achieve success in academic writing as they progress through their courses. How can we cultivate these strategies in our students? The results suggest that the *Framework* provides a key to the success of international students as they write for an American college audience. This research can improve our understanding of academic preparation and better inform faculty of international student needs. By incorporating the *Framework* into classroom practices, instructors can cultivate a more hospitable environment. Moreover, this insight will help students better prepare to write for an American college student audience, and for currently enrolled students to address potentially problematic areas.

First, instead of teaching discrete skills, such as counter-argument or citation, we can encourage students to be flexible to other perspectives and explain the importance of these underlying principles. When learning counter-argument in my second-language writing classes for instance, students sometimes initially believe that the goal is to change sides in the argument and argue both sides. Alternatively, other students avoid the counter-argument entirely, thinking it will weaken their position to bring up shortcomings. While native speakers of English may also have these characteristics to some degree, international students, especially those from non-Western cultural traditions, have a different understanding of cultural discourse, written English, organizational patterns, and styles.

Second, although emotional appeal was seen as a component of international student writing, the passion and voice of the students can be embraced as a strength. By capitalizing on their originality (creativity), voice, and diversity, international students add a dimension to the classroom that we otherwise might lack. If we harness the emotion by asking students to write from their own experiences, even evoking multiple rhetorics and explaining them clearly to their audience, we can all gain as readers. Specifically we can construct assignments with open-ended topics, ones that ask students to draw on their own experiences as evidence. Further, prompts that encourage multiple perspectives on a given issue incorporate multiple aspects of the *Framework*, such as curiosity, openness, engagement, creativity, and flexibility.

Finally, as always, the *Framework* provides us with specific strategies to emphasize in teaching international students. For example, international and local students can interview each other to discern how political or cultural information is perceived in different countries. For teaching rhetorical knowledge, for example, we have seen from this study that students' understanding of audience, including an audience of their peers, is helpful in academic success. To this end, I recommend constructing real-world assignments with accessible audiences that students engage with as directly as possible. These audiences can include their own peers, at times. Moreover, we note that cross-cultural instruction in ethos, pathos, and logos will help students establish credibility. If students engage audiences with personal and emotional experiences, they must also clearly organize and articulate the relevance of those experiences as evidence for a strong argument.

Another *Framework* component, critical thinking, is key to success. As we have seen, a key to success is trouble-shooting a text, considering multiple points of view, and presenting a fair-minded picture. This is done by encouraging the habit of metacognition, by having students critique a published text or a peer's paper. However, in many of our classrooms, we haven't discussed explicitly how to comment on peers' papers for revision. Our international and multilingual students may not be clear on the sorts of expressions that are permissible in academic writing, if not stated directly. Explicit instruction, modeling, and a guide for peer-review are extremely helpful in this regard. Peer-review guidelines that reflect the *Framework*'s habits of mind would be helpful to all our students. Although many native-speaking students are open to diversity, multilingualism, and multiculturalism, they may have not yet discovered ways to incorporate these notions into their own writing. Prompts that encourage students to write from their own experiences or that ask them to discover different perspectives on current issues will allow students to cross borders and develop open, creative, flexible habits of mind. By writing in liminal spaces, or in-between cultures, students can discover a translingual approach (Horner et al.), incorporating their voices and diverse experiences.

The *Framework* highlights writing processes and in fact, a key component to academic success appears to be revision, and bringing multiple perspectives to bear on the writing. As many international students may not be familiar with this process, one approach is to break down the steps of writing a paper in a formalized way (Bass), first thinking through how an expert constructs meaning, and then asking students to step into that process. By slowing down the writing process and making knowledge visible, students can overcome blocks and impediments.

Finally, knowledge of conventions is a part of the *Framework* that non-native speakers can use productively. Given that our native-speaking students do not focus as much on vocabulary, structure, or grammatical errors but pay more attention to meaning, we might see how students use words to create meaning in a new cultural context. For example, if the structures, vocabulary, and idioms they wish to use are unfamiliar to native speakers, they can explain them by analogy to their new environment.

We are nonetheless aware of the importance placed on these features in academic writing. As Horner et al. state,

> Writers' proficiency in a language will thus be measured not by their ability to produce an abstracted set of conventional forms. Rather, it will be shown by the range of practices they can draw on; their ability to use these creatively; and their ability to produce meaning out of a wide range of practices in their reading.

> Translingual fluency in writing would be defined as deftness in deploying a broad and diverse repertoire of language resources, and responsiveness to the diverse range of readers' social positions and ideological perspectives. (308)

The participants in this study consistently noticed that two of the three papers were non-native writers based in large part on surface errors, but were nonetheless appreciative of the creative and diverse approaches they presented. If we accept a translingual approach, we can only enrich the lives of all our students. By encouraging our students to incorporate and reflect on the views and language of their peers into their own writing, we can create a dynamic, open, metacognitive classroom.

The *Framework* also mentions the ability to compose in multiple environments. Though not addressed in this survey, composing in a multiplicity of settings, genres, and styles will increase the repertoire of our students. Many international students have recounted to me that they are accustomed to traditional pen and paper essays and commenting. Naturally students (both domestic and international) are composing outside the classroom on the Internet and social media where they find themselves negotiating meaning with those of diverse linguistic and cultural backgrounds. We behoove ourselves as instructors to harness those energies by encouraging our students to use these resources in the classroom, whether to critique or produce new texts for this globalized community.

Note

1. This research was funded in part by the Implementation of Multicultural Perspectives and Approaches in Research and Teaching Awards (IMPART) Program. I obtained IRB exempt certification for this study on August 6, 2013.

Works Cited

Bass, Randall. "Gathering Evidence to Improve Student Learning." Boulder, CO: Faculty Teaching Excellence Program Assessment Institute, University of Colorado, 7 January 2011. Guest Presentation.

Council of Writing Program Administrators, National Council of Teachers of English, and National Writing Project. *Framework for Success in Postsecondary Writing*. CWPA, NCTE, and NWP, 2011. PDF File.

Horner, Bruce, Min-Zhan Lu, Jacqueline Jones Royster, and John Trimbur. "Language Difference in Writing: Towards a Translingual Approach." *College English* 73.3 (2011): 303–21. Print.

International English Language Testing System. "Welcome to IELTS." IELTS, n.d. Web.

Matsuda, Paul Kei. "The Myth of Linguistic Homogeneity in U.S. College Composition." *College Composition and Communication* 68.6 (2006): 637–51. Print.

Matsuda, Paul Kei and Tony Silva. "Cross-Cultural Composition: Mediated Integration of U.S. and International Students." *Second-Language Writing in the Composition Classroom: A Critical Sourcebook*. Ed. Paul Kei Matsuda, Michelle Cox, Jay Jordan, and Christina Ortmeier-Hooper. New York: Bedford/St. Martin's, 2006. 246–59. Print.

Park, Haeyoun. "New to English." *New York Times*. New York Times, 13 March 2009. Web. 16 June 2014.

"Qualtrics." *Office of Information Technology*. N.p.: University of Colorado, n.d. Web. 24 July 2015.

Silva, Tony. *Writing Across Borders*. Oregon State University, 2015. Web. 24 March 2015.

TOEFL: Home. ETS, n.d. Web. 24 July 2015.

Thompson, Ginger. "Where Education and Assimilation Collide." *New York Times*. New York Times, 14 March 2009. Web. 16 June 2014.

United States. Census Bureau. *United States Census: An Older and More Diverse Nation by Midcentury*. US Census Bureau, 2008. Web. 16 June 2014.

Appendix: Steps to Collegiate Success Survey

Please fill out the consent form if you wish to participate.
>Informed consent form steps to collegiate success in second language writing

Please select one of the following options.
>I am a faculty member   I am a student

Please read one of the three linked papers:
>Paper 1
>Paper 2
>Paper 3

Complete the survey once for each paper you review. You may take this survey up to three times.

Which paper you are reviewing here:
>Paper 1   Paper 2   Paper 3

Is the formality (overall style) appropriate for academic writing?
>Strongly Agree   Agree   Disagree   Strongly Disagree

Comments?

Are the sentence to sentence transitions purposeful?
>Strongly Agree   Agree   Disagree   Strongly Disagree

Are the paragraph to paragraph transitions purposeful?
>Strongly Agree   Agree   Disagree   Strongly Disagree

Is the writing appropriate for an academic audience?
>Strongly Agree   Agree   Disagree   Strongly Disagree

Is the writing appropriate for its context and genre?
>Strongly Agree   Agree   Disagree   Strongly Disagree

Is the organization clear?
>Strongly Agree   Agree   Disagree   Strongly Disagree

Does the student provide a thesis?
>Strongly Agree   Agree   Disagree   Strongly Disagree

Does the paper demonstrate original thinking?
>Strongly Agree   Agree   Disagree   Strongly Disagree

Does the evidence show logical reasoning?
>Strongly Agree   Agree   Disagree   Strongly Disagree

Does the author use emotional appeal to support the points, if applicable?
Strongly Agree   Agree   Neither Agree nor Disagree   Disagree   Strongly Disagree

Are examples explained fully?
>Strongly Agree   Agree   Disagree   Strongly Disagree

Does the paper show original structure or wording?
    Strongly Agree   Agree   Disagree   Strongly Disagree

Is the counter-argument (if any) refuted?
    Not Applicable Strongly Agree   Agree Disagree   Strongly Disagree

Does the paper show a lack of bias?
    Strongly Agree   Agree   Disagree   Strongly Disagree

Does the paper use correct citations (if necessary)?
    Not Applicable Strongly Agree   Agree Disagree   Strongly Disagree

Does the conclusion either synthesize or summarize?
    Strongly Agree   Agree   Disagree   Strongly Disagree

What recommendations/suggestions would you give this student?

What is your overall reaction to this paper?

Do you think the author is a second language writer?
    Yes   No

What aspects of the essay might suggest that the author is or is not a second language writer?

6 A Writing Program's Teachers Speak: Metacognition and the *Framework for Success in Postsecondary Writing*

Dawn S. Opel

When a large university writing program uses the *Framework for Success in Postsecondary Writing*—specifically, the habits of mind—in its institutional training and discussion opportunities, what effect might those discussions have in the university classroom? In this chapter, I present a study of a large university writing program that explores how a writing program's teachers perceive this effect. I conducted this study in the summer of 2013 with a cross-section of a large research university's writing program teachers from various experience levels (TA, part-time faculty, and full-time faculty) and various areas of English studies (rhetoric and composition, linguistics, creative writing, and literature). The experimental design consisted of formal individual interviews with teachers. In these interviews, the teachers reflected on their first-year composition course syllabi and writing assignment prompts with an eye toward the habits of mind in practice. Through these interviews, teachers discussed the *Framework* and how they have experienced it: in teaching assistantship training, in the writing program's continued educational offerings and community conversations, and in professional development opportunities such as scholarly conferences.

These interviews yielded a rich data set uncovering the myriad ways in which the *Framework* shapes the pedagogy and practice of a writing teacher. While the aim of the study was to identify and evaluate discernable spaces for development of students' metacognitive skills (this aim was informed by writing transfer theory, specifically, Rebecca Nowacek's theory of meta-awareness in transfer as recontextualization), teachers universally offered information about practices relating to the other habits of mind as well—for instance, the effects of valuing particular habits of mind in student writing over others. In this way, the study did much more than simply identify how curricula is shaped by the habits of mind; similar to what Angela Clark-Oates provides in chapter 14 of this volume, it offers useful narrative feedback from the teachers themselves on their values vis-à-vis student writing and the teaching of writing. In essence, as Alice Johnston Myatt and Ellen Shelton also demonstrate in chapter 12 of this volume, the *Framework* offers a framework for teachers to share what they value.

First, this chapter presents this case study, describing this particular writing program, the teacher interviews I conducted, and the study's methods of data collection and interpretation. Second, the chapter discusses the findings, in terms of how writing program teachers became acquainted with the *Framework*, how they use and perceive the *Framework*, and then more specifically about their syllabi and the habits of mind. Finally, this chapter concludes with logistical considerations about the facilitation of habits of mind that the writing program's teachers articulated in these interviews, and how these might affect the influence and reach of the *Framework* more broadly.

Case Study Background and Methodology

In anticipation of interview process, I performed an institutional history from this large research university's writing program (hereinafter, "the writing program") as it related to its writing teachers, its teacher training offerings, and specifically, the habits of mind. To preface a discussion of the design of this study, it may be helpful to discuss some findings from this history as they relate to the writing program and the scaffolding it provides for its faculty in the teaching of writing. The writing program, which is one of the largest in the United States, teaches approximately 18,000 students every year. Of these, approximately 14,000 students are enrolled in first-year composition, although the writing program also offers advanced general education composition courses and workplace writing courses. The writing program is comprised of a faculty of 200 teachers, of whom 50% are graduate students and 33% are full-time contract faculty. The remainder consists of part-time faculty, who hold at least a master's degree in an area of English studies. The graduate student component of the faculty is a mixture of funded PhD students in literature, rhetoric and composition, and linguistics, as well as MFA students. This group is required to enroll in a yearlong training program that is comprised of a summer intensive orientation to the writing program followed by two semesters of one course each in the teaching of writing.

All writing program faculty are required to attend a fall and spring writing program convocation, which consists of ongoing training with multiple presentations and breakout workshop sessions. Finally, all writing program faculty have access to and participate in the writing program Blackboard site, which houses shared documents such as procedural forms and sample course documents for aid in curriculum design. All writing program teachers are required to post their syllabi in advance of a given semester on a group bulletin board site that is viewable by all teachers.

Following the publication of the *Framework for Success in Postsecondary Writing* in January of 2011, the writing program integrated the document into its formal training offerings. Across the US, as the chapters within this volume demonstrate, the *Framework* has entered institutions of secondary and higher education in various contexts, including discussion prompts for faculty in career development workshops and in reflective writing prompts for students (Rose). Prior to this study, the past three writing program convocation programs used the habits of mind as a training tool and conversation starter. The writing program circulated the document itself to all writing program teachers, as well as a *PowerPoint* presentation with the habits of mind and instructions for conversation starters. A series of small group exercises allowed writing program teachers the opportunity to discern how these habits might be addressed in the writing classroom. These small group exercises culminated in spring 2012 semester's "conversation starters," or a set of sample classroom lessons that teachers analyzed for their ability to attend to various habits of mind. Teachers then worked together to build upon these lessons for their various courses, and the writing program distributed this work via *Blackboard* shortly thereafter for teachers' use in their own classrooms if they so chose.

Interviews

I designed this study with the goal of talking one-on-one with writing program teachers about their experiences with institutional training offerings that focused on habits of mind, and a discussion of teachers' goals and values when teaching first-year composition in the writing program. After IRB application for exemption was approved, the study moved forward as I solicited all writing program teachers for interviews with subsequent requests for participating teachers' first-year composition syllabi and writing assignment prompts. I conducted interviews in April and May of 2013. The participating teachers included nine graduate students (two literature PhD students, one linguistics PhD student, and six rhetoric and composition PhD students) and three full-time faculty members (one tenured faculty member, one lecturer, and one instructor). All of these teachers have taught first-year composition at least one semester in the last two years and have participated in all writing program convocations. Participants in the study volunteered and submitted their syllabi in advance, along with specific reflective assignment prompts, and then participated in a 30- to 45-minute audiotaped interview in which the materials were discussed.

The focus of the interview protocol was the habit of mind of metacognition, in order to determine to what extent metacognition is actually finding a space in the writing program's first-year composition classroom. The interview questions began with a general question about which first-year composition courses the teachers teach or have taught in the writing program. I then asked about their teaching philosophy and the habits of mind, with specific emphasis on metacognition. Teachers were asked to identify specific instances in their syllabi and assignments where an exercise facilitated the development of metacognition, and asked to describe how this was done and why it was beneficial. I asked teachers if there was a specific point in their FYC course design sequencing in which a metacognitive exercise was most beneficial, and if so, when and how was the exercise employed. The interviews concluded with open-ended questions about the major course assignments in their syllabi, with specific discussion of what pedagogical goals are met with each assignment. This final portion of the interview allowed teachers to direct the focus of the discussion to teaching practices that they felt were most beneficial to their students.

Data Analysis

Subsequent to the interview process, I hand coded the syllabi and transcripts from the interviews using a descriptive first-cycle coding approach (Saldaña 70). I chose the descriptive codes according to specific areas of metacognitive research interest (e.g., identifying where rhetorical genre theory or rhetorical dimensions of genre appeared). I then analyzed these results thematically to discern trends in cultivation of metacognitive spaces in these first-year composition classrooms. It is important to note that this portion of the study was not evaluating the efficacy of these spaces, but instead was limited to how a large research university's writing program attends across classrooms to an identified habit of mind for success in postsecondary writing.

In this data-analysis process, I discovered that other habits of mind were discussed by teachers and used in classrooms in important ways. Rather than limiting the analysis to metacognition as my original experimental design anticipated, I chose instead to employ a grounded theory approach wherein this observation caused me to inductively take into consideration emerging codes from the data analysis process (Saldaña 85). The interviews were subsequently coded in a second cycle to capture data on all habits of mind—giving each habit of mind a descriptive code—and allowing a wider vantage point for observing and analyzing the practices and values of writing program teachers. This vantage point also more suitably reflects what teachers desired to discuss in this set of interviews. In essence, the teachers' practices as they described them in their interviews more readily fit into descriptions of other habits of mind.

From Training to Practice: the Habits of Mind in Teacher Narratives

Not surprisingly, given the emphasis on the *Framework* in the writing program's recent convocations, all twelve teachers interviewed expressed familiarity with the habits of mind and the convocation trainings that involved these concepts. Six of twelve teachers spoke enthusiastically about the benefits they gleaned from breakout discussion groups that focused on the habits of mind at the most recent writing program convocation. These breakout groups involved discussion around specific classroom activities (submitted in advance by writing program teachers) and connecting them to the habits of mind they may or may not facilitate. The six teachers that found these breakout discussions helpful offered different rationales for why these were helpful. One teacher found it a practical exercise to match specific activities with habits of mind, or to see how habits of mind were performed "in real life" (rather than theoretically). Another found it useful to see how other writing program teachers instantiate habits of mind in their classrooms. Three spoke about how their breakout groups were formed around an affinity for a specific habit of mind or classroom activity, and their groups were able to spend time talking about what they value as a collective.

Of the teachers who did not explicitly state that the writing program activities benefitted them, two offered the reason that the conversations were not helpful due to the disparate beliefs of the teachers in the breakout groups. Their breakout groups were unable to form traction as a result of either a lack of consensus on what habits of mind to discuss or value or incompatible classroom practices suggesting very different ways of knowing and enacting the habits of mind. This made the discussion a less enjoyable and/or useful exercise. Nevertheless, none of the six teachers equated their negative experiences with these convocation exercises with negative beliefs about the habits of mind or *Framework*; and discussions of metacognition and other habits of mind in the interviews reveal that the teachers' familiarity with these concepts stemmed from the exercises, regardless of the teachers' stated beliefs on their utility.

When asked about teaching assistantship training, the results were less instructive as pertaining to the habits of mind or the *Framework*, which is not surprising given that all but three teachers interviewed had gone through teaching assistantship training before the *Framework* came into being. Nine of the twelve teachers indicated that so much time had elapsed since their training that they could not remember much about it, or, that their masters' programs at other institutions had prepared them to teach, and as a result, they did not recall a connection between that early training and their pedagogy or values as a teacher. The other three teachers, all graduate student teaching assistants, spoke about specific lesson plans that they still teach in their first-year composition classrooms. These teachers believed that these lesson plans gave them confidence as new teachers, and that since these lesson plans resulted in successful outcomes they continue to use them. These outcomes were not linked to pedagogy per se, but instead, in confidence in their teaching abilities or the classroom activity's ability to answer what Paul Lynch calls the "Monday morning question," or, "the question that asks, 'This theory (or idea, or philosophy) you're proposing is great and everything, but what am I supposed to do with it when the students show up on Monday morning?'" (*xi*).

METACOGNITION AND THE FIRST-YEAR COMPOSITION CLASSROOM

As Angela Rounsaville, Rachel Goldberg, and Anis Bawarshi note, in writing studies, education studies, and psychology, researchers are pointing to metacognition as "crucial to knowledge transfer, especially across dissimilar contexts of the sort students will encounter between FYW courses, courses in different academic disciplines, and workplace settings" (97–98). Rebecca Nowacek, in *Agents of Integration: Understanding Transfer as a Rhetorical Act*, discusses the role of meta-awareness in "transfer understood as recontextualization" (30). The most benefit derived from metacognitive awareness occurs "when the process of connecting knowledge, ways of knowing, identities or goals from one activity system to another" (30) takes place. Nowacek's theoretical framework suggests that "conscious awareness of the rhetorical dimensions of genre is not necessary for transfer—but is helpful" (142). She indicates that more research could help us understand the degree to which this awareness aids in students' ability to act as agents of integration—connecting their "seeing" of genre to their "selling," and how we as teachers may better aid in the development (142). In the *Framework for Success in Postsecondary Writing*, the Council of Writing Program Administrators (CWPA), the National Council of Teachers of English (NCTE), and the National Writing Project (NWP) articulate eight habits of mind that foster said success, one of which nods in the direction of high road transfer. The eighth habit, metacognition, is defined in the document as "the ability to reflect on one's own thinking as well as on the individual and cultural processes used to structure knowledge" (5).

Data from the study fell into five broad categories where rhetorical genre interfaces with first-year composition, or perceived metacognitive spaces in the teacher's course (see Table 1). The first involves the first week of the course and the course description in the syllabus. Of the teachers interviewed, seven make explicit—both on the syllabus page and in discussion—the connection between first-year composition and other contexts such as the major or career. They read and discuss with their students in class their syllabi course descriptions such as, "English 102 is designed to help you develop sophisticated, situation-sensitive reading and writing strategies" and "writing for various discourse communities requires various rhetorical conventions." Interestingly, for three syllabi that did not include text related to context or genre, these teachers self-described their exercise reading the syllabus as group work in which small student groups "translate" the syllabus and presented it to other students to explain what first-year composition meant to them. These three all indicated that applying goals of first-year composition to the major or other coursework was a component of these discussions.

Table 1. Metacognitive Spaces in Writing Program's FYC Courses

Metacognitive "space"	Teachers Utilizing	Teachers Not Utilizing
Course description in syllabi with explicit transfer-informed content (may include genre theory)	7/12	5/12
WAW curriculum (entire course)	1/12	11/12 (First-Year TA textbook chosen by WP)
WAC/WID/transfer-informed project assignment prompts	7/12	5/12
WAC/WID/transfer-driven reflective writing prompts, or informal "meta-moments"	7/12	5/12
End-of-course reflection (looking back)	12/12	0/12 (required per WP policy for FYC courses)
End-of-course reflection with transfer-informed prompt (looking forward)	5/12	7/12

The second category involves the curriculum of each first-year composition course. Of the twelve interviewed, only one was utilizing a Writing About Writing (WAW) curriculum. This teacher's syllabus, as a result of the textbook and curriculum utilized, involved writing assignments and classroom activities that nearly all directly and explicitly related to metacognition and transfer. (This teacher is coincidentally also an advanced rhetoric and composition PhD student who conducts research in composition studies.) A large factor in these data on curriculum is the writing program's policy on textbook choice: newer teachers and non-rhetoric and composition-educated teachers must teach from a selected rhetoric, none of which are a WAW-based textbook. However, more advanced rhetoric and composition PhDs and faculty may select their own textbooks.

The third and fourth categories contain data about writing across the curriculum and writing in the disciplines-based work in the FYC classroom. It is important to note that the writing program has WAC-specific and WID pilot courses as well. These courses were not analyzed in this study. That being said, data found here indicate that teachers in regular first-year composition courses are informed by these concepts when planning first-year composition coursework. For large project assignment prompts, these ranged in design. Three involved literacy narratives that asked students to draw metacognitively on writing knowledge acquired before entering the first-year composition classroom, to ask Rounsaville et al.'s question of "how outcomes are related to incomes" (99). Some were informed by WAC/WID methods, such as asking students to apply a set of prompts from first-year composition to the intended major. The prompt asks that the student "interview a professor in your major to understand how you will be asked to write in that discipline, then write a research paper in first-year composition that satisfies disciplinary requirements." Finally, some projects required selection and engagement of digital literacies that may be used in students' everyday lives or technical writing careers, such as building Web sites, blogs, and making short films. In the latter type of assignments, several teachers asked for students to draw on literacies acquired in other contexts and look for ways to apply them in first-year composition and, then again later, in other courses or work/life contexts. Two teachers used reflective journaling or blogging assignments to reflect on the manner by which these literacies could be recontextualized into the larger project. In all of these cases, this project was used as a large, culminating assignment to complete the first-year composition experience at the end of the first year.

The remaining spaces all rendered a time for reflection to some degree in the first-year composition classroom. Throughout the semester, seven teachers assigned *meta-moments* (a term borrowed from Elizabeth Wardle and Doug Downs' WAW curriculum). These were metacognitive spaces interwoven throughout the semester to reflect on the knowledge acquired in first-year composition and its usefulness outside of the first-year composition classroom. Many more teachers beyond seven are asking their students to reflect on readings or completed assignments, but seven make a larger connection to transferring this knowledge across contexts. The latter was often as simple as asking "how may this help you in the future," but in WAW and WAC-specific curricula, a more instantiated description was asked for. One such example of this type of assignment is as follows: " . . . respond to Carter's article ["Ways of Knowing, Doing, and Writing in Disciplines"]. Which of the four metagenres he describes do you think your major would fit within? What does the metagenre you identify suggest about the ways of thinking and making arguments that are valued in your discipline?" This homework assignment, like others in this category, asked students to recontextualize knowledge of metagenre gained in a rhetorically informed first-year composition course with the processes used to create knowledge in the major.

Finally, the end-of-semester course reflection—an assignment required by all first-year composition courses per the writing program's policy—fell into two data sets after reconciling assignment prompts and interviews with teachers. All twelve teachers interviewed used the assignment in a fashion that asks students to reflect back on the semester and identify gains and continued challenges in their writing processes, based on a narrative of the large writing assignments completed in the course. A third of these further specified that students connect these reflections to the goals of the course as outlined in the front matter of the syllabus. The second data set includes five course reflection assignments that also asked of students that they look forward to future writing—in the university and beyond—and connect knowledge acquired in the first-year composition classroom to that future writing. Selections from these types of prompts include the following: "How do you plan on transferring ideas learned in this class to future courses? How have you already used ideas from this course in other courses? What has been most valuable for you from this semester? How do you see writing playing a role in your life after this course?" The difference between the first set of data and the second is reflection versus reflection explicitly designed for metacognition in support of transfer.

Results from this study indicate that the writing program training clearly made teachers aware of the habit of mind of metacognition and how to identify it ("I know it when I see it"), and that materials posted on the writing program's Blackboard site influence favorably front matter of syllabi and course content with regards to reflective spaces in first-year composition courses. However, other factors, such as disciplinarity and the experience level of the teacher also affect curriculum design and the degree to which metacognitive space is reflective in general or reflective specifically with an aim for transfer as recontextualization. It is important to remember that metacognition is but one habit of mind in the *Framework*, and it is also possible that competing course goals can complicate the focus on this particular habit. This is the issue taken up in the section below, as other habits of mind are addressed.

While many spaces are being opened and explored metacognitively in the writing program's first-year composition classroom, there are always more opportunities and possibilities for continued improvement. The data render a further suggestion that in the same manner that students need to be told explicitly *how* transfer might occur, so might teachers of writing need to consider explicitly the move from reflection on writing to reflection on writing transfer, and the possibility that getting at that kind of metacognitive work may require explicit verbal and textual acknowledgement of the question of *how* students might recontextualize knowledge acquired in the first-year composition classroom. This is consistent with findings from Linda Adler-Kassner, John Majewski, and Damian Koshnick's recent study on threshold concepts in general education classrooms, for example (Adler-Kassner et al.). Praxis is difficult in enacting principles such as explicit direction about metacognition across the classrooms of two hundred writing teachers in multiple areas of English studies.

Beyond Metacognition: Other Habits of Mind and Related Values

As the interviewer, my concern with the study was initially that teachers would attempt to conform their answers to my desired result; that is, to describe as many metacognitive practices for students in their classrooms as they could muster. However, as this section indicates, this concern did not manifest itself in the data collected. My questions were worded around concepts connected to rhetorical genre theory: I specifically asked about syllabi entries or assignments that appeared (or might possibly appear) to connect the knowledge or goals of first-year composition to other activity systems, whether it be other courses in college, student majors, or career or life outside of the university. Teachers did not stretch answers to meet these criteria, and were frank about their attention paid in each instance or about their attention to other valued areas of writing instruction. For example, one teacher, when asked about the course reflection and its contents, said that he "ran out of time" to create a prompt for the assignment. This atmosphere of frankness offers much in the way of getting beyond the syllabus page itself and into the lived experience of the classroom.

The "ran out of time" statement also speaks to an important finding in this study: that while metacognition was found to be an important habit of mind or value in the first-year composition classroom (particularly for those teachers with a rhetoric and composition background), it was not the only one. Four teachers spoke about the inherent time limitations in a first-year composition semester. It is impossible to do it all, and, as one teacher stated, "We have to cut things out." The concept that connected these four teachers' responses was the notion that certain habits of mind were more important than others at specific times in the course of the semester. While the other eight teachers did not speak explicitly to this point, they implicitly spoke to it by talking at length in the interviews about other values they held with regard to specific classroom activities and outcomes. That is, even though I as the interviewer asked a question that was intended to evoke a response about metacognition, the response reflected a different habit of mind or a different value that the teacher chose to foreground instead.

What follows is narrative feedback that writing program teachers provided, without prompt, about what they value in student writing. These values have been connected to the other habits of mind (see Table 2), but what is more revealing is how the habit of mind of metacognition provided a jumping off point for the discussion of these other values.

Here, I highlight narrative comments from writing program teachers that I have grouped into the three habits of mind of creativity, persistence, and responsibility.

Table 2. Other Habits of Mind in Writing Program's FYC Classrooms

Habit of Mind	*Framework*'s Description	Teachers Who Discussed Activities in this Category
Curiosity	the desire to know more about the world	7/12
Openness	the willingness to consider new ways of being and thinking in the world	7/12
Engagement	a sense of investment and involvement in learning	8/12
Creativity	the ability to use novel approaches for generating, investigating, and representing ideas	9/12
Persistence	the ability to sustain interest in and attention to short-and long-term projects	9/12
Responsibility	the ability to take ownership of one's actions and understand the consequences of those actions for oneself and others	12/12
Flexibility	the ability to adapt to situations, expectations, or demands	7/12

The most apparent of these narratives is the connection teachers made between multimodal composition and creativity. Of the nine teachers who discussed creativity as the *Framework* articulates it (see Table 2), the "novel approach" articulated by five of these teachers in some way involved the use of technology in the writing process. These teachers discussed projects on social media platforms, in non-traditional and non-alphabetic text formats, such as *imovie* or other visual applications, and visual presentation platforms, such as *Prezi* or *PowerPoint*. One teacher framed this work in terms of "breaking rules" for writing practices, while another discussed "real world" contexts that students could already place themselves and their writing outside of the classroom setting. Within these discussions of multimodality was also a theme of concern about teacher training (do I know enough technology to employ these lesson plans?) and devotion of time to technological skill development (should

I be teaching students to make infographics instead of spending time on discussion of theoretical concepts such as the rhetorical triangle?). Regardless of these practical concerns related to multimodal composition, this is a marked narrative of teachers' desires to teach creative approaches in the classroom and the belief in the use of technology to do so.

The second discernable trend in the teachers' narratives involved developing students' persistence in a process-based writing classroom. Nine of twelve teachers discussed concern for keeping students involved throughout the arc of a writing project, and the value in developing lessons that kept students working from invention to revision. Teachers expressed widely varying tactics to develop persistence in the writing classroom. Two teachers discussed keeping the focus on process rather than product by de-emphasizing the grade on the final draft in order to "reward" persistence throughout the writing process. Another teacher connected her course writing projects thematically, so that each student can choose a subject that appeals to him or her and she can develop it across the semester. This teacher believed that a student, in becoming an expert from research to advocacy, builds desire and commitment to see the projects through to completion. Two other teachers discussed specific in-class activities that assisted with persistence for students to see an idea through a specific stage in the writing process. One teacher mentioned collaborative planning as an exercise that benefitted her students. She felt that having each student's project workshopped by the entire class for a class period, with the student at the front of the classroom, dedicated time, resources, and effort that moved a paper beyond a concept and into a tangible outline. Other teachers mentioned in-class activities, such as in-class writings and layering of homework and in-class writings, to move the writing process forward. After reflecting on all of the interviews, it becomes evident that best practices to build students' commitment to the writing process is an important theme, whether or not explicitly defined as "persistence."

The final habit of mind that garnered sustained treatment in the interviews was responsibility. As a result of the study's focus on first-year composition, as well as the focus on the first-year composition syllabus, a sustained portion of the interviews were dedicated to the front matter of these teachers' syllabi and the ways in which teachers try to instill in their students a desire to perform the tasks therein in a responsible manner. All writing program teachers gave this subject some consideration in their interviews, whether they make a point to emphasize the attendance policy and how it differs from other courses at the university (writing program courses have an automatic failure for absences that total more than two weeks of the semester), to an emphasis in an online course of the importance of purchasing and reading the textbook, as the textbook in an online class "becomes the tangible teacher." One teacher valued responsibility so weightily that he had developed an in-class activity, group reflection reports to be filed for each writing project of the semester, with 360-degree evaluations (here, multi-source feedback from peers, teacher, and self) of each student in the group, both for the course and his or her participation in each project. While there are workplace studies in industrial psychology and human resources with a variety of conclusions on the effectiveness of this feedback, 360-degree evaluations are increasing in popularity because they widen the perspective of evaluation beyond just the immediate supervisor (Hazucha, Hezlett, and Schneider 326). In the classroom, they may also heighten a sense of responsibility to peers as well as self and teacher. Taken together, the overall narrative from all twelve teachers was their belief in their own responsibility in developing first-year composition students' sense of responsibility, both in their classroom and in the academy more generally.

Conclusion

I return to the question that began the chapter: What effect might a training program discussing the habits of mind have in the first-year composition classroom? In this study, the most readily apparent answer is that it provides a framework to analyze the narratives of writing program teachers across disciplines, pedagogical models, and practices. What began as a study of the instantiation of the habit of mind of metacognition to facilitate writing transfer became a collection of twelve conversations with writing teachers of all ages, positions, backgrounds, and experience, each teacher valuing different habits of mind in different ways in different first-year composition classrooms. The preliminary conclusion drawn from the data is that more time explicitly discussing writing transfer may be needed to successfully facilitate it, which conflicts with teacher concerns that not all habits of mind can be attended to simultaneously and effectively. Teachers must "cut things out" in a finite semester of instruction, and that is why the narratives in the second part of this chapter are so important: to visualize the competing claims on a writing teacher's time and focus, and what stands to be lost in the possibility of one habit of mind being privileged in the writing classroom.

Despite this apparent tension in the study's results, the writing program's offering of teacher trainings and breakout sessions provide a shared vocabulary for discussion of in-class activities, and a framework to examine what is happening in the writing classroom and why teachers choose specific activities over others. The habits of mind and the *Framework*, in conjunction with formal training and discussion offerings, offers a space for teachers to share with one another what they value as writing teachers (in which some reach consensus and some not, as evidenced in the teacher narratives). While it may complicate a study on metacognition and writing transfer, it also provides a necessary context that may enable a pragmatic examination of writing instruction based on the lived experience of teaching.

This study points to a possibility for the applicability of the *Framework* as an organizing document for this kind of examination of writing instruction. Teachers in this writing program were trained with this document in such a way that they could identify which habits of mind and experiences with writing, reading, and critical analysis serve to foster the development of those habits. Beyond this study, teachers also might articulate which habits of mind and which experiences they choose to focus their energies on in their particular classroom. What is possible, then, is for teachers across secondary and post-secondary institutions to name and map their unique classroom experiences in such a way that students may determine which specific classroom environments are best suited for their personal development as writers. The reach of the *Framework*, in this manner, could extend beyond a shared language for teachers, to make a shared map for students, teachers, and advisors to plot the course of a writer's growth.

Works Cited

Adler-Kassner, Linda, John Majewski, and Damian Koshnick. "The Value of Troublesome Knowledge: Transfer and Threshold Concepts in Writing and History." *Composition Forum* 26 (Fall 2012): n. pag Web. 9 February 2017.

Carter, Michael. "Ways of Knowing, Doing, and Writing in the Disciplines." *College Composition and Communication* 58.3 (2007): 385–418. Print.

Council of Writing Program Administrators, National Council of Teachers of English, and National Writing Project. *Framework for Success in Postsecondary Writing*. CWPA, NCTE, and NWP, 2011. PDF File.

Hazucha, Joy Fisher, Sarah A. Hezlett, and Robert J. Schneider. "The Impact of 360-Degree Feedback on Management Skills Development." *Human Resource Management* 32.2/3: 325–51. Print.

Lynch, Paul. *After Pedagogy: The Experience of Teaching.* Urbana, IL: NCTE, 2013. Print.

Nowacek, Rebecca. *Agents of Integration: Understanding Transfer as a Rhetorical Act.* Carbondale: Southern Illinois UP, 2011. Print.

Rose, Shirley K. "How Do Teachers of Academic Writing Value Creativity in Student Writers? A Report from the Largest First-Year Writing Program in the United States." 2012 Higher Education Creativity Conference. Chengdu, China. June. 2012.

Rounsaville, Angela, Rachel Goldberg, and Anis Bawarshi. "From Incomes to Outcomes: FYW Students' Prior Genre Knowledge, Meta-Cognition, and the Question of Transfer." *WPA: Writing Program Administration* 32.1 (2008): 97–112. Print.

Saldaña, Johnny. *The Coding Manual for Qualitative Researchers.* Thousand Oaks, CA: Sage, 2009. Print.

Wardle, Elizabeth and Douglas Downs. *Writing about Writing: A College Reader.* 2nd ed. New York: Bedford/St. Martin's, 2014. Print.

7 Messy But Meaningful: Using the Habits of Mind to Understand Extracurricular Learning

Faith Kurtyka

The *Framework for Success in Postsecondary Writing* makes the goals of college composition transparent to a wider audience, allowing for the identification of allies for these goals. As such, the *Framework* has been presented to constituencies outside of composition, including the Association of American Colleges and Universities and the National Alliance for Concurrent Enrollment Partnerships (O'Neill et al. 524). One possible additional group of allies consists of professionals in student affairs, who are charged with managing students' extracurricular involvement in clubs, groups, and organizations. In fact, the National Association of Student Personnel Administrators (NASPA), the national organization for student affairs administrators, espouses an explicitly holistic and "transformative" idea of learning (Keeling 9). For student affairs professionals, "the purpose of educational involvement is the evolution of multidimensional identity, including but not limited to cognitive, affective, behavioral, and spiritual development" (Keeling 9), a view of learning that resonates with the habits of mind.

Both student affairs professionals and the authors of the *Framework* seek to change public discourses that represent learning as the transmission of static knowledge, instead viewing education as an experience that profoundly influences students' identities. In this chapter, I demonstrate how the habits of mind can be used as a tool to name and interpret extracurricular learning experiences, which are normally under the purview of student affairs professionals. In doing so, I show how the extracurricular learning of student affairs offers composition scholars and teachers a deeper and broader understanding of the social and interconnected aspects of the habits of mind.

In this chapter, I use the habits of mind to analyze twenty-one narratives about learning from fifteen alumnae of a social sorority, ranging in age from mid-twenties to mid-fifties. For composition scholars and teachers, the sorority experience offers ideas for supplementing and expanding the habits of mind to account for the inherently social nature of learning, including the value of mentoring, social skills, community engagement, and self-knowledge from watching and observing other people. The sorority experience also presents an opportunity to think about the connections between the habits of mind because students in these situations often use many habits of mind at once. In particular, I demonstrate how the clearly defined leadership roles within many sororities lead students to an interesting interplay of engagement, persistence, responsibility, and metacognition.

I have divided this chapter into two sections pertaining to expansions of the habits of mind and the connections between the habits of mind. Each section introduces a research question, explains the methodology by which I sought an answer to that question, offers findings, and makes suggestions for how to apply this research to the teaching of composition. Because one of the aims of this collection is to showcase the malleability of the habits of mind, I adopt an imaginative and creative attitude toward their use. This means that at the expense of a single investigation, I introduce varied research strands and inquiries for teaching to inspire other researchers to also view the habits of mind as a generative tool for understanding messy but meaningful learning experiences.

Expanding the Habits of Mind

Carol Severino expresses concern that the habits of mind focus too much on individual traits and individual betterment, eliding the important role of sociality in learning to write (e.g., peer review, group workshops, or class discussion) and being a "good classroom citizen" (535). One solution to this problem is to imagine as researchers how we can expand the habits of mind to account for social learning experiences. My own interest in the social learning experiences began when I was invited to serve as the faculty adviser for a social sorority on my campus, even though I had never been in a sorority myself and like many academics, tended to view fraternity/sorority involvement as an opposing force to the academic experience. Doing more research, however, I found that the 2006, 2007, and 2008 National Survey on Student Engagement (NSSE) shows that fraternity/sorority members are more likely than non-members to engage in campus activities, community service, and leadership opportunities, and more readily take on academic challenges (Bureau et al.). The NSSE shows that sorority involvement and academic involvement can work as centripetal forces, generating a positive energy that engages students deeper into the university experience.

On the advisory board of the sorority, I met a group of sorority alumnae who had found their own sorority experiences to be personally and professionally transformative. As Kristine Johnson points out, assessing the habits of mind "asks writing teachers and other stakeholders to discern mere performance from actual cultivation" (533). I wanted to hear these women's stories because they demonstrated the extent of this cultivation, as the women were reflecting on learning experiences that continued to hold meaning for them five, ten, and twenty years after they had left college. Through a project approved by my university's institutional review board, I conducted focused oral histories with fifteen sorority alumnae, whose ages ranged from mid-twenties through mid-fifties. I asked the women to explain their initial involvement in the sorority, narrate some of their memorable experiences, and reflect on their most substantial outcomes from the sorority.

I worked with an undergraduate research assistant, Krysta Larson, to read through the interview transcripts with the fifteen alumnae. To narrow the data set, we identified moments where the participant discussed learning experiences that helped her grow or develop, and/or an experience that continued to resonate for her personally, socially, or professionally. We referred to these interview segments as learning narratives, although we did not limit ourselves to stories told in a chronological order. Of the fifteen interviews, we found twenty-one learning narratives. Each narrative was labeled with a pseudonym for the speaker (e.g., "Marcia") and a short title (e.g., "New Friends").

Krysta and I independently coded each learning narrative for the three habits of mind that we thought best encapsulated the learning experience, selecting the habits of mind in the order we thought they were best represented. For example, a learning narrative coded as (1) metacognition, (2) responsibility, and (3) flexibility meant that metacognition was the most important or most obvious habit of mind present in the narrative, and flexibility was still present but less important or less obvious. We also had the option of using zero, one, two, or three habits of mind for each narrative. Then, Krysta and I met to compare our codes. We discussed each difference and similarity in our coding, what we had been thinking when we coded, and how we interpreted both the habits of mind and the learning narratives. As we went along, we modified each existing definition of the habits of mind (see Table 1). By listening to each other's reasoning, we were able to agree upon an ordering of three codes for each narrative.

Once we had revised the habits of mind to fit the sorority experience, we wanted to use the revised habits of mind to determine one learning narrative that best encapsulated or represented each habit of mind. By finding this "best narrative" for each habit of mind, we could study it closely to think about how the learning process in the narrative could be applied to the classroom. We wanted to determine the best narrative by finding which narrative was ranked highest for each habit of mind; Krysta and I were concerned, however, that our eagerness to see the habits of mind in the data would skew our coding. We decided to invite other people to code our data who were not invested in the project. I crafted a Google survey with the twenty-one learning narratives and our revised coding scheme. I sent the survey to six coders, who, like the interviewees, ranged in age from mid-twenties to mid-fifties. I asked the coders to read the coding scheme, and then read each narrative and rank the habits of mind it displayed, as Krysta and I had done. The coders had the option of selecting zero, one, two, or three habits of mind and placing them in order of most-to-least significant. Krysta uploaded each narrative into *Dedoose*, a quantitative and qualitative analysis software program, and created a chart demonstrating whether coders selected the habit of mind first, second, third, or not all for each narrative (see Table 2). The x-axis is the title of the learning narrative and the y-axis is the number of coders who gave the ranking of first, second, or third. For example, five coders gave Dawn's story titled "Leadership" a first ranking for metacognition, and one coder gave it a second ranking for metacognition.

For the most part, our coders were consistent in their coding. On average, each narrative received 5.28 different codes (ranging from as few as four to as high as seven). With eight codes (plus the option to select no codes) and having each of six coders pick three, we felt that 5.28 meant that the coding was not overly dispersed. The last question on our survey asked the coders to reflect on the accuracy of the coding scheme, and

Table 1. Adaptation of the *Framework*

Habit of Mind	Existing Definition from the *Framework*	Additions from Sorority Research
Responsibility – the ability to take ownership of one's actions and understand the consequences of those actions for oneself and others	Recognizes her own role in learning Acts on the understanding that learning is shared among the writer and others Engages and incorporates the ideas of others, giving credit to those ideas by using appropriate attribution	Learns she has a responsibility to other people (individuals or a larger community) Engages in leadership of others Recognizes that something has to be done, regardless of how one feels about it
Openness—the desire to know more about the world	Examines their own perspectives to find connections with the perspectives of others Practices different ways of gathering, investigating, developing, and presenting information Listens to and reflects on the ideas and responses of others	Expresses a new way of being in the world or a change of heart Learns that other people have valid viewpoints Learns or concludes something about herself from other people Learns how to work with or get along with other people
Engagement—a sense of investment and involvement in learning	Makes connections between her own ideas and those of others Finds meanings new to her or builds on existing meanings as a result of new connections Acts upon the new knowledge that she has discovered	Recognizes her involvement as above and beyond the normal level of engagement in the sorority Stresses the depth of her involvement, or the all-encompassing nature of her involvement
Metacognition – the ability to reflect on one's own thinking as well as on the individual and cultural processes and systems used to structure knowledge	Examines processes she uses to think in a variety of contexts Reflects on the work that she has produced in a variety of contexts Connects choices she has made to audiences and purposes Uses what she learns from reflection to act differently on subsequent projects	Learns something about herself as person—how she works, thinks, acts, etc. Reflects on her own skills, abilities, etc. Learning how the world works Feels like a part of a larger community

the only consistent issue noted was that almost every segment could reasonably have been coded for "metacognition" because the social circumstances of an interview (asking someone to reflect on a past experience) naturally lead to metacognition. This does mean that metacognition skewed higher in our data.

Table 2. Ranking for Each Habit of Mind

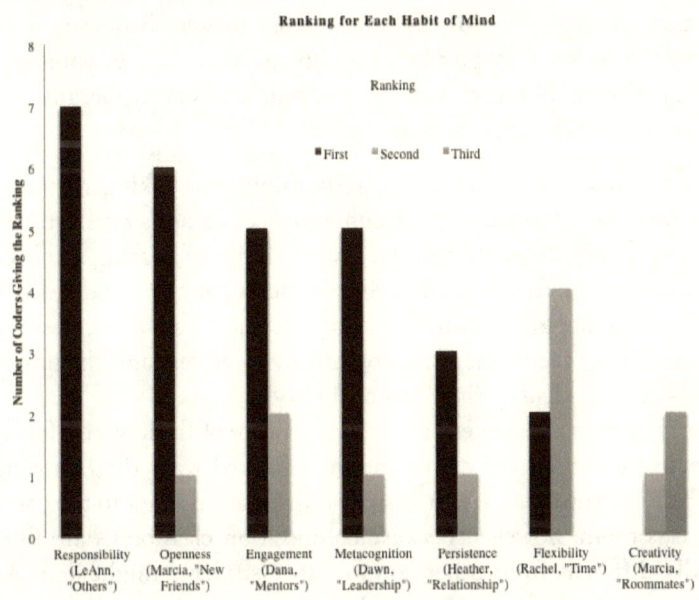

In my analysis here, I put into conversation the adaptations we made to the definitions of the habits of mind (Table 1) with narratives that received the highest weights for responsibility, openness, engagement, and metacognition (Table 2) to understand how the habits of mind work in the sorority experience and consider how the habits of mind might be applied to the classroom. LeAnn, a woman in her mid-thirties who was a university administrator and who served on the advisory board of her sorority, told a story about negotiating individual and collective identity that received the highest score for "responsibility." LeAnn noted that her sorority identity challenged her to take responsibility for herself because her actions reflected on others who held the same organizational identity:

> [I realized that] what I do reflects on the national president and the national officers in this area. We would go to basketball

games, and I wasn't 21 yet. All of my friends would drink, and I was like, "No, I'm not gonna." Whatever I do reflects not only on me but on the other thousands of women who are part of this organization . . . It's not just about me, it's about the group of alumni we've had since 1952 and this is about making sure that this chapter is here in 2052. It kind of brought that greater picture, it was more of a responsibility, it was more of a promise that I kept when we went through. You're part of an organization so what you do reflects on other people. It doesn't only reflect on your chapter here or your members here or your best friend here. No, it reflects on me, four states away, because we are part of the same culture.

While the habits of mind define responsibility as taking responsibility for one's *own* learning or the consequences of one's *own* actions, LeAnn's experience demonstrates the responsibility of bearing a collective identity that she finds valuable. She connects her collective identity and the values of her group to her everyday actions. In short, a collective identity challenges the learner metacognitively to understand the implications of her own identity (her "responsibility").

LeAnn's story is a testament to the importance of finding and forming collective identities as part of the multifaceted ways that students engage their communities. LeAnn's story is difficult to adapt to the composition classroom, however, because composition classrooms are fundamentally different from other communities students might join. As Roxanne Mountford writes, "In the classroom, students see themselves not as 'joining' a cause or group or community but rather as joining a coincidental grouping of individuals who are developing skills for future employment or self-interest" (305). Other scholars have similarly criticized the often idealized and abstract concept of classroom community (Harris; Horner). Although it may be unrealistic to expect students to form a community around shared values in the classroom, it may be reasonable to form a classroom community as a way of helping students to make meaning from a public identity. For writing program administrators (WPAs), Linda Adler-Kassner recommends putting on writing program events that change the conversation on campus about students' writing and what goes on in writing classroom, like a "Celebration of Student Writing" (153). In addition to positive publicity for writing programs, my research suggests that such events might help develop the identity of the writing program and students' identities as writers, part of the community of the writing program. Offering students these identities, as LeAnn's story suggests, may serve as a precursor to deeper forms of civic engagement, as it teaches students the implications of public identities for one's everyday life.

Although sororities are often associated with conformity, the highest-ranking story for "openness" (Marcia, "New Friends") and the highest-ranking story for metacognition (Dawn, "Leadership") were both stories about not fitting in with the group. The serious commitment to a sorority means that women often find themselves stuck with a certain group of people, which leads them to be open to other people and think about who they are in relation to others. Marcia, a woman in her fifties who now works as a hospital administrator, considered herself a quiet person when she first joined her sorority, but had to learn to be open to the more gregarious members of the sorority.

> Interviewer: How else did [your sorority] help you?
>
> Marcia: The random rooming. Getting to know people you wouldn't normally have known. In high school I never got to hang out with cheerleaders. I tell [women going through sorority recruitment] now that they'll get to meet people from other high schools whom they normally wouldn't meet and it's a good experience to be thrown together randomly with new people.

The women learn about how to be tolerant of different kinds of people and branching out to meet people who might not normally be in one's friend group. While Marcia sees the good in a general openness to different kinds of people (like cheerleaders), Dawn, a woman in her thirties who works in university residence life, more clearly specifies the takeaways from learning to work alongside other people. In observing others, Dawn realized her leadership style was atypical for the leadership she saw in most of the women:

> I think that with my personality, just some of the cattiness that goes on in a sorority . . . I just didn't want to have to deal with some of that. I don't think I'm a very good leader when it comes to women's organizations, [I'm] a better leader when there's co-ed involvement. You know, men and women are different and I think sometimes that my leadership style. . . . I don't want to say "harsh" but I am the type of person who is not afraid to call people out and to speak my opinion . . . I just think that

there are some leaders who are really good making sure everyone's voice is heard and "Let's have this be a communal decision," and I really see value in that but when you're a leader for just a year, that type of leadership is [too slow] and I'm the type of person who would want to see results.

The leadership style of the other women in the sorority was a useful contrast for Dawn in recognizing her own leadership style. In this way, metacognition comes about not via individual reflection, but by watching how another person lives, works, and leads, spurring the women to reflect on themselves and the kind of person they want to be.

For the rhetoric and composition classroom, this confirms the importance of reading and critiquing the work of others as acts of metacognition, but also, watching what others do, which Ellen Carillo and Alice Horning also argue in their respective chapters in this volume. While the knowledge students learn from watching each other may not always drastically change their behaviors, it can grow their awareness of who they are (like Dawn, they can confidently use phrases like "I'm the type of person"). It seems that *not* fitting into a community spurs as much if not more metacognition as finding a group with which you identify. Although there is much to critique about the sorority experience promoting uniformity, students may also be able to critique that uniformity (as Dawn does) and meaningfully define themselves in relation to it. Students learn about themselves from both positive and negative communal learning experiences, whether it be how to get along with difficult people or how to be open to mentoring from someone with a different area of expertise.

Working with others also requires openness to peers as an important source of learning—an act of humility and vulnerability—not just instructors and published sources, as articulated in the habits of mind. The women I interviewed were much less likely to remember the specific project or task they were working on in a story as much as the relationship they were working on with their collaborators. Women learn laterally in the sorority by forming relationships and finding role models among peers, instead of a centralized authority. We often think of sororities as massive groups, but the women formed individual connections with both peers and mentors, and these relationships continued to influence them throughout their lives. Dana's story about mentoring and role models was coded highest for engagement. Dana, a woman in her thirties who works in personnel management, deeply valued access to mentors and role models in the sorority experience:

> I didn't come away from [the sorority] with a hundred best friends, but I came away from it with one very best friend and probably three true mentors that totally helped me grow as a person, get involved, bloom as a leader, and just a lot of great experience of how to get along with people and organize people and especially at a time in their lives when they don't always want a lot of direction. The community made all the difference and, I think, if you look at people who are really successful at [my university], I would say at least 70% of leaders on campus are Greek. And so there's something about having this community that supports you but also challenges you where you have mentors in the house who help you know what to do and where to go and where to get involved, and so I think that it was a real reason why I was so involved and had so much success at [my university].

The sorority provides mentors for women—members of the same sorority who are two or three years older—to help them navigate campus life. The sorority demonstrates the importance of mentoring and developing meaningful relationships, which often segue into lifelong friendships and professional networks. Additionally, Dana's story is a testament to the role of peer-to-peer engagement, noting the significant way that students might involve other students in learning. Part of the reason the women form this bond is that they share more than the happenstance of landing in the same classroom together; one interviewee told me that the real value of sorority participation was the sharing of values. The sorority, she said, "is a platform, a way women can 'hook in.' Here's what we stand for, that's part of who you are, you'll have that for a lifetime." The women come together around shared values—not that they necessarily embody them at all times, but those to which they aspire.

What significance does this hold for composition? For WPAs, these findings resonate with what Adler-Kassner calls "values-based organizing," a long-term and strategic grassroots organizing method that unites allies around common values (107). As Lori Ostergaard, Dana Driscoll, Cathy Rorai, and Amanda Laudig powerfully demonstrate in chapter 16 of this volume, developing a common set of values in the writing program is important so that these values can influence writing program instructors and students in the writing program. Although it would be difficult to replicate the mentoring and deep relationships of the sorority, finding ways to build relationships among students—beyond first-day icebreakers—can be a means of holding students accountable to each other and helping them find those mentors and role models in the class.

Connecting the Habits of Mind

The habits of mind have also been criticized for their form of "parataxis," a jarring juxtaposition of seemingly unrelated items that prohibits deep thinking about how the habits of mind might fit together (Summerfield and Anderson 544–45). Extracurricular learning environments provide one window into how the habits of mind work together because in these types of learning environments, students may be learning many habits of mind all at once. Krysta and I also wanted to see how the habits of mind worked together in the narratives. Which habits of mind tended to occur together and why? What could these co-occurrences tell us about the habits of mind and how they work together in social learning? We cannot, of course, demonstrate that correlation means causation, but we felt that looking at the co-occurrences of the codes might help to complicate the compartmentalization of the list format. Using *Dedoose*, we designed a chart (Table 3) that showed how often a narrative was coded for two habits of mind together.

Metacognition and responsibility occur together eighteen times, the highest of any pairing. (Though metacognition does skew somewhat high because of the interview format.) Metacognition and responsibility tended to occur in narratives where women were speaking about leadership positions in a sorority. A sorority is mostly driven and organized by the women themselves, meaning that each member must have well-defined roles for the organization to function (e.g., director of recruitment, director of marketing), each of which comes with substantial responsibility. The definition of the leadership role, and the way it expands and contracts in different social contexts and as the school year goes along, seems to make the women more metacognitively aware of their responsibility. Throughout my work with this sorority, I was consistently surprised at the gravity of responsibility the women took on, from organizing events for three hundred people to making decisions about women's health and safety. Dana's story about leadership scored high in both metacognition and responsibility:

I really refined my leadership skills, my interpersonal skills, my ability to orchestrate groups and also to kind of, when I think about some of my stuff that I did as a [vice president], you just don't get those kind of opportunities to work with people on really personal things, discipline people but in a really loving way and help run an organization of sixty women with a set of six executives. . . . So I use so many of those skills I learned about leadership and mentorship and orchestration and how to use our network to do the things that you need to do.

Table 3. Code Co-Occurrences

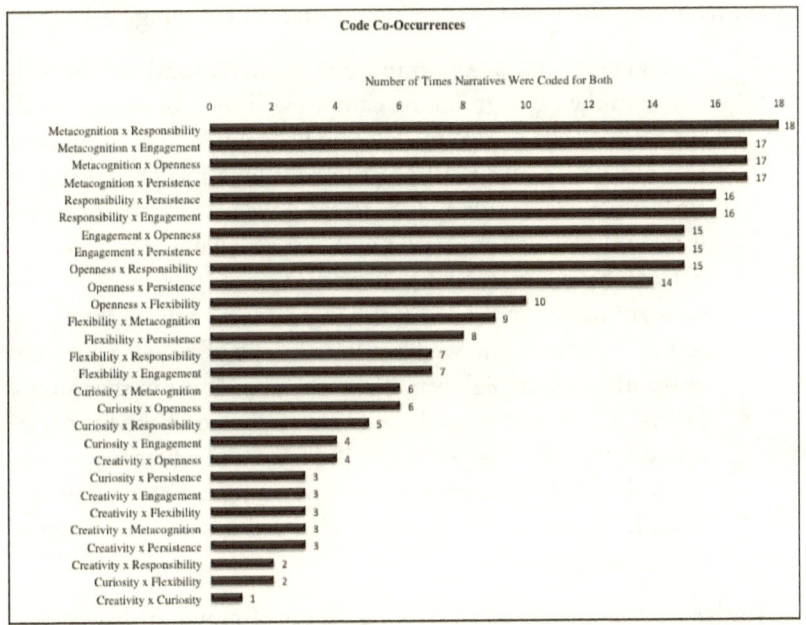

Having specific responsibilities in the sorority means that one is inclined to reflect on how successfully one fulfills those responsibilities. In addition to metacognition, responsibility also tended to occur with persistence. Having clear-cut responsibilities of leadership seems to build in students a stronger sense of commitment and responsibility to pursuing the goals of the group.

Metacognition and openness occur together seventeen times, which may happen because of the mentoring relationships mentioned earlier: once you are open to learning about and from other people, you begin to learn about yourself. Based on the women's narration of learning from peers and mentors, the three descriptions of openness—"Learns or concludes something about herself from other people," "Examines their own perspectives to find connections with the perspectives of others," and "Listens to and reflects on the ideas and responses of others"—could be applied to metacognition as well (*Framework* 4).

Ruth's story about recruiting for her sorority captures well the interplay of engagement, persistence, responsibility, and metacognition. If a sorority is particularly small, the members are allowed to recruit outside of the regular sorority recruitment (or "rush"), through a process where they meet with women individually. Ruth, who continues to work for her sorority in a national leadership position, found that her responsibility for recruiting women individually presented an engaging challenge:

> Our sorority was small, so in order to survive and be competitive with the other groups on campus we had to be recruiting all the time. When you go to class you have think, "Let me sit next to a girl who I admire [sic] or someone who I might be able to strike up a conversation with, to see if we have any similarities, if I could make a connection with her somehow." I'm a person, if I can have a mission I will work towards that mission very strongly and I also believe in the "big picture" reason, the philosophical reasons why we have institutions of higher education or sororities. So at eighteen, nineteen, when I was in that group, I could see those things. I could see the value of the history of the sorority, where we were coming from and where we wanted to go. I took it upon myself: we have to recruit so we can stay alive. It was important to me. It changed my interactions even in the classroom.

Ruth's story points to an interesting aspect of group affiliation and identity: Ruth takes on the weakness and vulnerability of the group (its small membership) as a personal challenge. As a naturally persistent person, Ruth is attracted to a group with a weakness that carves out a role for her: the group needs membership and she has the ability to connect with others. To return to the habits of mind, Ruth's persistence and responsibility offer her a group identity suited to her strengths—the one who recruits—as a means of engagement in the group's formation.

For the composition classroom, this research challenges us to consider the roles students adopt in classrooms because having a clearly defined role was an important part of the sorority women finding a place in the group and using their strengths to benefit the group. We need to consider how students' roles in the classroom are defined and undefined and how their roles expand and contract as the semester goes along. We should also consider whether or not the role of student carves out a space where students can exercise their strengths for the betterment of the group, as Ruth's strengths fulfill a weakness in her sorority. Furthermore, students often perceive academic discourse communities as monolithic and unchanging (Wardle), and worse, unwelcoming (Dryer). It is possible that if students were offered more clearly defined roles in discourse communities, roles that drew on their strengths rather than amplified their weaknesses, they would be more willing to feel like and act as an actual member.

The Habits of Mind as Points of Reference Between Spaces of Student Life

The habits of mind are a flexible tool that can be applied productively to a variety of learning experiences. They are not meant as a prescriptive list but instead can serve as what Peter Khost calls in this collection a "shared point of reference" between seemingly disparate aspects of the college experience. In the case of composition classrooms and sororities, the habits of mind showed the value of mentoring, social skills, community engagement, and self-knowledge from watching and observing other people. The clearly defined leadership roles of the sorority suggest interplay between engagement, persistence, responsibility, and metacognition, which informs the way we think about the roles offered to students in our classrooms.

The mission of student affairs, focused on transformative, holistic education, echoes the political function of the habits of mind to change the oversimplified ways that students are represented in the public discourse about education. As Kristine Johnson puts it in her analysis of the *Framework*, "Introducing habits of mind into the landscape of American education asks writing teachers to consider not only what student writers should know and be able to do but also how students write, think, and move in the world" (518). This is a challenge we share with student affairs professionals, and by paying attention to this shared point of reference, we can create a more holistic college experience for students. NASPA notes that students' curricular and extracurricular lives have grown increasingly fragmented on college campuses: "developmental experiences like leadership in student organizations or volunteer service simply orbit the student's world with little sense of their relationship one to another or to academic courses" (Keeling 8). We cannot replicate peer-driven and highly social learning environments, such as sororities, but using the habits of mind, we can theorize them as part of our same "orbit," scaffolding and reinforcing learning that we also value.

Works Cited

Adler-Kassner, Linda. *The Activist WPA: Changing Stories about Writing and Writers*. Logan: Utah State UP, 2008. Print.

Bureau, Dan, Helen Grace Ryan, Chad Ahren, Rick Shoup, and Vasti Torres. "Student Learning in Fraternities and Sororities: Using NSSE Data to Describe Members' Participation in Educationally Meaningful Activities in College." *Oracle: The Research Journal of the Association of Fraternity/Sorority Advisors* 6.1 (May 2011): 1–22. Web. 18 Apr. 2013.

Council of Writing Program Administrators, National Council of Teachers of English, and National Writing Project. *Framework for Success in Postsecondary Writing*. CWPA, NCTE, and NWP, 2011. PDF File.

Dryer, Dylan. "Taking Up Space: On Genre Systems as Geographies of the Possible." *JAC: A Journal of Rhetoric, Culture, and Politics* 8.3/4 (2008): 503–34. Print.

Harris, Joseph. "The Idea of Community in the Study of Writing." *College Composition and Communication* 40.1 (1989): 11–22. Print.

Horner, Bruce. *Terms of Work for Composition: A Materialist Critique*. Albany: State U of New York P, 2000. Print.

Johnson, Kristine. "Beyond Standards: Disciplinary and National Perspectives on Habits of Mind." *College Composition and Communication* 64.3 (2013): 517–41. Print.

Keeling, Richard, ed. *Learning Reconsidered: A Campus-Wide Focus on the Student Experience*. Washington, DC: National Association of Student Personnel Administrators, 2004. PDF File.

Mountford, Roxanne. "Classrooms as Communities: At What Cost?" *JAC: A Journal of Rhetoric, Culture, and Politics* 15.2 (1995): 304–07. Print.

O'Neill, Peggy, Linda Adler-Kassner, Cathy Fleischer, and Anne-Marie Hall. "Creating the *Framework for Success in Postsecondary Writing*." *Symposium: On the Framework for Success in Postsecondary Writing*. Spec. issue of *College English* 74.6 (2012): 520–33. Print.

Severino, Carol. "The Problem of Articulation: Uncovering More of the Composition Curriculum." *Symposium: On the Framework for Success in Postsecondary Writing*. Spec. issue of *College English* 74.6 (2012): 533–36. Print.

Summerfield, Judith, and Philip M. Anderson. "A Framework Adrift." *Symposium: On the Framework for Success in Postsecondary Writing*. Spec. issue of *College English* 74.6 (2012): 544–53. Print.

Wardle, Elizabeth. "'Mutt Genres' and the Goal of FYC: Can We Help Students Write the Genres of the University?" *College Composition and Communication* 60.4 (2009): 765–789. Print.

8 Experience, Values, and Habitus: Twelfth Graders and the *Framework*'s Habits Of Mind

Rebecca Powell

As the chapters within this volume attest, it is hard not to like the *Framework*. As Bruce McComiskey writes, "Who *wouldn't* want creative, persistent, responsible students with lots of rhetorical knowledge and flexible writing processes?" (537). Indeed, the *Framework*'s habits of mind and writing experiences speak to a variety of stakeholders; they celebrate the liberal arts tradition and focus on the experience and development of the student, long held rhetoric, and composition values, supported by research and tested in the classroom. Most importantly, the *Framework* productively shifts education reform conversations from test scores to students, from curriculum to experience.

Because the *Framework* values experiences and habits, it encourages the development of a certain type of student. For Kristine Hansen, this is the work of education: "I believe education is the development of certain kinds of people rather than the accumulation of so many credit hours or a list of skills to check off as students reach some minimum level of proficiency" (540). In Hansen's assessment, and my own, the *Framework* steps beyond prescribing curriculum to prescribing actual ways of being in the world. By attending to experiences and habits of mind, the *Framework* describes students who succeed in postsecondary writing, encouraging the production of those students. However, students are already shaped by writing experiences in a standards-based school system, by an increasingly digital world, and by particular communities who have their own relationships to writing. This chapter explores the gap between actual students and the students envisioned by the *Framework*.

Students write during an era of unprecedented proliferation of textual material, in an economy, as Kristine Johnson notes in chapter 1 of this volume, that is tied to writing's production and circulation and amid school reform movements' competing desires to both equalize opportunity and manage resources. The year 2014's twelfth graders attended twelve years of standards-based education under the *No Child Left Behind Act* and the Common Core State Standards while simultaneously living through an explosion of mobile technologies. In the year they were born (1996), 36% of households in the United States had Internet access, and 91 million used cell phones (Newberger 1; FCC). In 2014, 70% of households have internet access and 306 million use cell phones (Pew; FCC). These changes in education and the materiality of writing, how it is circulated and produced, shape students' access to writing experiences, influencing how students' use and value writing. As the *Framework* articulates the writing experiences and values preferred by rhetoric and composition, so should we describe the existing writing experiences and values of students negotiating powerful forces in their writing lives.

In this chapter, I claim students' writing experiences and values reflect their negotiation of community circulation, family uses of writing, school curriculum and climate, and the opportunities these contexts do, or do not, afford. These values matter because they shape students' predispositions, the habitus, they bring to universities and subsequent writing tasks. To make these claims, I explain how Pierre Bourdieu's theory of the social sphere and habitus may be an important lens for understanding the possibilities of the *Framework*. Next, I describe the larger study of two high schools in the Southwest of the United States from which I draw the findings. Then, I analyze these findings through the lens of habitus and the *Framework*. Finally, I end with a call to shift the *Framework*'s focus from shaping the "student" to shaping environments and the circulation of writing.

Habitus, Writing, and the *Framework*

The *Framework* recognizes that students' values and experiences form their predispositions to writing. By naming the habits of mind (curiosity, openness, engagement, creativity, persistence, responsibility, persistence, flexibility, and metacognition) and the writing experiences that form them, the *Framework* opens the conversation of what it means to foster engagement with learning and writing (1). Others, like Dana Lynn Driscoll and Jennifer Wells, have also recognized the importance of dispositions and their effect on transfer and writing development. Drawing on the work of educational psychologists Urie Bronfenbrenner and Pamela Morris, Driscoll and Wells define dispositions as "personal characteristics such as motivation and persistence." Those dispositions "allow or prevent successful development" and "transfer to take place." To move beyond defining and identifying the dispositions of writing success to fostering their formation, I turn to sociology, specifically Bourdieu.

Bourdieu's concepts of *field*, *capital*, and *habitus* and their resulting interactions, a logic of practice, provide a dynamic heuristic for envisioning how students' negotiate writing experiences within a standards-based education system, a digitized world, and specific geographical and socioeconomic locations. These concepts fit within Bourdieu's framework of social space, in which habituated agents struggle for capital to play a game where a winner is never determined. In this chapter, I see students, and indeed the field of rhetoric and composition, as habituated agents with varying relationships to a form of capital, writing. Their relationships to writing are structured by the various fields of school, community, family, and technology, to name a few.

Fields provide "a structure of probabilities—of rewards, gains, profits, or sanctions—but always imply a measure of indeterminancy" (Bourdieu, *Logic* 89). In *Invitation to a Reflexive Sociology*, Bourdieu and Loïc Wacquant liken the field to a card game with unspoken rules. Like a game, a field has something at "stake," a "product of competition," and by playing the game, the players agree "that the game is worth playing" (Bourdieu, *Other* 98). Fields may overlap, but all obey their own set of relations, reflecting external forces according to their own "internal structure" (Bourdieu, *Field* 75). Adolescents participate in many fields where the rules shift and what is at stake (capital: popularity, acclaim, money, or honor) differs. These fields hold different relationships to writing experiences and value and use writing differently. Thus, adolescents must necessarily negotiate their use and value of writing in accordance to a field's values or lose the game.

Students negotiate their use and value of writing in particular fields through habitus. Bourdieu defined habitus as "durable, transposable dispositions" (*Outline* 72). The habitus is "generative," "transposable," and "durable," but also limiting, meaning it can produce a variety of practices in different situations by different agents (generative); it works across fields (transposable); and it lasts across a person's lifetime (durable) (*Outline* 72). Habitus does not predict behavior, but it does condition agents to respond in particular ways in particular situations. Previous experience limits the available responses in any situation. This study assumes that certain contexts, locations, and histories (fields) produce a habitus in response to different writing experiences and seeks to describe the workings and practices of such habitudes.

Bourdieu posits that we can see the habitus at work as agents respond to the benefits of capital in different fields. To explain a dynamic social position, Bourdieu names four types of capital: economic, cultural, social, and symbolic (Bourdieu, "Forms" 243). Using Bourdieu's game metaphor, capital gains its value because it counts in a particular game/field. Without capital, one is not just losing the game, one's perceptions and experiences of opportunity and mobility are affected: "The lack of capital intensifies the experience of finitude: it chains one to a place" (Bourdieu, *Weight* 127). In certain fields, particular writing experiences and habits of mind count as capital, and therefore, encourage or discourage their production and opportunity and mobility. The *Framework* articulates the writing experiences and habits of mind that count as capital within postsecondary education. How, and if, students respond to the forms of capital named in the *Framework* tells of their habitus.

THE STUDY

To explore the writing habitus of 2014's twelfth graders, I draw on data from surveys, focus groups, and interviews that sought answers to the question, "What writing experiences do twelfth graders near the US/Mexico border report, and how do they value them?" I used a survey with a genre inventory, open-ended response, and reflective questions developed from the work of Anis Bawarshi and Mary Jo Reiff. Participants were asked to identify for what purposes they wrote each genre (school, personal, or extracurricular), thereby highlighting the places of writing. In addition, the survey's open-ended questions asked what experiences participants enjoyed and felt were successful. By articulating enjoyment and success, participants addressed their values surrounding writing, a disposition identified by Driscoll and Wells that leads to transfer and persistence. The focus groups sought to explore writing experiences and values in more detail by asking what participants valued about their writing experience thus far, how they came to those values and where, and what they remember writing. Interviews also explored values and their link to place by involving participants as researchers through photo-elicitation interviews and asking them to select and discuss a writing artifact that mattered to them.

Between September 2013 and January 2014, 171 twelfth grade students participated in this study. Fifty-two of the students attended a rural high school, Arroyo High School (pseudonym) while 119 attended a small city high school, La Vista High School (pseudonym). Participants ranged in age from sixteen to nineteen. Two participants from each school participated in interviews, and fifteen in focus groups. 67% of respondents participated in the research at both sites. Located near the US/Mexico border, La Vista and Arroyo High Schools are predominantly Hispanic-serving schools. At La Vista, 67% of participants identified as Hispanic, 25% as bilingual. At Arroyo, 88% of participants identified as Hispanic, 63% as bilingual. La Vista's average parent income was reported to be $64,359.00, and parent education levels were reported to be 72% with some college or more, which were significantly higher than the reported Arroyo parent income of $41,364.00 and education levels of 53% with some high school. These numbers were gained from participants' survey answers but were also matched to government census reports.

In the next section, I present each site's values and attitudes toward writing, give a brief overview of participants' reported writing experiences, and I share findings and analysis gathered from the following reflective open-ended questions: (1) What types of writing do you most enjoy? Why? (2) What types of writing do you least enjoy? Why? (3) What do you consider to be your most successful piece of writing (in school or out) and why? (4) What do you consider your least successful piece of writing, and why? I also analyzed focus group and interview transcripts, paying particular attention to responses related to the following questions: (1) What will you take with you from your high school writing experiences? (2) What do you value about writing? Throughout the chapter, participants have been given pseudonyms.

The Habitus of the Small City High School

La Vista High School is located in a small city with a land-grant university. La Vista High School's 2300 student population includes students from affluent outlying areas, rural *colonias* without infrastructure, and densely populated urban neighborhoods. Students from these neighborhoods are the children of university professors, recent immigrants, farmers, government personnel, and government aid recipients. Their heterogeneity mirrors that of the community. La Vista participants' values and attitudes towards writing were positive and self-interested. They believed in their ability to succeed at writing (self-efficacy); conveyed valuing writing experiences that allowed for expression, choice, and freedom; and appreciated writing experiences that garnered grades, positive feedback, and recognition.

La Vista participants' writing experiences were varied, many, and rich. More than 80% of participants wrote in more than fifteen categories of the forty-category genre survey. Their homes were sites of writing. Parents kept participants early writing experiences as mementoes. They wrote thank you notes, newsletters, and emails to extended family members and friends. La Vista interviewees took pictures of their writing solely within their homes, signifying that while writing may be assigned at school, what they consider worthy of documenting happens at home. They wrote in an array of genres for an array of purposes, but most participants claimed to write five paragraph essays, emails, book reports, text messages, and summaries. They wrote least in public writing genres (blog, Web-page design, Web-page text), mostly writing to an audience of one, a teacher, evaluator, friend, or family member. A Few participants wrote to large-scale audiences, an affordance of the Web. They wrote different genres in different settings, associating informal writing, such as texting and journals, with personal purposes, essays with school, and PowerPoint and work-related writing with extracurricular activities. Writing counted as capital in their homes, their communities, and their school.

La Vista participants also felt they were able to attain this capital through hard work and effort. They claimed a successful or unsuccessful writing experience was a direct consequence of their work and effort, demonstrating their self-efficacy, a disposition linked to the habits of mind of persistence and engagement. In response to open-ended questions about (un)successful writing experiences, 22% of La Vista participants, the highest percentage of any value or success-related code, wrote that writing was successful if they "put a lot of time, work, and thinking on it" or "because I literally spent a whole semester writing and perfecting this essay." Similarly, writings were unsuccessful if they felt rushed:

"Probably any essay I've done because it has always been rushed." Participants equated a lack of time, work, and effort with unsuccessful writings: "My least successful piece of writing is my argument essay in 11th grade. I just didn't spend enough time on it." When the "should haves" of writing were firmly in their control, so was the outcome of the writing. With enough time, work, and effort, La Vista students felt they could produce an effective piece of writing.

While participants demonstrated their self-efficacy through their belief that they could improve a piece of writing with work, time, and effort, they also valued writing by how much work, time, and effort they had expended on the piece. Rosalinda, an interview participant, noted the effect of time and effort on her judgment of her writing:

> I don't know if you can see this picture, but it's a really thick folder and sophomore year this is the main piece of writing that we worked on. Like every single day. Rough draft after rough draft after rough draft and then um it's probably like, I don't even know how many pages long I think like eight pages or ten pages [sic]. I don't know. But it's like revised a lot, and so I found it was important to me just because I put so much effort into it.

Rosalinda's commentary notes how time ("every single day") and effort ("rough draft after rough draft") contributed to her valuation of the writing. La Vista participants had experienced success through drafting and had been given time and space to reflect on the drafting process. These writing experiences predisposed them to value the writing process and writing itself, in accordance to the *Framework*, further positioning themselves as students who succeed in postsecondary writing.

Participants believed they could write a successful piece through work and effort, and their attitude of self-efficacy extended to their evaluations of their own writing. La Vista participants referred to their own judgment criteria when identifying effective writing. For example, when asked about their most successful piece of writing, participants wrote the following statements:

> "My free writings because they have the more [sic] meaning to me."

> "My name poem because I liked how it was very interactive." "The poem I wrote in Junior year because I actually liked it."

> "A poem, because it was amazing for my standards."

> "Analytical essays, to me, they reflect my abilities as a writer to comprehend data and synthesize writing about the data."

> "I said exactly what I wanted to say."

In identifying their own criteria for success, La Vista participants exhibited a confidence about writing, what makes good writing, and saw themselves as the authority on that definition. By claiming the definition of successful writing, they demonstrated their writing self-efficacy and their engagement. Participants' survey answers didn't always explain what made writing good, but in focus groups and interviews, La Vista participants categorized good writing with expression and successful identity performances.

La Vista participants (18%) valued writing's ability to express identities and capture experiences important to those identities. Identity, its performance and development, was a recurring theme used to characterize successful writing, justify why writing was important to them, and explain why they didn't value or enjoy certain genres or genre categories. Writing in creative genres allowed participants to "convey who I am," "get [myself] on paper," and have "a chance to be me." Essays also allowed participants to express aspects of their identity: "One of my college essays. Nothing like I've written. It is truly me"; "I wrote a satirical paper on how to better the school. I believe it was my best because it was witty and thoughtful and right up my alley." They valued writing experiences and writing forms that allowed them to display parts of their personality: "Slang because it shows your personality," and another survey participant, "Creative stories and poetry. It allows you to say what you feel in ways that do not conform to modern society." Participants also valued writing that embodied future identities: "I consider my research paper to be the best work of all time because I was writing like a college student." Successful writing allowed them to display and/or develop aspects of their identity. By associating effective writing with identity and expression, the La Vista participants were stepping into the metacognition valued by the *Framework* and displaying a habitus predisposed to value individual displays of identity.

Participants equated enjoying, or not enjoying, the writing of certain genres with identity traits. For example, participants wrote, "I am not a very poetic person and have difficulty writing poems," and "creative writing because I have a good imagination and creativity." What they are (poetic, creative) was linked to what genres they valued and enjoyed.

Similarly, success in writing was often linked to identity traits. "I am" phrases indicated that the participants inhabited an identity that led to success or failure of their writing experiences. For example "I haven't had a successful piece of writing because I am not very strong at it," and "I'm not an analytical thinker." The relationship between who students are and what type of writing they enjoy or feel they do well indicates the workings of habitus. Students identify as certain types of writers, echoing Hansen's belief that education develops "certain kinds of people" (540). In these cases, receiving praise or recognition for writing a particular genre shaped not only how they felt about the writing but also who they thought they were.

Participants also valued writing experiences that tracked their identity development. Diaries, journals, and writings saved by parents were valued for the record they kept of participants' evolving identities. For example, Rosalinda favored a piece of writing because it tracked her decision to study medicine:

> I guess I'm kind of proud of this because it's like an essay I submitted to my college. And so it's kind of talking about how culture intertwines with medicine and how I want to go into medicine and things like that. So this was kind of what I came up with and I am proud of it to a certain extent because it does encompass my experience and going to India and how I felt when I saw the people there and how it kind of impacted me and my drive to do what I wanted to do. And that's why I am proud of it, not really the writing itself.

Rosalinda valued the essay because it articulates an experience that contributed to her evolving identity formation and pre-professionalism. Participants valued writings that helped them articulate or remember an identity, but identity and its expression are not easily matched to the habits of mind or the writing experiences named in the *Framework*. Yet, participants most cited expressive writings and their link to identity formation as successful or enjoyable writing experiences.

Closely tied to students' appreciation of identity was writing's expressive capacity. As one participant wrote, "I thought it was successful because I felt like it expressed my feelings." 33% of participants valued writing's expressive capacity. They linked the expressive capacity of writing to a variety of genres, the exercise of creativity, and a generative capacity for thought and language. An interview participant, Aria, noted the generative capacity of writing and its allowance for revision and finding meaning:

> Sometimes I feel like I can't talk well. I don't have enough time to really form what I want to say . . . through writing I can go back and erase and go back scratch that out or I don't like whatever I just said so I can just take it all out like do you see what I mean? [*sic*]

Aria uses writing to express what she cannot communicate through speaking.

In their appreciation for expression, participants went beyond defining expression as an outpouring of feeling and thoughts and stated a joy in using different genres to form expression. Participants found the genres of newswriting, creative genres, argument, and blogs were conducive to forming expression.

> "Creative writing and news. It allows me to express my thought in a style I love."

> "My successful pieces deal with opinion paper [*sic*] because I get to express my own full views on topics."

> "Songwriting because I can get all my feelings out on paper."

> "Blog writing and creative nonfiction are the most enjoyable to me because they are different ways I can express myself."

Any genre could facilitate expression, if the parameters of the assignment or occasion allowed for it. Nevertheless, the most used genres for expression were freewriting and journaling. In the words of Rosalinda, journal writing allows her to express herself "because you don't have the audience, because the audience is yourself and you're just kind of working. You can get it out and you don't have to worry about it." Getting it out and kind of working, signs of creativity and flexibility, were features of participants' journal writing experiences, experiences they valued.

When noting what writing experiences they enjoyed, La Vista participants reported writing experiences that let them choose topics and explore possibilities. They preferred writing experiences that let "you choose what you want to write about," associating creative writing, freewriting, and essays with choice. For example, participants wrote, "I enjoy fictional writing the most because then the possibilities in your story are endless"; "Freewriting because I can write about whatever I want"; and "Essays/papers because it's easiest when you can write about anything." Conversely, the lack of choice was associated with their least liked writing experiences. Participants disliked "when a teacher gives you a topic and you can't choose" or being "being limited to specific topics." Participants' preference for choice extended to formatting and assignment constraints. They disliked assignments where they felt there were "too many rules and a tight procedure." They most enjoyed writing experiences that allowed them "to be creative with few restrictions." Perhaps because they saw themselves as an authority on effective writing or so prized expression and identity, La Vista participants wanted flexibility in the writing task, not to adapt to the writing task.

Participants valued writing experiences that they associated with a lack of rules and parameters. In focus groups, when asked to make a metaphor for writing in school, participants said the following:

> Focus Group Two, Derek: Writing for school is like you're a dog with a really long chain and you can kind of go out and explore and eat a few things to the range of your chain, but you have to stay inside a certain zone.
>
> Focus Group One, Aria: Writing is freedom.
>
> Focus Group Three, Taylor: It's like driving without speed limits. Pedal to the medal.
>
> Tori: Freedom to explore. To let your feelings out.

Writing that allowed students "off the chain" was valued, and perhaps more importantly, sought after. Their past writing experiences inside and outside of school had predisposed La Vista students to see writing as an act of possibility, where curiosity and individuality were rewarded.

Writing experiences that garnered high grades, praise, publication, and prizes were also valued by participants. Praise from teachers and peers was equally prized. Participants valued writing "that was highly recognized by a teacher," and participants had "won first place in a contest," ten in all. Reports of award-winning writing experiences usually appeared in response to the open-ended survey question about the most successful piece of writing and were accompanied by full and copious answers to other questions. La Vista participants lived in a community that held regular writing contests, attended a school that publicized those contests, and had teachers that gave ample feedback on their writing. This environment fostered their values and attitudes toward writing.

The writing experiences of La Vista participants reflected the circulation of writing experiences in their homes and community. They used writing to achieve goals in extracurricular activities, writing essays to gain leadership positions in cheerleading, band, and football. The winners of essay contests, city-sponsored ad campaigns and the writers of comics, news scripts, songs, and raps produced for friends, La Vista students experienced writing outside of school as an important part of their creative, personal, and spiritual lives. Their writing was oriented to their own goals, communication, and personal growth. They exhibited a strong sense of efficacy in writing and valued writing that allowed them to perform or develop their identity, gained them recognition, and allowed for expression.

The Habitus of the Rural High School

Arroyo High School lies four miles beyond the border patrol checkpoint, a station where travelers are inspected, and seventy-five miles from the US/Mexico border. The school serves 396 students, of whom 92% are Hispanic. Located in an agricultural-based community, Arroyo students are familiar with fieldwork, farming, and ranching. Arroyo students participate in Future Farmers of America, athletics, and civic service activities, such as preparing for community festivals and parades. Arroyo Valley participants' values and attitudes towards writing were ambivalent and pragmatic. Writing fulfilled a function in school success and sometimes had added benefits of expression and communication, benefits they valued in relation to their families and friends. Arroyo participants' defined successful writing as writing that fulfills the audience's expectations of topic and length, receives a good grade, and takes the least amount of effort. However, they most valued writing that maintained relationships and expressive writing, although they had few expressive writing experiences.

Arroyo participants' writing experiences were uniform, few, and surface. 53% of participants wrote in more than fifteen genres of the forty category survey. Arroyo participants' earliest writing experiences took place in school, and they were not saved by family members. Writing was not reported as a part of their family communication patterns. When asked to take photographs of their writing experiences, interviewees took all but one picture on school grounds, signifying that writing is considered a school activity. Genres ranging from creative writing, to informal journals, and to five-paragraph essays were written in school. They wrote in digital and school-based genres, the most participants claiming to write text messages, five-paragraph essays, argument essays, PowerPoints, and emails. Computer and Internet access were mostly afforded through school access. Writing counted as capital within school.

Arroyo Valley participants viewed writing as a rhetorical endeavor meant to fulfill audience expectations that were measured by grades and length. However, this same rhetorical bent meant some participants demonstrated an openness and flexibility like that named in the *Framework*. In an example of participants' rhetorical orientation to writing, an interview participant, Marie, said she valued writing about her personal experience in school essays. Yet, she also worried that beginning her essay with personal anecdotes would not work in college.

> Marie: I think after high school I am going to have a little more problem [*sic*] with writing personal stuff. I have a feeling that once I am out of here that it would be better to write informative.
>
> Me: Why do you say that?
>
> Marie: I guess it's because right now, like, like most of the students can relate to the stuff that I'm going through so it's easier to write having someone relate to it and um I guess when I get to college it's going to be more about what I know than what I feel.

Marie names her current audience as peers and anticipates future audiences that will require a knowledge demonstration. This conception of audiences that need to "relate" and be satisfied also ran through survey participants' responses. One survey participant equated successful writing with having an impact on the audience: "If I can change one's mind, I've succeeded." Other participants equated audience success with grades and length requirements. Arroyo participants' awareness of audience demands superseded their desire to express an identity.

Although participants demonstrated a rhetorical awareness of audience, many participants also wanted to ensure that audience demands were met with the minimum amount of text. When asked what writing they most and least enjoyed, Arroyo participants (52%) often justified their responses with "easy":

"A five paragraph essay because it's short and easy."

"Texting is easy."

"RACE [respond, answer, cite, explain, a standardized test formula for answering short answer questions], short and easy."

"Informative writing because it is hard to find the information."

Arroyo participants approach writing as a task to fulfill a school requirement, not for their own purposes, and therefore, writing should be completed in the most efficient manner, easily.

While Arroyo participants valued the easy, they also valued the expressive capacity of writing. Arroyo participants associated freewriting with expression and choice and tied expression to writing "what's on your mind," writing "whatever you like," and as "a way to let everything go." One focus group participant, Marie, used personal writing to "put down the emotions of what happened." Another, Turquoise, conveyed the value of expression as part of navigating life: "Expression began to matter when I realized communication was a big part of life." For Turquoise, being able to express herself well meant succeeding at relationships. Arroyo participants valued writing experiences in so far as they fulfilled their goals in other areas of their lives. Thus, if keeping in touch with friends and family was important to the participant, then so were texting, personal letters, and social networking. If school was important to the participant, then so was writing. Writing was a means to an end.

SITES AND HABITUS

To close these findings, I share focus group participants' answers to the question, "As you look back over your school career and think about the writing you've done, what you've learned, what do you think you'll take with you to your next phase either college or work or whatever you're going to do next?" These answers illustrate the major themes of the findings on both sites.

Arroyo Valley Participants: "Definitely learning how to cite."

"Oh my gosh yes."

"It's a big thing and you like get in trouble for making mistakes."

For Arroyo Valley participants, writing is and will be (as far as they can see thus far) a school-based activity, where they can "get in trouble for making mistakes" and will need to cite their sources. La Vista focus groups answered in different ways.

> "I learned how to write better."

> "You know how to construct a paragraph. You know how to do it."

> "I feel like most of my education has revolved around my writing skills."

> "I feel like all the writing skills are the only thing I am going to take with me because writing is like important to me not just for school, but also me personally. . . . Whether it is an essay or this or that, it impacts me a lot. And it's the written word. It's like everything that's going on up here (points to head) and going through here (points to heart). It's like so important."

For La Vista students, writing is a skill and form (vocabulary and paragraphs), but it's also about being able to understand, and for some "It's like everything." These writing habitus were formed from different environments.

The *Framework* and Habitus

In listing eight habits of mind that are "essential for success in college writing," the *Framework* writers sought to turn the focus of conversations about college readiness from test scores to students, their development and their capacity as human beings (1; See Foreword). In a sense the *Framework* returns agency to students. However, this study notes that students' differing habitus creates differing senses of agency surrounding writing. Through writing to learn, process-based, community and family-endorsed writing experiences, La Vista participants had improved their writing and created their own criteria for what writing well meant. Through performance-based, test-mandated writing experiences, Arroyo participants wrote to evaluators. These habitus were forged in different communities with different relationships to writing. In La Vista, writing experiences circulated through homes and the community. In Arroyo, writing experiences circulated primarily through the school.

The habits of mind outlined by the *Framework* match what La Vista students wanted from their writing experiences. La Vista participants wanted to experience curiosity about a topic of their choosing, explore new ways of being in the world, and involve themselves in writing tasks through displays of identity. They felt they had flexible, working writing processes that would allow them to persist through writing projects, and they used writing to reflect on their own experience and to comment on the workings of their community and political processes. This is not to say that those students embodied all the habits of mind or always displayed them, but they wanted and valued writing experiences that allowed them to explore, to engage with what they cared about, that were flexible. They valued writing experiences by how they had persisted through the process.

Arroyo Valley participants did not demand much from their writing experiences, nor did they want much to be demanded of them. Their pragmatic, rhetorical approach to writing and their past writing experiences told them that there would be an adjustment, that the audience would change and so would the evaluation of their work. They were not sure what writing in the university would look like, but they were sure it would be different, perhaps arbitrary, and definitely full of pitfalls and punishments. Arroyo Valley participants' values most match one of the habits of mind: responsibility. Writing irresponsibly could get them in trouble and keep them from their overall goal of success in school. This is not to say that Arroyo Valley participants were not engaged, curious, and creative people, only that they did not associate those habits of mind with writing, or school at large. They associated writing with grades, with tests. They understood assessment could be, and sometimes was, mysterious and arbitrary. Arroyo participants' pragmatic, rhetorical approaches pushed one step further might lead them to investigate those shady, hidden criteria for writing that they thought abided in the audience.

Results from the 2013 National Council of Teachers of English sponsored "Listening Tour" throw this study into relief. Administered by the Conference on College Composition and Communication, as part of the "Listening Tour," college instructors around the country interviewed 2200 freshman composition students about their views on writing. Results indicated that students associate writing with performance and assessment (Collier 10). These results mark Arroyo Valley participants' writing experiences and values as typical of students across the country, and situate La Vista participants as outliers. In other words, the habitus of the typical student attending the university most closely matches the habitus of Arroyo participants, those least engaged in and by writing. Interestingly, it's the writing experiences and habits of mind that the *Framework* does not mention (expression and identity) that was most displayed by La Vista participants. Although expressive writing may not be the focus of postsecondary writing, its practice may foster an appreciation of writing and its uses that lead to the habits of mind noted in the *Framework*.

The socioeconomic differences between Arroyo and La Vista most likely contributed to the differences in writing circulation in the home and community. During my time in these two communities, families in both communities expressed hopes for their children's success in postsecondary education. For La Vista, success was tied to identity and behaviors, who students were, what they would become, and what they should and would do. In Arroyo, success was tied to an external audience, the judgment of the school. The *Framework* can aid both communities, but to do that it must actually be a framework, a supportive structure.

The *Framework*'s emphasis on habits of mind and writing experiences across the curriculum takes an important stance on the importance of writing and elevates the development of the student. However, the focus on students puts the onus of preparation on teachers and students: individuals. My study indicates that the habits of mind encouraged by the *Framework* are not attained through individual grit or the work of a lone teacher, but through the circulation of writing experiences through different fields: schools, homes, and communities. A framework implies a supportive structure, but currently the *Framework* describes an ideal habitus shaped by ideal writing experiences provided by an ideal teacher. The structure to support those ideals is missing. If the *Framework*'s goal is to develop "certain kinds of people," we must go beyond naming the habits of mind and the writing experiences that foster them, for people are not formed solely in classrooms (Hansen 540). We must describe how schools, communities, and families can support the formation of these habits of mind through the circulation of writing experiences, and aid communities and families in the creation and circulation of those writing experiences.

Works Cited

Bawarshi, Anis, and Mary Jo Reiff. "Tracing Discursive Resources: How Students Use Prior Genre Knowledge to Negotiate New Writing Contexts in

First-year Composition." *Written Communication* 28.3 (2011): 312–337. Web. 3 June 2015.

Bourdieu, Pierre. *In Other Words: Essays Toward a Reflexive Sociology*. Stanford: Stanford UP, 1994. Print.

—. *Outline of a Theory of Practice*. New York: Cambridge UP, 1977. Print.

—. "The Forms of Capital." *Handbook of Theory and Research for the Sociology of Education*. Ed. J.G. Richarson. New York: Greenwood P, 1986. 241–258. Print.

—. *The Logic of Practice*. Cambridge: Polity P, 1990. Print.

—. *The Field of Cultural Production*. New York: Columbia UP, 1993. Print.

—. *Weight of the World: Social Suffering in Contemporary Society*. Trans. Priscilla Ferguson, Susan Emmanuel, Joe Johnson, and Shoggy T. Waryn. Stanford: Stanford UP, 1999. Print.

Bourdieu, Pierre and Loïc Wacquant. *An Invitation to Reflexive Sociology*. Chicago: U of Chicago P, 1992. Print.

Bronfenbrenner, Urie, and Pamela A. Morris. "The Bioecological Model of Human Development." *Handbook of Child Psychology*. 6th ed. Ed. Richard M. Lerner and William Damon. Vol. 1. New York, NY: Wiley, 2006. 793–828. Print.

Collier, Lorna. "Listening to Students: New Insights on Their College-Writing Expectations." *The Council Chronicle* 23.3 (March 2014): 10–12. Web. 6 June 2016.

Council of Writing Program Administrators, National Council of Teachers of English, and National Writing Project. *Framework for Success in Postsecondary Writing*. CWPA, NCTE, and NWP, 2011. PDF File.

Driscoll, Dana Lynn, and Jennifer Wells. "Beyond Knowledge and Skills." *Composition Forum* 26 (Fall 2012). Web. 3 June 2015.

Federal Communications Commission. *Local Telephone Communication Report 2013*. Government Printing Office. Web. 3 June 2015.

Hansen, Kristine. "The Framework for Success in Postsecondary Writing: Better than the Competition, Still Not All We Need." *Symposium: On the Framework for Success in Postsecondary Writing*. Spec. issue of *College English* 74.6 (2012): 540–43. Print.

McComiskey, Bruce. "Bridging the Divide: The (Puzzling) Framework and the Transition from K–12 to College Writing Instruction." *Symposium: On the Framework for Success in Postsecondary Writing*. Spec. issue of *College English* 74.6 (2012): 537–40. Print.

Newberger, Eric. "Computer Use in the United States: Population Characteristics." *Current Population Reports*. October 1997. PDF File.

Pew Research Foundation. "Mobile Technology Fact Sheet." *Pew Internet Project*. January 2014. Web. 3 June 2015.

9 The *Framework for Success* as Rhetorical Common Denominator

Peter H. Khost

> . . . they who have no arms / Have cleanest hands
> —Dylan Thomas

In this chapter, I issue a proposal on the basis of two preconditional positions: first, that teachers of writing ought to agree to some extent on a basic policy of college readiness in our subject area, and second, that the *Framework for Success in Postsecondary Writing* should be that policy. For some, these claims may appear to be self-evident on account of the very publication of the *Framework* in 2011 by National Council of Teachers of English (NCTE), Council of Writing Program Administrators (CWPA), and National Writing Project (NWP), but for others, both points are debatable for any number of reasons. For one thing, composition theorists do not seem to be settled enough on the merits of the *Framework* or on an apparent alternative. Although we should of course protect academic freedom, as Lauren Ingraham demonstrates in her chapter in this volume, I believe we must learn to negotiate with non-specialists about college-level writing from a standpoint of demonstrable unity. Questions of what it means for students to be college-ready and how important that is, who determines that, and how that is determined certainly warrant more complexity than simple *us vs. them* thinking, but in this case there is still indeed a powerful external *them* (i.e., policy makers and various special interests) and a much less powerful, variegated *us* (i.e., teachers), a point made by Peggy O'Neill, Linda Adler-Kassner, Cathy Fleischer, and Anne-Marie Hall in the Foreword to this volume. Like it or not, aware of it or not, they and we are competing to influence practices and views of college-level writing, but despite being largely a rhetorical matter, this dispute has not elicited much effective public debate from teachers of rhetoric and composition.

To improve our performance in this context, I propose a strategy of applying the *Framework* as what I am calling a rhetorical common denominator for our field, an approach that seeks both to unify writing instructors, and thereby strengthen our external negotiations about college readiness, and to preserve our vital internal pedagogical diversity. My strategy additionally intends to generate more visibility and evidence for the *Framework* in the hope of making this statement a household name among teachers as well as a more viable policy to present to concerned publics. After laying out some background, I make my proposal for establishing rhetorical solidarity, and I conclude with recommendations for readers.

EXIGENCY FOR THE *FRAMEWORK*

Though it does not say so explicitly, the *Framework* was clearly composed in response to the Common Core State Standards (CCSS), whose main theme of college readiness belies the fact that postsecondary teachers were paid no more than lip service in the policy's drafting.[1] The history and controversies of the CCSS should already be familiar or easy enough to find out without requiring summary here except to remind readers that many teachers remain concerned about how these standards may negatively impact student writing practices. Our worries run especially deep where high-stakes assessments are concerned, which spans a huge spectrum of influence including K–12 learning outcomes in forty-plus states; "college placement tools" for supposedly 640 institutions, "including most of the largest state systems," according to the Partnership for Assessment of Readiness for College and Careers (PARCC); and "an agreed-upon achievement level" in an unspecified number of postsecondary institutions partnering with Smarter Balanced Assessment Consortium (SBAC), so they hope. Teachers' worries run even deeper where automated essay scoring may be involved, a practice favored by testing companies but whose implementation status is currently (im)pending (see Human Readers). If there is any doubt about the extent of the threat to college-level writing beliefs and practices caused by what Harry Denny calls the "corporate-assessment-education industrial complex" (187), here are two telling testimonies to that effect from recent past presidents of the CWPA.

The first is from Linda Adler-Kassner published in the *WPA* journal in 2012:

> [If] "college and career readiness" is the frame within which discussions about education are taking place, and we know that it is, we need to be the drivers of the meaning of "college readiness." . . . We need to outline what we think is critical for students to be prepared for college level writing. . . . If we have a chance to make our case, then make it we must . . . because right now, ours is hardly the loudest voice in conversations about what "writing preparation" means, and "how well" that preparation has been achieved. . . . [T]hese movements [including the CCSS] are larger, more powerful, and better funded than any writing teachers, or even any group of writing teachers, will ever be. ("The Companies" 134–36)

The second is from Rita Malenczyk posted on the WPA listserv (WPA-L) on March 7, 2014:

> the alien takeover is nearly complete. ETS . . . controls *both* the curriculum of the elementary and secondary schools as well as The Big Test . . . and it uses our language to hoodwink the public into thinking it's getting something else. . . . I think as university professors, let alone as WPAs, we need to be aware of this and design curricula accordingly. That's the optimistic view. The pessimistic view is that only the private schools will now be producing independent thinkers and, therefore, the ruling class. The *really* pessimistic view is that we all need to move to Finland.

As of now, the possibility of postsecondary writing teachers driving the meaning of college readiness in public discourse seems about as likely as our expatriating en masse to Finland. But this is not for a lack of good intentions. We have easily enough imagined constructive responses to the predicament that are *pedagogical* in nature. For example, some of those who are familiar with the *Framework* speak of authoring assignments that involve its recommended habits of mind and experiences, and I have presented on using the *Framework*, as others have surely done, in graduate education, teacher training, and professional development

(Khost, "The 'Habits'"; "Open"; "Original"; and "Why"). As commendable as these may be as internal actions, such *pedagogical* uses of the *Framework* comprise little to nothing of a *rhetorical* response to the threat of large-scale external mischaracterizations of college-level writing and questionable assessment practices in the name of college readiness. More precisely, pedagogical responses are only a start to what must become a more robust rhetorical campaign. Responding to the present concern only in our classrooms might be likened to tidying up inside of one's house while disregarding a storm that rages ever bigger and nearer outside. In our busy and difficult professional lives it is understandably easy for many of us to forget, ignore, or give up on the political contexts in which our teaching occurs, but we do so at our own risk (Adler-Kassner, *Activist WPA*). For if we are not careful, we may lose our ability to make some pedagogical decisions autonomously or at all. To persuasively affect public discourse about college readiness, then, we need to think of ourselves not only as teachers and scholars, but also as advocates for our work, or, if you prefer, as *teachers* of our scholarship to parties beyond our ordinary student body.

I propose that upon developing this identity, we compositionists draw on the field's late arriving but gradually emerging sense of collective strength. Given rhetoric and composition's troubled institutional history and our widespread ongoing labor inequities, we may not yet be accustomed to regarding our collective identity as a particularly powerful force, yet considerable rhetorical potency might be generated if the many thousands of writing teachers nationwide were to achieve, demonstrate, and take action on a basic consensus about college readiness.

NEED FOR DISCIPLINARY ADVOCACY

Over the past five to ten years, publishers, investors, so-called *reformist* policy makers, and testing companies (some of which are non-profit but nevertheless garner huge sums of money) have put considerable effort into manufacturing or maintaining a crisis about students' lack of college readiness. With help from the media and government funding, the story has been widely bought by publics and schools—as have been its attendant high-stakes tests, curricular resources, and test-prep materials—despite a number of contending but lesser-known realities that initially existed or have since been revealed. These include the fact that the crisis-callers and would-be resolvers are generally not educators; that national test scores may not be declining but rising (Ravitch 44); that Americans today are being admitted to postsecondary institutions at all-time high or near highest percentages, with enrollments projected to increase for at least the next decade (National Center for Education Statistics); and that as of 2013 only 22% of the population believed that more testing improves students' performance in school, according to a forty-fifth annual Gallup/Phi Delta Kappa poll (Bushaw and Lopez 9). For these reasons alone, it is tempting to simply refuse the given terms of debate about college-readiness and declare the conversation moot. But the ship may have already sailed on that opportunity, as the technocrats backing the CCSS continue to effectively push their agenda.[2] Those of us interested in counteracting this crisis hype would probably now do better to operate within the existing construct of readiness, which we might like to believe would be as easy as saying to concerned parties: *If you want to know if a student is ready for college-level writing, just ask some college writing instructors.* But nobody seems to be asking our opinion, and we might not be able to present a very convincing one even if they were to ask us.

Can we compositionists point to anything that definitively identifies and explains college-level writing? We may know it when we see it in local situations, but there are at least two problems with this answer: (1) we likely won't convince many external stakeholders with only constant deference to the local, and (2) gut feeling-type evidence, even by seasoned scholars and teachers, does not count for much in today's age of accountability. NCTE has recently dedicated a two-volume collection called *What Is College-Level Writing?* to exactly this subject area (Sullivan and Tinberg; Sullivan, Tinberg, and Blau). In spite of offering generally thoughtful and provocative essays, the contributors to these volumes come down thoroughly inconclusively on the eponymous question. In an exchange about his review of the NCTE collection, one of a very few rhetoric and composition luminaries to have attracted large numbers of public sales of his own books (which might suggest a different opinion would follow here) goes as far as to rejoice at our field's insistence on an indeterminate approach to college-level writing: "I praise and indeed celebrate what could be called chaos and anarchy in standards for college-level writing" (Elbow 173). We specialists see this kind of continuous ambiguity as the healthy sign that it is, but lay people probably see it as indecisiveness, administrators as incompetence, policy makers as cause for reform, and investors as vulnerability and opportunity. Furthermore, none of these parties wants to engage us in perpetual academic dissensus.

Of course, by holding out against a fixed definition of college-level writing, we are admirably trying to protect students from surrendering to rigid standards and our pedagogy from devolving into mere test preparation. But is our method achieving these intended results? Are the CCSS not increasingly yoking high school curricula across the country to static and sometimes arbitrary standards (e.g., 30% literary and 70% informational texts for seniors)? Are high-stakes test scores not determining primary and secondary school teachers' reappointment and promotion, and thereby encouraging, increasing, and normalizing test preparation in classrooms—as may be competency-based programs without need of classrooms at all? Do college compositionists believe we are impervious to such encroachment on our domain: we whose course offerings consist of many expensive sections of relatively low-capped courses, whose institutional status often occupies the lowest spot in the disciplinary pecking order, whose programs may very well include only one or even no tenure lines, and whose subject matter is so poorly understood by external stakeholders? (The encroachment is already happening, by the way; see Smith.) SAT and AP exams, dual credit courses, and other such entities have long since blurred the secondary/postsecondary boundary in writing,[3] and for-profit enterprises and MOOCs are only a few recent signs that this corporate-backed effect may intensify further.

Meanwhile we know that non-formative high stakes writing assessments and corresponding test prep can easily corrupt students' academic composing practices, distort their view of college-level writing, and prompt gaming of the system (Kolowich; Perelman). Think of the common related complaints: five-paragraph essays; quantity over quality; writing to non-audiences; vague, canned, or unrealistic thesis statements; unrevised work; inflated voice; overblown vocabulary; fixation on grammar; and so on. For just one of any number of sources I could turn to for support in assuming the deterministic effect of value systems, I invoke psychologist Carl Rogers, of Rogerian argument fame to rhetoricians. He studied what happens when young people's sense of their "positive regard" depends on their being obedient to "conditions of worth" (225), as opposed to, say, being valued unconditionally for their uniqueness. Rogers found that under conditional circumstances children tend to censor their behavior to exclude aspects that are not approved. Perhaps to some degree this influence seems inevitable and even reasonable, but not so on a grand scale. When an entire public educational system centers its apparent values on outcomes rather than on experiences, it should come as no surprise to find that it yields inauthentic writing executed out of obedience to the telos of an exam-driven curriculum that reflects a deficit model approach to literacy.[4]

To help counteract the problem of over-standardized writing instruction, while also preserving definitional indeterminacy and pedagogical freedom, the *Framework* cleverly represents college-level writing exclusively in terms of individual, authentic habits of mind and composing experiences. I believe these habits and experiences can represent at least a working disciplinary consensus that may be supplemented as need be with locally relevant values. They are hardly the total but they may represent a base of what postsecondary writing teachers prize.

My Proposal

I propose that writing teachers endorse the *Framework* as a useful, general, and flexible enough policy to unite around as a basis for rhetorical solidarity in discourse about college readiness. I encourage readers to figuratively regard the *Framework* as a discipline-wide rhetorical common denominator: most certainly *not* a set of universal standards, but rather a shared point of reference (and instructional tool) that enables a broad diversity of supplementary goals and methods to be regarded as *numerators*. By using the phrase "common denominator," I mean a minimal set of values that the field would collectively agree to commit to, regardless of whether individuals teach them explicitly or implicitly, or wholly or partly. It's hard to believe that effective writing teachers do not promote these values at least implicitly and partly. My call borrows from a tactic associated with Gayatri Chakravorty Spivak, called strategic essentialism or strategic universalism, with which minority groups temporarily put aside internal differences at times of need for rhetorical solidarity. Spivak explains: you should "see what in the universalizing discourse could be useful," and "pick up the universal that will give you the most power to fight against the other side (183–84).

With apologies for the mathematical metaphor, I remind you that a denominator is the number below the line in a fraction and a numerator is the one above it, as in $1/8, 2/8, 3/8, 4/8, 5/8$, where 8 is the (in this case, common) denominator and 1–5 are the numerators. According to the *Oxford English Dictionary*, a denominator is an entity that gives a name or value to something, and in its figurative usage, a common denominator is "something common to or characteristic of a number of things, people, etc." ("denominator" defs. 1 and 2b). Using these definitions, the *Framework* in my view would be "characteristic" of the values that specialists ascribe to college-level writing. Although college-level writing is such a highly variable thing that its teachers understandably hesitate to definitively identify it, I feel we must nevertheless present some kind of authorized marker of it or else live with the unsatisfactory representations being made by other parties (Graff 1049; Smagorinsky 96). This marker itself should embody variability, within the limits of basic signification. What I mean to suggest is that the *Framework*'s habits and experiences can and should be used to "give a name" to college-level writing values but only by partial *description*, not by definitive *prescription*; that is, "by telling a different story about student writers," as Kristine Johnson notes in her qualified endorsement of the *Framework* (518).

The *Framework*'s authors say they want the statement to provide a "voice" for "college writing teachers and researchers" in readiness discourse (O'Neill et al. 522), and at the heart of this statement are the habits of mind it promotes. So, the presumption seems to be that we should speak with others about these eight habits. For this, I encourage you to commit them to memory using the following acronym I derived from many permutations: CREMPCOF—Creativity, Responsibility, Engagement, Metacognition, Persistence, Curiosity, Openness, and Flexibility. I have presented this admittedly awkward acronym at conferences at least a half dozen times as well as to my graduate classes, and it always gets a laugh, but it's the best we've got, and those inclined to memorize it will find that easy to do. It helps that the first three initials of the acronym are also the first three letters of the initial habit, *cre*ativity. With its emphasis on habits, the *Framework* transforms the concept of "success" (or readiness for success) from an outcome measured by external parties to something embodied, ongoing, and determined largely through one's own agency and in one's own terms (but not always *on* one's own terms, of course, since contexts and other contingencies of lived experiences apply). Habits are ways of being, and although one might produce a good piece of writing without having drawn on all eight of them listed in the *Framework*, one cannot *be* a good college-level writer without drawing on any of those habits. This distinction likely reveals a key difference between how educators and how many external stakeholders view the matter at hand. A similar divide exists regarding assessment.

Johnson makes a very strong case against assessing the habits of mind as outcomes. Doing so would not only be "antithetical to . . . the vision projected in the *Framework*," she claims, but would also potentially encounter confounding issues of validity, fairness, appropriateness, surveillance, overabundance of outcomes, expropriation on the "large-scale," and dubiousness of necessity (531–33). I agree with this essential point. We should not evaluate students' habits of mind; they are at work behind any number of outcomes that writing programs already regularly assess (see the "WPA Outcomes Statement for First-Year Composition"). Instead, the habits must be treated, as Johnson notes, as "practices" of individual "writers and persons" rather than as "objective content" (534–35). Objective content, which we should register at the numerator level, most likely correlates in some ways with denominator-level habits of mind, and this potential link should be researched, but that will not be easy to do. In 2013–14, as part of another study I am conducting, I piloted such an effort on a small scale in my own program using the trait of rhetorical competency. What I found was that before any correlations between habits of mind and this outcome could be effectively investigated, my writing program would need to do a better job of pinpointing rhetorical competency. Such a finding is important, and it somewhat exemplifies what *Framework* task force chair Peggy O'Neill means in encouraging writing programs to use the *Framework* to assess our assignments and assess our assessments.

As Chris Anson points out, "the Framework wasn't designed as (yet another) template for creating alphanumeric outcomes for student performance but as a guide to think about 'how *teachers* can foster these habits of mind.'" One of the ways such a general "guide" can be effective in specific contexts, as I have stated above, is through supplementation with local numerators. So, for example, basic or business writing programs would promote creativity, responsibility, engagement, and so on through the respective lenses of basic or business writers and contexts. Faculty who favor critical pedagogy would consider how issues of power relate to students' creativity, responsibility, engagement, metacognition, persistence, curiosity, openness, and flexibility. I, for one, would like to supplement the *Framework*'s habits of mind holistically with habits of body, spirit, and environment.

My proposal regarding the *Framework* is not just hypothetical; I have already taken two important steps toward gradually actualizing this plan. First is my initiation of an empirical study of student writers' habits of mind in first-year postsecondary writing courses at my own university. I began this ongoing project with IRB-approval in spring 2013, and in fall 2015 I expanded it to include secondary schools with support from a CWPA research grant, and two-year and baccalaureate institutions with support from a CCCC research grant. In part because of a recent general decline in sociopolitical esteem for the American teacher, it seems that our mere anecdotal support for the habits of mind cannot match strength with the psychometrics often used by testing companies and policy makers to advance their agendas. So in addition to engaging publics with other rhetorical strategies, I believe we should support our positions with evidence that is "replicable, aggregable, and data-supported" (Haswell 201), not only to remain competitive but also because it is good practice to do so. Because of space constraints, I must forego a detailed explanation of my study, but I can say that my approach has been to get a sense of where students themselves are on this issue by examining the self-efficacy of their habits of mind, on an optional basis, in the context of first-year writing courses. I have generated statistically significant results suggesting that some students' self-efficacy of their habits can be improved by even a very minor intervention, that this improvement does not seem to happen on its own within the given context, and that such self-regard may very well be highly correlated with students' overall satisfaction with their first-year writing course.

My second step, initiated in fall 2013, has been to form and to chair the WPA Task Force on Publicizing the *Framework for Success in Postsecondary Writing*. Among other projects this task force has taken on, we plan to create a Web-based platform where writing instructors from any level can post their ideas and comments signaling endorsement of the *Framework*. With support from a robust outreach and advertising campaign that takes advantage of the national network of NWP sites and WPA regional affiliates, this effort could generate a substantial and visible discipline-wide appearance of agreement about the *Framework* as being foundational to college-level writing. We can think of this forthcoming Web resource as providing a forum for sharing and discussing numerators with which to supplement the denominator habits of mind and experiences.

Conclusion

Many different kinds and ranks of educators have a stake in counteracting missteps taken by external stakeholders in the name of college-level writing, and for this we bear a responsibility to advocate as such to the degree that we can. But (as familiar as this call may be) it behooves senior faculty to take the lead in this effort. I acknowledge how busy they often are, especially as their numbers decrease in particular departments, yet they do possess job security and (often) the authority to form committees for dispersing workload. Job security is an umbrella term for several reasons why I believe that tenured faculty must take charge of this campaign. Junior tenure-track faculty are typically rewarded only for writing within their field's specialized publications, which is the opposite of addressing mostly external lay audiences as I am calling for.[5] Non-tenure track instructors often struggle with agendas that are more difficult to manage, especially freeway-flying adjuncts and graduate teaching assistants. This is not just a matter of having insufficient time but also of maximizing effort in the areas that pertain most to their precarious reappointment. Furthermore, a good deal of communicating the *Framework* as a common denominator will be directed at university administrators and policy makers who, for one thing, may be more apt to give time and credence to senior faculty and, for another, might well be displeased by resistance to their differing views of college readiness in writing.

To cite an example that came to my attention while I was writing this chapter, a WPA without tenure or a union reported on the WPA-L that her program (and other departments) is being "pushed" to consider Pearson's automated Propero platform for, in her words, "outsourcing . . . 'composition' courses [in which] writing accounts for only 20% of the grade, [with] no revision, many multiple-choice questions, and so forth" (Cassity). The administration at this WPA's private Master's-L institution, which has been cutting faculty and staff, clearly maintains a very different interpretation of college-level writing than does the person it hired to coordinate first-year writing. I am not alone in having immediately recognized in this case an example of our field's widespread vulnerability and corresponding need to take action. Two responses to the original listserv plea diagnosed the field's PR problem right away: "We have done a terrible job making clear to our publics what constitutes educational quality" (Hesse), and "[t]he profession . . . has done a poor job of articulating the value of our work" (Bleck). Ensuing were a number of calls to seize the "kairotic moment" (Cleary) by seeking "wider public exposure," "local media involve[ment]" (Ingraham), and even a "National Teachers Strike Day" (Fox). But after just three days this listserv thread ceased receiving posts.

The WPA in this example deserves (and all members of the field should possess) a clear indication of consensus that has been sanctioned by the field's most prominent organizations, against which we can expose, contrast, and correct wide varieties of misrepresentations and malpractices of college-level writing. The important difference to me between merely having a *document* that posits the field's agreement—which we arguably already possess in the *Framework*—and having a *consensus* on that is the human element: that is, the will to declare endorsement, the sociality of speech act, and especially the performance of rhetoric in lived contexts rather than only in abstraction. The *Framework* itself, with its focus on habits and experiences, calls for no less than such responsible, engaged, and persistent activity. Advocacy must become a more prominent aspect of our professional lives, and that begins with speaking out.

I am a lifelong hanger-back, having chronically shied away from declaring commitment to ideals for theoretical misgivings and inevitable exceptions that always seem to occur to me. I like to think this hesitation often serves me well. Perhaps many scholars feel similarly; after all, to invoke this chapter's epigraph, theory is to some degree *armless*. That is to say, it need not be accountable to action. In fact, not long ago, talk of blending theory with praxis was nothing short of anathema to many humanists. But if only because external threats have pushed the present issue to such a degree, I believe writing scholars will have to put our arms to work and get our hands dirty by more (pro)actively entering the college-readiness debate. We stand little chance of making a difference, however, without the collective force of agreement on a clear policy to put into contention with timed writing tests, inauthentic prompts, automated scoring, et cetera. So for any of its conceptual and structural shortcomings, despite (and also because of) its content-neutrality, and with acknowledgment of the chance for any number of contingencies to which my limited perspective blinds me, I hereby declare my endorsement for the *Framework for Success in Postsecondary Writing* as a basic (not exhaustive) set of values for promoting (not measuring) college readiness in writing. That's the tortured qualified version for the insiders who will read this chapter. We'll have to work on a catchy bumper-sticker version for everyone else.

Although we will never be able to match the financial, marketing, and political resources of the external parties that are challenging our views of college readiness in writing, we might be able to compete on ideological, experiential, experimental, and rhetorical grounds. But we need to sharpen, support, and spread our messages more effectively, including: (1) that reaching a cut score on a timed, single-draft essay exam will not produce college-ready writing nearly as well as will engaging in the practices outlined in the *Framework*; (2) that the natures of language, composing, and subjectivity vary with shifting purposes, audiences, and contexts of which fixed (or even computer-adaptive) standards can never accurately capture the value; and (3) that teaching to tests impedes students' ability and willingness to develop healthy habits and engage in authentic writerly experiences: the very things that *will* ready them for college writing.

My aim in this chapter has been to establish a rhetorical common denominator for disputing college readiness in writing and to inspire members of our field to take action with it. The former will amount to little good without the latter. In some cases this action may need to be taken collectively, or else individual retribution may occur, as is potentially the case cited above with Propero and the untenured WPA, who was rightly seeking collective support by writing to the WPA-L. The valuable conversation that ensued on that listserv included worthwhile advice, moral support, and disclaimers; indeed "all politics are local," as Bradley Bleck noted there. As I have argued above, individual writing programs and faculty members have very little power in these local contexts. In that example case, another respondent called for "NCTE to make a loud statement about Propero" (Beltran), which Maja Wilson then pointed out is not likely and probably not advisable. But NCTE (and/or CCCC, WPA, NWP, etc.) *could* form a kind of advisory committee to be anonymously called upon to help negotiate in such circumstances. This body, which would represent the individual program or WPA as well as the consensus of many thousands of professionals in the field, could be engaged perhaps not so much as to trumpet a "loud" *no* but as to employ a subtler rhetoric, say, of consultation, or if need be, to negotiate a satisfactory compromise. In cases focusing on college readiness or college-level writing, the *Framework* could serve as a common denominator with which to secure a vetted foundation of values and in relation to which to discuss locally relevant numerators.

In addition to declaring your own (and your program's) endorsement of the *Framework* and taking part in corresponding collective actions, the following is a partial list of ways you can get involved in advancing this cause. Download the *Framework* from the CWPA website, read it, and determine your own numerator values to append to it. Speak with your administrators, colleagues, and students about the *Framework*. Conduct professional development sessions regarding the habits of mind and experiences. Use the statement, as O'Neill recommends, to assess your assignments (e.g., to what degree does a given task call for and support the habit of creativity?) or to assess your assessments (e.g., do your colleagues and you value the habit of engagement as you read student portfolios?). Memorize and teach others my habits of mind acronym: CREMPCOF. Seek opportunities to use and spread word of the *Framework* as a rhetorical common denominator, including through contact with concerned publics across various media.[6] Look for more information on this subject, including forthcoming reports on my empirical research on the *Framework*'s habits of mind, and six columns about the *Framework* and advocacy that I will be editing for volume 106 of NCTE's *English Journal*. Please also send me your comments, questions, and ideas.

NOTES

1. My comments extend only as far as rhetoric/composition scholars and the English Language Arts standards are concerned. For primary evidence of NCTE's token role in and toothless response to the development of the CCSS, see Beers; Gilyard.

2. Thomas Newkirk warns that if anything in this scenario is to be perceived as moot, it will likely be the complaints of critics because the "deft rollout" of the Common Core "portrayed [the CCSS] as so consensual, so universally endorsed, so thoroughly researched and vetted, so self-evidently necessary to economic progress, so broadly representative of beliefs in the educational community—that they cease to be even debatable" (1).

3. See the *CWPA Position Statement on Pre-College Credit for Writing* for more information.

4. The "high" stakes of assessments can also extend beyond college entrance and placement. *The New York Times* reports that "many employers are still asking job applicants for their [SAT] test scores, even if they are years out of date," to screen applicants and predict job performance (Dewan). I have been emphasizing college readiness, but career readiness plays in here as well.

5. Because of my insufficient knowledge about contract responsibilities at teaching institutions and high schools, my scope here is limited to postsecondary faculty at research institutions. It should be obvious, though, that I believe writing teachers everywhere should do whatever they can to contribute to the collective effort.

6. Linda Adler-Kassner can serve as a model, having at least twice participated in talk radio programs about the *Framework* and college readiness ("New Approaches"; "The Expectations").

Works Cited

Adler-Kassner, Linda. *The Activist WPA: Changing Stories about Writing and Writers.* Logan: Utah State UP, 2008. Print.

——. "The Companies We Keep Or The Companies We Would Like to Try to Keep: Strategies and Tactics in Challenging Times." *WPA: Writing Program Administration* 36.1 (2012): 119–40. Print.

Anson, Chris. "Re: Measuring the 'Habits of Mind.'" *WPA-Listserv.* Council of Writing Program Administrators, 8 Nov. 2011. Web. 10 July 2014.

Beers, Kylene. "An Open Letter to NCTE Members about the Common Core State Standards." *NCTE.* NCTE, 17 Aug. 2009. Web. 27 Dec. 2012.

——. "An Open Letter to NCTE Members about the Release of the September Public Draft of the Common Core State Standards." *NCTE.* NCTE, 21 Sept. 2009. Web. 27 Dec. 2012.

Beltran, Diane Quaglia. "Re: Anyone being pushed to use Propero?" *WPA-Listserv.* Council of Writing Program Administrators, 6 July 2014. Web. 7 July 2014.

Bleck, Bradley. "Re: Anyone being pushed to use Propero?" *WPA-Listserv.* Council of Writing Program Administrators, 6 July 2014. Web. 7 July 2014.

Bushaw, William J., and Shane J. Lopez. "Which way do we go?" *Phi Delta Kappan* 95.1 (2013): 8–25. Web. 7 July 2014.

Cassity, Kathleen J. "Anyone being pushed to use Propero?" *WPA-Listserv.* Council of Writing Program Administrators, 4 July 2014. Web. 4 July 2014.

Cleary, Daniel J. "Re: Anyone being pushed to use Propero?" *WPA-Listserv.* Council of Writing Program Administrators, 4 July 2014. Web. 5 July 2014.

Council of Chief State School Officers and National Governor's Association. *New York State P-12 Common Core Learning Standards for English Language Arts & Literacy.* CCSSO and NGA, 10 Jan. 2011. PDF File.

Council of Writing Program Administrators. *CWPA Position Statement on Pre-College Credit for Writing.* CWPA, 2014. PDF File.

——. "WPA Outcomes Statement For First-Year Composition." CWPA, 2014. PDF File.

Council of Writing Program Administrators, National Council of Teachers of English, and National Writing Project. *Framework for Success in Postsecondary Writing.* CWPA, NCTE, and NWP, 2011. PDF File.

Denny, Harry. "A Queer Eye for the WPA." *WPA: Writing Program Administration* 37.1 (2013): 186–98. Print.

"denominator." *Oxford English Dictionary.* Oxford UP, 2014. Web. 6 July 2014.

Dewan, Shaila. "How Businesses Use Your SATs." *NYTimes.com.* New York Times, 29 Mar. 2014. Web. 8 July 2014.

Elbow, Peter. "Response to Kelly Ritter." *WPA: Writing Program Administration* 35.1 (2011): 172–74. Print.

"The Expectations of College Level Writing." *Blogtalkradio.* BlogTalkRadio.com. 2014. Web. 7 July 2014.

Fox, Stephen. "Re: Anyone being pushed to use Propero?" *WPA-Listserv.* Council of Writing Program Administrators, 5 July 2014. Web. 6 July 2014.

Gilyard, Keith. "NCTE President Keith Gilyard Talks about NCTE and Common Core Standards." *NCTE.* NCTE, 9 Feb. 2012. Web. 27 Dec. 2012.

Graff, Gerald. "Scholars and Sound Bites: The Myth of Academic Difficulty." *PMLA* 115.5 (2000): 1041–52. Print.

Haswell, Richard. "NCTE/CCCC's Recent War on Scholarship." *Written Communication* 22.2 (2005): 198–223. Print.

Hesse, Doug. "Re: Anyone being pushed to use Propero?" *WPA-Listserv.* Council of Writing Program Administrators, 5 July 2014. Web. 6 July 2014.

Human Readers. "Professionals Against Machine Scoring Of Student Essays In High-Stakes Assessment." *Human Readers.* Human Readers, 12 Mar. 2013. Web. 15 Jan. 2014.

Ingraham, Lauren. "Re: Anyone being pushed to use Propero?" *WPA-Listserv.* Council of Writing Program Administrators, 5 July 2014. Web. 6 July 2014.

Johnson, Kristine. "Beyond Standards: Disciplinary and National Perspectives on Habits of Mind." *College Composition and Communication* 64.3 (2013): 517–41. Print.

Khost, Peter H. "The 'Habits of Mind' (and More) as Grad Seminar Teaching Tools." 128th Modern Language Association Annual Convention. Sheraton Boston Hotel, Boston, MA. 4 Jan. 2013. Conference Presentation.

—. "Open To Debate: Research-Based Strategies for Disputing 'College-Readiness' in Writing." Sixty-Fifth Annual Convention of the Conference on College Composition and Communication. JW Marriott, Indianapolis, IN. 22 Mar. 2014. Conference Presentation.

—. "Original Research and Positions on the Framework for Success's 'Habits of Mind.'" Annual Conference of the Council of Writing Program Administrators. Coastal Georgia Center, Savannah, GA. 20 July 2013. Conference Presentation.

—. "Why and How the Framework for Success Should Become Writing Studies' Common Denominator." 103rd Annual Convention of the National

Council of Teachers of English. Hynes Convention Center, Boston, MA. 23 Nov. 2013. Conference Presentation.

Kolowich, Steve. "Writing Instructor, Skeptical of Automated Grading, Pits Machine vs. Machine." *The Chronicle of Higher Education*. The Chronicle of Higher Education, 28 Apr. 2014. Web. 8 July 2014.

Malenczyk, Rita. "CWPA and the new SAT announcement (related to 'Revision of the SAT')." *WPA-Listserv*. Council of Writing Program Administrators, 7 Mar. 2014. Web. 8 Mar. 2014.

National Center for Education Statistics. "Undergraduate Enrollment." *The Condition of Education*. US Department of Education. May 2014. Web. 4 July 2014.

"New Approaches to Teaching Postsecondary Writing." *Central Standard*. Kansas City Public Radio. KCUR, Kansas City. 18 Jan. 2012. Radio.

Newkirk, Thomas. "Postscript: Speaking Back to the Common Core." *Heinemann*. N.p., 2013. PDF File. 7 July 2014.

O'Neill, Peggy. "Re: Measuring the 'Habits of Mind.'" *WPA-Listserv*. Council of Writing Program Administrators, 9 Nov. 2011. Web. 27 Dec. 2012.

O'Neill, Peggy, Linda Adler-Kassner, Cathy Fleischer, and Anne-Marie Hall. "Creating the *Framework for Success in Postsecondary Writing*." *Symposium: On the Framework for Success in Postsecondary Writing*. Spec. issue of *College English* 74.6 (2012): 520–33. Print.

Partnership for Assessment of Readiness for College and Careers. "Postsecondary and PARCC." The Partnership for Assessment of Readiness for College and Careers, 2014. Web. 15 July 2014.

Perelman, Les. "Information Illiteracy and Mass Market Writing Assessments." *College Composition and Communication* 60.1 (2008): 128–41. Print.

Ravitch, Diane. *Reign of Error: The Hoax of the Privatization Movement and the Danger to America's Public Schools*. New York: Vintage Books, 2014. Print.

Rogers, Carl C. "A Theory of Therapy, Personality and Interpersonal Relationships as Developed in the Client-centered Framework." *Psychology: A Study of a Science Vol. 3: Formulations of the Person and the Social Context*. Ed. Sigmund Koch. New York: McGraw Hill, 1959. *Archive.org*. N.p., n.d. Web. 3 July 2014.

Smagorinsky, Peter. "Speaking Out in the Public Sphere: Why, What, Where, and How Teachers Can Enter the Fray." *English Journal* 104.3 (2015): 91–96. Print.

Smarter Balanced Assessment Consortium. "Higher Education Involvement." *Higher Education*. Smarter Balanced Assessment Consortium, n.d. Web. 15 July 2014.

Smith, Ashley A. "Common Core Gets a Footing." *Inside Higher Ed*. Inside Higher Ed, 28 Apr. 2015. Web. 12 May 2015.

Spivak, Gayatri Chakravorty. "Criticism, Feminism and the Institution: An Interview with Gayatri Chakravorty Spivak." *Thesis Eleven: Critical Theory and Historical Sociology* 10/11.1 (1985): 175–87. Print.

Sullivan, Patrick, and Howard Tinberg, eds. *What Is "College-Level" Writing?* Vol. 1. Urbana: NCTE, 2006. Print.

Sullivan, Patrick, Howard Tinberg, and Sheridan Blau, eds. *What Is "College-Level" Writing? Volume 2: Assignments, Readings, and Student Writing Samples*. Vol. 2. Urbana: NCTE, 2010. Print.

Thomas, Dylan. "Was there a time." *Collected Poems 1934–1952*. New York: New Directions, 2003. Print.

Wilson, Maja. "Re: Anyone being pushed to use Propero?" *WPA-Listserv*. Council of Writing Program Administrators, 6 July 2014. Web. 7 July 2014.

10 The *Framework for Success* Goes Online: Integration of the *Framework* into Online Writing Courses

Beth Brunk-Chavez

As Kristine Johnson notes in her article "Beyond Standards: Disciplinary and National Perspectives on the Habits of Mind," the *Framework for Success in Postsecondary Writing* "reframes a widespread public narrative about written projects and quantified achievements with an alternate narrative about writers and their development" (518). As the chapters within this volume demonstrate, since the *Framework*'s publication in 2011, many first-year writing programs have recognized these habits of mind as behaviors and experiences that already guide their curriculum development and delivery; other programs have actively sought to incorporate them when they were missing. Indeed, Amy Kimme Hea, Jenna Pack Sheffield, and Kenneth Walker in chapter 2 and Lori Ostergaard, Dana Driscoll, Cathy Rorai, and Amanda Laudig in chapter 16 provide good examples of such important work. Many of these composition programs and individual courses are taught in face-to-face settings with students and instructors sharing the same physical space. With online education seeing an increase in enrollment, we can also look to the *Framework* as a guide for online writing course development. To paraphrase Barry Maid and Barbara D'Angelo, online is not necessarily special; it does not have a special curriculum; and students and faculty should not be evaluated any differently from their face-to-face counterparts (15). It stands to reason, then, that the guidelines that influence face-to-face courses and programs should also guide online ones. Specifically, the *Framework* can be integrated into an online writing course's goals and design; it can also serve as a guide for both students in the class and the instructors teaching it. This chapter, then, combines the *Framework* with characteristics of successful online learners to promote student persistence in online courses as well as success in learning the content and becoming effective writers.

ONLINE LEARNING

According to the 2012 Survey of Online Learning conducted by the Babson Survey Research Group, over 6.7 million students took at least one online course in fall 2011; that is 570,000 more students than in fall 2010 (Allen and Seamon 17). Additionally, 32% of students enrolled in institutions of higher education now take at least one course online during their undergraduate education (19). Finally, over 69% of the chief academic leaders surveyed find online learning is critical to their institution's long-term strategy (4). In other words, more online classes are offered, more students are enrolling in them, and more universities are counting on online course offerings to sustain or increase overall enrollments than ever before.

The Babson report additionally indicates that 62.4% of higher education institutions are moving from offering individual online courses to fully online programs (20). While undergraduate writing classes, particularly first-year composition courses, may not be part of an online major, they are often an institutionally required course at the core level or are offered as an elective at the upper-division level. With the growing demand to deliver online writing courses, instructors assigned to teach them may not have the enthusiasm of early adopters and might not believe that online learning is as effective as face-to-face learning experiences.

In 2010, drawing on studies from the previous decade, Credence Baker notes that research has consistently found no significant difference between face-to-face and online learning. Not all studies concur, however. Some recent research finds that online students at community colleges persist at lower rates and achieve lower course grades compared to those students enrolled in face-to-face courses. Di Xu and Shanna Jaggers suggest, therefore, that while online courses and programs have provided increased access to education, they "must also improve the academic success of these students" (634). Appropriately, then, Baker notes that "researchers are now delving into the realm of identifying which instructional strategies are most effective for an online learning environment" (2). She argues that attention should be focused on "specific learner characteristics, learning models, and curriculum restructuring" to further increase the efficacy of online courses as a benefit to all students enrolled in them (2).

Similarly, online education experts Diane Oblinger and Brian Hawkins as well as Kelli Cargile Cook, Beth Hewett, and Christa Ehman and Micheal Callaway recognize the importance of combining both pedagogical and technological expertise when developing a course. Understanding both the allure of technology as well as the possible confusion it can cause, they remind us that learning outcomes and pedagogy should drive course development; the technology should assist the instructor and student in meeting those outcomes. In the words of Hewett and Ehman, instructors are advised to "first identify *pedagogical principles* for training that supersede specific technology platforms and then choose training methods adaptable to particular platforms" (5). In addition to course design considerations, such as linking learning objectives to course activities and measurable outcomes, the *Framework*, as Johnson argues, "asks writing teachers to address the person behind writing products and processes—to consider intellectual agency and ethical aims of writing instruction in an increasingly technocratic educational landscape" (527). When coupled with the 2014 revised "WPA Outcomes Statement for First-Year Composition" (WPA OS) and programmatic goals, the *Framework* is appropriate for developing a "philosophically sound, yet situationally adaptive" online writing course so students have a positive learning experience and so instructors are confident that they have developed a robust learning environment for students (Hewett and Ehman 5).

Uses of the *Framework* in Online Course Design and Delivery

As the *Framework* states, "habits of mind refers to ways of approaching learning that are both intellectual and practical and that will support students' success in a variety of fields and disciplines" (1). In other words, while the intent of the *Framework* is to propose a set of behaviors and experiences that will prepare students for literacy work in higher education and beyond, it has applications that stretch beyond this context. Similarly, many researchers and organizations have determined the ideal characteristics for successful online learners. In Table 1, the Illinois Online Network (ION) successful online student characteristics are mapped to the habits of mind. While all the habits of mind are significant to student learning, not all are immediately relevant to ION's framework. Of the eight habits of mind, six most directly apply to online course development and delivery: engagement, persistence, responsibility, flexibility, openness, and metacognition. (While curiosity and creativity are also useful habits of mind in an online class, they do not immediately apply to the framework articulated in this chapter.)

Table 1: Comparison of ION's Characteristics of Successful Online Students to the Habits of Mind

Online Network's Characteristics of Successful Online Students	*Framework*'s Habits of Mind
Be open minded about sharing life, work, and educational experiences as part of the learning process	Openness
Be able to communicate through writing	Addressed through the WPA Outcomes Statement
Be self-motivated and self-disciplined	Responsibility
Be willing to "speak up" if problems arise	Responsibility, Flexibility
Be willing to commit to 4 to 15 hours per week per course	Engagement, Persistence
Be able to meet minimum requirements of the program	Responsibility, Metacognition
Accept critical thinking and decision making as part of the learning process	Engagement, Metacognition
Have practically unlimited access to a computer and internet service	Responsibility
Be able to think ideas through before responding	Metacognition
Feel that high quality learning can take place without going to a traditional classroom	Openness, Flexibility

Just as students who develop ION's characteristics are poised to be successful in online classes, "students who come to college writing with [the *Framework*'s] habits of mind . . . will be well positioned to meet the writing challenges in the full spectrum of academic courses and later in their careers" (*Framework* 2). These characteristics and habits are not only useful during the design phases of an online course, but also appropriate to discuss with students both as they begin the online course and throughout the semester when they may feel disconnected from their instructor and classmates as well as overwhelmed by the workload. In addition to providing goals for student behavior and attitudes, the *Framework* provides a guideline for instructors to follow throughout the duration of a course. The remainder of this chapter discusses how these characteristics and habits can be built into, foregrounded, and practiced in online writing courses.

Engagement

Instructors new to online teaching often express concern over how to engage students. If students do not have the opportunity to enter a classroom and sit in physical proximity to their instructor and classmates, how can they become engaged and sustain that engagement throughout the duration of the class? The *Framework* defines engagement as an "investment and involvement in learning." It can be fostered when writing students have the opportunity to "make connections between their ideas and those of others," as well as find new meanings or build on previous meanings, and "act upon the knowledge they have discovered" (4).

Engagement in online learning can be reflected, most basically, in the time students are willing and able to invest in their class. ION suggests that students should commit between four and fifteen hours per week per class and says, "basically, the student has to want to be there and needs to want the experience." While there is only so much an instructor can do and control for in terms of engagement (perhaps, for example, a student may want to complete an online degree program but may not be engaged in the subject matter of an individual course), it can be encouraged through the design and content of the class. An interactive course design is preferable to a course dominated by a presentational delivery mode in which students work independently as passive recipients of teacher-provided content. As Cook outlines, in an interactive course, students have regular opportunities to engage with the instructor and with each other; they must cooperate and collaborate with their classmates to achieve course goals through a variety of activities assigned by the instructor. Students can also be afforded the opportunity to provide course content and comment on or assess others' work (59). A balance between presentational and interactive design may be achieved by asking students to read a chapter or view an instructor-generated video summarizing the weekly content. This can be followed by whole class or small group discussions in which students locate examples, post them to a discussion thread, answer and/or ask analysis questions about their examples, and then respond to classmates' postings. In this sequence, instructors provide the conceptual framework, and students' work becomes a significant portion of the course content.

With interactive delivery design, students also have the opportunity to demonstrate ION's characteristic of accepting "critical thinking and decision making as part of the learning process" rather than memorizing course content and reporting back what the instructor articulates. When students understand that their work in a discussion board post or a video or audio presentation of a chapter contributes to the course in a meaningful way (versus being hidden in a dropbox that only the instructor will see), they may become increasingly engaged in the learning process.

Of course, instructors must also demonstrate the habit of engagement in an online writing course. An unfortunate critique that students sometimes have about online classes is the instructor isn't available when they have questions or need feedback, and they aren't sure that the instructor is regularly viewing their work. When an online instructor seems absent, students often lose interest in the course and their engagement with the content and each other diminishes as well. The habit of engagement is made evident by an instructor's virtual presence in the course. Just as an instructor wouldn't stare blank-faced at students during an in-class discussion, the online instructor shouldn't fail to respond appropriately to online discussions and should provide frequent positive and corrective feedback as appropriate. While feedback should not be overwhelming, it should demonstrate to students that the instructor is reading what they write and appreciates their engagement in the course.

Persistence

When students are engaged in an online class, this often translates to the habit of persistence. The *Framework* defines persistence as "the ability to sustain interest in and attention to short- and long-term projects" (5). It is developed when students commit to an idea or task; grapple with challenging ideas in any form; follow through on tasks, processes, and projects; and consistently rely on in- and out-of-class opportunities to improve their work (5).

Persistence is clearly an important habit of mind for any student at any level in any type of class, and it is especially significant for online students. As mentioned previously, ION indicates that online students should be willing to commit between four and fifteen hours per class per week. Online writing instructors can encourage students to practice the habit of persistence by developing course activities and projects that require regular, visible participation in the course. This will not only help students scaffold the work required for long-term projects, but also keep them engaged in returning to and participating in the course at regular increments.

Particularly for online students, closely related to the habit of persistence is the practice of consistency. Hilda Patron and Salvador Lopez's study, "Student Effort, Consistency, and Online Performance," found that more than overall effort, consistency is a significant influence on not only persistence but also student success. Patron and Lopez define consistency as the frequency at which a student engages with the course coupled with stability in the amount of time spent during each login. In other words, what matters is how often the student logs in and is engaged and if the amount of time spent on the course is roughly the same during each visit; rather than students spending one hour in the class each week and then twenty hours working on a final project in the last week, their learning experience will be more productive if they spend a consistent five hours on the class each week (7). To foster consistent, persistent learning behavior, courses need to be developed in such a way to encourage it. Perhaps each week follows the same general pattern: write short whole class response, read chapter, watch video, participate in whole class discussion, participate in group discussion, and work on project draft. Although some faculty might find the repetition uninspiring, students will know what to expect each week and will be able to allocate their time accordingly. On weeks that do break the pattern—with either less or more time on task—faculty can notify students of the change on the syllabus or a week ahead of time.

The *Framework* additionally states that persistence is fostered when students regularly rely on opportunities to improve their work—both in and out of class. For on-campus students, this might mean encouraging students to attend office hours or visit the library and writing center. For online students, however, the options may not be as obvious unless their campus has established robust student support services along with instructions for accessing them. To be sure students can access these opportunities to improve their work, online instructors should encourage a variety of communication practices. This could be using chat or video during online office hours, providing a link to and instructions for accessing online tutoring through the campus writing center, and encouraging students to rely on each other by providing the forums for doing so when appropriate. The best way to cultivate students' habit of persistence is to provide the assistance and feedback they need when they seek it.

Responsibility

Closely related to persistence is responsibility. The habit of responsibility, according to the *Framework*, is the "ability to take ownership of one's actions and understand the consequences of those actions for oneself and others" (5). Students need to cultivate the habit of responsibility to log into the class consistently, complete all their work, and follow-up with the collaborative work they do with their classmates. ION's online learner characteristics of being "self-motivated and self-disciplined," being "willing to speak up if problems arise," being "able to meet the minimum requirements of the program," and having "practically unlimited access to a computer and internet service" are reflective of a responsible learner.

Although students should develop and demonstrate responsibility for their learning in the characteristics and actions mentioned above, it is the instructor's responsibility to develop a course that helps them to cultivate and practice that habit of mind. One way this can be done is through the "pacing and predictability of the course" (Warnock 143). Although variability may be a strength for face-to-face courses where the instructor can maintain a certain level of control and provide additional guidance, too much variability can work against student success in an online course. Obviously, learning activities should not become rote and boring. However, establishing a predictable work pattern, such as the sequence of assignments mentioned above and regular deadlines, will help students "feel anchored to the weekly work in the course" (Warnock 143). In turn, they will have an easier time bearing responsibility for the learning tasks they are assigned. Patterns should be explained at the start of the semester (i.e., each week you will complete these assignments; they will always be due on Sunday at midnight). And, exceptions to the pattern should be announced in advance so that responsible students can plan for the changes. Additionally, back-up plans should be announced should the technology be unavailable. This way, students are not scrambling and frustrated trying to find a solution.

In *The Checklist Manifesto*, Atul Gawande writes about the value of checklists for professionals, such as surgeons, pilots, and investors. Something as simple as a checklist can also be useful for online instructors and learners. At the start of each module, week, or unit, instructors can provide a checklist of readings, discussions, mini-assignments, and major tasks the students are to complete. Checklists can also help instructors stay responsible when it is time to comment on and grade their work. Using a checklist will ensure that some assignment or discussion post does not go overlooked. Figure 1 illustrates a weekly checklist where students are instructed to "Start Here!" During the first week of class, instructions suggest that they copy the checklist into a word processor or print it so they can check-off the tasks as they are completed. Following the checklist are links to each reading or task along with detailed instructions.

Week 3 Checklist: START HERE!

Week 3 Checklist

Below are the tasks to complete for Week 3. If you have questions, please post them to the Helpboard.

As before, all of the "e-activities" have links in the Module Section.

___ 1. **CLASS DISCUSSION**: Post your thoughts on the images of argument ("Baseball") in the "Baseball" discussion thread.

___ 2. **READ**: Read Chapter 3 (Tools for Analyzing Arguments) in Herrick.

___ 3. **WATCH**: Watch the video on Herrick's Chapter 3.

___ 4. **WATCH**: Watch the "Introduction to Rhetoric" vidcast.

___ 5. **CLASS DISCUSSION**: Go to the "Week 3: Rhetoric" class discussion and respond to the prompts. Be sure to write thoughtful responses and to respond to your classmates as well.

___ 6. **READ**: Read the webpages on the rhetorical appeals.

___ 7. **GROUP DISCUSSION**: Go to the group area, click on "Group Blog" and follow the directions. This weeks' group discussion involves a Lego advertisement. Be sure to work together to create one solid answer by the end of the week.

___ 8. **MINI-ASSIGNMENT**: Turn to the exercises at the end of Chapter 3 in Herrick (page 51). Scan, standardize, and diagram the passage from C1 (the one that starts "Americans are switching..."). You may attach this one as a Word document in order to complete the diagram.

___ 9. **ANALYSIS PROJECT 1**: Continue working on the first analysis project. Remember to get to work on it early, use lots of details, and post questions to the HelpBoard.

Figure 1: Weekly Checklist

Flexibility and Openness

In an online writing course, the habits of flexibility and openness are complementary. The *Framework* defines flexibility as "the ability to adapt to situations, expectations, or demands" (5). Students accustomed to traditional face-to-face learning environments will need to be both flexible and open to a different approach to learning about writing. Flexibility can be fostered when writers are encouraged to approach writing tasks in multiple ways, consider their "purpose and audience," recognize that conventions depend on the discipline and context, and reflect on their choices (5). Warnock suggests that a significant advantage of online writing courses is that students are writing constantly. They are not just writing to fulfill project requirements; they are also writing in discussion boards, for clarification on a help board, in emails to the instructor, or to share information. Says Warnock, "they must always be thinking about their writing practices in their course interactions" (4), and they are always writing for an audience. This shift in the purposes of their writing to multiple audiences in an online class encourages them to practice the habit of flexibility.

Practicing the habit of flexibility in an online learning environment is dependent upon the habit of openness. In the *Framework*, openness is defined as "the willingness to consider new ways of being and thinking in the world" (4). This correlates well to the successful online student characteristics of both "be[ing] open minded about sharing life, work, and educational experiences as part of the learning process" and "feel[ing] that high quality learning can take place without going to a traditional classroom" (ION).

The *Framework* mentions that openness can be developed when students are encouraged to examine their own perspectives; practice multiple ways of researching, writing, and delivering information; and participating in honest feedback about theirs and others' writing. An online writing course lends itself very well to developing the habit of openness. At a basic level, online courses encourage students to examine their perspectives on learning. To be successful, students need to be open to the concept that their instructor isn't physically present, that they need to be responsible for their learning, and that the dynamic of the course may be different than their previous learning experiences.

One way instructors can foster openness in an online class is through the use of discussion boards. Because discussions are presented and archived in writing, all students have the opportunity to participate and to consider their classmates' points and perspectives more carefully than in a rapid-paced in-class discussion. However, openness may not necessarily be automatic for students; in fact, they may be more reticent about sharing their thoughts in a more visible, more permanent way. Instructors should frame discussion board questions in ways that encourage students to articulate a well-formed perspective and to respond thoughtfully to classmates participating in the thread. Students may also need some guidance in how to read their classmates' ideas or analyses and provide open, thoughtful feedback.

Of course, openness is appropriate for faculty to practice as well. Although many writing faculty are adept at designing student-centered, active-learning courses in the face-to-face environment, Helen Grady and Marjorie Davis suggest that a significant challenge in the transition to online is "developing an authentic [online] interactive learning environment " (101). Therefore, instructors new to teaching writing online need to be open to trying new pedagogies as well as assuming new roles as the instructor. This includes considering alternative means for generating and delivering course content. Perhaps an in-class mini-lecture with notes on the whiteboard becomes a short narrated slideshow available through a link on YouTube. The related in-class group work becomes posts to a group wiki where one group member reports the results to a whole class discussion board at mid-week. Then those group reports are synthesized by a class member and provided as notes to the whole class. This sequence provides learning opportunities from both presentational and interactive perspectives, and because all the work is completed in writing, students are able to reflect, discuss, negotiate, synthesize, and then later study the ideas they generate. In other words, with an openness to different learning opportunities and careful planning on the instructor's part, students have the opportunity to become engaged with the content and then responsible to one another for their learning.

Metacognition

Finally, online learners have the opportunity to engage in metacognition, "the ability to reflect on one's thinking as well as on the individual and cultural processes and systems used to structure knowledge" (5). This habit relates to ION's successful online student characteristics of "accepting critical thinking and decision making as part of the learning process" as well as "being able to think through ideas before responding." Metacognitive activities are an important part of any writing class and are easily incorporated in class discussions both formally and informally. Online, however, the activities may need to be more deliberately incorporated. Instructors should make clear the metacognitive goals at the start of the course, along with each project assignment, and at the end of major projects. Halfway through the term, students could be asked to reflect on the variety of writing they have done (for projects, in discussion boards, backchannel emails to the instructor and classmates) and then "connect the choices they have made in texts to audiences and purposes for which texts are intended" (*Framework* 5). Just as with any learning experience, calling attention to students' thinking processes, rhetorical choices, and learning habits can enhance their experience. It gives them the opportunity to continue what they are doing well and improve on the challenges they are facing. Table 2 provides an overview of how students and instructors can use the habits of mind in an online class.

Table 2: Suggestions for Developing the Habits of Mind for Students and Instructors

Habit of Mind	What instructors can do	What students can do
Engagement	—use interactive delivery model —be visible in the class —provide regular and encouraging feedback	—commit to the appropriate amount of time to work on the class —interact with instructor and classmates
Persistence	—provide reasons for students to check in more than once a week —scaffold projects and require students to submit or post them —provide resources for students outside of the course	—log into the course regularly and spend a consistent amount of time in the course each week —break projects into manageable chunks —access additional support for writing
Responsibility	—develop a well-organized, structured course —give assignments that encourage all students to participate equally —provide a weekly checklist	—ask for assistance when appropriate —follow through on collaborative discussions or projects —possess reliable access to the course
Flexibility	—adapt to teaching online —prepare students to make rhetorical choices when communicating online	—adapt to learning online —reflect on rhetorical choices when communicating online for different purposes and audiences
Openness	—appreciate the value of online teaching —provide scaffolding students can use to formulate discussions —provide guidelines for responding to classmates' ideas	—appreciate the value of online learning —share ideas willingly in discussions —respond thoughtfully to classmates' ideas
Metacognition	—introduce and discuss the habits of mind —provide frequent opportunities to reflect on the habits of mind	—monitor uses of the habits of mind —participate in opportunities to reflect on the habits of mind

Getting and Staying Connected

The habits of mind provide an effective guideline for designing online writing classes and for encouraging successful student behaviors. However, as Carol Severino commented in her 2012 *College English* symposium article, "The Problem of Articulation: Uncovering More of the Composition Classroom," one appropriate addition is the "creation of social ties so important to composition" (535). Social ties are also important to online course development and delivery. An online instructor needs to develop, respond to, and sustain social presence in an online class both between the instructor and students as well as among students. Similarly, Aimee Whiteside, Amy Garrett Dikkers, and Somer Lewis find that, "the power of human connectedness for learning" is an essential element for success in online learning. Social presence involves a "level of connectedness" between the student and instructor as well as between students that can motivate them to take an active role in their learning. There are several ways to develop social connectedness in an online writing class, and many of them are techniques we already practice in our face-to-face classes. Online writing instructors can develop social and help-board discussion threads where students have the opportunity to socialize with and assist one another. Discussion boards that ask students to post thoughtfully and respond to one another also help students get to know one another. Collaborative projects encouraging students to write together can be assigned with careful guidelines on doing the work from a distance. Finally, instructors can provide some content through audio and/or video so that they become more than words on a screen; students can be encouraged or required to do the same. Many of the suggestions for encouraging engagement above are dependent upon a social connection in the online class. Similarly, flexibility, openness, and metacognition will lead to richer learning experiences with social presence.

Conclusion

As suggested earlier, students should be introduced to the *Framework* at the start of an online writing course along with discussion on how practicing the habits can help them be successful learners in their online writing courses. As Peter Khost discusses in chapter 9 of this volume, it would not be an easy task, and perhaps not an appropriate one, however, to formally evaluate student performance on the habits of mind. Instead, students might practice the habit of metacognition by evaluating their successes and challenges in these areas at various points throughout the course. They can reflect in writing on their level of responsibility and openness, for example, when submitting a major project or at mid-term and then consider how their current practices are leading to success or not. After the instructor has reviewed these, measures can be put into place to praise what they are doing well and encourage those habits that seem to be less easily achieved.

Although the *Framework*, in conjunction with other guidelines for online course development, can be useful for developing robust online writing courses, certain cautions are in order. For example, the habits should be interpreted according to the diversity of students enrolling in online courses. Responsibility to an eighteen-year-old student living on campus is not the same thing as responsibility to a thirty-something student with a family and a full-time job. Additionally, students with learning accommodations may also need to interpret the habits in slightly different ways as well. (See Christopher Wyatt for an excellent dissertation on how online learning affects students with autism in particular.) An online writing instructor who is engaged and socially present in the course can gauge these differences and guide students towards practicing the habits in ways that work for them.

Although an online course is different in many ways from a face-to-face course, the principles that guide the course don't have to be. In fact, they should not be. Students are still expected to reach the same goals but through different or adjusted learning experiences. Additionally, just as with face-to-face classes, there is no one way to teach an online class. However, using the *Framework* and other guidelines for student success can make a course a more valuable learning experience for students and a more enjoyable experience for instructors.

Works Cited

Allen, I. Elaine, and Jeff Seamon. "Changing Course: Ten Years of Tracking Online Education in the United States." Babson Survey Research Group, 2013. Web. 16 July 2014.

Baker, Credence. "The Impact of Instructor Immediacy and Presence for Online Affective Learning, Cognition, and Motivation." *The Journal of Educators Online* 7.1 (2010): 1–30. Web. 27 June 2014.

Callaway, Micheal. "The WPA Learning Outcomes: What Role Should Technology Play?" *The WPA Outcomes Statement: A Decade Later*. Ed. Nicholas Behm, Gregory Glau, Deborah Holdstein, Duane Roen, and Edward White. Anderson, SC: Parlor Press, 2013. 271–84. Print.

Cook, Kelli Cargile. "An Argument for Pedagogy-Driven Online Education." Cook and Grant-Davie 49–66. Print.

Cook, Kelli Cargile, and Keith Grant-Davie, eds. *Online Education: Global Questions, Local Answers*. Amityville, NY: Baywood, 2005. Print.

Council of Writing Program Administrators. "WPA Outcomes Statement For First-Year Composition." CWPA, 2014. PDF File.

Council of Writing Program Administrators, National Council of Teachers of English, and National Writing Project. *Framework for Success in Postsecondary Writing*. CWPA, NCTE, and NWP, 2011. PDF File.

Gawande, Atul. *The Checklist Manifesto*. New York: Metropolitan Books, 2009. Print.

Grady, Helen, and Marjorie Davis. "Teaching Well Online with Instructional Procedural Scaffolding." Cook and Grant-Davie 101–22. Print.

Hewett, Beth, and Christa Ehman. *Preparing Educators for Online Writing Instruction: Principles and Processes*. Urbana: National Council of Teachers of English, 2004. Print.

Johnson, Kristine. "Beyond Standards: Disciplinary and National Perspectives on the Habits of Mind." *College English* 64.3 (2013): 517–41. Print.

Maid, Barry, and Barbara D'Angelo. "What Do You Do When the Ground Beneath Your Feet Shifts?" *Online Education 2.0: Evolving, Adapting, and Reinventing Online Technical Communication*. Ed. Kelli Cargile Cook and Keith Grant-Davie. Amityville, NY: Baywood, 2013. 11–24. Print.

Oblinger, Diane, and Brian Hawkins. "The Myth about Online Course Development." *Educause Review Online* 41.1 (January/February 2006): 14–15. Web. 14 June 2014.

Patron, Hilda, and Salvador Lopez. "Student Effort, Consistency, and Online Performance." *The Journal of Educators Online* 8.2 (2011): 1–11. Web. 25 July 2014.

Severino, Carol. "The Problems of Articulation: Uncovering More of the Composition Curriculum." *Symposium: On the Framework for Success in Postsecondary Writing*. Spec. issue of *College English* 74.6 (2012): 533–36. Print.

Warnock, Scott. *Teaching Writing Online: How and Why*. Urbana: National Council of Teachers of English, 2009. Print.

"What Makes a Successful Online Student?" Illinois Online Network. University of Illinois, 2010. Web. 25 June 2014.

Whiteside, Aimee, Amy Garrett Dikkers, and Somer Lewis. "The Power of Social Presence for Learning." *Educause Review Online*. May 2014. Web. 14 June 2014.

Wyatt, Christopher. "Online Pedagogy: Designing Writing Courses for Students with Autism Spectrum Disorders." Diss. U of Minnesota, 2010. Web. 25 July 2014.

Xu, Di, and Shanna Jaggers. "Performance Gaps Between Online and Face-to-Face Courses: Differences Across Types of Students and Academic Subject Areas." *The Journal of Higher Education*. 85.5 (2014): 633–59. Web. 2 June 2015.

11 Using the *Framework* to Develop a Common Core State Standards-Aligned Curriculum for First-Year Composition

Lauren S. Ingraham

The year 2010 brought significant changes to the landscape of K–12 education and first-year college composition. It was the year that thirty-eight out of fifty states enthusiastically adopted the Common Core State Standards—an effort to establish common standards for K–12 math and English learning initiated by the National Governors Association but supported by a multitude of nonprofit and for-profit education-related organizations. The ultimate goal of the Common Core State Standards (CCSS) was to establish a nationwide consensus about the knowledge and abilities American students needed to be "college and career ready" regardless of the state where they lived (National Governors Association). As Peggy O'Neill, Linda Adler-Kassner, Cathy Fleischer, and Anne-Marie Hall note in the Foreword to this volume, in 2011, the *Framework for Success in Postsecondary Writing* appeared in response to business-driven education initiatives—like the Common Core State Standards—that seemed to be gaining monumental influence without being clearly connected to actual research and best practices for teaching writing.

Tennessee was an early and enthusiastic adopter of the CCSS when it signed on to the initiative in 2010. The state's commitment to the CCSS got a massive infusion of resources that same year when Tennessee received over $500 million in the first phase of President Obama's "Race to the Top" awards, one of only two states to earn grants in the first round of funding ("Delaware"). A significant portion of this four-year grant enabled the state to launch the most comprehensive training program in the country to help K–12 teachers understand how to teach with the Common Core State Standards; more than 70,000 teachers participated (Camera). By the 2013–2014 school year, all public schools in Tennessee had fully implemented the CCSS.

In early 2013, a representative from Tennessee's Higher Education Commission (THEC) posed an interesting question to me: Once students complete high school using a Common Core-aligned curriculum, how will our college and university first-year composition courses adapt to build upon the knowledge and skills these students will bring with them to college? Although I had been working on several state committees related to CCSS implementation at the middle and high school levels, I hadn't thought about the potential consequences for first-year composition instruction. The Common Core emphasizes nonfiction texts and evidence-based writing and analysis—the same kinds of texts and critical writing at the heart of many college composition courses. I wondered if we could really expect better prepared students who would need a more challenging course than the existing first-semester course.

His challenge was two-fold. First, design a first-year composition curriculum that aligns with the last year of the Common Core State Standards (grades 11–12) and builds upon the skills and knowledge that high school graduates who are rated "college and career ready" bring to our introductory writing course. Second, determine the types of professional development that faculty around the state would need to teach this curriculum effectively. Once piloted and revised, the curriculum and professional development would be offered to—but not mandated for—college writing instructors and dual enrollment high school teachers state-wide. This multi-year effort, he told me, had already been funded by a grant from Rockefeller Philanthropy Advisors (RPA) as part of the Core to College initiative, an effort to increase collaboration between K–12 and higher education partners and thus improve students' readiness for college (Rockefeller).

This proposal was rife with potential risks that could blow up in my face. Would college faculty be willing to explore anything that was associated with the Common Core State Standards? Would a state-initiated course re-design be welcomed anywhere in the state? Would I, as course re-designer, face professional scorn from colleagues for working on a project that gets dangerously close to interfering with academic freedom? I had any number of reasons to turn down the project, but I didn't. What the state saw as a course re-design, I saw as a well-funded teachable moment. The RPA grant would fund work with college composition faculty across the state, many of whom still teach a modes-driven curriculum, to bring them up to speed on basic best practices for teaching first-year writing. In addition, this project offered the opportunity to address two other important concerns. First, the English Language Arts standards of the CCSS are completely content-based and do not speak to the kinds of classroom environments or student and teacher behavior and attitudes that lead to optimal student learning—the habits of mind and learning experiences specified in the *Framework*. As Kristine Johnson writes, "the *Framework* asks writing teachers to address the person behind writing products and processes—to consider intellectual agency and the ethical aims of writing instruction in an increasingly technocratic educational landscape" (527). More pointedly, Peggy O'Neill et al. contend that "if the goal is to make certain that all students are prepared to succeed in college and career, then, at least in terms of writing, it's imperative that the Standards and the assessments promote the experiences and habits of mind outlined in the *Framework*" (524).

Second, as Peter Khost notes elsewhere in this volume and as Bruce McComiskey suggests in his response to the *Framework*, it is not as helpful as it could be because of its low profile among rank-and-file college and high school writing teachers. Whether I participated or not, a state-initiated re-design of first-year composition rooted in the Common Core State Standards was moving forward. I signed on because I saw this project as an opportunity to promote the *Framework* in the professional development offered to support this re-design. This chapter details the process used to shift the focus in the course re-design from the CCSS to the *Framework for Success in Postsecondary Writing*.

GETTING STARTED / CHANGING THE PROJECT'S FRAME

The THEC staff member who recruited me for the project also tapped two other faculty with whom he had worked on a number of professional development projects in the state. The team leader was our state's newly hired alignment director, a former high school English teacher who had a deep knowledge of and commitment to the CCSS English Language Arts standards but little background in composition theory and pedagogy and no experience working as a peer with college faculty or administrators.[1] From our first meeting, the differences in our perspectives were apparent. As we studied sample first-year composition syllabi from across the state to understand what was actually going on in our state's composition programs, the college faculty on the team were disheartened to see that modes-based teaching—using rhetorical strategies (i.e., description, narration) as discrete purposes for writing—was much more common than we had anticipated. The alignment director didn't understand our concern because she also had taught writing largely from a modes-based approach. We also clashed about how to involve the consultant assigned to our project from the nonprofit, nonpartisan agency contracted to evaluate the entire Core to College initiative. Like our alignment director, our consultant had also been a high school English teacher, and she had directed assessment projects for a state department of education, but she was candid with us about having no experience with college-level writing instruction. Despite this admission, the alignment director would often solicit her opinion when our team was debating the next move forward by saying things such as, "Let's get _____'s take on this before we make a decision."

The alignment director's enthusiasm for bringing the Core to College was matched by our insistence that college faculty would not embrace a state-initiated, Common Core-aligned course presented as such. Instead, following Johnson's argument, we believed that the *Framework* "reframe[d] a widespread public narrative about written products and quantified achievements with an alternate narrative about writers and their development" (518). The alignment director had a mission: to deliver a course that the project funders could see was aligned with the CCSS. But she also had a team with expertise in and experience with teaching college writing according to research-supported best practices—expertise and experience she did not have. Acknowledging the rhetorical situation she faced, we all agreed that the course could begin as an extension of the last year of the CCSS, but the substance of the course had to be based on the *Framework*. In the final product, the only reference to the Common Core State Standards was a table identifying how our course objectives were related to and extended the CCSS for grades 11–12. Below, because of space constraints, we present an abridged version of that table.

Table 1: Course Objectives Compared to CCSS for Grade 11–12 Writing

Common Core Writing Standards Grades 11–12	Course Objectives for CCSS-Aligned Composition I
11–12.1 Write arguments to support claims in an analysis of substantive topics or texts, using valid reasoning and relevant sufficient evidence.	13.1 Drawing on a variety of texts, complete writing tasks that demonstrate an understanding of the rhetorical situations presented in those texts. Students will use critical thinking processes such as abstracting, representing, incorporating, and synthesizing ideas from diverse points of view.
11–12.4 Produce clear and coherent writing in which the development, organization, and style are appropriate to task, purpose, and audience.	13.2 Write arguments to support claims in an analysis of two or more texts on the same topic, synthesizing information learned in order to convey complex ideas and incorporating evidence into the student's argument.
11–12.5 Develop and strengthen writing as needed by planning, revising, editing, rewriting or trying a new approach, focusing on addressing what is most significant for a specific purpose and audience.	13.3 Develop the skill of constructive critique focusing on higher order concerns, including matters of design, during peer workshops.
11–12.6 Use technology, including the Internet, to produce, publish, and update individual or shared writing products in response to ongoing feedback, including new arguments or information.	13.4 Use technology to practice and develop writing processes pertaining to invention, revision, organization, drafting through multiple drafts, editing, and adjusting for rhetorical context (purpose, audience, persona, social context, and genre).
11–12.7 Conduct short as well as more sustained research projects to answer a question including a self-generated question or solve a problem; narrow or broaden the inquiry when appropriate; synthesize multiple sources on the subject, demonstrating understanding of the subject under investigation.	13.5 Compose viable research questions and conduct research required to answer them using library databases and other credible sources.

INCORPORATING THE *FRAMEWORK*

We designed a fifteen-week course in five modules that progressively guides students to meet each of the course objectives.[2] Built into each module is a variety of learning opportunities that allow students to develop the essential habits of mind identified in the *Framework*: curiosity, openness, engagement, creativity, persistence, responsibility, flexibility, and metacognition. As Matthew Heard notes, the habits of mind detailed in the *Framework* "do not spontaneously appear in the minds of composition students: these habits must be framed carefully by thoughtful, attentive designers who shape curricular experiences to engage and challenge students" (315); thus, our week-by-week schedule explicitly identifies opportunities to develop the knowledge and abilities identified first in the "WPA Outcomes Statement For First-Year Composition" and subsequently in the *Framework*: rhetorical knowledge, critical thinking, writing processes, and knowledge of conventions. We did not identify the *Framework*'s "abilities to compose in multiple environments" because the course would be taught in a myriad of classroom settings whose particulars would determine how the course supported that experience.

Module 1: What Is Rhetoric and the Rhetorical Situation?

In this three-week period, we want students to understand writing as a *rhetorical practice* and a *recursive process* that includes revision and reflection. As such, it reinforces the *Framework*'s focus on developing rhetorical knowledge; critical thinking, writing, and reading; and to some extent, writing processes. Students (and their teachers, in some cases) learn in the first week that traditional writing modes (narration, description, etc.) are not stand-alone purposes for writing but rather techniques used to achieve larger writing purposes. Students focus on five elements of effective writing: purpose, audience, genre, tone, and social context. The major writing project is an analysis of a print text that examines its facility with these five elements of effective writing.

Module 2: Rhetorical Appeals

This two-week module introduces the concepts of ethos, pathos, logos, and kairos. The major writing project is a rhetorical analysis of a visual or multimedia text. This module also invites students to develop rhetorical knowledge; critical thinking, writing, and reading; and to some extent, writing processes.

Module 3: Inquiry

In this five-week module, students compose a research question, conduct research to address the question, evaluate the sources they find, and practice crafting effective paraphrases, summaries, and quotations. The module ends with an annotated bibliography that prepares students to write a thesis-driven researched essay in Module 4. Knowledge of conventions becomes especially important in this module as students attend to details of formatting their bibliographies.

Module 4: Taking a Position

This three-week module focuses on developing claims and counterclaims, marshaling compelling evidence, understanding and avoiding fallacies, and avoiding plagiarism by accurately paraphrasing, summarizing, and quoting sources. Students write a researched position paper during this module, which focuses on all four writing experiences we adopted from the *Framework*.

Module 5: Showcase

The final two weeks of the course have students deepening their reflection and revision abilities by designing either a final portfolio that demonstrates their growth during the course or a re-mix of an earlier project that is substantially transformed by addressing a different audience, taking a different side, changing the genre, etc. Because this is the showcase module, more emphasis is placed on students demonstrating knowledge of writing conventions. In each module, we identify each *Framework*-related concept or ability at the end of every course activity. Module 1 in the appendix serves as an example of how we keyed each activity to the *Framework*.

Course Rollout: From Deciding Committee to Pilot Testing

Our initial pilot (a very small-scale pre-pilot) occurred in spring 2014 with two instructors—one at a university and one at a community college. We were looking for impressionistic feedback from the instructors simply to gauge if the general approach we were taking was resonating with students. Both instructors reported success with the course, in large part because students were highly engaged throughout the semester. The most significant insight for the university instructor was that the course resulted in the lowest DFW rate—the number of Ds, Fs, and Withdrawals—in her teaching career. Two out of her three sections had no DFWs, which was a first for her. The community college instructor also noted a high level of engagement from her students in the three sections she taught. She told us that these student portfolios were more impressive than all others in her career, a distinction she attributed to students being heavily invested in the course. She specifically credited the focus on the *Framework*'s habits of mind to create more engaged students. She discussed these habits of mind explicitly with students, and they wanted to see even more emphasis on them in her class and their other college classes. While her pass rates in the pilot sections were comparable to those in her two non-pilot sections, she noticed that student engagement was noticeably higher in the pilot sections.

Beyond the pre-pilot semester, the alignment director's enthusiasm for a CCSS-aligned composition course—and her inexperience with the ways of higher education—led to a rocky introduction of the re-design to college and university administrators. Coming from the K–12 world where teachers and administrators frequently believe they have no option but to capitulate to mandates from one authority or another, she assumed a high level of cooperation when she contacted various campus administrators about piloting the new course. In summer 2014, she emailed college and university administrators across the state requesting that they identify two or three instructors to pilot the re-designed course in fall 2014. For most of the people she contacted, that email was the first they had heard of this course re-design. They were taken aback by what they perceived as a very presumptuous request and on principle, were highly resistant to the idea of piloting the course.

Around that time, a publisher representative emailed me to ask about the "deciding committee" I was on that would be creating the new mandated curriculum and choosing required textbooks for first-year composition across the state. The vendor wanted only to make sure that her company's products would be considered, but her understanding that a three-person committee had the power to mandate a state-wide curriculum for a college course was disturbing. Her (mis)information had come from a faculty member in our state—one who was clearly concerned about being forced to teach a course as instructed by the state's higher education commission. The alignment director's presumptuous demand for campus administrators to name instructors for the pilot sections increased the feeling that the state was infringing on academic freedom. In fact, my own university was hesitant to run pilot sections for fear of contributing to what they feared might turn into a takeover of individual faculty-driven curricular decisions. After receiving—and feeling insulted by—the alignment director's rather overconfident email about piloting the course, the only reason the pilots were allowed on my campus was because I appealed directly to the local parties involved. I explained the project in more faculty-friendly language and reassured them that this project was not a threat to academic freedom.

Based on my experience getting my campus to participate in pilot testing, the re-design team believed that if we could speak directly with college writing instructors, we could explain the merits of the course and recruit them to pilot it. We offered to travel to campuses over the summer to work with faculty and introduce the course personally, but the alignment director resisted that idea. She had cobbled together a small group of instructors to attend a one-day workshop in June 2014 to learn about the course and—ideally—agree to pilot it in the fall. However, our state's two-year college English association called an emergency meeting to discuss a variety of "state-driven challenges" that affect English faculty on the same day as our planned workshop. When more than half the faculty who had planned to attend our workshop cancelled, citing the need to attend the community college ad hoc meeting, the alignment director agreed to postpone our workshop. We asked to speak at the community college meeting to explain the re-design work we were doing. We started by acknowledging the legitimate concerns they had about our work and tried to put them at ease by sharing the "deciding committee" myth and assuring them that no one would be mandated to teach the course. We knew several faculty in the room—my team member had been an officer in the organization a few years prior—so we appealed directly to them by stressing that the course was designed by *us*, their colleagues—well-trained composition faculty, not education consultants or administrators with no experience of teaching college writing. From that meeting, we recruited volunteers to pilot sixteen new sections of the course at four institutions in fall 2014.

We convened a two-day professional development workshop in July 2014 to introduce the details of the course to piloting instructors, a group that ranged from faculty with doctoral degrees in rhetoric and composition and years of composition teaching experience to faculty with masters degrees in literature and limited, if any, background in composition theory and best practices. To avoid singling out individuals as the "bad" teachers who still teach modes-driven assignments, our strategy for the workshop was to frame our course as a response to several problems most any writing teacher could easily identify: disengaged students, students who give up too quickly, students who come into class with rigid ideas about what is and isn't "good writing," and students who lack the self-awareness needed to identify and understand specific challenges they need to overcome to make progress. In short, we started with the *Framework*, a document that few instructors were familiar with. We also invited the pre-pilot instructors to speak to the group about their positive experiences and share some student writing, and workshop participants seemed genuinely excited about the possibility the pilot course presented. After a session on "minimal marking," one teacher said she felt freed from her focus on sentence-level error and was looking forward to being able to enjoy her students' writing before she responded to it. In doing so, she had adopted some of the habits of mind central to the *Framework*: curiosity, openness, and engagement, among others. A few days after the workshop, we received the following email from a participant who attended with three other instructors from her campus:

> We just wanted to thank you for including us in the pilot. We discussed on the ride back to [our institution] just how pleased we were with the curriculum and the promise of this pilot.
>
> We also very much appreciate the faculty development of this 2-day workshop—even without the curriculum, the exchange of ideas, techniques, and inter-campus discussion was very, very productive (so, the curriculum was a bonus).
>
> We look forward to working with you this fall and helping to make the case.

Instructors had left the workshop looking forward to the pilot, and this email was further confirmation of their optimism.

Consistently, students and faculty pointed to the course's use of the *Framework* as key to its success. While pass rates and other quantitative measures of student success were relatively stable in pilot sections of the course, instructors reported much higher levels of student engagement in the pilot sections, which they attributed to the course's focus on revision and reflection. As one instructor wrote, "The majority of students are fully engaged and appear to understand the writing process better than previous classes have." Another pointed to the metacognitive work built into the course for its success: "The pilot program's emphasis on reflection gave students a tangible sense of their skill level and what they need to do to continue their development beyond the scope of the class." Teachers with strong backgrounds in teaching rhetorically—

about three-quarters of the group—embraced the course, making few or no changes. However, those teachers without a strong background in teaching writing as rhetoric modified the course by adding elements in their comfort zones, such as lengthy, non-contextual lectures on thesis statements and paragraph development, with little opportunity for students to practice these concepts.

MOVING THE *FRAMEWORK* BEYOND THE COMPOSITION COMMUNITY

I would like to say that we expanded the course rollout following the success of the fall 2014 pilot sections. Instead, the work ground to a halt. In fall of 2014, the anti-Common Core sentiment that had been sweeping the country finally prevailed in Tennessee. Under enormous pressure from state legislators and constituents, the governor who had so spectacularly championed the CCSS as the ticket for turning around our troubled public education system announced a full review and public vetting of the CCSS with an eye toward recommending changes by the end of 2015. With his announcement came an acknowledgement from most at the state level that anything related to CCSS was dead in the water. The Core to College grant that funded our course re-design ended in December 2014 and was not extended to fund a similar re-design of the second semester course, as we had once hoped it would. The alignment director, whose salary was paid from the grant funds, left the Core to College program in November to take a new position with another education reform-minded nonprofit. Her absence left the pilot program without a formal means of analyzing data beyond the end of the grant period. The end of 2014 also signaled the end of the Race to the Top funding that had sustained Tennessee's embrace of the Common Core State Standards. Between the loss of Core to College funding and the intense antipathy toward the CCSS in Tennessee and several other states who have dropped the CCSS, I don't see the "Core" coming to college anytime soon, though in chapter 12 of this volume Alice Johnston Myatt and Ellen Shelton provide an example of how they productively and effectively applied the *Framework* at the collegiate level in Mississippi.

Conclusion

I got involved in this project because I wanted to increase awareness about the *Framework* among our state's college writing faculty. By that measure, we realized some success. When discussing the central role the *Framework* played in our course development at the ad hoc meeting the two-year faculty association called, we were able to reach dozens of faculty who had been unaware that such a document existed. And, when we worked directly with piloting faculty, we were able to dive deeply into the *Framework* as part of our professional development work with them. Even the handful of college administrators and state bureaucrats with whom we discussed the *Framework* were impressed with its potential to transform what and how we teach writing once they learned about it. All these stakeholders want students to cultivate the habits of mind and have the kinds of reading/writing/thinking experiences outlined in the *Framework*.

However, for the *Framework* to be of broader use beyond the composition community—to influence public policy discussions and get the attention of potential funders of writing-related research, for example—we need to re-frame it to expand its audience, and as Kristine Johnson avers in chapter 1, we need to understand the intended and unintended consequences of the frames we choose. We need to help potential stakeholders and allies see it not as an isolated document that is limited by its focus on student writers, but rather as an important piece of the larger conversation in which they are already deeply involved and (in the case of funders) literally invested: how do we help students (and faculty) develop habits and practices that lead to academic success (See Farrington; Headden and McKay)? The heavy hitters in education reform funding—the Lumina, Carnegie, Gates, and Hewlett foundations, among others—regularly refer to the need to develop the kind of "mindset" that leads to academic achievement. In doing so, they routinely cite Carol Dweck's groundbreaking book *Mindset: The New Psychology of Success*, which argues that success is largely dependent on the kind of mindset one adopts. A "fixed mindset" assumes that we are born with a finite amount of talent and intelligence, so that when we fail at something, it's because we are incapable of achieving it. In this mindset, success comes from innate talent, not achievement that results from focused effort. Conversely, a "growth mindset" assumes that achievement comes from hard work rather than innate talent. From this mindset, failure presents an opportunity to learn and get better; it's not a reflection of a person's ultimate worth, intellect, or ability. Adopting a growth mindset develops many of the habits of mind included in the *Framework*, notably persistence, resilience, and flexibility.

Dweck's fixed and growth mindsets parallel the way students, some faculty, and much of the public view student writers—and as such, creates an especially important opportunity to link the *Framework* to existing initiatives and funding areas. Too often, students arrive in a college writing class believing that they "can't write" because they have experienced past writing failures as measures of their innate ability (fixed mindset) not as opportunities to learn and improve (growth mindset). In other words, people with a fixed mindset believe that writers are "born, not made," while those with a growth mindset see that writers are "made, not born." Helping audiences beyond the composition community see the *Framework* as an extension of work they already admire is critical for its wider acceptance. And by adopting a growth mindset, those of us who have been frustrated by the difficulty the *Framework* has had in gaining a higher profile can turn that frustration into new ways of thinking about best ways to promote it to wider audiences.

Notes

1. The Rockefeller Philanthropy Associates grants to all Core to College states funded an alignment director position for every state. These administrators were responsible for coordinating all core-alignment work in their states and sharing information and data with their counterparts in other Core to College states.

2. Both the concept of modular organization and the term *module* became another site of contention for the team. For me, the word strongly connoted remedial or gatekeeping activities that students completed online. I didn't want the course we were developing—which was not developed for an online environment—to have that stigma. Others on the team, however, experienced the idea of "modules" in a more straightforward way as small units of instruction that build upon each other to guide students through an entire course. I deferred to the group, but I confess to some latent unease with the modular organization of the course.

Works Cited

Camera, Lauren. "Tennessee on Dogged Path to Race to Top Finish." *Education Week*. Editorial Projects on Education, 8 Jul. 2014. Web.12 Feb. 2015.

Council of Writing Program Administrators. "WPA Outcomes Statement for First-Year Composition." CWPA, 2014. PDF File.

Council of Writing Program Administrators, National Council of Teachers of English, and National Writing Project. *Framework for Success in Postsecondary Writing.* CWPA, NCTE, and NWP, 2011. PDF File.

"Delaware and Tennessee Win First Race to the Top Awards." *U.S. Department of Education.* US Deptartment of Education, 29 Mar. 2010. Web. Press Release. 13 Feb. 2015.

Dweck, Carol. *Mindset: The New Psychology of Success.* Ballentine Books: New York, NY. 2006. Print.

Farrington, Camille A. "Academic Mindsets as a Critical Component of Deeper Thinking." William and Flora Hewlett Foundation: Chicago, IL. Apr. 2013. PDF file.

Giles, Sandra. "Reflective Writing and the Revision Process: What Were You Thinking?" *Writing Spaces: Readings on Writing.* Vol. 1. Ed. Charles Lowe and Pavel Zemliansky. West Lafayette, IN: Parlor Press, 2010. 191–204. Web. 24 Feb. 2014.

Headden, Susan, and Sarah McKay. "Motivation Matters: How New Research Can Help Teachers Boost Student Engagement." Stanford, CA: Carnegie Foundation for the Advancement of Teaching, July 2015. PDF File.

Heard, Matthew. "Repositioning Curriculum Design: Broadening the *Who* and *How* of Curricular Invention." *College English* 76.4 (2014): 315–36. Print.

Hess, Amanda. "To Prevent Rape on College Campuses, Focus on the Rapists Not the Victims." *Slate.com*. The Slate Group, 16 Oct. 2013. Web. 23 Feb. 2014.

Johnson, Kristine. "Beyond Standards: Disciplinary and National Perspectives on Habits of Mind." *College Composition and Communication* 64.3 (2013): 517–41. Print.

McComiskey, Bruce. "Bridging the Divide: The (Puzzling) *Framework* and the Transition from K-12 to College Writing Instruction." *Symposium: On the Framework for Success in Postsecondary Writing.* Spec. issue of *College English* 74.6 (2012): 537–40. Print.

National Governors Association Center for Best Practices, Council of Chief State School Officers. *Common Core State Standards.* National Governors Association Center for Best Practices, Council of Chief State School Officers, 2010. Web. 5 June 2016.

O'Neill, Peggy, Linda Adler-Kassner, Cathy Fleischer, and Anne-Marie Hall. "Creating the *Framework for Success in Postsecondary Writing*." *Symposium: On the Framework for Success in Postsecondary Writing.* Spec. issue of *College English* 74.6 (2012): 520–24. Print.

Reid, E. Shelley. "Ten Ways to Think About Writing: Metaphoric Musings for College Writing Students." *Writing Spaces: Readings on Writing.* Ed.

Charles Lowe and Pavel Zemliansky. Vol. 2. Anderson, SC: Parlor Press, 2011. 3–23. Web. 24 Feb. 2014.

Rockefeller Philanthropy Advisors. "Core to College." *Rockpa.org*. Rockefeller Philanthropy Advisors, n.d. Web. 24 Aug. 2015.

Ruecker, Todd. "Writing Process." *Uwc.utep.edu*. University of Texas at El Paso University Writing Center, July 2010. Web. 10 Feb. 2015.

United States. Dept. of Education. "Race to the Top: Tennessee Report Year 1: School Year 2010–2011." Washington, DC: US Department of Education. Jan. 10, 2012. Web. 10 Feb. 2015.

Yoffe, Emily. "College Women: Stop Getting Drunk." *Slate.com*. The Slate Group, 15 Oct. 2013. Web. 23 Feb. 2014.

—. "Emily Yoffe Responds to Her Critics." *Slate.com*. The Slate Group, 18 Oct. 2013. n. pag. Web. 23 Feb. 2014.

Appendix

Module 1: What Is Rhetoric and the Rhetorical Situation? Suggested Progression of Concepts/Skills

Key: *R=Rhetorical Knowledge, T=Critical Thinking, Writing, and Reading, P=Processes, C=Conventions of Writing; #=Learning Objective*

Week 1

Engagement

1. Opening Discussion: "Can "bad writing" be effective?" Use the discussion and samples of effective and ineffective writing in different genres/styles/tones/levels-of-correctness to introduce the five elements of effective writing. *(R; 13.7) (30 minutes)*

Putting "Modes" into Perspective

2. Mini-lecture/discussion to identify traditionally-taught modes: narration, description, exposition, compare/contrast, and persuasion. Outcome: students should understand that for many years, these modes have been taught as stand-alone purposes for writing. *(R; 13.7) (10 minutes)*

3. Writing activity to illustrate the problem with stand-alone modes: Assign groups of students to individually write one of the following: (1) a narrative paragraph with no description; (2) a compare/contrast paragraph with no exposition (explaining); (3) a persuasive paragraph with no exposition (explanation). Share and discuss paragraphs and process. *(R; 13.7) (30 minutes)*

4. Mini-lecture on these various modes as a *means to an end*. That "end" is the writing's purpose, which is always an infinitive verb (i.e., to inquire or explore, to analyze or interpret, to take a stand, to evaluate or judge; to propose a solution; to seek common ground; to inform or explain; to express or reflect, etc. *(R; 13.7) (5 minutes)*

5. Read, annotate, and discuss model paragraphs from contemporary or older publications that incorporate several modes to achieve a larger purpose. *(T; 13.1) (30 minutes)*

Understanding Writing as a Rhetorical Practice:

6. Discuss using students' annotations "Purdue OWL, "Understanding Writing: The Rhetorical Situation" *(T; 13.1) (15 minutes)*

7. Discuss using students' annotations Reid, Shelley, "Ten Ways to Think About Writing" *(T; 13.1) (30 minutes)*

Week 2

Understanding Writing as a Recursive Process That Includes Reflection and Revision:

1. Discuss using students' annotations Ruecker, "Recursive Writing Process"

Discuss using students' annotations Giles, "Reflective Writing and the Revision Process"
(T; 13.1) (20 minutes)

Formal Writing Assignment

2. Introduce first major writing assignment (for our purposes, an analysis of a text's use of the five elements of effective writing). Read and discuss models of the genre(s) students will write. Focus on features that students will need to include in their piece. *(R; 13.1) (30 minutes)*

3. Based on students' reading annotations, discuss how pieces of a **text set** address these five elements:

   a. Original piece: Yoffe, Emily. "College Women: Stop Getting Drunk." Salon.com. 15 Oct. 2013.

   b. Response: Hess, Amanda. "To Prevent Rape on College Campuses, Focus on the Rapists, Not the Victims." Salon.com. 16 Oct. 2013.

c. Rebuttal from Original Writer: Yoffe, Emily. "Emily Yoffe Responds to Her Critics." Salon.com. 18 Oct. 2013. *(T; R; 13.1; 13.2) (50 minutes)*

In-class (and) out of class pre-writing for major assignment. *(P; 13.1; 13.6) (50 minutes)*

Week 3

Writing Workshop

1. First draft and reflective writer's statement workshopped by peers. *(P, W; 13.4; 13.3; 13.7) (50 minutes)*
2. Revision work in and out of class. *(P, W; 13.4) (100 minutes)*

Teacher draft with reflective writer's statement due at end of week. (Teacher will provide feedback to facilitate student revision. At teacher's discretion, students complete a final draft within a few days or revise for a final portfolio.) *(P, W; 13.4) (0 minutes)*

12 Applications of *the Framework for Success in Postsecondary Writing* at the University of Mississippi: Shaping the Praxis of Writing Instruction

Alice Johnston Myatt and Ellen Shelton

As authors of this chapter, we appreciate the opportunity to share with readers the ways in which the *Framework for Success in Postsecondary Writing* became a vehicle for planning recurring writing symposia, supported the redesign of writing program curriculum, and served to improve the delivery of writing instruction across educational settings in Mississippi by its use in a variety of K–16 professional development activities. At the University of Mississippi, Alice is the associate director of the Department of Writing and Rhetoric in the College of Liberal Arts, and Ellen is director of the University of Mississippi's Writing Project, housed within the Division of Outreach. Both of us are actively involved with writing instruction and curriculum, and we began incorporating the *Framework* into relevant projects and writing instruction immediately after its release in 2011.

In this chapter, we describe how the *Framework* helped us shape the advancement of writing instruction in secondary and postsecondary educational settings in Mississippi. Our purpose is to provide insight into how the *Framework* informed the University of Mississippi's campus-wide quality enhancement plan (QEP) initiatives and the inaugural and subsequent programs of annual Transitioning to College Writing (TCW) symposia. Like Angela Clark-Oates notes in chapter 14 of this volume, we posit that the *Framework* can be an effective document to use in designing professional development activities for K–16 writing instructors; it is also an excellent reinforcement of the "WPA Outcomes Statement for First-Year Composition" (WPA OS), as evidenced in the curricular revision we undertook.

BACKGROUND

The Department of Writing and Rhetoric (DWR) at the University of Mississippi (UM) is an independent writing program within the university's College of Liberal Arts and home of its first-year composition program, advanced composition courses, and the university's writing centers. The University of Mississippi's Writing Project (UMWP) is deeply involved in community outreach programs and takes the lead in the planning and delivery of K–12 professional development workshops and the UMWP Invitational Summer Institute in north central Mississippi. Among recent developments in Mississippi has been the state's adoption of the Common Core State Standards (CCSS), and with the release of the *Framework*, we recognized its value as a lens for understanding and integrating the CCSS in K–12 classrooms and beyond, though we share the same degree of caution that Lauren Ingraham expresses in chapter 11 of this volume. In addition to its value as a resource for our respective units and K–12 teachers, we found expanded application for it in our collaboration as program planners for annual symposia held at the University of Mississippi. Since 2011, we have jointly planned and hosted annual Transitioning to College Writing (TCW) symposia that bring together high school and postsecondary writing teachers from Mississippi and nearby areas to share resources, attend workshops, and have round-table discussions connected to writing instruction.

The TCW symposia were developed specifically to encourage dialogue and build connections between high schools and postsecondary schools in Mississippi, while introducing such curricular-enhancing elements as writing across the curriculum and digital literacy. An important goal of the symposia is to share resources that help prepare students for college readiness. A foundational element of the symposia has been—and continues to be—workshops on curricular and assignment development for writing teachers from K–16 settings that incorporate elements of the *Framework* and the CCSS. In addition to distributing the *Framework* document to symposia attendees, we integrate discussion of habits of mind and experiences emphasized in the *Framework* in the annual programs we develop.

Additionally, the release of the *Framework* supported the ongoing implementation of UM's 2009 quality enhancement plan (QEP), which, underneath the umbrella of "improving student writing" (2), had as its purview curricular redesign and ongoing professional development of the writing instructors teaching for the DWR, where writing instructors meet in small groups to discuss current classroom issues, pedagogy, and assessment; undergraduate writing consultants who work in the university's writing centers also participate in ongoing professional development activities.

The publication of the *Framework* in 2011, with its focus on habits of mind and its emphasis on the value of such characteristics as curiosity, inquiry, invention, and creativity, foregrounded a resource we believed would help us support writing instruction in a beneficial and productive manner. At the time, though, we weren't quite certain how to use it. Although we were fully committed to the concepts and ideas that led to the adoption of the *Framework* by the Council of Writing Program Administrators (CWPA), the National Council of Teachers of English (NCTE), and the National Writing Project (NWP), in what practical, useful, and sustainable ways could the statement be used to encourage Mississippi's K–12 teachers to mindfully incorporate these important habits of mind into their classrooms? How would the statement support or add to the often high-stakes transition from high school to college writing? Given that our work also included working with a community of writing instructors and writing center consultants at UM, how could we mindfully use the *Framework* to support ongoing professional development? We found the answer by matching the habits of mind and their attributes to the outcomes of the foregoing questions.

Using the *Framework* to Cross Boundaries: The Transitioning to College Writing Symposia

The phrase "college and career readiness" has been floating in the education world for over ten years, but, ironically, as Nicholas Behm, Sherry Rankins-Robertson, and Duane Roen note in the introduction to this volume, high school teachers and college instructors are rarely given the opportunity to discuss what "college ready writers" actually means. Are high school teachers teaching writing for the demands of community colleges or universities? Are community colleges and universities sharing the same expectations for students who matriculate into their programs? What do college teachers expect students to be able to write? Without articulation or discussion, high school teachers are left with only their own experiences as students in college writing classes to guide them. For many of us, that experience was long ago, and expectations have changed. As Katherine Nolan, education researcher and former executive director of Project Align, observes, "Colleges have rarely defined what students need to know and be able to do in order to be successful writers" (qtd. in NWP and Nagin 64). We needed to understand the landscape of where students were coming from: we needed to appreciate that we could, and should, as the state's flagship university, play a role in communicating our core values and expectations to those teaching in the places from where our students were coming. We needed to understand how the mandates in the K–12 world were affecting university writing instruction. In short, we needed a way to dialogue with writing teachers in Mississippi's schools: primary, secondary, and two- and four-year colleges.

For several years, the University of Mississippi Writing Project (UMWP) talked about creating a day-long conference for high school teachers, community college, and university instructors to discuss what writing best prepares students for the demands of college and career writing. We knew from research in professional development that "teachers who get help from colleagues who are more expert than they are may also gain important new information from those interactions that extends what they learn from formal professional development experiences" (Ball and Cohen 14). If we as teachers are to reach an understanding of what college readiness is, we must communicate with each other. The prevailing mindset on the university level seemed disconnected to the K–12 world with the idea that, ultimately, students would only receive writing instruction once they had matriculated to the college level. Both teachers and instructors assumed they knew what the other expected; in reality, there was a disconnect between student writing in the K–12 world and the writing happening in college classrooms. How would we communicate the *Framework* to our colleagues in primary and secondary school settings? Given the adoption by Mississippi's legislature of the CCSS, how could we encourage writing teachers to use the *Framework* without overwhelming them with perceived demands on their time, energy, and resources?

As a writing project site, we knew that we could bring high school teachers to the discussion, and when we first decided to hold the first Transitioning to College Writing (TCW) symposium, we wanted to be very careful that this space was one of mutual respect, of all sides valuing the work of the others. We did not want the symposium to become a top-down model of university instructors directing the conversation. This concept had to be–and remain–at the core of our planning. Otherwise, the whole program could very well unravel into a top-down model program, something we wanted to avoid. The symposium planning committee was aware of this danger, knowing that any success of these relationships might be diminished by feelings of frustration from high school teachers if they were not part of the planning and execution of the symposium. Fortuitously, while at the 2011 CCCC conference in Atlanta, one of us attended a small, impromptu meeting that focused on partnerships and transitions across K–16 settings. During that meeting, Alice met then high-school writing center director Jennifer Wells and other educators from secondary and postsecondary schools. As would later be articulated by Peggy O'Neill, Linda Adler-Kassner, Cathy Fleischer, and Anne-Marie Hall in their July 2012 *College English* article "Creating the *Framework for Success in Postsecondary Writing*," this meeting, while productive on many levels, was outstanding in helping us appreciate that "writing instruction is an activity shared by K–16 teachers, not one in which teachers at lower levels 'teach up' to those at higher levels or instructors at higher levels 'blame down' for what students 'should have learned' by the time that they arrive at college" (520). We became committed to including as many voices as possible in planning the symposium.

While the WPA OS articulates what students "should know and be able to do at the end of a first-year composition or writing course" (1), the *Framework* "identifies the habits of mind and the kinds of writing experiences that will best prepare students for success as they enter courses in which they will work to achieve those outcomes" (3). Thus, we saw a vital connection between the *Framework*, our TCW symposium, and the strong interest our target symposium audience had in the recently released CCSS, which was adopted by the Mississippi legislature in 2010. We wanted to ensure that our symposium attendees would engage with more than just the narrow focus of the CCSS but also have the resources to engage with the deeper habits of mind and needed writing experiences the writers of the *Framework* connected to students who would be ready to write at both college and career levels. As we worked with the planning team comprised of the CWR writing instructors, high school teachers, and community and university instructors to develop that first symposium, we distributed the *Framework* to the planning team and asked for ideas and suggestions on how best to create awareness of how useful it would be in supporting the educational goals all of us had. Because it was written in collaboration with NCTE, NWP, and CWPA, we knew that the document was in line with the position of the committee that convened to plan the inaugural TCW symposium. We both felt that by recognizing and collaborating with all of the constituencies represented by K–16 writing teachers, our TCW symposium would become a place and space where meaningful exchanges could take place across boundaries, not from one boundary to another in a vertical give and take, but in a flat, horizontal exchange of values and ideas that would emphasize the common values and ideas that we all cherished.

We realized the potential for the *Framework* to be the key to opening discussion with those attending the symposium. The fact that all educational levels are the audience for the *Framework* led us to see the document as a leveling text for the symposium. The *Framework*'s design of breaking writing instruction into habits of the mind and writing experiences would give participants a language with which to share writing strategies across all instructional levels. As echoed again by Bruce McCominsky, in the symposium, "with the help of the *Framework*, then, K–12 teachers and college teachers can discuss openness in local contexts *without relying solely on documents written for their own educational levels*, bridging the concerns of all involved" (529, emphasis added). In essence, we had found our vehicle for honest and respectful discussions about writing instruction.

The elements of the habits of mind and writing experiences from the *Framework* drove our planning for that first symposium in 2011, and they continue to be a part of what we wish to model through our planning. We wanted those habits and experiences to be at the core of this work. As we were developing the program for the first symposium, we wanted one focus to be on the preparation of high school students and the transitioning to the requirements of college writing. As stated in the *Framework*'s introduction, "Students who come to college writing with these habits of mind and these experiences will be well positioned to meet the writing challenges in the full spectrum of academic courses and later in their careers" (2). Part of that preparation had to be on finding out what each institution expected from their students, and that discovery could only happen through dialogue and sharing assignments. We wanted the participants to be curious about each other's classrooms, so we purposefully placed high school teachers, university instructors, and community college instructors on panels and presentations together, a format that we refer to as the triad concept. For example, we made a conscious decision not to include the place of instruction on the name badges: we wanted all teachers to be on the same level. We were all writing instructors in Mississippi. No titles were used for this same purpose. We wanted to reinforce the idea that the responsibility for teaching writing fell not on any one group of teachers: we all have a responsibility to teach writing to our different classrooms with the understanding that we are preparing our students for the next step of college and career.

In planning annual symposia, we settled on the roundtable format for topics such as integrating digital learning, beginning writing centers, discussing the then-rumored CCSS and its subsequent impact on higher education classes, and incorporating relevant connections from the *Framework* in the conversations we facilitated. We wanted teachers to be engaged in discussions at all levels. Such roundtable discussions would ultimately challenge attendees to identify the resources and strategies they plan to use once they are back at work in their local communities. We typically began the day with a presentation demonstrating writing across our state. The standard opening called "Starting the Conversation: Mapping our Academic Writing Landscape" focused the spotlight on writing instruction in the high school, community college, university, and writing centers across our state. Our intent was, and is, to ask participants to realize that we are all teaching writing for the same purpose with the same goals in mind. Ultimately, this is about the local place of instruction while building the community of the symposium, an honoring of what each teacher brings to writing instruction. Often, the conversations we share become opportunities to map connections to the habits of mind articulated by the *Framework*.

In addition to identifying habits of mind relevant to writing instruction, the *Framework* calls for learning experiences that meet certain objectives, among which are that "teachers can foster these habits of mind through writing, reading, and critical analysis experiences" (1). Thus, we crafted workshop sessions that mirrored the Experiences with Writing, Reading, and Critical Analysis outlined in the *Framework* (6–10). Reflecting on this, we don't believe this was as much a conscious decision as much as a shared philosophy of writing instruction. A powerful element of the *Framework* document lies in its grounding in writing pedagogy. These are processes in which all writing teachers engage. These elements exist at the heart of what we do, and for many teachers are points of inquiry for instruction. As a result, session topics consistently address the positions outlined in the *Framework*. Unspoken in this discussion is the fact that most instructors attend this symposium, or any conference for that matter, in an attempt to gather strategies to implement in their own classrooms. We are all looking for new layers of learning.

Session topics across the years have addressed the experiences in writing instruction such as peer review, reading and writing connections, research processes, building community in a writing classroom, using e-Portfolios in the writing classroom, multiple genres of writing, multimodal writing, and writing across the curriculum. The strength of the sessions comes from the triad concept of ensuring that we have three audiences represented in the presenters for the sessions. As teachers and instructors share ideas, they are able to see the writing instruction continuum set for their students. Each level comes to an understanding of what assignments came before and what assignments will come after and how to build the skills needed for next level.

In our planning, we started to think about who could be the most effective messengers of our mission. While the roundtable breakout session presenters are Mississippi teachers and instructors, we wanted to invite plenary speakers who are recognized for their success in the experiences discussed in the *Framework*. After consideration, the first year we invited composition scholars Richard 'Dickie' Selfe and Lil to join us, as we knew both speakers could ground us in writing in all grade levels and modes. Dickie and Lil connected their presentations and workshops to relevant characteristics of the *Framework*. For example, Lil, a long-time member of the NWP, described one of her symposium workshops this way: "Research is all about being curious—of asking questions, exploring possibilities, wondering" ("Mapping the Intersections"). In her keynote address, she described the use of daybooks in writing classrooms, and in so doing, she connected implicitly to curiosity, one of the habits of mind, when she said, "We, like our students, need a place where our writing can be messy, where we can think out loud on paper when we don't know what to say, where we can collect our thoughts and feelings, explore ideas that matter to us without penalty, where we can just try things out just to see what happens" ("Mapping the Realities"). She followed her address with a workshop for attendees to gain experience with practical application of the strategies and ideas presented in her keynote talk. And again, she connected to that essential habit of mind, curiosity. The abstract she wrote for the event described it as follows: "In this workshop, we will explore how daybooks are used as tools for inquiry. We will use daybooks to map stories that we live by and then to see how those stories can be mined as data so that our stories matter" ("Mapping the Intersections").

Dickie Selfe's focus on digital composition mapped well to the *Framework*'s inclusion of the need for students to experience composing in multiple environments with a workshop that featured digital compositions. The title of his workshop was "Working with Digital Assignments in the Composition Classroom" and he described it by saying, "How do we help students who have been 'born digital' to recognize the challenges and rewards of writing and learning in digital environments? This workshop offers attendees practice in developing and working with a variety of digital composition assignments." Even now, several years past that day in October 2011, those teachers who attended his workshop speak of the profound influence his suggestions and practical modeling had, and continue to have, on their own teaching and working with student writers.

Those participating in planning our first TCW symposium had the *Framework* very much on their minds; from their questions, it is also clear that they did not quite grasp the intent of the *Framework*. In referring back to our notes at the time, we found this question from one of the planners, followed by another that shows the connection teachers were making, even then, between the *Framework* and the CCSS. First, the question was asked, "What is the *Framework for Student Success in Postsecondary Writing* and why should we care? And, What exactly are the Common Core State Standards and how will they affect our work?" To respond to those questions, especially since the planners had the needs of their colleagues in mind, the program for that fall's symposium included a workshop titled "Common Core/*Framework* in Practice" and was described this way: "In this workshop, attendees will map the CCSS to the *Framework for Success in Postsecondary Writing*, and they will discuss how to incorporate these best practices into their own classrooms." That workshop had the highest number of attendees of all the sessions on that year's program; years later, we still hear from teachers who are still using those workshop resources in planning their lessons and curricula.

As we moved into the second year of planning for the symposium, we turned again to the *Framework* as our guide. From the first year's comments, we heard that teachers wanted to see more of how other teachers implement those writing experiences that build on the habits. Again, our guide was the *Framework* as we planned for "the habits of mind and the kinds of writing experiences that will best prepare students for success as they enter courses in which they will work to achieve those outcomes" (3). Again, we wanted to keep the format of roundtables because of the rich discussion and sharing of assignments that happen in those sessions. For our second symposium, we offered roundtables with a focus on peer response, the realities of writing instruction, bridging transitions, the implementation of the CCSS, grammar, and MLA documentation. We also added a strand for supporting writing centers in all three levels with two visiting scholars, Amber Jensen, Edison High School, Virginia, and Kerri Jordan, Mississippi College. This popular strand encompassed the idea of helping teachers and students develop flexible writing process experiences. Our keynote speaker, Chris Anson, gave a relevant address on "It's All About Location: Reflections on Student Preparedness and the Transfer of Knowledge" that focused on what habits students have acquired from their writing experiences and whether or not they transfer those to another writing experience, a discussion that is particularly reflective of the *Framework*'s message.

No matter how consciously or unconsciously we applied the *Framework* as a document to our planning of the first and subsequent symposia, we feel that all of the programs have been grounded in the tenets set forth by the developers of that document. So much of what we hear teachers who participate in our writing project site's projects discuss is a desire to foster the habits of mind in their student writers. While planning for each symposium, we keep those at the forefront of our thinking. However, broader connections sometimes require space be consciously made. If the standards are the goals we want our students to achieve before they leave high school and enter college, the *Framework* provides the habits of mind and articulates the vital writing experiences that will carry them through college and career readiness.

IMPLEMENTING THE *FRAMEWORK*: CURRICULAR DEVELOPMENT

In 2009, The University of Mississippi (UM) began implementation of a quality enhancement plan (QEP) that had the lofty and potentially enriching goal to "improve student writing" (iii). As a result of that implementation, the administration of first-year composition, along with an advanced composition class intended for sophomores, became the responsibility of a new unit, the Center for Writing and Rhetoric (CWR). The center, in addition to its administration of first-year writing courses, was also the administrative home of the university's writing centers, and it was an independent unit whose director (given equal status to department chairs) reported to the dean of the College of Liberal Arts. The QEP articulated the three-fold approach the CWR would use as "reshaping freshman writing curriculum," "improving writing support services and resources," and "enhancing the teaching-learning environment" (iii). Though the *Framework* was not released until after the implementation of the QEP began, the QEP incorporated the WPA OS into the mandated curricular revision it called for, observing that the "desired student learning outcomes reflect and in some areas converge with the five key writing knowledge areas identified by the WPA: (1) rhetorical understanding, (2) critical thinking and reading, (3) processes, (4) conventions, and (5) use of digital technologies" (22). The *Framework* thus supported the QEP and added dimension and depth to the revisions undertaken by the CWR's curricular committees.

Alice recalls how the *Framework* influenced the implementation of the QEP:

> One of the first actions I took upon accepting the position at UM was to join the Council of Writing Program Administrators (CWPA). I read about the release of the *Framework* via WPA-L, a listserv for all interested in writing program administration. Although later critiques of the document would question the value of its stating the obvious, for me, being a relative newcomer into the WPA world, my reading of the document

> helped me to connect the thinking and learning I had engaged in regarding pedagogy and best practices in writing instruction to the work I was doing in curricular redesign. In the summer of 2011, at the CWPA conference in Baton Rouge, Louisiana, I attended the session during which those on the task force of the *Framework* discussed how the statement developed and how they hoped it would be used by educators at all levels. Since my introduction to the *Framework*, it was and continues to be a guiding instrument in my thinking about curricular development and in working with our writing instructors and writing directors to develop effective teaching and tutoring practices.

The publication of the *Framework* in 2011, with its focus on habits of mind and its emphasis of such characteristics as curiosity, inquiry, invention, and creativity, foregrounded a resource that supported our curricular development. As mentioned earlier, the QEP at UM included curricular revision as one of three ways to improve student writing. The first two years of the QEP saw the formation of curricular committees that undertook this complex and difficult task. In addition to enhancing the curriculum, committees had to meet the sometimes-unrealistic expectations of its external audience that was comprised not only of the university's faculty and staff but also of students who often came into first-year composition thinking of it as one of the best GPA boosters available to them. This work, beginning as it did in 2009, of course was well underway by the time the *Framework* statement was published in 2011. However, it was to have a strong influence on a course that would undergo curricular revision in 2012 and 2013, as both of us were on that particular curricular committee.

The course had been around for some time. Previously taught as English 250, it had the name Applied Writing. Much confusion existed among students and faculty about the specific purpose of the course, and the course (which is a requirement for graduation in many majors) lacked curricular consistency. It tended to be taught according to the whim of the instructor, with varying assignments and thus with few specific reliable outcomes. The curricular revision committee was a large one comprised of faculty and adjuncts who had taught or were teaching the course. We had both taught the course, and serendipitously, the release of the *Framework* offered us a roadmap to use in establishing specific student learning outcomes for the revised course. A benefit of having and using the *Framework* was that it gave us a way of pulling together the seemingly disparate and even dichotomous objectives the committee (which at one time included ten people) tendered. It also gave us a way of offering positive recognition for certain outcomes that would support the QEP goals, offering as it did a bridge between the WPA OS (which the QEP had incorporated) and the praxis of teaching the course to students who had diverse majors and various levels of preparedness.

The committee elected to take an approach that supported the habits of mind and learning experiences featured in the *Framework*. Although this was not made an explicit mandate of the committee, sharing the *Framework* with that early committee gave all involved some clear direction. They looked for ways to foster students' abilities in the areas of curiosity, openness, engagement, flexibility, creativity, persistence, responsibility, and metacognition. Ultimately, the committee would adopt a curriculum designed to meet the needs of students coming into an advanced composition course (the name of the course actually changed to Writing 250, Advanced Composition) by asking students to begin by examining and discovering how knowledge was made and shared within their particular discourse communities (incorporating curiosity, requiring openness to new ideas, fostering engagement with their chosen major, and requiring persistence in discovering existing research and writing in their fields), and incorporating in the curriculum the use of a mini-research component that asked students to design and test a small primary research project. Again, although not explicitly written into the course outcomes as habits of mind, the outcomes feature verbs and actions that would draw on and foster the use of the habits in productive and generative ways.

Implementing the *Framework*: Professional Development

Similar to what Peter Khost expresses in chapter 9, both of us have found the *Framework* of immense value in planning and executing professional development initiatives and activities. Our section on using the *Framework* to cross boundaries, which discussed the Transitioning to College Writing symposia, also serves to illuminate the use of the *Framework* to support cross-institutional professional development; the University of Mississippi Writing Project hosts a number of workshops and short institutes each year for K–12 teachers, and the *Framework* document is an important resource we share with them. We have also found the document to be a useful resource for departmental professional development, some of which we present here.

The third component of the university's 2009–2014 QEP was that of "enhancing the teaching-learning environment," and one of the ways to do this was by the creation of small groups within the Center for Writing and Rhetoric's (CWR) teaching community and writing centers that would be a space for professional development and the exchange of ideas. Here again, the value of the *Framework* was the grounding it provided for discussion about some of the best practices we wanted to find enacted in our classrooms and writing centers. Of particular benefit were the "writing, reading, and critical analysis experiences" (2) the *Framework* emphasized. By weaving discussion of how best to accomplish or integrate such experiences into the existing curriculum (which was guided by the WPA OS), the CWR teaching and tutoring community acquired the practical knowledge, language, and scaffolding that best supported those experiences. One example is the experience summarized in the *Framework*'s executive summary: the "[a]bility to compose in multiple environments—from traditional pen and paper to electronic technologies" (1). All of the curricular committees adopted one assignment that fell into the genre of multimodal composition. This assignment, in whatever form it takes under the direction of individual instructors, fosters (it is hoped) an awareness in students not only of the rhetorical purpose of different modes, but it also introduces students to an awareness of the affordances and drawbacks of different modes of composition. In executing this curricular advancement, the CWR hired an instructional designer whose primary focus is to support the pedagogical aims of the program, assisting instructors to effectively implement the multimodal composition assignment. Such work is well supported by the habits of mind and experiences identified in the *Framework*.

This focus of the *Framework*'s habits of mind and experiences also extended into the professional development of our undergraduate writing center consultants. For some years, the training and development given to the writing center consultants had been, for the most part, based on one-on-one and weekly staff meetings with the director combined with observations of more experienced consultants. However, this method opened the door for working more with the product of the session rather than with the student writer. By offering and engaging the writing consultants in more structured consultant education, the culture within the writing center gradually shifted to one that took advantage of the traits of the habits of mind. Consultants now regularly use a facilitative, inquiry-based approach to help emerging student writers gain confidence, persistence, and commitment in their own writing. Additionally, we developed and teach a credit-bearing course for writing center consultants, and we provide the *Framework* as a resource for the course and for the continued professional development we do with writing center consultants.

Lessons Learned: Combined Reflection

As our CWR transitioned into a department, the demands of supporting the three goals of the 2009 QEP encouraged us to draw on the habits of mind as well as look for ways to provide students with the writing experiences espoused by the *Framework*. Further, the collaborative development of annual writing symposia call on us to apply the *Framework*'s language and ideas. We recognize much of this in retrospect, and while we made the *Framework*'s potential explicit in our first TCW symposium, it remains an integral, although more implicit, part of our thinking as we, along with the program planners we recruit from Mississippi's high schools and college settings, design and execute sessions and activities that best support the acquisition and development of the habits of mind and provide our students with enriching experiences that, we hope, will help them to become lifelong writers who, having learned to write, continue writing to learn.

As Bruce McComiskey notes, "There isn't a thing in the *Framework* with which I disagree. Who *wouldn't* want creative, persistent, responsible students with lots of rhetorical knowledge and flexible writing processes? Who *wouldn't* want curious, open, engaged students who are able to compose in multiple environments? But why another document about writing instruction when there are others already floating around?" (537). In short, we believe the strength of the *Framework* not only lies in what it states, but also in its application to the classroom and to our professional development. It is not a mandate or a call to arms, such as The National Commission on Writing's 2003 publication *The Neglected R*, which was helpful in talking with administrators but not so helpful in starting discussions with teachers. Rather, it is a set of principles that defines good writing instruction; one that provides multiple entry points for supporting dialogue among writing teachers in various institutional settings.

As it gave us a beginning for discussion, the *Framework* has continued to provide our different schools and departments with a common language. Both the UM writing project and the Department of Writing and Rhetoric continue to provide professional development to schools via workshop, support for developing writing centers in high school, and in-school modeling and mentoring teachers and writing center tutors. Again, the *Framework* grounds our thinking about writing and research as a process, a reminder "that writing activities and assignments should be designed with genuine purposes and audiences in mind (from teachers and other students to community groups, local or national officials, commercial interests, students' friends and relatives, and other potential readers) in order to foster flexibility and rhetorical versatility" (3). We live and teach in rural, urban, and suburban areas of Mississippi, and we continue in our commitment to reach all teachers of writing to create better writing in Mississippi. The *Framework* is an integral part of that commitment.

Works Cited

Anson, Chris. "It's All About Location: Reflections on Student Preparedness and the Transfer of Knowledge." 2012 Transitioning to College Writing Symposium Program. Oxford, Mississippi: U of Mississippi Center for Writing and Rhetoric, 2012. Keynote Address.

Ball, Deborah L., and David K. Cohen. "Reform by the book: What Is—or Might Be—The Role of Curriculum Materials in Teacher Learning and Instructional Reform?" *Educational Researcher* 25.9 (1996): 6–14. Print.

Brannon, Lil. "Mapping the Reality of Writing." 2011 Transitioning to College Writing Symposium Program. Oxford, Mississippi: U of Mississippi Center for Writing and Rhetoric, 2011. Keynote Address.

—. "Mapping the Intersections of Stories and Data." 2011 Transitioning to College Writing Symposium Program. Oxford, Mississippi: U of Mississippi Center for Writing and Rhetoric, 2011. Workshop.

Council of Writing Program Administrators. "WPA Outcomes Statement For First-Year Composition." CWPA, 2014. PDF File.

Council of Writing Program Administrators, National Council of Teachers of English, and National Writing Project. *Framework for Success in Postsecondary Writing*. CWPA, NCTE, and NWP, 2011. PDF File.

McComiskey, Bruce. "Bridging the Divide: The (Puzzling) Framework and the Transition from K–12 to College Writing Instruction." *Symposium: On the Framework for Success in Postsecondary Writing.* Spec. issue of *College English* 74.6 (2012): 537–40. Print.

National Governors Association Center for Best Practices, Council of Chief State School Officers. *Common Core State Standards, English Language Arts*. Washington, DC: NGA Center for Best Practices, Council of Chief State School Officers, 2010. Web. 18 April 2013.

National Writing Project and Carl Nagin. *Because Writing Matters: Improving Student Writing in Our Schools*. San Francisco: Josey-Bass, 2003. Print.

O'Neill, Peggy, Linda Adler-Kassner, Cathy Fleischer, and Anne-Marie Hall. "Creating the *Framework for Success in Postsecondary Writing*." Symposium: On the Framework for Success in Postsecondary Writing. Spec. issue of *College English* 74.6 (2012): 520–24. Print.

Selfe, Richard. Abstract. "Working with Digital Assignments in the Composition Classroom." 2011 Transitioning to College Writing Symposium Program. Oxford, Mississippi: U of Mississippi Center for Writing and Rhetoric, 2011. Keynote Address.

The National Commission on Writing in America's Schools and Colleges. *The Neglected "R": The Need for a Writing Revolution*. Princeton, NJ: College Entrance Examination Board, 2003. Print.

University of Mississippi. "Write Here. Write Now. The University of Mississippi 2009 Quality Enhancement Plan." University of Mississippi, 2009. Print.

University of Mississippi. "UM / 2020 Strategic Plan." University of Mississippi, 2010. Print.

13 Metacognitive Persistence and Cultural Knowledge: Application of the *Framework* with Preservice Teachers for Writing Instruction in Secondary Schools

Rodrigo Joseph Rodríguez

The need for more metacognitive approaches and openness to cultural knowledge in writing instruction, particularly in courses that train preservice teachers, has been established in the last decade (Culham 13). Increasingly, educators are finding ways to engage preservice teachers in assignments and projects that call for them to apply habits of mind and to learn about linguistic and cultural pluralism in preparation to work with diverse populations in public education. An important area of concern is defining the role of writing and the teacher in secondary and post-secondary education. For instance, in *10 Things Every Writer Needs to Know*, Jeff Anderson asks, "What is writing? . . . And how do you do it well? And, as a teacher, just how do you teach writing effectively? What do I need to adjust? And, in making adjustments, what stays?" (ix).

Currently, there exists a strong need for perspectives on the *Framework for Success in Postsecondary Writing* that explore teacher education and preservice teachers' preparation. More specifically, it is important to know how literacy is defined in English education projects and to demonstrate how writing with cultural knowledge is enacted for teaching readiness and rigor. If educators can understand preservice teachers' perceptions about writing and approaches for reflection on the writing instruction they received in the past, this knowledge can provide insights into how to operationalize documents, such as the *Framework*, and how to integrate and actualize the habits of mind as part of a new generation of writing pedagogy that privileges and values metacognition and cultural knowledge (Nieto 4). For instance, such pedagogy could integrate Michael Martinez's definition of metacognition and how it promotes self-regulatory practices and persistence: "[M]etacognition is the monitoring and control of thought" (696) and "making thinking audible" (699). His definition emphasizes individual effort with deliberate expression and communication often in the face of obstacles with solutions governed by self-regulation and self-awareness through reflective practice. Martinez's definition mirrors the habits of mind found in the *Framework* that emphasize reflective thinking and those that we espouse "on the individual and cultural processes and systems used to structure knowledge" (O'Neill et al. 529).

Through metacognitive modeling and persistence, educators can engage preservice teachers and secondary-school students to make their "thinking audible" to themselves and to their peers as they self-regulate effectively, cultivating their ability to activate and adapt the metacognitive behaviors and actions in a world driven by writing on demand and for quick consumption (Martinez 699). In support of the act of writing and thinking like an emerging writer, culturally relevant and responsive teaching advanced by Gloria Ladson-Billings and Geneva Gay challenge deficit-thinking practices and conditions toward a learning environment that is democratic. This means that professionals possessing cultural competencies in the language arts classroom recognize the knowledge that students possess to complement learning. Cultural knowledge is further deepened with metacognitive habits and decision-making that students adopt toward thinking critically through their writing, reading, and research. In teacher education, students' cultural and prior knowledge significantly informs instruction and can advance learning in and out of school settings (Summerfield and Anderson), particularly if that instruction attends to language users' struggles by valuing and calling on the multiple languages and rich experiences learners bring to the classroom. This can be complemented by Ron Ritchart and Mark Church's call for "directing our mental activity and planning" with types of thinking that identify patterns, generate possibilities, evaluate evidence, monitor actions, identify bias, and clarify priorities (14).

To help discern the manifestations of cultural knowledge in writing instruction and production, I conducted an IRB-approved study that examined the writings of preservice teachers who participated in a methods course on writing instruction. The study was designed to understand preservice teachers writing beliefs, particularly how they believe writing is influenced by habits of mind and cultural experiences. The following research question guided the study: How do preservice teachers communicate their writing beliefs while engaged in conversations about habits of mind and linguistic and cultural knowledge? The *Framework* serves as the guiding document, but at the same time in my role as a teacher educator I note the interconnectedness of three documents—*Framework*, Common Core State Standards (CCSS), and *Beliefs about the Teaching of Writing* (*Beliefs*), which was developed by the National Council of Teachers of English (NCTE) Writing Study Group of the Executive Committee. Overall, these three documents were triangulated for the benefit of preservice teachers' preparation for the English language arts classroom and the students with whom they will work in secondary schools. This chapter presents a qualitative, single-case study project that examines the perspectives of preservice teachers studying in a university along the US-México border in Texas and how they conceptualize writing beliefs to support metacognitive persistence and cultural knowledge.

Methodology

Grounded in the culturally relevant and responsive pedagogy advocated by Gloria Ladson-Billings, Geneva Gay, and Sonio Nieto, this study advanced critical pedagogy to privilege literacy and self-actualization as articulated by Paolo Freire. Mary P. Sheridan and Lee Nickoson argue that literacy is "learned and practiced in complicated, seemingly invisible ways, yet we carry the values of complex activity networks with us as we learn and research, as we move from space to space" (2). Gholnecsar E. Muhammad advances how English language arts educators can "reconceptualize the roles and purposes of writing accentuated in the histories, identities, and literacies of youth. Without wider views, other voices continue to become the dominant or the outwardly solitary narrative" (225). Overall, these thinkers strengthened my examination of metacognitive persistence and cultural knowledge in teacher preparation and writing beliefs.

As an illustration about questioning and habits of mind, Kimberly Tanner observes, "The importance of metacognition in the process of learning is an old idea that can be traced from Socrates' questioning methods to Dewey's twentieth-century stance that we learn more from reflecting on our experiences than from the actual experiences themselves" (113). Furthermore, some of the earliest thoughts about metacognition include "introspective observation" by William James, "consciousness of cognizance" by Jean Piaget, and "inner speech" and "reflective thought" by Lev Vygotsky (qtd. in Silver 8–9). A qualitative, single-case study was conducted to examine how six preservice teachers presented their writing beliefs while participating in an undergraduate seminar I taught in 2014. The course, named Teaching Composition and Literature in the Secondary Schools, is part of the Literacy and English Education Program in the Department of English at The University of Texas at El Paso. The six students, who were part of a larger class of eighteen students classified as either juniors or seniors, had been assigned field placements at either middle or high schools in an English language arts classroom in the greater El Paso del Norte school communities. A qualitative, single-case study provides opportunities to gain descriptive and observational insights about learning in and out of the classroom. For example, Robert Yin describes a case study as an "empirical inquiry about a contemporary phenomenon (e.g., a 'case'), set within its real-world context—especially when the boundaries between phenomenon and context are not clearly evident" (*Case Study Research* 18). Moreover, the adoption of this methodology can reveal phenomena about the influences of metacognitive persistence and cultural knowledge in writing beliefs and instruction.

The six participants (see Table 1) were most candid in their teaching journals and open classroom deliberations about their past writing experiences, current struggles, and instructional readiness in their quest to become professional English language arts teachers in secondary public schools.

Table 1. Demographics of Participants (All Names Reflect Pseudonyms)

Participant and Academic Classification	Age	Race/Ethnicity	Sex	School Setting
Esmeralda, senior	22	Mexican American	F	Public, urban
Holly, junior	24	White American	F	Public, suburban
Rosalba, senior	22	Mexican American	F	Public, urban
Sebastian, senior	21	White American	M	Public, urban
Susana, junior	21	Mexican American	F	Public, urban
Timoteo, senior	23	Mexican American	M	Public, suburban

I am a benefactor of public schools in urban communities of Houston, Texas. My experiences in bilingual education during elementary school and later in a magnet career-oriented secondary school provided me with multiple learning and teaching experiences. As a Latino male of Mexican origin, I believe that teacher education can be strengthened by communicating to our students our identity awareness and positionality, which informs cultural knowledge. Teaching in a community that is home to one of the longest and most complex international borders of North America required that I examine my own writing beliefs while engaged in conversations about habits of mind and linguistic and cultural knowledge, particularly discerning how my pedagogical practices include concepts defined in the *Framework* and how those concepts enable students to gain more sophisticated rhetorical and twenty-first-century skills.

Although I maintained my professor role, I also became a teacher-action researcher, documenting direct observations, reflections, dialogues, and writings in the classroom that informed my students' habits of mind, experience, and writing. Gerald Pine explains action research as seeking to "achieve concrete change in a specific situation, context, or work setting to improve teaching/learning" (30). Pine adds, "Action research empowers teachers to own professional knowledge because teachers—through the process of action inquiry—conceptualize and create knowledge, interact around knowledge, transform knowledge, and apply knowledge" (30). Thus, as a teacher-action researcher, the field notes that I generated while working with preservice teachers were revealing about their writing beliefs, joys, and frustrations toward self-discovery.

My field notes relate the preservice teachers' dual citizenship, geographies, and environments in the Paso del Norte Region, or greater Texas-México borderlands, in the Chihuahua Desert; these are significant identifiers that the preservice teachers espoused in regard to their sense of self. Maisha Winn and Latrise Johnson argue, "[Culturally relevant pedagogy] welcomes students' voices, demands their reflection, and pushes them toward discovery of self. Culturally relevant pedagogy validates students' existence regardless of class, race, ethnicity, economic status, or academic level" (15). The six students struggled sharing their beliefs about the act of writing, their thoughts about the writing process, and their own apprehensions about teachers identifying themselves as critics, researchers, and especially as writers.

DATA COLLECTION AND ANALYSIS

The purpose of gathering data was to gain insights into students' writing beliefs and how their beliefs related to and were enriched by the habits of mind, such as openness, persistence, and metacognition, in the *Framework*. Various data sources were collected: two audiotaped interviews were conducted in early March 2014 and twenty-four writing artifacts were collected throughout the semester until May 2014. Each preservice student provided four artifacts: a personal belief narrative, a narrative poem, an information-based essay, and a personal letter written and addressed to an adolescent self. The following prompts encouraged the preservice teachers to cultivate and apply their habits of mind:

1. The purpose of this assignment is to learn about your writing beliefs. Read and then, in an essay, summarize the *Beliefs* in order to explain them to someone unfamiliar with writing instruction. As you read, pay attention to any of the beliefs which may seem either applicable or counterintuitive. Compare these beliefs to the writing instruction you received as a high school student. To what extent did your high school English language arts and reading teachers follow these beliefs and practices? Write one belief statement of your own about the teaching of writing that you espouse and include your rationale.

2. The purpose of this writing assignment is to assess your application of close reading of a poem. Read the poem "The History Teacher" by Billy Collins and pay attention to the use of literary elements, figurative language, and cultural knowledge. Also, note the pedagogical role, choices, and consequences of the teacher's (speaker's) actions found in the poem. Write a four-stanza poem of your own with Collins's poem as your mentor text. Begin with

the first two lines in a first-person point of view as follows: "Trying to protect my students' innocence / I tell them . . ."

3. The purpose of this assignment is to examine action research led by two experienced teachers on reading and writing and to identify strategies we can adopt in our teaching. In *Reading in the Wild: The Book Whisperer's Keys to Cultivating Lifelong Reading Habits*, Donalyn Miller and Susan Kelley argue,

> Reading is nothing remarkable or special for [my students]; it is a regular part of their lives. They are readers, but they are also artists, athletes, writers, gamers, and musicians. For me, this is what worthwhile reading is: readers who incorporate reading into their personal identities to the degree that it weaves into their lives along with everything else that interests them. . . . Reading is a big deal to us because we know that reading well unlocks academic, professional, and social opportunities, but for readers themselves, reading is just part of who they are. (3)

Using this quotation, write a narrative essay in which you describe your own identity as a reader and perceptions of adolescent reading. Illustrate with two references from our course readings either your agreement or disagreement with Miller and Kelly's point of view. Lastly, describe two strategies or approaches that you will use to advance reading and writing habits of mind in your classroom.

4. The purpose of this assignment is to reflect on our individual and cultural processes. If you could send a personal letter to yourself between the ages of 13 and 19, what would you write in it? What would you reveal, share, understand, and/or question? Write a friendly, personal letter to your adolescent self, including the *Framework* habits of mind you've adopted and adapted this semester. Apply personal letter-writing conventions. Consider the narrative excerpts as mentor texts from *Dear Me: A Letter to My Sixteen-Year-Old Self* and *The Letter Q: Queer Writers' Letters to their Younger Selves* that offer advice about remaining committed and persistent as you brainstorm and craft your letter.

These assignments were *Framework*-informed and designed to elicit metacognitive persistence and cultural knowledge from the preservice teachers and to help them "move past obvious or surface-level interpretations and use writing to make sense of and respond to written, visual, verbal, and other texts that they encounter" (O'Neill et al. 530). In addition to the artifacts, my observational notes and teaching reflections provided rich data sources. The interviews were transcribed and analyzed with the writing artifacts to determine primary themes and categories related to teaching, writing, thinking, and ethnicity/culture. The primary categories that emerged were writing beliefs, persistence, and instruction. Practicing triangulation, each participant confirmed the coding and categories, "establishing converging lines of evidence" (Yin, *Applications* 13).

In supporting college-level critical analysis, the first writing assignment asked students to develop a belief statement about the teaching of writing that they espoused with evidence from personal experiences and published research on writing instruction for bilingual and multilingual writers. With this assignment, I was curious to know what they believed writing is and how it works in relation to reading. The assignment asked them to consider how being successful came at a cost to what they hoped to learn. I wanted students to examine if the secondary-school assignments supported their own college readiness and success, and to think about how these contributed or restricted them.

An additional part of the assignment called for reading and discussing the document titled *Beliefs about the Teaching of Writing*. The document launched a conversation about our own belief systems as they related to writing instruction and production. In my field notes, I noted that the students described the beliefs outlined in the NCTE document as "easy to read," "helpful," and "give perspective." The individual perceptions about the teaching of writing and how their beliefs either created or dispelled myths about writing instruction were insightful. For instance, all six preservice teachers participating in the study agreed with the first outlined belief: "Everyone has the capacity to write, writing can be taught, and teachers can help students become better writers" (NCTE). Timoteo, one of the preservice teachers, explained, "Writing is NOT a formulaic five paragraph structure, or three paragraph structure."

A few challenges experienced by the six preservice teachers were regarding objectivity, subjectivity, and agency. Rosalba, a preservice teacher added, "I'm not supposed to use 'I' in my writing, or it will be looked-down upon. I gave up writing about myself. That's something

I learned in high school about writing." For the six preservice teachers, persistence was characterized as sustaining selfhood in the act of writing.

Findings

The preservice teachers' reflections on writing beliefs and instruction supports what Lucy Calkins shares in *The Art of Teaching Writing*. Calkins explains, "Writing gives me awareness and control of my thoughts. It allows me to hold onto ideas long enough to scrutinize them, to think about my thinking. . . . I think by writing and I want students to do likewise" (485). The preservice teachers communicated the need to build up secondary-school students toward their own self-importance, freedom, and authority to speak and nurture their writing voice.

The preservice teachers' writings and communications on the application of the *Framework* were divided into three areas: (1) conceptions about writing, (2) metacognitive persistence, and (3) cultural knowledge/wealth. The six preservice teachers were driven to rethink their (mis)conceptions about writing, while also adding new perspectives that reflected research-based and classroom-tested beliefs for writing instruction in the secondary-school classroom. Furthermore, the writing assignments—as organized and aligned with the *Framework*—were much richer and stronger about the preservice teachers' evolution of their thinking.

Conceptions about Writing

All six preservice teachers explained that they had not met any secondary school teachers who wrote with them when they attended secondary school and who made academic writing engaging and purposeful. The intellectual, rhetorical, and compliance work required from writing competed in different spheres and circumstances for them. The preservice teachers explained in detail that they had not met teachers who openly shared their metacognitive persistence and writing curiosity, flow, deliberations, interruptions, and progress. Instead, all writing effort was centered on persuasive techniques and scaffolding and thus governed by scripted, formulaic, standardized, and structured approaches. In addition, point-based rubrics and penalties in all stages of a five-step writing process were followed with a required final submission for scoring by their teacher.

Rosalba, a preservice teacher, recalled her public schooling as heavily dominated by standardized assessments and rote learning and no self-regulation. She explained, "All they cared about was that I practiced and passed tests. Then, we all were retained or promoted. I lost friends due to this, too. That's just how it works. I didn't like writing for this main reason mostly." These learning conditions driven by rote memorization confirm what Ruth Culham exhorts for teachers: "Our rallying cry should be, 'Texts not tests.' Every student deserves a highly qualified writing and reading teacher and a wealth of reading and writing resources—no matter where they live: urban or rural; the North, South, East, or West" (12).

On the other hand, specific writing forms held certain ideas about writing that influenced the preservice teachers' beliefs about learning to write and teaching it. For instance, Susana, a preservice teacher, detailed a specific writing form with techniques she had to master and added, "You had to know what you were going to persuade somebody about in your writing, or else you'd fail. If I couldn't argue my thoughts very well on paper, well, I was totally screwed. Really. I'm not kidding." In contrast, her colleague Holly who attended two, high-performing secondary schools, insisted,

> Look, I was ready to do the writing for tests, because we had studied this long before high school. Audience was significant for our writing, and we were trained to write to get it over with. My teachers felt interrupted by tests, because they had more excitement about the authors they wanted us to read, know, and like like they did.

In contrast, creative writing was perceived as limiting and abstract and thus unwelcome in the English language arts classroom of their secondary schooling. Creative writing was not held in regard for promotion and college readiness, since it was not academic enough in the eyes of their teachers. They explained that while students wrote, teachers handled administrative responsibilities in their classes and monitored their task-based lessons. Writing became a solitary labor with punitive consequences and, for some, rewarding results. Holly continued, "It was sink or swim, and you had to be ready to adapt to [the course assignments and state tests]."

Overall, students did not observe their teachers poised as writers, critics, editors, and researchers with think alouds and elaborative rehearsals, which are relevant to writing as design and process. In the interviews, the preservice teachers recalled their secondary schooling being dominated by authority, control, and compliance. To write became a laborious, and even regimented, task with an absence of personal expression and a looming threat of point deductions or, even worse, the risk of course failure. Their beliefs and experiences dug deeper into the convictions they held about writing as future teachers. Some of the convictions noted by the preservice teachers in their first assignment during the semester were as follows:

> Esmeralda: "Writing is the key to success in the professional world."
>
> Holly: "Writing is complex, and reading and writing are intrinsically linked together."
>
> Rosalba: "Writers develop through encouragement and support."
>
> Sebastian: "Writing draws on every aspect of human knowledge."
>
> Susana: "All students need positive feedback with their writing."
>
> Timoteo: "To become a writer requires lots of reading. Imitate others."

As their professor, I wanted to work with them to either sustain or expand their stated beliefs about writing. It would be helpful if they gained *Framework* concepts and contexts for "making adjustments," as noted by Jeff Anderson, to define and enact a writing life with expertise and rigor as professionals, creative educators, and writers (10).

Metacognitive Persistence

All six preservice teachers explained that metacognition as defined by Martinez helped them notice their thinking and ways to regulate and assess their thinking habits. At the same time, Rosalba and Holly explained that they, who had adapted to the task-based, regimented assignments, could now exercise the habit of mind of persistence to reach a goal of their choosing. To take a case in point regarding a change in thinking, Sebastian explained that he had not questioned the writing instruction he received, and thus without the *Framework*'s habits of mind, he believed his academic and writing challenges were strictly of his own making. He confirmed that other factors affected his writing processes and even disdain for the act of writing toward deficit perspectives.

The preservice teachers were assigned *Several Short Sentences about Writing* by Verlyn Klinkenborg to examine the study and teaching of writing, especially to revisit what emerging writers endure when metacognitive persistence is neither supported nor modeled for students. Klinkenborg asserts that the role of metacognition and self-regulated learning is paramount: "Who's going to give you the authority to feel that what *you* notice is important? It will have to be you" (37). The *Framework* notes that "writers think through ideas, problems, and issues; identify and challenge assumptions; and explore multiple ways of understanding; . . . move past obvious or surface-level interpretations and use writing to make sense of and respond to written, visual, verbal, and other texts that they encounter" (O'Neill et al. 530). This can be fostered through writing as a process as Klinkenborg states: "Being a writer is an act of perpetual self-authorization. No matter who you are. Only you can authorize yourself" (37). The self-authorization leads to self-discovery and self-regulation for the writer.

Consequently, there was shared agreement in the interview and writings I reviewed from the six preservice teachers about becoming caring, professional teachers who are committed to new methods about how students learn and approaches to writing that include metacognitive persistence. They were interested in adopting the *Framework* and designing instructional and learning situations that have students in multiple roles as writers, editors, reviewers, publishers, thinkers, and researchers. The interviews revealed that students can reflect on their own learning history and experience. To elaborate further, in "Reflective Pedagogies and the Metacognitive Turn in College Teaching," Naomi Silver argues, "Students benefit from metacognition because it enables them to reflect on their own thinking and learning processes, to accurately assess what they know and don't know, and then to make good choices for self-regulated learning" (20). Silver's position is instructive and telling in the assignment submitted by Sebastian, a preservice teacher, via a poem. His revisionist poem, "The English Teacher," is a rendition of Collins's, and reads:

> Trying to protect my students' innocence
>
> I tell them the truth about life,
>
> because the most harm to their innocence
>
> are the lies I could tell.

> Ignorance won't prepare them for the harsh realities of the world,
>
> but a proper education will give them a fighting chance at least.
>
> They will meet Jim Crow in Harper's *To Kill a Mockingbird* and write about where he lives today.
>
> They will meet Big Brother in Orwell's *1984*, and reflect on where he stays.

The poem communicates a preservice teacher's teaching beliefs as he engages students' habits of mind, encouraging them to question what they read and value cultural knowledge across the disciplines. Based on the critical literacies of noticing and questioning, the preservice teachers possessed, like Sebastian, an acumen that communicated they were "well positioned to meet the writing challenges in the full spectrum of academic courses and later in their [professional teaching] careers" (O'Neill et al. 526).

Cultural Knowledge/Wealth

The writing assignment about reader identity and the teaching of reading revealed the six preservice teachers' motivations to read and write and the diverse background knowledge they possessed and believed could benefit their reading and teaching experiences and their students' engagement, too. In particular, they found Miller and Kelley's advice and strategies to cultivate a lifelong love of reading among "wild readers" as relevant and instructive for building a community of readers and writers—in and out of school settings (11). One discussion focused on Miller and Kelley's key habits that wild readers follow: (1) dedicate time to read, (2) self-select reading material, (3) share books and reading with other readers, (4) have reading plans, and (5) show preferences. Rosalba explained,

> It makes sense to dedicate classroom libraries and to welcome students' interests, preferences, and critiques about what they read and seek to read. I want students to know they can value and that I value Spanish as their home language or any other language. Although it may be hard for some of us to recall our adolescence, our students need understanding and support with an open mind from us and that we value how they see and interpret the world in and out of school. By keeping this in mind,

> I want to be able to build trust with my students, learn from them and their writing, and teach with an understanding that will help them find their own reader-writer identity.

For the preservice teacher Esmeralda, the literature written by US writers of Mexican descent and from the Paso del Norte Region were absent in her public schooling and thus were not studied in her English and Spanish language arts classes. She explained, "I would have wanted to read Dagoberto Gilb, Rafael Jesús González, Gloria López-Stafford, and Pat Mora, but we didn't. I am reading them now as a student teacher, but these weren't choices for me as a reader and beginning writer then. Now that I'm learning about how to use mentor texts, I can teach these writers to speak with more texts my students can consider in an open dialogue." Esmeralda's schooling experiences confirm how dominant cultural values and belief systems influence historical narratives, a point made cogently by Antonia Dardner: "[A]ll readings of history are constructed within a set of values and beliefs that shape the ontological and epistemological interpretations given to particular societal relationships and events" (15).

One preservice teacher in the field, Timoteo, embedded literary works with excerpts into his *Julius Caesar* and *Antigone* lesson plans that he co-taught with a mentor teacher at his assigned high school. Timoteo worked closely with his mentor teacher, and he introduced classic literary works with modern, digital perspectives through Thug Notes, which is a literary web series that summarizes and analyzes various literary works through comedy and contemporary linguistic innovation advanced by youth. His explanation about why he would need to remain abreast of popular culture and digital technologies affirms the *Framework*'s emphasis on adolescents being able to "create writing using everything from traditional pen and paper to electronic technologies" (O'Neill et al. 532). Timoteo wrote,

> As a teacher, I have to make sure I do not fall behind and lose my connection with students. I want them to use self-regulation and to notice their thinking. While volunteering in a few high schools, I noticed that many of the students had negative views on reading and writing. The reason I believe is because so few can relate in any way to the reading material and writing assignments that can include media and what they watch and know outside of school. I will make sure to keep challenging myself

and never forget that writing and reading are a continuous process. If I lose my connection with students and what they like and dislike, it will be much harder to approach them with reading or writing.

Timoteo recognized the need to foster promising reading and writing conditions that allow adolescents to apply their cultural knowledge while negotiating secondary classrooms in which they are often unfairly scrutinized. He made connections to students' lives that are more holistic and useful with key experiences noted and even absent in the *Framework* and *Beliefs*. Timoteo was perceptive about the attitudes, conventions, and environments that are conducive to writing instruction and literary studies and will seek to embed these in his lesson planning.

Conversely, the *Framework* articulates openness as a habit of mind, yet as Andrea Feldman gently critiques the document in chapter 5 of this volume, native and diverse cultures of the US, including international influences and concepts, are not mentioned in the document in a way that informs educators about possibilities for integrating diverse perspectives that welcome students' prior knowledge and ways of knowing that are independent of the schooling process and dominant cultures and hierarchies that can create disparate treatment of students home languages in English language arts classrooms. As teachers in formation, Esmeralda and Timoteo realized that they can directly influence students' interests and engagement in their English language arts classroom. Essentially, they argue that all literature can be culturally relevant and responsive to students' lives if it explores inner and external conflicts across time.

Conclusion

With opportunities to question the writing instruction they received that informed their belief system, the preservice teachers expanded the conversations to include *Framework*-influenced habits of mind and cultural knowledge that inform their learning, teaching, and self-reflection. In the preparation of these language arts teachers, metacognitive persistence and cultural knowledge became hallmarks of the habits of mind. In rhetoric and composition, language hierarchies once placed the English language as the supreme language of argument and intellect, but the *Framework* attempts to offer ways to expand our thinking with an openness to the "perspectives of others" (4). However, the *Framework* would benefit by including global awareness and linguistic diversity in the development of rhetorical skills. In "It Is All in the Attitude–The Language Attitude," Isabel Baca notes, "A bicultural individual, for example, a Mexican American, is not two monoculturals; the bicultural individual combines and blends the two cultures to produce a unique cultural configuration" (152). The configuration Baca describes is central to the human diaspora, world languages, and cultural knowledge that preservice teachers and secondary-school students bring into our classrooms. Students with bicultural or multicultural inquiry possess habits of mind that are altogether diverse and significant and can complement our writing instruction and literary studies when we design instruction that values students' background and prior knowledge.

A central premise of the *Framework* is that "teaching writing and learning to write are central to education and to the development of a literate citizenry" that reflects our democratic principles and beliefs in the twenty-first century (O'Neill et al. 526). By examining students' conceptions about writing, building students' metacognitive persistence, and integrating students' cultural knowledge in teacher education courses, teacher educators can use the *Framework* to advance concepts and build assignments that adopt and critique the *Framework* toward realizations of their own that work. Through the development of writing assignments and by modeling the habits of mind that value culturally relevant pedagogy, students can gain rhetorical awareness for the twenty-first century as identified in the *Framework*.

Nieto's description of what it takes to thrive as classroom teachers includes, and with no surprise, two habits of mind that appear in the *Framework*. Nieto acknowledges, "[Teaching] takes humility, a willingness to learn, an openness to acknowledging and valuing the tremendous assets of students of diverse backgrounds, and a commitment to public education" (xiv). As such, our work is yet to be done as we build more communities of writers toward a reading and writing life that sustains them through metacognitive persistence and values their cultural knowledge.

Works Cited

Anderson, Jeff. *10 Things Every Writer Needs to Know*. Portland, ME: Stenhouse P, 2011. Print.

Baca, Isabel. "It's All in the Attitude—The Language Attitude." *Teaching Writing with Latino/a Students: Lessons Learned at Hispanic-Serving Institutions*.

Ed. Christina Kirklighter, Diana Cárdenas, and Susan Wolff Murphy. Albany, NY: State UP of New York, 2007. 145–67. Print.

Calkins, Lucy McCormick. *The Art of Teaching Writing*. Portsmouth, NH: Heinemann, 1994. Print.

Council of Writing Program Administrators, National Council of Teachers of English, and National Writing Project. *Framework for Success in Postsecondary Writing*. CWPA, NCTE, and NWP, 2011. PDF File.

Culham, Ruth. *The Writing Thief: Using Mentor Texts to Teach the Craft of Writing*. Newark, DE: International Reading Association, 2014. Print.

Dardner, Antonia. *Freire and Education*. New York: Routledge, 2015. Print.

Freire, Paulo. *Pedagogy of the Oppressed*. Trans. Myra Bergman Ramos. New York: Bloomsbury Academic, 2000. Print.

Galliano, Joseph. *Dear Me: A Letter to My Sixteen-Year-Old Self*. New York: Atria Books, 2011. Print.

Gay, Geneva. *Culturally Responsive Teaching: Theory, Research, and Practice*. 2nd ed. New York: Teachers College Press, 2010. Print.

Klinkenborg, Verlyn. *Several Short Sentences about Writing*. New York: Vintage, 2013. Print.

Ladson-Billings, Gloria. *The Dreamkeepers: Successful Teachers of African American Children*. 2nd ed. San Francisco: Jossey-Bass, 2009. Print.

Martinez, Michael E. "What Is Metacognition?" *Phi Delta Kappan* 87.9 (2006): 696–99. Print.

Miller, Donalyn, and Susan Kelley. *Reading in the Wild: The Book Whisperer's Keys to Cultivating Lifelong Reading Habits*. San Francisco, CA: Jossey-Bass, 2014. Print.

Moon, Sarah. *The Letter Q: Queer Writers' Letters to their Younger Selves*. New York: Arthur A. Levine Books, 2012. Print.

Muhammad, Gholnecsar E. "Searching for Full Vision: Writing Representations of African American Adolescent Girls." *Research in the Teaching of English* 49.3 (2015): 224–47. Print.

National Council of Teachers of English. *NCTE Beliefs about the Teaching of Writing*. Writing Study Group of the Executive Committee of the National Council of Teachers of English, 29 July 2014. Web. 14 May 2015.

National Governors Association Center for Best Practices and Council of Chief State School Officers. *Common Core State Standards for English Language Arts and Literacy in History/Social Studies, Science, and Technical Subjects*. Washington, DC: National Governors Association and Council of Chief State School Officers, 2010. Print.

Nieto, Sonia. *Finding Joy in Teaching Students of Diverse Backgrounds: Culturally Responsive and Socially Just Practices in U.S. Classrooms*. Portsmouth, NH: Heinemann, 2013. Print

O'Neill, Peggy, Linda Adler-Kassner, Cathy Fleischer, and Anne-Marie Hall. "Creating the *Framework for Success in Postsecondary Writing*." *Symposium:*

On the Framework for Success in Postsecondary Writing. Spec. issue of *College English* 74.2 (2012): 520–53. Print.

Pine, Gerald J. *Teacher Action Research: Building Knowledge Democracies*. Thousand Oaks, CA: SAGE Publications, 2009. Print.

Ritchart, Ron, and Mark Church. *Making Thinking Visible: How to Promote Engagement, Understanding, and Independence for All Learners*. San Francisco: Jossey-Bass, 2011. Print.

Sheridan, Mary P., and Lee Nickoson. "Introduction: Current on Writing Research." *Writing Studies Research in Practice: Methods and Methodologies*. Ed. Lee Nickoson and Mary P. Sheridan. Carbondale: Southern Illinois UP, 2015. 1–12. Print.

Silver, Naomi. "Reflective Pedagogies and the Metacognitive Turn in College Teaching." *Using Reflection and Metacognition to Improve Student Learning: Across the Disciplines, Across the Academy*. Ed. Matthew Kaplan, Naomi Silver, Danielle LaVaque-Manty, and Deborah Meizlish. Sterling, VA: Stylus, 2013. 1–17. Print

Summerfield, Judith, and Philip M. Anderson. "A Framework Adrift." *Symposium: On the Framework for Success in Postsecondary Writing*. Spec. issue of *College English* 74.2 (2012): 544–47. Print.

Tanner, Kimberly D. "Promoting Student Metacognition." *CBE—Life Sciences Education* 11 (2012): 113–20. Print.

Winn, Maisha T., and Latrise Johnson. *Writing Instruction in the Culturally Relevant Classroom*. Urbana, IL: National Council of Teachers of English, 2011. Print.

Yin, Robert K. *Applications of Case Study Research*. 3rd ed. Thousand Oaks, CA: SAGE Publications, 2011. Print.

—. *Case Study Research: Design and Methods*. 5th ed. Thousand Oaks, CA: SAGE Publications, 2013. Print.

14 Using the Eight Habits of Mind to Foster Critical Sustained Reflections: Active Teaching and Learning

Angela Clark-Oates

Systematically and critically reflecting on pedagogical choices can provide teachers opportunities to engage in a praxis-oriented approach to teaching and to redefine teaching as an action and a reflection. Reflective habits have the potential to encourage practitioners to explore, grapple, improve, and refine their practice over time, but for practitioners to use a reflective practice to hone pedagogical, practical, and theoretical knowledge, they must be intentional about recording and documenting, collecting and sorting, and reading and analyzing. By collecting, organizing, and reflecting on these artifacts, reflective practitioners can make informed decisions about curriculum revision, assessments, and students' engagement/disengagement. They also are able to produce knowledge and theorize their practice. This praxis-oriented approach—developed through critical reflection—also illuminates the recursive process of teaching and can help foster a kind of professional stamina (Martin 23).

But, the process for engaging in systematic reflection can be elusive, especially when considering the ubiquity of the idea. More than twenty-five years ago, Lee Shulman, past President of the Carnegie Foundation and Emeritus Professor at Stanford University, fleshed out a cycle for pedagogical reasoning and action. He defined reflection as "reviewing, reconstructing, reenacting, and critically analyzing one's own and the class's performance, and grounding explanations in evidence" ("Knowledge and Teaching" 15). Since then, universities, colleges, departments, units, and teaching and learning centers have used reflection as a necessary component in building an "active scholarship of teaching" (Shulman, "From Minsk to Pinsk"). Similarly, qualitative research approaches that call for rigorous reflective habits—action research, practitioner research, teacher research/teacher inquiry—have emerged from the same research paradigm championed by Shulman, what he called the study of "classroom ecology" (qtd. in Cochran-Smith and Lytle, *Inside/Outside* 6). Teacher research/inquiry is a deliberate *seeing*, a documenting of a teacher's ability to make the familiar strange through research and writing by pursuing curiosities of the classrooms (Cochran-Smith and Lytle, *Inside/Outside* and *Inquiry as Stance*). In crafting an insider's eye to research, teachers commit to re-craft classrooms, students, and schools, and as these research approaches were taken up by teacher scholars and championed in K–12 schools, post-secondary institutions, and community sites, reflection—as a systematized and rigorous practice—became less amorphous. Reflection was not merely improvisation in the classroom based on an emotion or instinct or a curriculum revision based on a hallway conversation with a colleague. As a result, practitioners were (are) using rigorous reflective habits to generate local knowledge. Moreover, this critical and sustained practice, when coupled with other methodologies, also has the potential to lead to what Cochran-Smith and Lytle call "the interplay of teaching and learning, the synergies of learning and leading, the synthesis of theorizing and acting, and the continuous reinvention of ways of connecting to and allying with colleagues, parents, and communities" (*Inquiry as Stance* 132).

When integrated into the research process, reflection becomes a much more tangible practice, but how do practitioners, particularly those who are new to the field, begin to develop daily habits of teaching that allow for the deliberate development and growth of reflective habits? How do they sustain an active and engaged practice that allows for teaching to become what Garth Boomer calls a "deliberate learning"? (5). First, practitioners must have a clear understanding of how reflection can support their teaching. Second, they must construct reflective habits that are critical and sustainable. Finally, they need a framework for focusing their reflective habits. In this chapter, I first define the term *critical sustained reflection*, grounding this definition in my knowledge and research as a teacher educator and practitioner researcher to illustrate the importance of reflection. I then turn to the eight habits of mind—curiosity, openness, engagement, creativity, persistence, responsibility, flexibility, and metacognition—in the *Framework for Success in Postsecondary Writing*, a document drafted to support the teaching and learning of writing in universities and colleges, to show how practitioners can use these habits to focus their reflective habits. Although the *Framework* has traditionally been used to support students in the writing classroom, I argue that it is also a document that can be used to support faculty development, an argument that is well-supported by other scholars in this volume, like Peter Khost in chapter 9 and Alice Johnston Myatt and Ellen Shelton in chapter 12. By using the eight habits of mind to foster a critically sustained reflective practice, practitioners are encouraged to renew their engagement with students and curriculum and to make visible their responsibility to ask critical questions about their practice, their classroom, and their students. Because critical sustained reflection, as I define it below, asks practitioners to explore and engage with other teachers and scholars, practitioners will also have more opportunities to construct new habits of knowing and ways of being, which can eventually lead them to disrupt assumptions guiding what they know and how they practice. In short, by embedding the language of the habits of mind into their reflections, practitioners may have more opportunity to engage new epistemologies for teaching and learning.

Defining Critical Sustained Reflection

I define *critical sustained reflection* as the theoretical, pedagogical, and practical investigation of beliefs, values, and experiences, where constructions of reality are examined and imagined possibilities are explored with others. To conceptualize *critical sustained reflection*, I also reimagine a practitioner as someone who understands teaching and learning as a stage in motion, where the actors are always unfinished in their movement to become *the* student or *the* teacher (Bahktin 348), which means as a practitioner structures learning opportunities for students to appropriate new knowledge, new discourses, and new academic mores, she is also always grappling with her own ideas and beliefs about this knowledge, these discourses, and these academic mores. It is in the moment of choosing—to agree to meet a curriculum or a text, deciding on text-based or new media projects, requiring peer review or group projects—where a practitioner should be engaged in critical sustained reflection, reflection that is informed by the eight habits of mind.

To articulate a definition for reflection that has the potential to be critical and sustainable, my definition also has Deweyan undertones. The idea of reflection that is so prevalent in the literature on teaching and learning and teacher research, which is where I first discovered it, can be traced back to John Dewey when he writes that, "Active, persistent, and careful consideration of any belief or supposed form of knowledge in light of the grounds that support it, and the further conclusions to which it tends, constitutes reflective thought" (6). Carol Rodgers reminds us in "Defining Reflection" that Dewey understood reflection to be "a complex, rigorous, intellectual, and emotional enterprise that takes time to do well" (844). Similarly, she relies on Dewey again in "Seeing Student Learning" when she defines the processs of reflection as "rigorous and systematic and therefore distinct from ordinary thought . . . [as] slow[ing] down the teaching/learning process, revealing rich and complex details, allowing for appreciation, and paving the way for a considered response rather than a less thoughtful reaction" (232).

Situating Critical Sustained Reflection: A Pilot Study

To situate and support my assertion about critical sustained reflection, I share data (collected under a standing IRB) from an action research project I designed to study the relationship between fostering the habits of mind and the reflective habits of undergraduate and graduate students working in a writing fellows program embedded in an online first-year composition program at a large public university. As the writing program administrator for the Writers' Studio, an online first-year composition program, I hired, supervised, and mentored these students, who also took a fifteen-week practicum course from me during their first semester as a writing fellow. I designed the practicum course to support their development as emerging practitioners because in their role as writing fellows, they foster discussion among students, provide asynchronous written and audio feedback on students' text-based and new media projects, and participate in one-on-one writing conferences with students.

My research questions were as follows: How do the eight habits of mind from the *Framework*, used as a guiding framework for structured reflective prompts, encourage a more in-depth reflection from the writing fellows? As the program manager, how can I support writing fellows to sustain a daily practice of systematic reflection using the habits of mind as a framework? In using the eight habits of mind as a framework for reflection, how will this better prepare writing fellows to foster these habits in students?

THE WRITERS' STUDIO, THE EIGHT HABITS OF MIND, AND A PRACTICE OF REFLECTION

The Writers' Studio is a fully online first-year composition program housed in the College of Letters and Sciences at Arizona State University (ASU). The courses offered by the Writers' Studio are available to any student seeking a face-to-face degree on any of ASU's four campuses or any student seeking a degree from ASU Online. The Writers' Studio has approximately 2,600 students enroll per year in one of our first-year composition courses across fall, spring, and summer terms. We offer the standard two-semester course sequence as English 101 and 102, as well as English 105, an accelerated one-semester course, and for each course, students have a choice of enrolling in either a fifteen-week or a seven-and-a-half-week version.

During the semester, we ask each student to complete two projects and design and curate an e-portfolio for their projects, drafts, and reflections. Both major projects include a substantial academic essay and a new media text. For each project, students also reflect on their learning through the lens of the *Framework*, addressing the WPA outcomes and the habits of mind. As I have written elsewhere, metacognition is "an indispensible element of the Writers' Studio" (Clark-Oates, Boggess, and Roen 135). And, because the habits of mind are foundational to how we approach learning in the Writers' Studio, using them as foundational to how we approached teaching allowed me to align my vision for learning and teaching in our first-year composition courses.

Based on my experiences as a teacher educator and a teacher researcher, in the spring of 2013, a semester after I began my tenure as the administrator for the Writers' Studio, I asked the writing faculty—instructors, faculty associates, and course coordinators—to commit to crafting weekly reflections about their online teaching practice. My goal was to design meaningful faculty development opportunities from ideas that emerged from their reflections while encouraging them to assign structured time to look critically at their practice in an online classroom. I did not make this a programmatic requirement; I asked the faculty to participate voluntarily. In our spring meeting, I briefly discussed the value and virtues of teaching from a reflective space. Two faculty took the challenge, so the three of us spent seven-and-a-half weeks sporadically documenting our practice. Our reflections weren't structured or sustained. We shared our reflections with one another, which prompted a rich exchange of ideas and encouraging words of support, but we did not produce substantial or critical reflections. This experience led me to think deeply about the importance of approaching reflection as a more structured process, much like the process of reflection in which we asked our students to engage. Moreover, this experience influenced my decision to design an action research project, a project that would move my gaze from the faculty teaching in the program to the undergraduate and graduate writing fellows hired to work as embedded writing tutors. In this way, I could require writing fellows to craft weekly reflections for a teaching journal. This was a much more accessible and controlled research site because all new writing fellows are required to participate in a fifteen-week internship with me.

An Unstructured Approach to Critical Sustained Reflection: Writing Fellows Reflect

My mentorship of writing fellows, whether in training sessions, one-on-one conferences, or through the course curriculum, emerges from the idea that "the most productive starting place for teachers' professional development is their own classroom experiences" (Rodgers, "Seeing Student Learning" 232). And, although in the internship course I asked the fellows to read and discuss foundational texts in the fields of rhetoric and composition, literacy studies, English education, and writing center work, I also asked them to craft a teaching journal focused on their experiences in the online classroom. Additionally, I asked them, much like the students in our first-year composition courses, to design and curate an e-portfolio where they reflected on their teaching experiences through the lens of the *Framework* and the learning outcomes for the course. I did provide some minimal structure for the e-portfolio, such as giving examples from prior semesters, instructions on how to access and use Web page creation tools like Google Sites and Wordpress, a rubric, and suggestions for organizing artifacts. But, for the first few semesters I taught the internship course and much like my approach to faculty reflections, I provided minimal guidance on the content or form for the reflective, teaching journal beyond some guiding questions (that they were not required to use): How are you incorporating the language of the *Framework* into your feedback practices? What strategies work the best or the worst for providing feedback that allows students to practice their literacy practices differently? What are your goals for the following semester given your success and failures? Regardless of these guiding questions, the writing fellows' entries were crafted either as a list of tasks they had completed or a list of complaints about students. For most of the fellows, neither the e-portfolio nor the teaching journal fostered critical sustained reflections.

Instead, the majority of the fellows' reflective practice can be described as, what Rodgers calls, "an imprecise picture," one that revealed an easy dismissal of the practice instead of what Dewey identifies as "a complex, rigorous, intellectual, and emotional enterprise that takes time do well" (qtd. in Rodgers, "Defining Reflection" 844). To address this dearth of rigor and complexity in the writing fellows' reflections, similar to what I had experienced when working with the faculty, I redesigned the process for the reflective practice, focusing specifically on writing fellows' teaching journal. To craft a process that would foreground the habits of mind, I used Rodgers' reflective cycle to construct a more structured approach for the writing fellows to engage in.

A Reflective Cycle and The Habits of Mind

Carol Rodgers identifies four phases of reflection as a framework for fostering practitioners' abilities "to 'see' the world, to be present to it and all its complexities" ("Seeing Student Learning" 230): (1) presence in experience: learning to see; (2) description of experience: learning to describe; (3) analysis of experience: learning to think from multiple perspectives and form multiple explanations; and (4) experimentation: learning to take intelligent action. She describes the cycle as fostering presence that is "inclusive of several disparate acts that together comprise the whole process of reflection . . . *in the moment and from moment to moment*" ("Seeing Student Learning" 235). And it's her focus on presence and its implications for how to be in the world that illustrates the importance of using a practice of reflection to foster the habits of mind in practitioners.

Presence in Experience: Learning to See

In this phase, reflective practitioners learn to be present in students' learning so that they can respond with thoughtful and informed instruction. In her explication of the phase, Rodgers refers to Dewey's concept of being alive in the classroom. By being aware of students' emotional, cognitive, and bodily expressions, practitioners are able to do more than cover the material ("Seeing Student Learning" 236). Moreover, when teachers construct a presence undergirded by the qualities of love and passion, their reflective process emerges from their curiosity, openness, and engagement. And when curiosity, openness, and engagement are fostered, practitioners are much more likely to disrupt their positionality and model these habits for their students. These three habits of mind have the potential to develop a passion for connecting with others, which can translate to many more academic, professional, and personal successes.

Description: Learning to Describe and Interpret

In this phase of the reflective cycle, practitioners should craft thick descriptions (Geertz) of their experiences, which means being descriptive and interpretive (Ely et al.). First, practitioners should observe writing details about the context, the participants, the tone of the environment, and even snippets of discourse, reserving their interpretation as a separate experience, one that moves reflection from observation to inquiry. This phase of the cycle encourages creativity and responsibility. This distinction between description and interpretation is the hallmark of an experienced teacher researcher, and understanding this distinction, as a reflective practitioner, is critical to developing an ethnographic eye. Therefore, the reflective practitioner must experiment and play—fostering creativity—to find a method for capturing moments through a craft of description. Once the practitioner begins to interpret the observation, then she begins interpreting these moments, and it is through the craft of interpretation that responsibility can be fostered, especially when these reflections are shared in a community, when reflection is made public. Rodgers describes reflections made public as opportunities for others to "coax the teacher beyond the boundaries of her own necessarily limited perceptions by fleshing out the details, filling in the missing pieces, and looking at the incident from a number of different standpoints" ("Seeing Student Learning" 240). And finally, in this phase, the reflective practitioner also opens herself up to feedback from peers and students. When participating in a practice of reflection that fosters creativity, responsibility, and openness, a teacher allows for shifts in her curriculum, her relationships with students, and in her methods for engaging students in learning. And this type of openness, I would argue, has the possibility to construct relationships and ideas that might allow practitioners to do what Ken Macrorie calls, "doing something that makes a difference in a researcher's life and the lives of others" (54–55).

Analysis of Experience: Learning to Think Critically and Construct Theory

This phase of the cycle focuses on developing a practice of analysis, one that emerges from the practice of interpretation. This phase fosters persistence and metacognition, as the practitioner must be in constant movement among the moment, making meaning of the moment, and experimenting to shift the meaning. It takes a sustainable practice and commitment to participate in a meaning-making process that "moves a learner from one experience into the next with deeper understanding of its relationships with and connections to other experiences and ideas" ("Defining Reflection" 843), but it also depends on a developed capacity for metacognition.

Experimentation: Learning to Take Intelligent Action

In this final phase of reflection, the practitioner acts on the reflection, engaging in what I called earlier in this chapter a praxis-oriented approach to teaching. In this last phase, the practitioner must rely on a confluence of the habits of mind to participate in the cycle of reflection that begins again the moment the experimentation occurs, what Rodgers describes as taking risk and persisting "for second, third, and fourth tries, each of which is text for further reflection and offers an opportunity to practice being present to the dazzling intricacy of teaching and learning" ("Seeing Student Learning" 250).

Structured Critical Sustained Reflections: A New Practice for Writing Fellows

Rodgers's articulation of a reflective cycle influenced my decision to construct a more structured and guided approach for writing fellows to use when crafting their teaching journals. Each week in the course, I designed a reflective prompt to guide their journal entries, prompts that emerged from their experiences with students, programmatic expectations for student learning, and their interpretations of both. Below, I share one prompt that aligns with each phase of Rodgers' cycle and provide examples from the writing fellows' teaching journals.

Learning to See

To provide opportunities for writing fellows to learn presence in the classroom, I asked them during week two to reflect on the connection between their digital literacy narratives and their writing fellow practice by noticing how key experiences tie those two things together, how their developing fellow practice was influenced by their past literacy experiences, and how their own relationship with literacy might impact their relationship with students. This structured prompt was designed to foster curiosity, openness, and engagement for writing fellows. Jason's response illustrates how this structured approach encouraged him to connect his past experiences with the current experiences of students, as well as articulate his desire to use empathy. I would argue that his use of the word empathy hints at his openness to find common ground between him and students as a way to establish a relatable space where he can engage with them and their work. He writes,

> The ability for me to intertwine my experiences with literature and finding my own narrative voice will allow me to become relatable to my students and to empathize with their own emerging writing style.

Similarly, Misty reveals the same sort of desire to do more than cover the material, to engage with them. She writes,

> I have also developed compassion and understanding for the struggles of others in some areas of literacy. I have had my own struggles in challenging courses . . . this impacts my relationship to the students in similar ways, by understanding them as peers who have authority over their own work and who also have literacy.

Both Jason and Misty, through the process of structured reflection, demonstrated a desire to be present with their students. They did not discuss their students as isolated skills that needed to be fixed. Instead, the prompt encouraged them to engage with their students with an openness that will allow them to see their own faces in the faces of their students.

Learning to Describe

In week 1, I asked writing fellows to describe their experiences with the habits of mind, describing contexts where they rely on them, describing their importance, and then finally moving to a more interpretive space by asking them to craft a rationale for why we should foster these habits of mind in our students. In focusing on description and interpretation—the idea of thick description discussed earlier in the chapter—I structured this prompt to foster responsibility and creativity.

Mary writes,

> The eight habits of mind are ways of thinking [sic] learning that are completely applicable to everyday life and can be used inside and outside the classroom. I rely on these habits everyday to [sic] the best version of myself I can be as college student [sic] and active member of society. . . . If you start off writing and learning with these habits, they will become second nature to a student's process and final product. . . . One of the habits I would emphasize with my students is engagement. . . . I would hone this habit in my students my [sic] asking many questions when I give feedback to get them involved in their writing. . . . Lastly, I would like to use tutor practices to instill creativity. I want my students to get out of their comfort zones in their writing and take a risk with it.

By participating in this structured approach to reflection, Mary moved from description to interpretation of how fostering creativity in her students would impact their learning. Mary is acting responsibly by observing the needs of her students and then relating those needs to her own experience as a student. Sharing in the teaching journal encourages Mary to live her idea about fostering creativity in a public space, where it can be examined and critiqued. This, too, fosters a practice of responsibility.

Learning to Analyze

Halfway through the semester, I asked writing fellows to critique the habits of mind, providing them with the following guiding questions: What are the weaknesses of using these habits as anchors for learning in our courses? Is our course curriculum designed to foster these habits? If not, should it be and how can we revise it to make sure we are fostering these habits? What is forgotten or left out when we focus on the habits of mind? These questions were crafted to foster persistence, flexibility, and metacognition. To answer these questions, the fellows had to reflect on both their presence in the classroom and their description of the habits from week one, and despite critiques, they would have to continue to foster a sustainable writing fellow practice that fostered these habits of mind, being flexible in their choice of methods. Misty writes,

> When we focus on the habits of mind in our classroom specifically, I wonder if perhaps students have a harder time anchoring their work to the concrete. For example, we work on rhetorical analysis to foster curiosity and metacognition, but students don't know how to analyze their own work rhetorically. Or we try to do things like the multimodal analysis to foster creativity, but students don't fully understand what the multimodal portion is or how it's relevant in the "real world." I think it might be real-world relevance I'm trying to get at here—we can try all we want to get students to have certain habits of mind, but until they understand concretely how what they're producing applies to what they will be doing in their careers or in the 'real world,' they won't be able to apply those habits outside the classroom.
>
> All in all, I'm not fully sure about the negative sides of the habits of mind. I don't know how they tie in to some of the failings I do see or if they are tied in at all. But I do think they perhaps focus too much on the abstract and don't focus enough on concrete points of success/improvement. After all, how do you measure how creative a student is or how much more engaged they've become over the course of the class? I'm not sure.

In this reflection, Misty is digging into not just the practical application of the habits of mind, but a more conceptual wrangling. She also feels comfortable admitting that her musings are still exploratory at this point, not ready for experimentation through action. In this way, her entry shows that the structured prompt fostered persistence and flexibility.

Experimentation

For week seven, I asked writing fellows to experiment with the idea of revision in the following prompt: In his memoir *Mentor*, Grimes writes, "Revision is an act of hope." How can the act of revision help students foster the eight habits of mind from the *Framework*? Or, better yet, what kind of revision practice could students construct that would foster their curiosity, openness, engagement, creativity, persistence, responsibility, flexibility, and metacognition? How can you mentor students to build a revision practice like the one you described? Opening a space for writing fellows to flex their expertise is an opportunity for them to participate in public feedback; it's an opportunity for me to mentor them by example by showing them that "the first step toward action takes place within the group, where teachers proffer different strategies for dealing with the classroom problems or questions at hand" (Rodgers, "Seeing Student Learning" 249).

In Jason's journal entry, he identifies a tension between the potential of revision being a meaningful practice for developing writers to participate and the actual practice of it in the Writers' Studio. He writes, "I am a tremendous advocate for the revision process. I believe there is no single tool that is greater in forming a successful paper, but also in preparing students to be successful writers." He continues for a few lines until he presents the dissonance:

> Yet I worry that these students don't have the foundation necessary to become successful revisers and editors . . . insofar as the 7.5-week term is concerned, I don't see a lot of room for development . . . to try to teach those [marginal skills] that need the 8 habits of mind most and to utilize an effective revising strategy in such a condensed amount of time seems as though we're not hav[ing] much "hope," as Grimes would say, for the students in the first place.

This tension for Jason needed to be addressed with an intelligent action, something that he could experiment with, but unfortunately, I think he was paralyzed by the semester structure, which neither of us could act on to change. In our one-on-one conference a few weeks later, I asked Jason to craft concrete actions for addressing this tension. How could he develop a feedback practice that allowed the students to experience what he viewed as the greatest potential for revision, which was the scaffolding of the learning of developing writers? He hesitated when I asked, but finally named the tension: "It's the mechanical participation in the revision process" that needed to be addressed. He said he could work more closely with the instructor to provide participation guidelines before peer review, craft more detailed feedback on the students' responses to their peers, and provide examples of students' responses that showed engagement (even in an accelerated course). This structured approach to reflection provided much more opportunities for the writing fellows to develop, hone, and flex their habits of mind.

Conclusion

The authors of the *Framework for Success in Postsecondary Writing* describe students who use the eight habits of mind—curiosity, openness, engagement, creativity, persistence, responsibility, flexibility, and metacognition—as active learners, but to engage these habits fully and hone them through practice, especially in schools, students need to encounter practitioners, whether faculty, teaching assistants, or tutors, who are prepared to develop and engage these habits through intentional curriculum design. To do this effectively, practitioners who foster these habits within themselves and rely on them as they pursue the work of teaching and learning are more likely to be engaged and active teachers. Active teachers are invested teachers, which will better position them to privilege these habits in their curriculum and classrooms.

Accordingly, the eight habits of mind are critical to developing an active teaching practice, a practice that can reclaim teaching spaces through inquiry and discovery. To foster the eight habits of mind through critical sustained reflection, I embedded well-defined opportunities for writing fellows to construct intentional moments in writing that would encourage them to act as agents, to reclaim the collaborative classroom as an intellectual space. When teachers use systematic reflection and design classroom-based research, they begin to authorize their teaching spaces, develop a deeper investment in their teaching and students' learning, and construct collaborative spaces where the value of teaching and learning are renewed.

Works Cited

Bakhtin, Mikhail. *Dialogic Imagination.* Trans. Carl Emerson and Michael Holquist. Austin,Texas: University of Texas Press, 1981. Print.

Boomer, Garth. "Addressing the Problem of Elsewhereness: A Case for Action Research in Schools." Goswami and Stillman 4–12. Print.

Cochran-Smith, Marilyn, and Susan L. Lytle. *Inquiry as Stance: Practitioner Research in the Next Generation.* New York: Teachers College Press, 1999. Print.

—. *Inside/Outside: Teacher Research and Knowledge.* New York: Teachers College P, 1993. Print.

Clark-Oates, Angela, Allyson Boggess, and Duane Roen. "Using the *Framework for Success in Postsecondary Writing to Foster Learning*." *The Next Digital Scholar: A Fresh Approach to the Common Core State Standards in Research and Writing.* Ed. James P. Purdy and Randall McClure. Medford, NJ: Information Today, Inc., 2014. 107–40. Print.

Council of Writing Program Administrators, National Council of Teachers of English, and National Writing Project. *Framework for Success in Postsecondary Writing.* CWPA, NCTE, and NWP, 2011. PDF File.

Dewey, John. *How We Think.* New York: D. C. Heath and Co., 1910. Print

Ely, Margot, Ruth Vinz, Maryann Downing, and Margaret Anzu. *On Writing Qualitative Research: Living by Words.* Philadelphia: Routledge/Falmer, 2001. Print.

Geertz, Clifford. *Interpretation of Cultures.* New York: Basic Books, 1973. Print.

Goswami, Dixie, and Peter Stillman, eds. *Reclaiming the Classroom: Teacher Research as anAgency for Change.* Dixie Portsmouth, NH: Heinemann, 1986. Print.

Grimes, Tom. *Mentor: A Memoir.* New York: Tin House Books, 2010. Print.

Macrorie, Ken. "Research as an Odyssey." Goswami and Stillman 49–60.

Martin, Nancy. "On the Move: Teacher-Researchers" Goswami and Stillman 20–27. Print.

Rodgers, Carol. "Defining Reflection: Another Look at John Dewey and Reflective Thinking." *Teachers College Record* 104.4 (2002): 842–66. Print.

—. "Seeing Student Learning: Teacher Change and the Role of Reflection." *HarvardEducation Review* 72.2 (2002): 230–53. Print.

Shulman, Lee. "From Minsk to Pinsk: What A Scholarship of Teaching and Learning." Annualmeeting of the Carnegie Academy for the Scholarship of Teaching and Learning(CASTL) campus affiliates hosted by the American Association for Higher Education(AAHE). Anaheim, CA. 29 March 2000. Address.

—. "Knowledge and Teaching: Foundations of the New Reform." *Harvard Educational Review* 57.1 (1987): 1–23. Print.

15 A *Framework*-Based "No-Text/Two-Text" Honors Composition Course

Martha A. Townsend

Since the *Framework for Success in Postsecondary Writing* was published, it—along with my university's summer "one-read" book for incoming first-year students—have been the primary texts I use in my first-year honors composition course. With just these two texts, neither of which is a traditional textbook, the students and I accomplish not only the outcomes established by our local writing program but also by the Council of Writing Program Administrators (CWPA) over a decade ago. Both of the *Framework*'s key features, the "WPA Outcomes Statement For First-Year Composition" (WPA OS) and the habits of mind, are integral to my honors course. Five years into the project (four with the *Framework*), the model I use to teach honors students seems to be working well enough to share. Combining observational, reflective, and quantitative data, I describe in this chapter how I use the *Framework* itself as a text; how we use the one-read book; what our assignments are; how students react to this idiosyncratic approach; and what assessment reveals about the class, students' growth as writers, and me as a teacher.

The Power of One Student Comment, or How I Came to This Model

In 2006, I stepped down from a fifteen-year tenure as director of my university's writing-across-the-curriculum program. This career move offered me an opportunity to return to my roots, to first-year composition (FYC) where I had begun my teaching life. The composition program at the large public Midwestern AAU institution where I work allows considerable flexibility for the graduate students and contingent faculty who deliver the vast majority of our writing curriculum. Because all instructors choose their own texts and build their own syllabi, I was free to employ whatever pedagogies I wanted.

One student's comment on a course evaluation years earlier had long stuck with me. Summing up her enthusiasm for the course, the student concluded, "She did all this *on purpose*!" This student's astonished recognition that I had somehow intentionally planned the semester's curriculum surprised me. Did students not think that what we do is by design? Didn't students know that we carefully consider learning outcomes, select texts, sequence assignments, and integrate theory and supplementary material to the best of our ability? What if I were to make "all this" clear to students at the outset of the course? Incorporate it throughout the course? Mindful of Joseph Williams and Gregory Colomb's "The Case for Explicit Teaching," I decided to find out. Even though Williams and Colomb's argument concerns itself with teaching forms and genres of writing, I find it worthwhile to extrapolate their argument to how courses themselves are presented to students. Making the tacit aspects of my course as explicit as possible seems like a worthwhile endeavor. Moreover, doing so is consistent with virtually all of the *Framework*'s premises, especially the habit of metacognition.

From 2007 through 2009, I taught my fall honors course fairly successfully using a highly regarded textbook. After these three iterations, however, I wasn't satisfied with integration of its chapters with the WPA OS. That, plus my university's announcement of Jean Twenge's *Generation Me* as the one-read book for 2010, along with my former student's "She did that on purpose," compelled me to create the "No-Text/Two-Text" course. Just a year later, when the *Framework* was published, I eagerly incorporated the habits of mind into my curriculum.

Syllabus

Front and center on the first page of the syllabus is the WPA OS in brief: (1) Rhetorical Knowledge; (2) Critical Thinking Through Reading, Writing, and Research; (3) Flexible Writing Processes; (4) Knowledge of Conventions; (5) Composing in Multiple Environments; and (6) Ability to Transfer This Knowledge to Other Courses You Will Take. (The revised 2014 WPA OS eliminates the fifth). My sixth outcome—emphasizing transfer of knowledge to other classes—shows how the WPA OS can be adapted by individuals. I explicitly build into the course multiple ways of exploring what it means to transfer learning to other contexts; this outcome meshes nicely with the *Framework*'s habit of metacognition as well. The syllabus's WPA OS section ends with a short description of the three professional organizations that developed the *Framework*. Discussing in class what the CWPA, National Council of Teachers of English (NCTE), and National Writing Project (NWP) are reinforces the idea that the principles on which the class is based have emerged from thoughtful deliberation by professionals who devote their scholarly careers to the teaching of writing. Most students aren't aware that rhetoric and composition is an academic discipline, nor that these professional organizations exist. The syllabus also notes that we will accomplish the outcomes "more or less automatically" as the course proceeds; that is to say, we will do this without benefit of a traditional textbook.

On the first day of class, I conduct a detailed syllabus review. Pedantic as this may seem, it is integral to letting students know what they are expected to learn. Doing this is part of my attempt to make the tacit knowable, to help first-year students who are still "inventing" the university, as Bartholomae would put it, become comfortable in my class. Not until the syllabus's second page do students see the one-read book announced as their text, followed by the usual requisite information: writing center contacts; attendance policy; my teaching philosophy (in a nutshell "classes will be highly interactive, with the responsibility for learning shared by all"); course evaluation schema; and finally, on page three, the university's ADA, plagiarism, privacy, and (now) Title IX policies.

Our composition program's flexibility in texts and methods is offset by a succinct set of parameters within which each instructor must work: a minimum of three formal papers, each requiring revision based on peer review and instructor feedback, along with whatever informal writing the instructor wishes to assign. My grading scheme comprises four parts, each worth 25% of the course grade: Paper 1 is a four-page rhetorical analysis of the entire one-read book; Paper 2 is a four-page research-based, critical "spin off" from the one-read book; Paper 3 is a four-page personal response to the one-read book for a public audience; finally, participation is based on contributions to our classroom community.

The papers are spaced evenly across our fifteen-week semester, into three five-week units. Along with background to contextualize the assignments, each paper is supported by informal writing (based largely on the *Framework*'s eight habits of mind); supplementary material; instructor review; peer review; optional one-on-one consultations with me; and writing center tutorial support, if desired. Papers are scaffolded such that each builds on the outcomes from the previous paper. So far, so good. But this is fairly standard fare, no doubt similar to what many writing instructors do. What's the big deal?

The One-Read Text

The concept of summer reading for first-year college students is hardly new. But the degree to which summer reading programs have changed over the years can be seen in a comparison with the texts that were assigned when I entered the University of Illinois as a freshman in 1965. A list of five books was mailed to my home, with the exhortation that I be ready to discuss them, if not in FYC (called Rhetoric back then), then in other courses as appropriate. The list included Friedrich Nietzsche's *The Genealogy of Morals*, Roger Garrison's *The Adventure of Learning in College: An Undergraduate Guide to Productive Study*, and three others I have blissfully forgotten. All were extraordinarily challenging—too much so for freshman to read without guidance, for which none was given. I certainly hadn't "invented" the University of Illinois well enough to understand what I read. To my immense relief, none of my professors invoked any of them in my freshman classes. I kept the books for years, thinking I would eventually re-read them, before donating them to our graduate students' annual book sale.

If summer reading programs are not new, neither are they without controversy. At the 2012 MLA Conference, for example, the National Association of Scholars and MLA representatives debated the concept with no particular resolution. The panel "Common First-Year Readings/Themes: Practice, Problems, Promise" highlighted the "vexed" nature of such programs (Golden). More problems than promises were raised: selections are too liberal, too easy, too recent, too similar, too far from the classics or the canon. That's just for starters. Although one might assume that the selection of a book would reflect the institution's values, that seemingly straightforward precept is also contentious. Perhaps it's noteworthy that my university's summer reading program lasted a full decade. Begun in 2004, the program resided in the office of the vice chancellor for student affairs. It succumbed after ten years due to increasing university enrollment combined with insufficient faculty and staff volunteers to facilitate the small-group discussions held during orientation week (Reilly).

Students are first exposed to the one-read book when they come to campus in June or July for advising and registration. They purchase the book at a discount at the bookstore, where copious quantities have been stockpiled, and they are told they will discuss it with peers and academic leaders during fall orientation before classes begin. They have one or two months to read the selection, which has been chosen by a committee of faculty, staff, and students. Three criteria guided the selection: the book had to be a topic of interest to incoming students, available in paperback, and the author or a related expert had to be available to give a fall lecture.

Theoretically, by the time students arrived in my class the week after fall orientation, they had already read the book, engaged in a group discussion about it, and (assuming sufficient intellectual curiosity) discussed it further with their peers. I discovered early on, however, that not all students had actually read the book, nor even attended their assigned group discussion, much less discussed it more widely. A few students came to class wondering why they found no required text on the bookstore shelf for our section. By year two of using the model, I began emailing each new group about a month before class to alert them to the book and to encourage them to participate in the fall orientation activities. Over the past five years, I have used six different books to teach eight sections of FYC to 148 students. Student evaluations are on a five-point scale.

Two of the sections (spring 2015 and one from fall 2012) were last minute additions and not honors classes. Barbara Ehrenreich's *Bright-Sided* and Mike Rose's *The Mind at Work* were not university one-read selections, though both fit the committee's guidelines and would have been worthwhile choices. By the time the spring 2011 class was added, the fall students from my pilot class had already unanimously recommended that I continue the model. Not wanting to repeat the same text (and knowing that even if the spring students had read *Generation Me* the previous summer, their memories of it would be fading), I presented several options to the fall 2010 students and invited them advise me on which to use. *Bright-Sided* turned out to be a popular "no-text" with the spring 2011 class. By fall 2014, the one-read program had been discontinued; to continue with the model, I simply chose my own. Inspired by Duane Roen's keynote address at the 2014 WPA Conference, I selected Mike Rose's *The Mind at Work*. It, too, worked well with the fall 2014 honors class, if slightly less so with the spring 2015 non-honors students.

Figure 1. Evaluations of "No-Text/Two-Text" Course

Year	Semester	Title	Author	Enrollment	Teacher Eval.	Course Eval.
1	Fall '10	*Generation Me: Why Today's Young Americans Are More Confident, Assertive, Entitled—and More Miserable Than Ever Before*	Twenge	19	4.84	4.53
1	Spr '11	*Bright-Sided: How the Relentless Promotion of Positive Thinking Has Undermined America*	Ehrenreich	20	4.70	4.50
2	Fall '11	*Zeitoun*	Eggers	19	4.94	4.94
3	Fall '12	*Nothing to Envy: Ordinary Lives in North Korea*	Demick	19	4.95	4.63
3	Fall '12	*Nothing to Envy: Ordinary Lives in North Korea*	Demick	18	4.57	4.29
4	Fall '13	*Start Something That Matters*	Mycoskie	18	4.06	3.94
5	Fall '14	*The Mind at Work: Valuing the Intelligence of the American Worker*	Rose	19	4.33	4.21
5	Spr '15	*The Mind at Work: Valuing the Intelligence of the American Worker*	Rose	16	4.25	4.19
			total (or) avg.	148	4.58	4.40

The only book that led to a less than fulfilling semester was *Start Something That Matters*. Through this book, Mycoskie, the founder of

TOMS Shoes (which famously gives away one pair of shoes for each pair purchased), aims to influence others to have a positive impact on the world. Although intended to inspire altruistic young people, the book lacks intellectual gravitas. As it turned out, the book was to become the university's final selection in the one-read program. Unfortunately, I didn't read it myself until right before the start of the semester, by which time it was too late to select another. Earlier selections, especially Dave Eggers' *Zeitoun* and Barbara Demick's *Nothing to Envy*, had proved to be intellectually stimulating and richly rewarding. No doubt the selection committee was well intentioned; still, by that time they were hoping to revivify a flagging program. Alas, *Start Something That Matters* simply could not live up to the pedagogical needs of an honors course. In sticking with it, I rationalized that we could use it as a negative example, as in, how *not* to write for college or the workplace. I thought we could still derive the needed rhetorical lessons from it. Unsurprisingly, that semester resulted in the lowest teacher ratings and lowest course ratings, which are discussed below, of any of the "No Text/Two Text" courses I taught.

Finally, to address an argument many compositionists might raise against using one-read books in FYC—one with which I completely agree—is that the job of FYC is to teach writing, not literature. I do not, however, approach any of the "no-text" books from a literary perspective. All of the one-read selections are works of creative nonfiction and, as I show below, I approach them from both a rhetorical perspective (e.g., Who is the author? Why did she write this book? What is its purpose?) and from a compositionist's perspective (e.g., What claims is the author making? What research undergirds the claims? Are the sources documented appropriately given the genre?). Literary features such as plot, theme, character development, and the like are not part of the "no-text" approach.

Assignments and Supplemental Material

The course begins with an informal research assignment students receive the very first day of class. Immediately after the syllabus review, I divide the class into four random groups. Each group of four or five students is assigned a different set of research questions, the results of which will be presented over the next two class periods. A one-page handout condenses all of the questions but offers minimal instructions. Questions are standard from year to year, but because the book changes, plagiarism isn't an issue, nor do I get bored. By group, they research (1) Who is Mike Rose and what are his credentials for having written *The Mind at Work*? What is his background? His education? (2) What else has Rose written? Where and by whom has his work been published? (3) How has *The Mind at Work* been critically received? Who are the reviewers, and what is their credibility? What is the impact of the book? (4) What kind of book is *The Mind at Work*? What genre is it? Where would you find it shelved, say, at Barnes and Noble? Why does genre matter? Is this an academic book? How do you know?

Assured that presentations constitute a low-stakes assignment, an unspecified percentage of which factors into the total class participation grade of 25%, students dive in. They decide what their question entails; where they will find the information they need (and if not online, how to find the library); how to divide up the work; and they make arrangements for meeting outside of class to follow up. The exercise is an inquiry-based assignment, so I answer only the most basic questions. Students know we will devote two full class periods to the four presentations.

In one way or another, this informal research assignment touches on all of the outcomes noted in the WPA OS, and depending on individual students, it can touch on any or all of the habits of mind. Given the bare bones instructions, students prepare surprisingly thoughtful reports on their research findings. We post bibliographic data and other links to the class Blackboard site. Most come with technologically sophisticated presentations that employ PowerPoint or Prezi, into which they've embedded text, audio, images, and video clips. I remind everyone that a key responsibility of being a curious college student is to "listen rhetorically" (Ratcliffe), and that everyone should be prepared with meaningful questions or comments following each presentation. I debrief each group by having students examine the process they used in doing their research and evaluate how effective they believe their presentation was.

By the end of all four presentations, students' knowledge of the book and author has grown substantially, they have learned who their classmates are and have begun to develop a classroom community, they have begun to collaborate and to conduct research individually and collectively, and they have some sense of what they might have done differently. More important, their engagement in the course is heightened, and we have begun to address virtually all of the outcomes and habits of mind that the *Framework* deals with. We refer back to discussions that occurred during these presentations for weeks to come.

In doing this informal assignment, students inevitably realize they have not read the book as closely as they might have, that there is more to be gained by doing a closer reading than they have done to this point. Not "close reading" in the literary New Critical sense, but close reading in a rhetorical sense, in the sense of the first two outcomes of the WPA OS: developing rhetorical knowledge and developing critical thinking, reading, and composing (1–2). So, the semester begins with a discussion of what reading in college means and how a rhetorical approach to reading, and writing, will benefit them in college and beyond. Without overt pedagogical instruction or textbook intervention, this inquiry-based, low-stakes research assignment lays important groundwork for the semester.

This initial assignment, the *Framework*-related informal writing discussed below, and some supplemental material posted to Blackboard, together with the three formal graded assignments address all of the learning outcomes for FYC. Except for subtle tweaking, the formal assignments have remained unchanged over the five-year history of the "No-Text/Two-Text" course. The outcomes for all three assignments are cumulative and overlapping. Descriptions of the assignments follow; a companion paragraph shows how they play out.

Paper 1—A Rhetorical Analysis of the Whole Book

This assignment plunges students directly into the first outcome: developing rhetorical knowledge—"the ability to analyze contexts and audiences and then to act on that analysis in comprehending and creating texts" (WPA OS 1). Because students often begin working on the details of assignments without looking at the bigger picture, this outcome, including its bullet points reproduced directly from the *Framework*, is printed prominently at the top of the assignment sheet, to foreground what they are to be learning. Although a few of the students have never heard of rhetorical analysis, most have done some sort of rhetorical analysis in high school, usually on poems or short texts. None, though, has been required to think in rhetorical terms about texts as large as a whole book. I post links on Blackboard to some of the excellent rhetorical analysis resources readily available on the Internet, which we discuss in class. Apart from these supplemental resources and the one-read book itself, no external sources are needed. For most students, this is their first in-depth exposure to the concepts of *audience* and *purpose*, as well as to *ethos*, *pathos*, and *logos*. One of the most challenging aspects of this assignment is that students are not allowed to express personal opinions about the book; often, this is the first time they have approached a text analytically without being asked to state a personal response. Thus, depending on the student, the assignment requires them to apply some combination of the habits of mind, which we discuss as they craft the paper. The hypothetical audience for the analysis is undergraduate students in another class who are reading the book for the first time.

This assignment is where the issue of reading emerges. One entire class, for example, stopped reading *The Mind at Work* at the end of Rose's "Conclusion," skipping the "Afterword: On Method" and "Notes" sections altogether. As a result, they failed to recognize this book as a scholarly product and Rose as an author with scholarly credentials—despite the research they had done on him for their earlier presentation. When presented with the concepts of qualitative research, this class, heavy on science majors, questioned the validity of Rose's interviews and observations because the book told stories and used the first person, but lacked numbers, charts, and graphs. Our resulting class discussions, then, drew on newly added supplemental material, comparing quantitative versus qualitative research. Genre, too, typically makes for robust discussion. Again, despite the initial presentation by group four ("What kind of book is this?), students tend to describe every book as a novel. Getting them to think about any book as something other than fiction has led to new insights.

Paper 2—Evaluation & Synthesis of Research

This assignment addresses the second outcome as it is reproduced in the *Framework*: "developing critical thinking through writing, reading, and research—the ability to analyze a situation or text and make thoughtful decisions based on that analysis" (7). Again, the outcome, with its bullet points, is displayed at the top of the assignment sheet. In contrast to Paper 1, this more open-ended assignment lets students step away from the book while they explore any issue that arouses their curiosity, as long as the issue is inspired in some way by the book. Students must find, evaluate, and synthesize six scholarly resources that answer a research question they develop. The assignment becomes students' introduction to designing research questions; exploring the many forms research can take (e.g., basic/applied, quantitative/qualitative/mixed methods), who uses them, and why; the varied venues in which research is distributed (e.g., scholarly conferences, journals, and books; popular sources such as trade books, newspapers, and magazines). This paper includes a library session on using scholarly databases, followed by an annotated bibliography. Supplemental materials address how to construct a working bibliography and critically evaluate sources. Finally, students practice synthesizing sources into a coherent document. The hypothetical audience is educated readers who care about social issues.

The assignment challenges honors students, who need help working their way through the multiple outcomes it addresses. Students design widely varied research questions. Intrigued by the unlawful imprisonment of Syrian-American businessman Abdulrahman Zeitoun following Katrina, a student from the fall 2011 class researched the phenomenon of extraordinary rendition (government-sponsored kidnapping and transferring of individuals to other countries for torture). Inspired by our use of the Burkean parlor metaphor (110–111) to illustrate that research occurs in the context of what has gone before, a student from the fall 2014 class researched studies of working-class citizens conducted prior to Rose's compelling portrayals.

Paper 3—A Personal Response to the Book

This assignment incorporates all of the learning outcomes and finally allows (in fact requires) that students express an opinion about the book. All of the outcomes are again listed at the top of the assignment sheet, but without the bullet points this time. Instead of simply expressing an opinion, though, students must take a critical perspective on the book and convey it to a specifically identified external audience; they turn their considered opinion into constructive action, via Burke's metaphor, by joining a conversation. Students may carry forward some of the sources from the second paper, but must also add newly researched sources to them. The most challenging aspects of this paper are formulating an opinion that is backed up by research and identifying an appropriate audience who cares about it.

An aspiring journalist from the fall 2010 class saw her response to this assignment published in her hometown *Chicago Tribune*'s weekly teen newspaper and website *TheMash.com*. A student from the fall 2013 class—inspired by a local company whose business model we contrasted with Mycoskie's—wrote a letter to her father, a newspaper publisher, suggesting ways to transform his paper's internship into a wider community outreach program. (Her father emailed me to say he was considering her ideas.) Other students have written blog entries to Huffingtonpost.

com, op-ed pieces for their local newspapers, and letters to state and national legislators.

Framework Assignments, Specifically

Beyond structuring the formal assignments around the WPA OS, the *Framework* has also inspired several informal assignments that are deployed throughout the semester. For instance, following the initial group research project on the one-read book, I have assigned the *Framework* itself as the text for another informal group project. Answering these questions reinforces both the outcomes and habits of mind: (1) what is the purpose and genre of the *Framework*? (2) Who is the audience for the *Framework*? (3) What is the content of the *Framework*? Summarize it. (4) Who are the authors/sponsors of the *Framework*? By using the *Framework* as a text that can be analyzed, students come to understand rhetoric and composition as a field of study, and they appreciate that they have understood a professional document for which they are not the primary audience while at the same time discerning the structure of their upcoming course.

Additionally, I have students select one or two habits of mind they most need to work on during the semester. An informal poll shows which habits students have chosen, and we strategize how to address them. The fall 2012 and 2014 classes, for example, overwhelmingly reported they most needed to work on persistence, with the other habits receiving only scattered attention. Apart from this observation, I have not perceived a pattern among responses and surmise that these would be as idiosyncratic as the students themselves. Whenever a free moment presents itself in class, we revisit the habits they are working on. Checking in on students' progress can yield anything from "I forgot" to "I practiced persistence in studying for my chemistry exam last night." In a conference on her final paper, one student, who had claimed flexibility as her habit to work on, asked, "You mean I can have more than five paragraphs and I don't have to have a quote in every paragraph?" This became an example of where she could practice flexibility.

Moreover, I have students write a poem to share with the class on the habit(s) of mind they have selected to focus on. Modeled on Art Young's poetry across the curriculum concept, this assignment doesn't seek to create works of art but to creatively contemplate the habits of mind students are working on. The fall 2011 class recommended by a vote of fifteen to two that I repeat the habit of mind poem with future classes. The fall 2013 class's poetry was so successful that they asked that the poems be collected and distributed to all.

I also combine metacognition with all six of the course outcomes by giving periodic "metacognition/transfer" quizzes. This occasional in-class assignment lists the five WPA outcomes reproduced in the *Framework* on a sheet of paper. For each outcome, students give an example of how they have applied each one in another class that semester. A fall 2013 student reported that he "used rhetorical knowledge in Mechanical and Aerospace Engineering when writing homework assignments by keeping in mind [his] audience and what they are expecting to hear." Another fall 2013 student reported that she "used critical thinking in [her] calculus class when interpreting a word problem."

Assessing the Model: What Students and Others Report

There are several ways to examine the effectiveness of the "No-Text/Two-Text" model described below with excerpts from the data: four from students (course evaluations, post-course feedback, an end-of-semester exercise, and end-of-course reflective memos) and three from departmental sources and beyond (a colleague's observational report, the department's annual review, and extra-departmental feedback).

Our students completed one-page, end-of-semester course evaluations, which generated the teacher and course ratings above. Of the 148 students who have taken the eight classes, 141 evaluations were submitted. Students answer three open-ended questions on course, instructor, and overall learning experience, then circle "excellent" (5 points), "good" (4 pts.), "fair" (3 pts.), "poor" (2 pts.), or "unsatisfactory" (1 pt.) for both course and instructor. On this 5-point scale, the average rating for all sections of the "No-Text/Two-Text" course is 4.4, with a high of 4.95. (The average for all FYC courses is 4.1). The average rating for all sections with me as an instructor is 4.58, with a high of 4.94. (The average for all FYC instructors is 4.1). Inasmuch as FYC is a required course, I am pleased with the homogeneity of these ratings and that they are above departmental averages.

Because the rating system offers no descriptors for "excellent," "good," and the rest, students' open-ended responses can help reveal the thinking behind the numbers. From the fall 2010 pilot class, which produced scores of 4.53 for the course and 4.84 for me as the instructor, students wrote: "Textbooks don't engage! Each day brought new knowledge . .

. I've learned to be more open-minded and am willing to try new approaches" and "I learned to view scholarly study as an ongoing conversation to which I can contribute." Worth noting is that during the Q & A after Twenge's guest lecture on *Generation Me*, one student from our class visibly stumped the author by asking, "Who exactly would you say is the audience for your book?"

From the top-rated class at 4.9, for both the course and for me (fall 2011, based on *Zeitoun*), one student wrote that the assignments were "difficult, but do-able." Others said, "I really liked . . . that the assignments were like nothing I had done before"; "The habits of mind . . . will help guide my writing in all other fields." And one student who had rated the course only "good," nonetheless concluded, "This was a perfect way to begin college English."

The fall 2013 class, which earned the lowest ratings for both the course (3.94) and for me (4.06), based on Mycoskie's *Start Something That Matters*, is worth extended commentary. One student wrote:

> I really like the way she uses the one-read book in her class. *SSTM* is not in any way an academic book, but by using it in her class she proved to us that any book can be analyzed for its rhetoric. So many English classes that I have taken use classics, like Shakespeare. It was refreshing to change it up.

Others said, "I wish I had learned more and I think that would have come from more [different] reading"; "I liked the book and it engaged me, but I'm not sure it was the best choice"; and "The 'textbook' . . . lacked content . . . but I learned many things . . . to apply to the rest of my college career."

In retrospect, I believe that using this book was misguided. Negative examples do not make for inspired teaching and learning, particularly when they must sustain an entire semester. That said, of the several guest speakers we hosted in the "No-Text/Two-Text" classes, Lawren Askinosie's remarks in fall 2013 generated the most spirited discussion. Representing her Springfield, Missouri family's bean-to-bar craft chocolate business, she diplomatically contrasted their business model with Mycoskie's, which had been a source of confusion and contention throughout the semester. Moreover, as a recent alumna, Askinosie spoke authoritatively about the value of a liberal arts education for the business world. One student chose, as the focus for her third paper, to write a letter to Askinosie summarizing what the class had learned. Askinosie replied, "I was impressed by the engagement and depth of [the class's] questions . . . Judging by the critical thinking, clarity, and passion displayed in your letter, I think it's safe to say you're on the path to success."

Post-course student feedback has also been positive. Several students have contacted me well after the class ended to say how the approach has continued to affect their learning. A fall 2011 student specifically mentions the outcomes from the *Framework* that structured Paper 1:

> I want to thank you for teaching me rhetorical purpose and audience first semester. In my writing intensive class, I have had to write two-page progress reports weekly and have had three major papers due . . . You have helped me become a much more efficient and effective writer; this is reflected by the comments on my graded papers for my internship class. My writing is focused and dense with quality information. I have no doubt that the stress on rhetorical purpose in your class is the reason why my papers are of college-level material.

A third measure that reveals the value of the *Framework* is the whole-class end-of-semester exercise I often use. "What We Learned This Semester" is an informal, in-class assignment in which students quickly create a bulleted list of everything they have learned throughout the term. After five minutes of silent brainstorming, we compile all responses until every item has been accounted for. The habits of mind are often obliquely, if not directly, invoked here, e.g., "the importance of self-reflection" echoes metacognition; "how not to procrastinate on my writing" echoes engagement and responsibility; "how to write in a noisy dorm" echoes persistence and flexibility; and "how to appreciate other authors' voices" echoes openness. When we finish, students often comment, "I can't believe we learned so much in this class." I email the compilation to them to keep as a reminder of what they collectively reported.

The last of the student-reported measures comes from in-class reflective memos, which I assign when I don't use the "What We Learned" exercise. For this informal assignment, students use a one-page summary of the *Framework*'s outcomes and habits of mind as a prompt to reflect on their semester's learning. The responses here come from the spring 2015 non-honors class—the students who rated both the class (4.19) and me (4.25) second-lowest of all eight sections:

- [The class] taught me to look at what an author was saying in a piece of writing and break it down . . . that when reading a book, or any piece of writing, I need to look into what the author is saying rather than just read line after line.

- The most important thing [I learned] was to be curious . . . to always question everything . . . that to truly understand things that people are saying, you need to listen and be engaged.

- Making my audience trust me never seemed all that important. I figured they just would.

- Learning how to do research helped me in my chemistry class when I needed to find sources for a project. This paper exercised some habits of mind for me . . . I had to have an open mind and no bias. It also required me to be flexible. As I did my research, my question and focus shifted . . . These are things that I have never had a problem with, but it's interesting to note that I am now conscious about what I am doing.

- I knew that persistence was my weakest habit of mind. When we talked about this in class, it made me think about why I jump around projects and leave them unfinished . . . I lose interest before I finish because I've already learned what I wanted to know. This doesn't really work for school, though. I can't stop writing a paper just because I feel like I've learned what I wanted to.

- The Habits of Mind were . . . essential to my writing this semester . . . the greatest is metacognition . . . I use almost every habit of mind throughout my studies every single day without even knowing it.

These and many more of the students' comments echo virtually all of the *Framework*'s outcomes and habits of mind. Finally, this extraordinary reflection from a student who had previously failed FYC: "I actually used many of the eight habits of mind in [my last] paper by being persistent with my argument, being open to new ideas, . . . using creative ways of capturing my audience's attention by using personal experiences, and engaging in an essay I wanted to write instead of one I had to . . . English has always been an uphill struggle for me . . . I finally look at English as a subject I can excel in."

An observational report by one of my colleagues also attests to the effectiveness of the "No-Text/Two-Text" model. English faculty are required to have our classes observed periodically by senior members of the department, who then submit a report to the chair. Awkward as this observation is to present here, keep in mind that the evaluator is commenting on methods inspired by the *Framework*. The observation occurred during the second day of students' group presentations and on only the third class meeting of the semester:

> Marty is very clear in telling students what the purpose of an assignment is. She articulates the goals and summarizes them again after the class session. I found this effective because it was evident to me that the students actually not only learned the material *but also understood how and why they learned it*. . . . It was clear that the students really "got" how Marty had given them a model for approaching and analyzing texts in all their future courses. I don't think I've ever seen a class where students were given such a useful model broken down like this that they could see for themselves would be easy and effective for all their reading. It opened their eyes in numerous ways—and what's more—they *knew* it opened their eyes. (Swick)

One other departmental evaluation, albeit indirect, comes from the committee charged with evaluating and ranking each faculty member's annual performance in research, teaching, and service. The committee scrutinizes student evaluations and colleague comments, both of which weigh heavily in their report. This committee, for example, would have taken into consideration a Commendation for Teaching awarded by the university-wide student association, a nomination put forward by a student from the spring 2011 class when we studied Ehrenreich's *Bright-Sided*. This committee consistently placed my teaching in the "high merit" category.

One final insight into the course's effectiveness, again indirect, is feedback from external constituents. These extra-departmental respondents have had contact with the students in some way. Here, I am thinking of the public venues in which student work has been published (e.g., *Chicago Tribune, Huffingtonpost*), parental and guest speaker feedback (mentioned earlier), along with state legislators, high school teachers, and others who have replied (either to me or to students) when student letters from the third assignment were addressed to them. Each time students received this external validation, their engagement in the course was heightened and their enthusiasm for written communication increased.

Conclusion

Notwithstanding my one semester's use of an unpopular book, my self-evaluation of the five-year-old "No-Text/Two-Text" model is highly positive. As I think the various forms of feedback demonstrate, the *Framework* helped me invite honors students into the discourse of the academy. I would use this model again, and I recommend it to others. Still, the following limitations remain.

The formal assignments are challenging for honors students; the same assignments were less successful when used with general population students in the two non-honors sections. More scaffolding of the assignments, or different assignments that address the same outcomes, might be warranted for general population students.

The "No-Text/Two-Text" model relies on using *students'* texts in lieu of textbooks when lessons need to be taught, especially those dealing with the Knowledge of Conventions outcome—and, concomitantly, recognizing when the need for those lessons arises and preparing supplemental handouts from students' texts to illustrate handling those conventions. Not least of all, students must be reminded continually to read—and re-read—the assignment sheets with outcomes at the fore.

Without having taught FYC off and on for twenty-five years before using this model, I question how successful the classes might have been. It helps to have an internalized sense of what the outcomes of FYC are and how to present them, a sense that best comes from experience. In each of the eight iterations of the course, for example, I made adjustments by adding or subtracting informal assignments, steering course discussions in new ways, or introducing new supplemental material—based on my professional knowledge of what that class, at that time, needed. A countervailing option would be for an experienced composition teacher to pilot the method for one or two semesters and then have a small cadre of newer instructors who wish to use it to join her in a teaching community where weekly conversations could offer support.

Not every instructor has the freedom to adopt alternative approaches. Nor is there one "right" way to teach FYC. Many others abound, and I am not advocating that the "No-Text/Two-Text" model supplant what others have found successful. But I enthusiastically recommend the deployment of the *Framework* for much more than just instructors' planning purposes. No doubt many other assignments, formal and informal, beyond those I've described could be created to reinforce students' awareness of the WPA OS and habits of mind. Similar to what

Beth Brunk-Chavez suggests in chapter 10 and Angela Clark Oates demonstrates in chapter 14, my experience offers compelling evidence that the *Framework for Success in Postsecondary Writing* can be integrated into FYC classes as a text itself to be read and rhetorically analyzed by students as well as teachers. The *Framework* need not be relegated to instructors' file cabinets but, instead, might just cause students to realize that "You did that *on purpose!*"

WORKS CITED

Askinosie, Lawren. Message to fall 2013 student, 13 December 2013. E-mail.

Bartholomae, David. "Inventing the University." *When a Writer Can't Write: Studies in Writer's Block and Other Composing Problems*. New York: Guilford, 1985. 273–85. Print.

Burke, Kenneth. *The Philosophy of Literary Form*. Berkeley: U of California P, 1941. Print.

Council of Writing Program Administrators. "WPA Outcomes Statement For First-Year Composition." CWPA, 2014. PDF File.

Council of Writing Program Administrators, National Council of Teachers of English, and National Writing Project. *Framework for Success in Postsecondary Writing*. CWPA, NCTE, and NWP, 2011. PDF File.

Demick, Barbara. *Nothing To Envy: Ordinary Lives in North Korea*. New York: Spiegel & Grau, 2010. Print.

Eggers, Dave. *Zeitoun*. New York: Vintage Books, 2010. Print.

Ehrenreich, Barbara. *Bright-Sided: How Positive Thinking Is Undermining America*. New York: Picador, 2010. Print.

Garrison, Roger H. *The Adventure of Learning in College: An Undergraduate Guide to Productive Study*. New York: Harper & Brothers, 1959. Print.

Golden, Serena. "Common Reading, Common Ground." *Inside Higher Ed*. Inside Higher ED, 11 Jan. 2012. Web. 1 June 2015.

Mycoskie, Blake. *Start Something That Matters*. New York: Spiegel & Grau, 2012. Print.

Nietzsche, Friedrich. *The Birth of Tragedy and The Genealogy of Morals*. Trans. Francis Golffing. Garden City, NY: Doubleday & Company, 1956. Print.

Ratcliffe, Krista. "Rhetorical Listening: A Trope for Interpretive Invention and a 'Code of Cross-Cultural Conduct.'" *College Composition and Communication* 51.2 (1999): 195–224. Print.

Reilly, David. Message to the author, 16 April 2014. E-mail.

Roen, Duane. "Writing Program Faculty and Administrators as Public Intellectuals: Opportunities and Challenges." Annual meeting of the Council of Writing Program Administrators. Normal, IL, 19 July 2014. Plenary Presentation.

Rose, Mike. *The Mind At Work: Valuing the Intelligence of the American Worker*. 10th Anniversary Edition. New York: Penguin Books, 2014. Print.

Swick, Marly. Letter to David Read, 29 August 2011.

Twenge, Jean M. *Generation Me: Why Today's Young Americans Are More Confident, Assertive, Entitled—and More Miserable Than Ever Before*. New York: Free Press, 2006. Print.

Williams, Joseph M., and Gregory G. Colomb. "The Case for Explicit Teaching: Why What You Don't Know Won't Help You." *Research in the Teaching of English* 27.3 (1993): 252–64. Print.

Young, Art. "Writing across and against the Curriculum." *College Composition and Communication* 54.3 (2003): 472–85. Print.

16 Bridging High School and College Writing: Using the *Framework* to Shape Basic Writing Curricula

Lori Ostergaard, Dana Driscoll, Cathy Rorai, and Amanda Laudig

Basic writing was first offered at Oakland University in 1972, and until recently, the course remained largely unaffected by disciplinary calls for rhetorical approaches to writing instruction. Prior to enacting the course redesign that we describe in this chapter, our basic writing curriculum at Oakland University (OU) shared few outcomes with the rest of our first-year writing (FYW) curriculum and had never been assessed. We believe this lack of professional support for the course contributed to increased first-to-second year attrition rates and decreased six-year graduation rates for our basic writing students ("Student" 13).

In this chapter, we describe how the *Framework for Success in Postsecondary Writing* shaped our 2012 redesign of the basic writing curriculum, goals, and assignments. In our redesign, we emphasized rhetorical knowledge, critical thinking, writing processes, and the eight habits of mind, blending the best practices outlined in the *Framework* with other pedagogical innovations designed to improve the college readiness of our students. Some of these other innovations included assigning an undergraduate embedded writing specialist to each class, designing course assignments to develop students' help-seeking behaviors (Williams and

Takaku), and working to improve students' metacognitive abilities to support the transfer of learning (Driscoll and Wells).

As the four of us researched, piloted, assessed, and revised our program's basic writing curriculum, we found a familiar comfort within the experiences outlined in the *Framework*—the "writing, reading, and critical analysis experiences" we were accustomed to constructing with our students (1). At the same time, it was unusually gratifying to conceive of a writing curriculum less as a set of assignments and activities designed to teach students a set of skills—researching, drafting, peer reviewing, revising, and reflecting—and more as a set of experiences designed to foster curiosity, openness, and creativity or to encourage persistence and responsibility. For our committee, an engagement with the habits of mind in our classes led us to a better understanding of the roles we play as educators: designing "landscapes—experiences with writing, reading, and critical analysis—that students must navigate freely" (Johnson 536). As we discuss in the sections below, however, while we found succor in designing and implementing assignments to foster the habits of mind, we also felt a growing sense of unease when we considered how best to assess our students' development of those habits over the course of the semester.

In the section that follows, we provide a brief history of basic writing at Oakland University to demonstrate the role this course has played at our university. Next, we describe some of the pedagogical challenges that have impacted the course. We also provide some background into the research that shaped our new curriculum and a description of that curriculum. Finally, we conclude by analyzing the effect of our redesign on student success, using both an assessment of student work and institutional retention data.

Basic Writing at OU

Oakland University is located in Rochester, Michigan, twenty-five miles north of Detroit. This Carnegie-ranked Doctoral Research University was endowed and founded in 1957 to provide local students with a "first-class undergraduate program" (*Catalog*). To early faculty and administrators, that first-class collegiate education did not include "courses of a sub-collegiate character," including courses in reading, first-year composition, and any math classes lower than calculus (*Catalog*). The university's inaugural years were shaped by a profound disconnect between faculty expectations and student abilities, resulting in high failure rates and emergency measures introduced by the administration to mitigate those failures.

Among the earliest interventions into student writing at OU was the founding of a writing center in 1964, and in 1972, a separate Department of Learning Skills was developed to offer classes in "effective writing, all modes of communication, including speech and reading, as well as other study-related activities" (*General Catalog* 365). Developing this new department for learning skills opened the floodgates on developmental education at OU: while the department began with only five courses, by 1979, learning skills faculty offered twelve distinct developmental reading and writing courses. The learning skills approach to writing instruction ended in 1982, when faculty from that department joined with faculty in communication and journalism to form a new Department of Rhetoric, Communication, and Journalism (RCJ). Finally, in 2008, rhetoric split from RCJ to form a separate Department of Writing and Rhetoric to support both the first-year writing program and a new major in writing and rhetoric.

While OU began with no developmental courses, but with a commitment by faculty to "place a strong emphasis on writing in all courses" (*Catalog*), by the 1980s the university offered a staggering array of such classes, including three 4-credit tutorials in reading and writing skills and two "Basic Writing Skills" classes. The writing program's developmental focus lasted into the twenty-first century, waning only with the establishment of more advanced undergraduate writing classes, graduate-level composition pedagogy courses, and a new writing and rhetoric major. In 2000, half of the rhetoric courses (seven) offered in RCJ were developmental reading, writing, and study skills courses, and while they were taught with less frequency than in years past, six of those courses remained in the course catalog until 2010 when faculty in the new department reduced the number of developmental courses to three (Basic Writing, Supervised Study, and College Reading).

Where We Are Today

Throughout its history, the first-year writing program at OU has struggled to address the issue of basic writing student attrition. In the past, only 30%-40% of our basic writing students returned for their sophomore year, compared with 70%-80% of students who initially enroll in Composition I. As they are at many universities, first-year student attrition rates are a university-wide concern and can be attributed to a number of causes, including financial concerns, work and family commitments, and academic preparedness. However, in their 2010 assessment of student performance in our first-year writing program, our university's Office of Institutional Research and Assessment (OIRA) suggested that even "after accounting for differences in academic preparedness, results suggest that there is some aspect of Basic Writing that reduced six-year graduation rates for Basic Writing students" ("Student" 13). While OIRA could not identify the "aspect," we knew the course was in need of revision.

In 2010–2011, Lori began an informal assessment of the basic writing course through a survey of course syllabi, and she was pleased to discover two recent developments in the course. Spearheaded by our writing center director, these initiatives included an embedded writing specialist program that put writing center tutors into every basic writing class and an instructor-developed common course syllabus. Although the embedded writing specialist program was commendable in that it encouraged help-seeking behavior that may lead to higher retention (Williams and Takaku) and provided students with additional in-class support for their writing, the standard syllabus was not in keeping with best practices in the field. Indeed, the presence of eleven distinct course goals that resulted from this effort at standardization suggested that a number of compromises had to be reached to satisfy the ideologies of our diverse basic writing faculty. Those course goals, many of which could not be easily assessed, ranged from the aspirational—"develop confidence in ability to accomplish a writing task"—to the pedantic—"write complete sentences in the four basic patterns (simple, compound, complex, and compound-complex)." Course goals both reflected some of our faculty's awareness of new movements in the field—"add visual literacy to your definition of composition"—and harkened back to an earlier age when students were taught "appreciation" of great works—"appreciate the complex and personal effort involved in the craft (art and science) of writing."

Despite this range of course goals, Lori's review of the existing program suggested that the majority of our faculty focused primarily on grammar and reading in basic writing. Students were required to read one to two books, along with anthologies of shorter non-fiction works. They also completed a variety of grammar exercises and took regular quizzes about assigned readings, vocabulary, punctuation, grammar, and usage. Basic writing students also completed a wide range of written assignments during the fourteen-week semester, including personal narratives, compare/contrast essays, reading summaries, multimodal works, letters to authors, position statements, and source syntheses. However, only the synthesis and position statements required rhetorical, analytical, and constructive work with more academic sources. Both university retention data and our own survey of the existing basic writing course, then, demonstrated the need for a change in focus, practices, and outcomes for this important first-year course.

In the section that follows, we detail the research that informed our redesign of the basic writing curriculum at Oakland University, with a particular focus on why we used the *Framework* to shape this class.

THEORIES THAT INFORMED OUR REDESIGN

Much basic writing research of the twenty-first century urges teachers to move away from the kinds of prescriptive grammar instruction and decontextualized writing assignments that we witnessed in our own basic writing classes at OU. Rather than isolating basic writing from the rest of the writing curriculum, contemporary researchers encourage mainstreaming, not of basic writing students, necessarily, but of basic writing assignments and course goals. As Ann Del Principe notes, basic writers do not "need special, different treatment," and writing instructors should not assume that these students "cannot handle certain types of assignments" (75–76). Del Principe's work is articulated against an "iconic position" in basic writing (75–76), a position that assumes basic writers cannot write essays until they have learned to write paragraphs, and they cannot write paragraphs until they have mastered the construction of grammatically correct sentences (see Gunner). In calling this linear approach to writing instruction into question, Del Principe draws on the 1986 research of David Bartholomae and Anthony Petrosky and on the 1987 explorations of Joseph Martinez and Nancy Martinez to emphasize the idea that sentence construction and error correction are not what basic writing students need to succeed in college. Thus, she argues for what she calls the "Basic Writers Aren't Basic Thinkers" paradigm wherein basic writers are "engaged in truly college-level reading and writing projects" (73).

Such college-level work has been outlined in a number of professional position statements, including the Council of Writing Program Administrators' "Outcomes Statement for First-Year Composition" (WPA OS). Published in 2000 and re-worked in 2008 and 2014, this document emphasizes the need for college writing students to engage in assignments designed to develop their (1) rhetorical knowledge; (2) critical thinking, reading, and composing; (3) writing processes; and (4) knowledge of conventions, and to assist students with learning how to compose in disparate contexts and with digital technologies. Each of these goals functions under the assumption that effective writing does not exist in a vacuum but is instead comprised of several interconnected, recursive acts. While teachers and researchers work to help students attain the outcomes outlined in the WPA OS, they have also emphasized the fact that effective writing instruction positions writing as an activity that is holistic, authentic, and varied. The most successful assignments take into account that students become stronger writers when they use flexible processes, when they are presented with real-world writing situations, and when they write to learn. To improve our basic writing curriculum, we first needed to mainstream our course assignments and goals by emphasizing process, providing students with authentic rhetorical challenges, and offering a variety of institutional supports for their development. Our new curriculum, in other words, needed to bring our basic writing course in line with the values of the discipline, as those values are expressed in both the WPA OS and the *Framework*.

Our first-year writing curriculum at Oakland University has undergone a number of assessments and revisions over the last six years as the program has moved away from theme-based composition courses and towards courses centered around instruction in what we call "the four Rs": rhetoric, research, revision, and reflection. Prior to the redesign, these changes had not impacted the basic writing course; thus, this course may have offered students what Sara Webb-Sunderhaus terms "equality of access," but we had yet to engage in "much critical attention to offering basic writers equality of success" (99). Such success, we believe, is rooted in the eight habits of mind outlined in the *Framework*.

The Council of Writing Program Administrators (CWPA), the National Council of Teachers of English (NCTE), and the National Writing Project (NWP) jointly produced *The Framework for Success in Postsecondary Writing* to serve as a companion to the WPA OS. As Peggy O'Neill, Linda Adler-Kassner, Cathy Fleischer, and Anne-Marie Hall observe in their article about the creation of this document, "While the [WPA] Outcomes Statement 'articulates what is expected at the *end* of the first year of college composition,' the *Framework* [was designed to] focus on what students need to know and be able to do at the beginning of the first-year course so they could reach the outcomes" (522). The *Framework* emphasizes "experiences with writing, reading, and critical analysis" (1), and prefaces these strategies with a list of "eight habits of mind essential for success in college writing"—curiosity, openness, engagement, creativity, persistence, responsibility, flexibility, and metacognition—as well as bulleted strategies to foster each habit (1). According to O'Neill et al., the *Framework* seeks, in part, to develop an agenda "that will articulate the experiences, knowledge, and habits of mind that students need to succeed as they begin the first year of college writing" (520). Patrick Sullivan notes that this list of habits contains the basis for intrinsic motivation (548), while Bruce McComiskey has observed that the *Framework* may function as a useful bridge between secondary-school writing and the WPA OS (538). Because our basic writing class must also serve as a bridge between high school English and our Composition I course, the *Framework*, and especially the eight habits of mind, provided us with a strong foundation for our basic writing curricular redesign.

Judith Summerfield and Philip Anderson posit that the *Framework* constitutes only half of Arthur Costa and Bene Kallick's better-known "16 Habits of Mind" (545); however, they sell the *Framework* a bit short with this assessment. Indeed, the bullets describing how each habit may be fostered provide additional information that, we believe, ties each of the eight *Framework* habits to one or more of Costa and Kallick's sixteen habits. For our committee, though, the question was never *how many* habits to emphasize in our new curriculum, but *how best* to do so. We wondered if these habits were intrinsic or if they could be learned. If they could be learned or developed, we wondered what kinds of assignments might foster that learning. And if we could design assignments to teach or strengthen the habits, we wondered how we might assess the effectiveness of those assignments. Finally, given how much we needed to accomplish in our revised basic writing class, we questioned whether or not this class, or any writing class for that matter, should even focus on habits of mind.

While we debated whether to incorporate these habits into our new curriculum, we began to notice that most of our discussions about our basic writing students' college preparation naturally veered into discussions about the eight habits. The more we talked about the kinds of successful and prepared writers we hoped our students would become, the more we found ourselves describing those students as curious, open, engaged, flexible, and persistent. We wished for our students to learn creativity, responsibility, and an understanding of their own thinking and writing processes. In other words, we realized that we were already invested in nurturing these habits with our basic writing students. In fact, we found that focusing on the habits of mind was not a distraction from rhetorical and writing instruction in the class, for, as Kristine Johnson observes, a focus on the habits of mind "provides an exigency for reinvigorating ancient rhetoric and the liberal arts" (519) and for countering constructions of "education as transactional (in which students are passive)" (519).

From these conversations, we designed a course wherein our students' first experiences in the class—their first journal entries and their learning narrative—focused overtly on discussions about the eight habits of mind. We continued that work throughout the semester through journal assignments and paper reflections. And while we do not question the value of these habits to emerging writers, as we illustrate in the final section of this chapter, we have still found it difficult to assess what our students may have learned through a focus on the eight habits in these assignments, a difficulty similarly expressed by Amy Kimme Hea, Jenna Pack Sheffield, and Kenneth Walker in chapter 2 of this collection.

How the *Framework* Shaped Course Goals

While the WPA OS helped to shape our Composition I and Composition II curricula, the *Framework*'s principles served as our guide for developing a new basic writing curriculum with six new course goals that were designed to be both student-centered and, for the most part, assessable. Over the course of the summer of 2012, we collaborated to write common course goals and a common syllabus that included assignments and activities that were in line with our larger department goals. In this section, we discuss each of those new course goals and provide descriptions of the assignments that we believe help us in attaining those goals with our students.

Basic Writing Course Goals

Our first goal asks students to approach writing as a multi-phase, recursive process that requires feedback. This goal recognizes the importance of the writing described in the *Framework*. Each assignment in the new basic writing course requires students to approach writing as a process: pre-writing, researching, drafting, editing, revising, and reflecting. This goal is especially important to basic writers who often struggle with pre-writing and revision. We wanted students to see that a new level of success was attainable if they followed a writing process that included frequent feedback—from their peers, their course instructor, and the undergraduate writing specialist—and developed healthy patterns of writing behaviors that would transfer to other courses.

Because rhetoric is a foundational part of our first-year and advanced writing curriculum, we incorporated the study of rhetoric into our basic writing curriculum as well. Thus, our second goal requires students to compose their texts to address the rhetorical situation. Throughout the new basic writing course, students are asked to use rhetorical analysis to determine how best to reach their audience and achieve their purpose. Each of the three major writing assignments in this course has a different audience, purpose, and context. Our goal is to demonstrate how important rhetorical knowledge is to success in writing and to scaffold this skill for the two composition classes that follow basic writing.

Our third goal requires students to demonstrate an ability to synthesize information/ideas in and between various texts—written, spoken, and visual. Critical thinking skills require that students read, process, and analyze multiple texts before using that knowledge to construct a new understanding of an issue. Each major writing assignment in the redesign asks students to read, analyze, and synthesize multiple primary and secondary sources.

Because we wish to support students' metacognitive abilities, our fourth goal requires that they reflect on their own writing processes and evaluate their own learning, much like the intensive critical reflection that Angela Clark-Oates describes in chapter 14. To evaluate their learning, students must have an awareness of their writing abilities—strengths and weaknesses—including their own habits of mind. Reflective writing throughout the semester asks students to accurately assess their writing processes and discuss what role the habits of mind played in those processes. They can then use this awareness to seek help with their own writing challenges and track their growth as writers.

Our fifth goal requires that students adapt prior knowledge and learning strategies to a variety of new writing and reading situations in college and beyond. The *Framework* recognizes the need for college writers to be able to adapt to environments that might be new or different. This goal emphasizes that transfer of learning is a critical goal for the course, both in terms of building upon prior knowledge and bridging between high school writing (Reiff and Bawarshi) as well as writing to other courses in composition and across the university (Wardle; Driscoll). Habits of mind are critical parts of this goal, as they are largely dispositional in nature and can encourage transfer of learning to a wide variety of circumstances (Driscoll and Wells; Perkins and Salomon). Flexibility, openness, and engagement are essential habits for writers who must learn to adapt to new writing challenges both in and out of the classroom.

Our sixth and final goal states that students will develop the habits of mind of effective college writers and readers. While we worried that this final goal might prove difficult to assess, we recognized the importance of these habits and their relationship to student success beyond the writing classroom. As a result, they are an explicit or intrinsic part of every writing assignment and class activity we designed.

Common Course Assignments

Students respond informally (one draft) to topics in a variety of media (print, visual, audio) in a writing journal. Although most of the journal prompts challenged our students to think critically about what others composed and to demonstrate their *openness* to other viewpoints, we incorporated a number of assignments asking that they also reflect directly on the habits of mind they witnessed in their own lives, in their descriptions of people they admire, and in the works they read.

We have found that basic writers often enter college with negative and unrealistic views of their writing abilities. The feedback they have received in the past centers on their deficiencies in content and conventions, rather than on their successes reaching an audience. An ACT English score of 15 or below and the resulting placement in basic writing often confirms their belief that they are not competent writers. We sought to challenge these negative perceptions and aid our students in their metacognitive awareness by encouraging them to develop more accurate assessments of their own abilities. We also sought to encourage our students to draw upon prior knowledge and to be boundary crossers rather than boundary guarders (Reiff and Bawarshi). To aid them in this work, we ask our students to read a variety of learning narratives wherein writers reflected on their own learning processes. Our students then compose their own narratives. In their *learning narratives*, our students assess their own habits and how those habits shape the way they learn. Instead of describing themselves simply as "poor writers," we encourage them to discover ways in which they have been curious, open to new ways of thinking, engaged in learning, creative, persistent, responsible, flexible, and reflective. We believe this assignment may help our students expand their views of themselves as writers and learners and see themselves as superior to their struggles with language. We believe this assignment also builds their confidence, makes them aware of their own agency as learners, and helps them to create a more accurate picture of their habits of mind.

A three-part community engagement project asks students to engage with one of fourteen campus services that provide support for first-year students. This assignment was designed to address Sara Webb-Sunderhaus's challenge that basic writing teachers provide their students with equal pathways to success (99). She cites John M. Braxton and Meaghan E. Mundy's 2001 retention recommendations that course assignments compel students to become well acquainted with each other and with campus and university programs and resources (110). This assignment requires that our students be open to new ways to research the world, exhibit curiosity in seeking out authoritative sources, persist with a single project through multiple steps, and exercise their creativity and flexibility through the presentation of their research in traditional print and multi-modal genres. Part 1 of the assignment requires that students research campus resources—including the counseling center, health center, academic skills center, and writing center—using both primary and secondary sources: an observation of the resource, an interview with someone who provides this resource, and an investigation of the resource's university website. Part 2 requires that our students use this research to write an essay that describes the most important services this resource provides and cites both their primary and secondary sources in MLA format. Part 3 of the assignment requires that they repurpose their research for a different medium, preparing a multi-modal presentation for their classmates and for incoming students. By the end of the project, our students have engaged in in-depth research on one campus resource and have seen presentations about a variety of other resources.

After informal and research writing, the final essay of the semester asks students to respond critically to readings. The course instructor introduces a series of five or six academic and popular essays about a controversial issue, and these works are analyzed in class. Then, students are asked to take a position on the issue and synthesize at least two sources to support their position. This assignment emphasizes the use of an academic voice that is supported by sources that are either paraphrased or quoted directly in MLA format. In this way, we hope the course bridges from the work students were asked to do in high school and the tasks that will be required of them in their university courses. Students are required to take responsibility for their positions, illustrate their flexibility in meeting the rhetorical expectations of their academic audience, and engage with the work of other thinkers and writers to construct their own arguments.

At the end of the semester, students submit a collection of their writing in a final portfolio that includes a metacognitive analysis of their own learning. This portfolio includes a copy of a first week, informal writing assignment that serves as a base line for their reflections. It also must include copies of all of their first drafts, peer review comments, final drafts, revisions, instructor comments, and essay reflections. Using this collection of writings, students are then asked to reflect on the process that they used to write one of the essays and to describe what they learned about their own writing, researching, and learning processes. Writing about their own writing is a new activity for most basic writers. We believe their ability to reflect on what processes work best for them as writers and how they will overcome challenges in the future are vital to their success in future composition courses.

Having provided the historical context for our basic writing course, the research that informed our course, and a description of how the *Framework* shaped our course goals, we conclude this chapter by describing the assessment methods and results that we believe demonstrate the efficacy of this approach.

Assessment

We elected to assess our students' learning in the class using two measures: analyses of their change in writing quality over the semester and examinations of self-reported learning behaviors and habits of mind. This assessment was then triangulated with retention and success data that we collected from our university's Office of Institutional Research and Assessment (OIRA).

Selection of Materials and Sampling

Our assessment focused on examining the first-week diagnostic essay (which asked students to write a letter taking a position on the use of ACT scores as college admission tools), their portfolio reflections, and their final critical response to readings papers. We collected all of the essay drafts, responses, and revisions so that we might later revisit this work to assess our students' progress over time and their revision processes.

After obtaining IRB approval, each of the four basic writing faculty in this study submitted three randomly selected student portfolios from each of their basic writing sections (n=11 sections for a total of 33 portfolios). Two portfolios were collected for assessment with an additional portfolio collected to aid in norming and rubric development.

Rubric Development

To assess the goals for the course, we developed a rubric for both the portfolio reflections and the quality of student writing. This rubric was adapted from our department's prior Composition II assessment and used the *Framework* as a guide. The rubric employs a Likert scale to rate the quality of the work, with one signifying low quality and five signifying high quality on the scale (see table 1). While rubrics that assess student writing are fairly well known, a short discussion of our reflective writing rubric is worth noting because it demonstrates our attempt to assess both the presence or absence of the categories in student work and the quality of their work in those categories. The categories we rated connected with our course goals, emphasizing students' ability to adapt prior knowledge, critically evaluate the writing of others, assess their own learning, and engage the habits of mind, which are embedded as 2b of the appended reflection rubric. We chose to use a rubric to assess habits of mind because it provided us with a baseline, some way to begin these conversations about what we were seeing, or not, in our students' reflective writing. Rubrics to evaluate other reflective processes have, in prior assessments, been used quite effectively by our program (see Allan and Driscoll), and given the constraints of time and the fact that this was a pilot assessment, we felt using such a rubric would help to focus our analysis and discussions. And in that effect, it was successful; although, other kinds of analyses, such as elaborated coding strategies, would have led to a more robust analysis. As this was a pilot assessment, for the habits of mind, we used the rubric in Table 1 (and this scale is similar for all areas).

Table 1. Rubric for Assessing Habits of Mind

1	2	3	4	5
Student demonstrates no evidence of effective habits of mind.	Student demonstrates slight evidence of one or two habits of mind, but no detail is given and/or student does not demonstrate success.	Student provides limited description of positive habits of mind, with some detail, but information may be missing, may only focus on positive.	Student provides good description of habits of mind, either one in detail or several in less detail.	Student provides excellent analysis of habits of mind, including critical understanding of integrating habits of mind into learning processes.

Assessment Process

Our assessment reading took place over a one-day period. For norming purposes, we read three sets of anchor essays demonstrating high, medium, and low work. Each set contained a first-day essay, a critical response to readings paper, and a portfolio reflection, which we read and rated individually using our prepared rubrics, and then collectively discussed as a group. After norming, we rated all sampled student portfolios (n=22); each portfolio had two raters. If our scores were off by more than one point on our five-point scale, the two raters discussed the differences and reached consensus on those scores (this happened with less than 15% of our portfolios). Otherwise, we averaged scores for analysis purposes.

Data Analysis and Assessment Results

Data were analyzed using Microsoft Excel and SPSS 20. Descriptive statistics (means and ranges) were calculated for all rubric areas. Additionally, paired samples t-tests (two-tailed) were conducted to examine change over the course of the term with regards to student writing. Additionally, we worked with OIRA to analyze course-taking patterns, retention, and grade distribution for students in our pilot course compared with previous years.

Students made statistically significant gains from their initial writing on our diagnostic essay to their critical analysis essay. Students had an overall mean score of 2.91 on their beginning of term diagnostic letters and a mean of 3.14 on their end-of-term critical response essays. A comparison of individual scores across the portfolios is displayed in Figure 1. Please note that the categories for figures 1 and 2 are shortened versions of our course objectives.

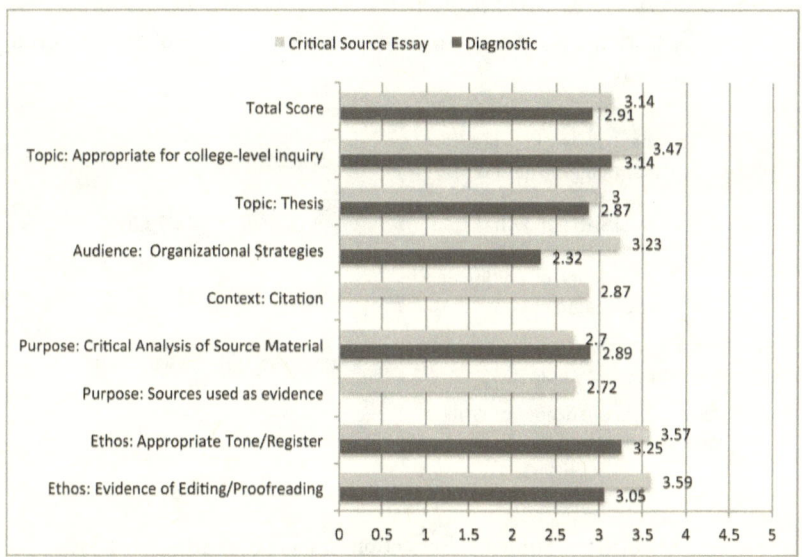

Figure 1. Assessment of Students' Academic Writing

As Figure 1 demonstrates, students made gains in all areas from the beginning to the end of the course with the exception of the "Purpose: Critical Analysis of Source Material" area; however, since the critical analysis with sources is a much more rhetorically challenging activity than the first day essay, this could explain the drop in scores in this area. Students made statistically significant gains in two categories: "Ethos: Evidence of Editing/Proofreading" ($p<0.01$) and "Audience: Organizational Strategies" ($p<0.002$). A third category approached significance, "Topic: Appropriate for College-Level Inquiry" ($p<0.07$). The other categories did show change, but that change was not statistically significant.

STUDENT REFLECTION ON WRITING PROCESS AND HABITS OF MIND

In addition to the quality of student writing, we examined a number of areas in students' reflective writing to see how effectively they were meeting a number of basic writing goals based on the *Framework*. Raters indicated whether and to what amount students demonstrated evidence of various practices, including writing process and learning strategies and habits of mind.

Figure 2 shows mean reflection scores for basic writing students' writing process as described in their reflective writing. As demonstrated in Figure 2, students scored a "meets expectations" score of at or around three for all areas.

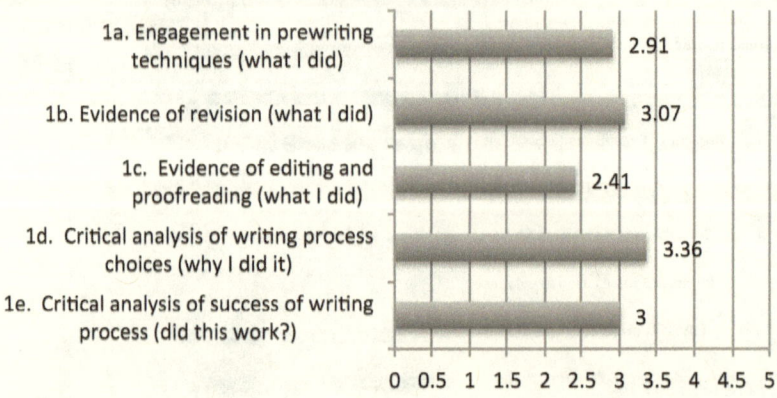

Figure 2. Assessment of Students' Reflections on Their Writing Processes

Figure 3 examines students' learning strategies and habits of mind. From this, we see that students engaged in moderate amounts of reflection concerning themselves and their learning processes (3.0), but that habits of mind were assessed as still in need of further development (2.25). We also see that our students are more able to anticipate future connections to writing content (2.87) than to consider transferring and adapting strategies from high school (2.25).

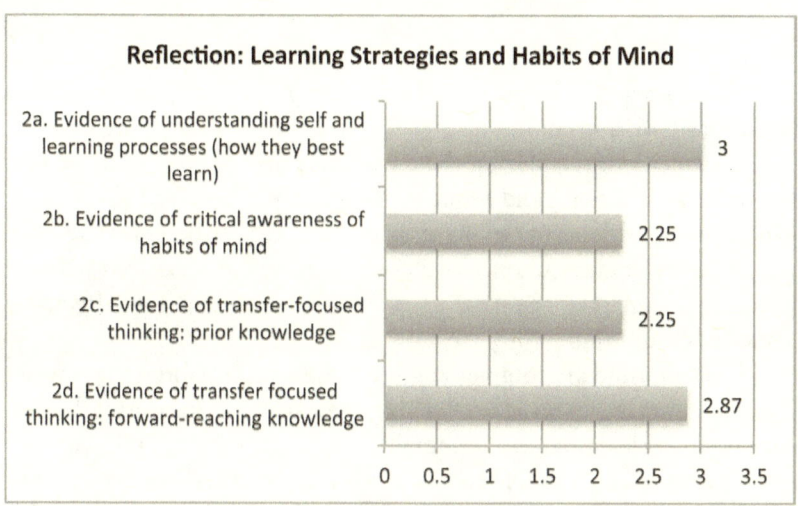

Figure 3. Assessment of Students' Reflections on Learning Strategies and Habits of Mind

Comparison Between Fall 2012 Pilot Cohort and Previous Years

In addition to our direct research on student writing and reflective writing for our basic writing course, we worked with OIRA to compare the course-taking patterns, retention, and grade distribution for students in the fall 2012 cohort with those in the fall 2011 cohort.

Students in the 2011 and 2012 cohorts enrolled and passed Composition I at comparable rates: 66% of student who enrolled in Composition I the semester following basic writing passed in both cohorts, and 90% of those students who took the Composition I course passed with a 2.0 or better in both cohorts.

Despite these similarities in pass rates and enrollment rates from 2011 and 2012, however, the number of students earning higher grades increased dramatically in our 2012 cohort. The 2011 cohort had 68% of students earning a 3.0 or better (a similar percentage to that found in previous years). The 2012 cohort had 90% of students earning a 3.0 or better, for an increase of 22% earning higher grades. Furthermore, an average of 2% of basic writing students earned a 4.0 in Composition I during the previous three years (1%, 3%, and 2%); however, in our fall 2012 cohort, 6% of our basic writing students earned a 4.0 in Composition I.

Discussion

The *Framework* provided us with a roadmap to enact positive change in our basic writing course, change that aided us in developing more effective student writers during the term, integrating habits of mind into the writing classroom, and improving student performance in more advanced composition courses. Our assessment results demonstrate both areas where our curriculum was successful as well as areas that we need to improve, but they also lead us to question how one may effectively assess habits of mind.

Habits of mind are complex cognitive and social qualities that impact students' learning to write and effectively transfer their writing knowledge to multiple domains; the complexity of these habits of mind are not easily measured by a simple rubric. However, the question of whether or not habits of mind can be assessed using traditional assessment methods is an important one, and our experiences suggest that Kristine Johnson may be correct when she suggests that these habits cannot be "fully captured in assessment instruments" (519).

Dana's recent experience in developing a taxonomy to measure metacognitive awareness, for example, suggests that each habit of mind is expressed in students' writing and lives in multiple ways, not all of which are easily measurable and not all of which can best be measured through reflective writing (Gorzelsky, Driscoll, Paszek, Hayes and Jones). Metacognition alone can be broken into multiple different aspects, such as metacognitive awareness of one's self, the task, or strategies to use versus actually using those strategies through regulation, control, or evaluation (see Scott and Levy for detailed descriptions of the difficulty in measuring metacognition and various metacognitive features). Furthermore, in examining metacognition, Dana's team found that complex expressions of metacognitive awareness, the kinds that facilitated transfer of learning, were often articulated after a FYW semester ended and teased out through interviews rather than through students' reflective writing during the term.

While our assessment of the habits of mind our basic writing students engaged with throughout the semester was incomplete and, perhaps, rightly so, we had hoped it would provide us with some insights into how to teach habits of mind effectively in a way that would make them meaningful and valuable to students—and while our data is inconclusive, we believe we met with some success in fostering these habits. Despite our emphasis on habits of mind throughout the course, our students seemingly demonstrated less understanding and application of habits of mind than in other areas of our rubric. This may be, in part, because we chose not to prompt students to discuss the habits of mind in their reflections; we hoped instead to locate those habits in how they discussed other aspects of their learning in the course. Given Dana's team's findings (Gorzelsky et al.), while we did learn something meaningful about habits of mind through our teaching and assessment, we feel that more elaborated examinations—and collection points during the writing process—would lead to a more effective assessment of habits of mind. We are left with several questions regarding our emphasis on habits of mind: Were we not able to effectively measure habits of mind through reflective writing or through our assessment materials? Or, were we less able to effectively teach habits of mind based on *Framework* guidelines? Or, did our students learn habits of mind effectively in the classroom but choose not to articulate them explicitly in their reflections?

We were able to see the useful and productive outcomes that our emphasis on habits of mind had in our own classrooms; however, we were not able to measure that accurately through reflective writing alone. Our rubric, (see Appendix), is our first attempt in measuring habits of mind in the context of basic writing. This rubric examined three features of habits of mind: how many habits of mind students displayed in their reflections, how nuanced and integrated their discussion of habits of mind was, and their critical awareness of how the habits of mind impacted their learning and writing process. In the future, if we want to emphasize habits of mind more explicitly in our assessment, we could create rubric areas for each of the habits of mind and prompt students to discuss these in their final reflections for the course. However, given the challenges of designing such a rubric, we are also considering employing a psychometric survey that could be administered at the start of the semester and again at the end of the semester, asking our students questions designed to elicit how they might respond to situations wherein curiosity, persistence, and openness were called for.

CONCLUSION

As teachers of writing and as a field, we tend to emphasize student writing, but we found the habits of mind provided our committee with an additional productive emphasis, especially for basic writing students. Specifically, the habits of mind appealed to us because of their ability to

> describe ethical relationships between writers and the world: *curiosity* says students should continually pursue new knowledge about the world; *openness* says they should understand diverse ways of being in the world; *responsibility* says that they should own the effects of the rhetorical action in the world. . . . (Johnson 524)

In short, the habits of mind helped our group to shift the conversation about our students' college readiness away from cataloging the kinds of skills that could be measured through traditional assessment instruments and towards the "intellectual behaviors and educational experiences" we already valued as writing teachers (Johnson 517).

We conclude this chapter with some takeaways that we hope are helpful to others. First, we believe the *Framework* provides a rich source of material for revising a basic writing course and it can be leveraged to aid basic writers in a multitude of ways, from writing outcomes to habits of mind. We see this at work in the grades our students earned beyond the basic writing course—this course, emphasizing the *Framework*, really seems to have worked for our students, especially using a scaffolding model where the entire first-year writing sequence already uses the WPA OS as a guide. Second, habits of mind in the *Framework* provide a useful emphasis for basic writing students and for the basic writing curriculum; however, they are not as straightforward as other kinds of writing practices. Third, as Peter Khost suggests in chapter 9, assessments of habits of mind should be designed very carefully and robustly, examining not only after the fact reflective activity but also ongoing work in the course and thinking through individual habits of mind and their effects on writers. While these assessments will take considerable time, a deeper awareness both for our program—and for the broader field—may result.

More significantly, perhaps, as Johnson suggests, focusing on the habits of mind in our writing classes may lead to a reassessment of the work we do in the field; to a reconsideration of our roles as educators within the liberal arts tradition; and, ultimately, to a necessary questioning of higher education's "obsession with objective content, standardized assessment, and credentialing" (536). None of us questioned the role the habits of mind would play in our basic writers' success throughout the university curriculum, and, like Johnson, we already embraced James A. Berlin's edict that to teach writing is to teach "a way of responding to experience" (qtd. in Johnson 537). However, it was not until we encountered the challenges of assessing the role our curriculum had played in fostering these habits that we began to understand how much of the valuable work we do with student writers can never be fully institutionalized, regimented, or measured. Such an understanding allows us to imagine a curriculum where the first question we ask is not, "Will it work?" but, "Do we value it?" and then, "Is it important?"

As we continue to refine and develop our basic writing curriculum, we look forward to the conversations that the chapters in this collection will initiate among writing program administrators and to learning more about how best to incorporate, teach, and assess the habits of mind outlined in the *Framework*.

Works Cited

Allan, Elizabeth G., and Dana Lynn Driscoll. "The Three-Fold Benefit of Reflective Writing: Improving Program Assessment, Student Learning, and Faculty Professional Development." *Assessing Writing* 21 (2014): 37–55. Print.

Bartholomae, David, and Anthony Petrosky. *Facts, Artifacts and Counterfacts: Reading and Writing in Theory and Practice*. Portsmouth: Boynton/Cook, 1986. Print.

Braxton, John M., and Meaghan E. Mundy. "Powerful Institutional Levers to Reduce College Student Departure." *Journal of College Student Retention* 3.1 (2001): 91–118. Print

Catalog. Michigan State University Oakland. Rochester, MI. 1959–1960: n. pag. Print.

Costa, Arthur, and Bene Kallick. "Describing 16 Habits Of Mind." *ASCD Edge*. Association for Supervision and Curriculum Development, n.d. Web. 10 June 2014.

Council of Writing Program Administrators. "WPA Outcomes Statement For First-Year Composition." CWPA, 2014. PDF File.

Council of Writing Program Administrators, National Council of Teachers of English, and National Writing Project. *Framework for Success in Postsecondary Writing*. CWPA, NCTE, and NWP, 2011. PDF File.

Del Principe, Ann. "Paradigm Clashes Among Basic Writing Teachers: Sources of Conflict And a Call For Change." *Journal of Basic Writing* 23.1 (2004): 64–81. *Academic OneFile*. Web. 5 May 2015.

Driscoll, Dana Lynn. "Connected, Disconnected, or Uncertain: Student Attitudes About Future Writing Contexts and Perceptions of Transfer from First-Year Writing to the Disciplines." *Across the Disciplines* 8.2 (2011): n. pag. Web. 4 June 2015.

Driscoll, Dana Lynn and Jennifer Wells. "Beyond Knowledge and Skills: Writing Transfer and the Role of Student Dispositions." *Composition Forum* 26 (2012): n. pag. Web. 4 June 2015.

General Catalog. Rochester, MI: Oakland University, 1972–1973. Print.

Gorzelsky, Gwen, Dana Lynn Driscoll, Joe Pazcek, Carol Hayes, and Edmund Jones. "Metacognitive Moves in Learning to Write: Results from the Writing Transfer Project." *Critical Transitions: Writing and the Question of Transfer.* Ed. Jessie Moore and Chris Anson. (Forthcoming).

Gunner, Jeanne. "Iconic Discourse: The Troubling Legacy of Mina Shaughnessy." *Journal of Basic Writing* 17.2 (1998): 25–42. Print.

Johnson, Kristine. "Beyond Standards: Disciplinary and National Perspectives on Habits of Mind." *College Composition and Communication* 64.3 (2013): 517–41. Print.

Martinez, Joseph G. R., and Nancy C. Martinez. "Are Basic Writers Cognitively Deficient?" Paper presented at the Annual Meeting of the Western College Reading and Learning Association, Albuquerque, NM, 9–12 April 1987. ERIC. Web. 2 May 2015.

McComiskey, Bruce. "Bridging the Divide: The (Puzzling) *Framework* and the Transition from K–12 to College Writing Instruction." *Symposium: On the Framework for Success in Postsecondary Writing.* Spec. issue of *College English* 74.6 (2012): 537–40. Print.

O'Neill, Peggy, Linda Adler-Kassner, Cathy Fleischer, and Anne-Marie Hall. "Creating the *Framework For Success In Postsecondary Writing.*" *Symposium: On the Framework for Success in Postsecondary Writing.* Spec. issue of *College English* 74.6 (2012): 520–24. Print.

Perkins, David N., and Gavriel Salomon. "Knowledge to Go: A Motivational and Dispositional View of Transfer." *Educational Psychologist* 47.3 (2012): 248–58. Print.

Reiff, Mary Jo, and Anis Bawarshi. "Tracing Discursive Resources: How Students Use Prior Genre Knowledge to Negotiate New Writing Contexts in First-Year Composition." *Written Communication* 28.3 (2011): 312–37. Print.

Scott, Brianna M., and Matthew Levy. "Metacognition: Examining the Components of a Fuzzy Concept." *Educational Research* 2.2 (2013): 120–31. Print.

"Student Performance in WRT 102, 104, 150, and 160." Oakland University Office of Institutional Research and Assessment. Rochester, MI: Oakland University. 2010. Print.

Sullivan, Patrick. "Essential Habits Of Mind For College Readiness." *Symposium: On the Framework for Success in Postsecondary Writing.* Spec. issue of *College English* 74.6 (2012): 547–51. Print.

Summerfield, Judith, and Philip Anderson. "A Framework Adrift." *Symposium: On the Framework for Success in Postsecondary Writing.* Spec. issue of *College English* 74.6 (2012): 544–47. Print.

Wardle, Elizabeth "Understanding 'Transfer' from FYC: Preliminary Results of a Longitudinal Study." *WPA: Writing Program Administration* 31.1/2 (2007): 124–49. Print.

Webb-Sunderhaus, Sara. (2010). "When Access is Not Enough: Retaining Basic Writers at an Open-Admission University." *Journal of Basic Writing* 29 (2010): 97–116. Print.

Williams, James D., and Seiji Takaku. "Help Seeking, Self-Efficacy, and Writing Performance among College Students. *Journal of Writing Research* 3.1 (2011): 1–18. Print

Appendix: Reflection Rubric

Area	1	2	3	4	5
1a.–1c. Prewriting Revision Editing techniques	Student demonstrates no evidence of techniques; no discussion is present	Student briefly mentions techniques but provides little to no detail (e.g. "I did some prewriting.")	Student provides limited description of techniques; discussion may lack detail or skip areas	Student provides good description of techniques; most areas are clear and detailed	Student provides excellent, clear, step-by-step description of techniques
1d.–1e. Critical analysis of writing process choices and success.	Student demonstrates no evidence of critical analysis of choices or evaluation of success	Student provides brief analysis / evaluation ("it worked") but provides little to no detail validating choices / success	Student provides some analysis / evaluation with moderate amounts of detail; some information may be missing; may only focus on positive	Student provides good analysis of their process and overall success; provides details of challenges and successes	Student provides excellent analysis of process and overall success; can clearly evaluate their choices and understand challenges
2a. Evidence of understanding self and learning	Student demonstrates no understanding of self and learning processes over time	Student demonstrates slight understanding of self and strategies, but is missing any detail and/or discussion of change over time	Student demonstrates adequate understanding of self and strategies, provides some detail, but does not demonstrate a nuanced understanding	Student provides a detailed description of self and learning strategies and describes changes over time	Student provides a superior description of self and learning strategies, clearly describes changes over time, and is able to engage in critically reflects on change
2b. Evidence of habits of mind	Student demonstrates no evidence of effective habits of mind.	Student demonstrates slight evidence of one or two habits of mind, but no detail is given and/or student does not demonstrate success	Student provides limited description of positive habits of mind, with some detail, but information may be missing, may only focus on positive	Student provides good description of habits of mind, either one in detail or several in less detail	Student provides excellent analysis of habits of mind, including critical understanding of integrating habits of mind into learning processes

Bridging High School and College Writing 281

2c. Evidence of Transfer: Prior Knowledge	Student demonstrates no evidence of adapting prior knowledge	Student briefly mentions prior knowledge ("I knew about grammar from high school") but provides no specifics	Student briefly discusses use of prior knowledge ("I used MLA from high school in writing my current paper"); may lack detail on specifics	Student discusses the use of prior knowledge and ("I used MLA from high school and it helped me"	Student provides specific details of prior knowledge and evaluates the success of that adaptation ("I learned about MLA high school. I used it in this paper through X and Y")
2d. Evidence of transfer: Forward-reaching knowledge	Student demonstrates no evidence of adapting prior knowledge	Student briefly mentions knowledge transfer but provides no specifics ("I expect to use what I learned in the future")	Student briefly discusses where knowledge may transfer may lack detail on specifics ("I expect to use rhetoric in my future writing."	Student discusses specifically what and where knowledge will be used ("The concepts of rhetoric will be useful to me in upcoming assignments, including WRT150")	Student provides superior, clear and specific details of (I learned about the importance of audience, and in every paper I write in the future, including in WRT150, I will start by analyzing my audience.")
3a. Self-evaluation of strengths as a writer	Student does not critically evaluate his/her strengths as a writer.	Student very briefly evaluates his/her strengths, suggests he/she does not have any strengths, or over-exaggerates strengths	Student provides an adequate description of strengths as a writer, provides a cursory description of struggles and what he/she did to overcome them.	Student provides a good description of his/her weaknesses as a writer; describes strategies to overcome weaknesses and shows progress	Student provides a superior description of his/her weaknesses as a writer, clearly describes how he/she worked to overcome, and gauges what he/she has left to do
3b. Self-evaluation of weaknesses as a writer	Student does not critically evaluate his/her weaknesses as a writer.	Student very briefly evaluates his/her weaknesses, but does not provide specifics or how to overcome weaknesses.	Student provides an adequate description of weaknesses as a writer, provides a cursory description of struggles and what he/she did to overcome them.	Student provides a good description of his/her weaknesses as a writer; describes strategies to overcome weaknesses and shows progress	Student provides a superior description of his/her weaknesses as a writer, clearly describes how he/she worked to overcome, and gauges what he/she has left to do

Criterion	(Poor)	(Below Average)	(Average)	(Above Average)	(Superior)
3c. Self-evaluation of quality of learning about writing and rhetoric	Student does not critically evaluate learning about writing and rhetorical knowledge.	Student very briefly evaluates his/her learning about writing and rhetoric, but this is cursory and non-detailed	Student provides an adequate description of learning about writing and rhetoric, details and specific may be lacking	Student provides a good description of his/her learning about writing and rhetoric, will include some details	Student provides a superior description of his/her learning about writing and rhetoric; includes details and critical evaluation of said learning
3d. Self-evaluation of quality of learning about paper topic	Student does not describe learning about topic.	Student very briefly describes learning about topic, but does not provide any specifics.	Student briefly describes learning about topic, may provide limited specific details.	Student provides good description of topic, including specific details.	Student provides superior and detailed description of topic, may include how topic connects to other areas or impact topic had on student.
3e. Overall quality of reflection (non-cumulative, a holistic "grade")	Poor or unacceptable quality, student lacks detail and has not invested effort.	Below-average quality. Student has not provided details, has not supported claims with evidence from his/her practice, and does not cover many points.	Average quality reflection. Student provides information requested, but detail and further in-depth analysis may be lacking.	Above average reflection. Student provides clear details, describes learning and writing processes, and provides some critical analysis of strengths and weaknesses.	Superior reflection. Student is able to critically reflect upon his or her learning, writing processes, and provides honest and clear analysis of strengths and weaknesses.

Afterword

Andrea A. Lunsford

I am writing this afterword in December, 2015, in the wake of the Paris and San Bernardino attacks carried out by followers of ISIS and of the ongoing immigration crisis in Europe and beyond. Some people within the United States seem caught up in extreme fear, expressed in isolationism, Islamophobia, and other bigotries. Certainly there is call for caution and for vigilance, but extremists don't particularly like these words: they want to ban Muslims from entering the United States, to put certain people in internment camps, to refuse to accept any refugees from Syria and other countries. It's a very dispiriting time, here at the end of 2015, and it's hard to find examples of people thinking clearly and cogently, which is one reason I have been so drawn to the work of this volume that is dedicated to developing young people's abilities to think clearly and cogently—and creatively and ethically as well.

In 2010, when leaders of the National Council of Teachers of English (NCTE), the Council of Writing Program Administrators (CWPA), and the National Writing Project (NWP) came together to discuss the lack of input from the writing community in forming the Common Core State Standards (CCSS) and to respond to that lack not just with criticism but with a positive contribution, I followed along with enthusiasm and gratitude. The months of intense work that went into forming a task force and articulating principles and vetting them with teachers and scholars around the country led, in January 2011, to the release of the *Framework for Success in Postsecondary Writing*. I was immediately impressed with the entire effort, and especially with the habits of mind, which I think brilliantly capture the capacities we want to enable in our students and that speak forcefully, if indirectly, to some of the blind spots in the CCSS. The *Framework* garnered a lot of attention and spawned a series of responses. Almost all were positive, but a recurring theme began to emerge: while researchers around the country recognized the need for such a *Framework* and applauded its richly expansive and rhetorically-based understanding of how writing (and reading) develop, they also noted a concerning lack of specifics: how should the eight habits of mind be most effectively taught and developed? How should such development be assessed? How could the *Framework* be effectively applied across a range of situations and institutions?

Enter Nicholas Behm, Sherry Rankins-Robertson, and Duane Roen, the editors of *The Framework for Success in Postsecondary Writing: Scholarship and Applications*, a volume dedicated to providing answers to some of these questions. From Kristine Johnson's compelling opening essay, "Framing the Framework," to Marty Townsend's powerful chapter on how she uses the principles of the *Framework* in her first-year honors writing course, readers of this collection are immersed in vibrant and stimulating explorations of scholarly, theoretical, and practical applications of the *Framework*. We've also been privileged to listen to the voices of smart, caring teachers who work every day with the *Framework* (not to mention the CCSS) and, even better, to the voices of their students (I savored every word those La Vista students said in chapter 8, for instance). We've learned of ways to improve on the *Framework*, especially in terms of focusing on deep reading as well as on writing (as in chapters 3 and 4). We've seen how to align the *Framework* with the CCSS, as Lauren Ingraham discusses in chapter 11, and how to apply the *Framework* to high school and basic writing curricula (chapter 16). And much, much more.

The work in this volume, along with the full *Framework*, demonstrate how serious professional organizations like CWPA, NCTE, and NWP can mount a response to and an intervention into discussions of national educational policy. Bravo and brava to all involved in this endeavor. If we have hope of educating a generation of ethically engaged, creative, and persistent critical thinkers, this volume's exploration of the *Framework*'s principles and habits of mind will be at the forefront of helping us to do so.

Contributors

Linda Adler-Kassner is Associate Dean of Undergraduate Education and Professor of Writing Studies at University of California Santa Barbara. She works with students and faculty on issues related to writing and learning, often drawing on the Framework and on threshold concepts. Her most recent book, co-edited with Elizabeth Wardle, is *Naming What We Know: Threshold Concepts of Writing Studies*. Currently, she serves as the associate chair of the Conference on College Composition and Communication and is a past president of CWPA. She led the Council on Writing Program Administrators subcommittee that worked on *The Framework for Success in Postsecondary Writing*.

Nicholas N. Behm is Associate Professor of English at Elmhurst College in Elmhurst, Illinois. He studies composition pedagogy and theory, writing assessment, and critical race theory. He is a former member of the CWPA Executive Board and served on the committee charged with revising the CCCC Statement on Preparing Teachers of College Writing. With Greg Glau, Deborah Holdstein, Duane Roen, and Ed White, he is co-editor of *The WPA Outcomes Statement—A Decade Later*. He can be reached at <behmn@elmhurst.edu>.

Beth Brunk-Chavez is Dean of Extended University at the University of Texas at El Paso. She is also a professor of Rhetoric and Writing Studies and directed the First-Year Composition program for five years. Her research has been published in *Writing Program Administration*, *Composition Studies*, *Written Communication*, and several edited collections. Brunk-Chavez was named to the University of Texas System Academy of Distinguished Teachers in 2013. Her forthcoming book, *Retention, Persistence, and Writing Programs* is co-edited with Todd Ruecker, Heidi Estrem, and Dawn Shepard.

Ellen C. Carillo is Associate Professor of English at the University of Connecticut and the Writing Program Coordinator at its Waterbury Campus. She teaches undergraduate and graduate courses in composition and literature, and she is the author of *Securing a Place for Reading in Composition: The Importance of Teaching for Transfer*. Her scholarship has been published in numerous journals including *WLN: A Journal of Writing Center Scholarship*; *Rhetoric Review*; *Feminist Teacher*; *Currents in Teaching and Learning*; and in several edited collections. Ellen is co-founder of the Role of Reading in Composition Studies Special Interest Group of the CCCCs.

Angela Clark-Oates is Assistant Professor of English at California State University, Sacramento, where she teaches undergraduate and graduate courses focused on research methods, composition pedagogy, and teaching writing in high schools. Her research is focused on high school-to-college transition, writing program administration, composition pedagogy and theory, and theories of literacy and teacher identity. While at Arizona State University, she directed the Writers' Studio, an online composition program. She has published on a variety of topics including writing assessment and faculty writing groups. As a co-director for Central Arizona Writing Project's summer institute, she has also worked extensively with English teachers in high schools.

Dana Lynn Driscoll is Associate Professor of English at Indiana University of Pennsylvania, where she teaches in the Composition and TESOL doctoral program and directs the Composition & TESOL mentoring program. Her scholarly interests include writing centers, writing transfer, RAD research methodologies, writing across the curriculum, and writing assessment. Her work has appeared in journals such as *Writing Program Administration*, *Assessing Writing*, *Computers and Composition*, *Composition Forum*, *Writing Center Journal*, and *Teaching and Learning Inquiry*.

Andrea Feldman is Senior Instructor and International Student Coordinator in the Program for Writing and Rhetoric at Colorado University-Boulder. She holds a PhD in Cognitive Linguistics, specializing in Language Acquisition. Formerly Director of Curriculum at the Academy of Languages in Seattle, WA, she developed a teacher-training program, foreign language and translation service, and full-service ESL Center. Her publications and national conference presentations are in the areas of linguistics, second-language writing, and cross-cultural rhetoric. She is the founder and continues to coordinate the Program for Writing and Rhetoric's second language writing program in scientific and professional writing and first-year writing.

Cathy Fleischer is Professor of English at Eastern Michigan University, where she teaches courses in writing and writing pedagogy, and she co-directs the Eastern Michigan Writing Project. She writes and presents widely on teacher research, disciplinary literacies, advocacy, and writing pedagogy and is the author of NCTE's website *Everyday Advocacy* and the editor of NCTE's Principles in Practice Imprint. She led the NCTE Task Force that contributed to the creation and writing of the *Framework for Success in Postsecondary Writing*.

Anne-Marie Hall is Emeritus Faculty at the University of Arizona, where she was Director of the Writing Program, Director of the Southern Arizona Writing Project, and a member of the Rhetoric, Composition, and the Teaching of English Program in the Department of English. Her ethnographic research on comparative pedagogies, ecological literacies, and developmental writing has been published in *Journal of Basic Writing, Reflections, Journal of Bilingual Research,* and *College English*. She led the National Writing Project Task Force that contributed to the creation and writing of the *Framework for Success in Postsecondary Writing*.

Alice S. Horning is Professor of Writing and Rhetoric at Oakland University, where she holds a joint appointment in Linguistics. Her research, that spans her entire career, has focused on the intersection of reading and writing and the impact of students' reading difficulties. Her work has appeared in major professional journals and in books published by Parlor Press and Hampton Press. Her most recent book *Reconnecting Reading and Writing*, co-edited with Beth Kraemer, was published in 2013 by the WAC Clearinghouse and Parlor Press. Her forthcoming book *What is College Reading?* is co-edited with Cynthia Haller and Deborah-Lee Gollnitz.

Lauren S. Ingraham is Professor of English and Director of Composition at the University of Tennessee-Chattanooga. She teaches courses in composition theory, writing pedagogy for pre-service teachers, and grant writing. Her work has appeared in *Writing Program Administra-*

tion, *Composition Studies*, *The Promise and Peril of Writing Program Administration*, and *The Ethics of Writing Instruction*.

Kristine Johnson is Assistant Professor of English at Calvin College, where she directs the Written Rhetoric program and teaches courses in composition pedagogy, linguistics, and writing. She studied Rhetoric and Composition at Purdue University, and her work has also appeared in several journals, including *Rhetoric Review*, *College Composition and Communication*, and *Writing Program Administration*.

Alice Johnston Myatt is Assistant Professor and Assistant Chair of the Department of Writing and Rhetoric at the University of Mississippi. She teaches composition classes and is the academic coordinator of the minor in Professional Writing; she also chairs the planning team for the department's annual Transitioning to College Writing Symposium. Among her research interests are the intersections between writing program and writing center administration and assessment, the role of independent writing departments and programs in the field of writing studies, and the key characteristics of effective cross-institutional collaborations. She earned her PhD in English with a focus on Rhetoric and Composition from Georgia State University.

Peter H. Khost is Assistant Professor in Stony Brook University's writing program, where he has been associate director, assessment coordinator, and writing center director. He co-edited the collection *Collaborating(,) Literature(,) and Composition* (Hampton Press) and his articles have appeared in *Composition Forum*, *Pedagogy*, *JAEPL*, and *Journal of Educational Technology Systems*. Peter is founding chair of CWPA's Task Force on Publicizing the *Framework for Success* and founding editor of the *English Journal* column "Reframing Readiness." He won grants from CCCC and CWPA to study the *Framework*'s Habits of Mind. Peter's forthcoming book is *Rhetor Response: A Theory and Practice of Literary Affordances*.

Amy C. Kimme Hea is Associate Dean for Instruction and Associate Professor at the University of Arizona. Her scholarly interests include computers and composition, writing program administration, and technical communication. Her work has appeared in numerous edited collections and peer-reviewed journals. Her collection *Going Wireless: A Critical Exploration of Wireless and Mobile Technologies for Composition Teachers and Researchers* was nominated for the *Computers and*

Composition best book award, and her social media issue of *Technical Communication Quarterly* is the most widely read in that venue. She serves as chair of the Consortium of Doctoral Programs in Rhetoric and Composition.

Faith Kurtyka is an Assistant Professor of English at Creighton University in Omaha, Nebraska. Her research combines quantitative and qualitative methodology to research students' extracurricular literacies. Her work on sorority literacies has appeared in *Composition Forum*, *Literacy in Composition Studies*, *Across the Disciplines*, *Peitho*, and *Composition Studies*.

Amanda Laudig is Special Lecturer in the Department of Writing and Rhetoric at Oakland University where she teaches basic, first-year, and business writing as well as creative nonfiction. Her current research interests include classroom support for basic writers, strategies for teaching the personal essay, and first-person accounts of the longgrass prairie.

Andrea A. Lunsford is Professor Emerita of English at Stanford University. The Director of Stanford's Program in Writing and Rhetoric from 2000 through 2012, she has designed and taught courses in writing history and theory, rhetoric, literacy studies, and women's writing and is editor, author, or co-author of more than twenty books, including *Essays on Classical Rhetoric and Modern Discourse*, *Singular Texts/Plural Authors*, *Reclaiming Rhetorica*, *Everything's an Argument*, *The Sage Handbook of Rhetorical Studies*, *Writing Together*, and *Everyone's an Author*. A long-time member of the Bread Loaf School of English faculty, she is currently at work on *The Norton Anthology of Rhetoric and Writing*.

Peggy O'Neill is Professor of Writing at Loyola University Maryland, where she teaches writing and rhetoric classes. She has also served as Director of Composition and Chair of the Writing Department. Her scholarship focuses on writing assessment, pedagogy, and disciplinary issues. She was the chair of the NCTE task force that drafted the *Framework for Success in Postsecondary Writing*.

Dawn S. Opel is Assistant Professor in the Department of Writing, Rhetoric, and American Cultures at Michigan State University. She also is a researcher with WIDE (Writing, Information, and Digital

Experience) and for a research center in the MSU College of Arts & Letters and teaches courses in Experience Architecture (XA), rhetoric, and professional writing. She is a former public interest lawyer and her research interests include health and medical rhetoric and the ethical design of communication. Her recent work has appeared in *Connexions: International Professional Communication Journal*; *Kairos: A Journal of Rhetoric, Technology, and Pedagogy*; and *Transformative Works and Cultures*.

Lori Ostergaard is Associate Professor and Chair of the Department of Writing and Rhetoric at Oakland University in Rochester, Michigan. She is a former member of the CCCC Executive Committee and served on the committee charged with revising the CCCC Statement on Preparing Teachers of College Writing. Her co-edited collections include *Transforming English Studies: New Voices in an Emerging Genre*; *Writing Majors: Eighteen Program Profiles*; and *In the Archives of Composition: Writing and Rhetoric in High Schools and Normal Schools*. Her work has also appeared in *Rhetoric Review*, *Composition Studies*, *Composition Forum*, *Studies in the Humanities*, and *Peitho*.

Jenna Pack Sheffield is Assistant Professor of English and the Coordinator of Writing Across the Curriculum at the University of New Haven. Her research interests include multimodal composing, writing program administration, and professional writing pedagogy. Her recent research has appeared in *Computers and Composition International*; *NANO: New American Notes Online*; and *College English*.

Rebecca Powell is Assistant Professor of English at the University of Southern Mississippi. Her research interests include adolescent writing experiences, K–16 writing pedagogy, community literacy, and place studies. Her studies and reviews have appeared in *A Guide to Composition Pedagogies*; *Environmental Rhetorics and the Ecologies of Place*; *Teaching English in the Two Year College*; and *Xchanges*.

Sherry Rankins-Robertson is Associate Professor of Rhetoric and Writing at the University of Arkansas at Little Rock (UALR). She has served as Associate Vice Chancellor of Academic Affairs and Writing Program Administrator at UALR. Her research and publications explore designing writing assignments to respond to the national learning outcomes, developing curriculum and assessing learning in online environments, offering instruction to incarcerated writers, and using multimodal instruction. Recently, she was one of the co-editors of *WPA: Writing Program Administrator*. She is currently working on an edited collection with Joe Lockard titled *Prison Pedagogy: Teaching and Learning with Imprisoned Writers*. Her publications have appeared in *The Journal of Writing Assessment*; *Kairos: A Journal of Rhetoric, Technology, and Pedagogy*; *Computers and Composition*; *Academe*; *WPA: Writing Program Administration*; and *Journal of Basic Writing* and include nearly a dozen book chapters. She can be reached at sjrobertson@ualr.edu.

Rodrigo Joseph Rodríguez is Assistant Professor of Literacy and English Education in the Department of English at The University of Texas at El Paso, which is located in the borderlands across from Ciudad Juárez, Chihuahua, México. He has taught English and Spanish language arts in public schools and at various levels in higher education. His research interests include academic writing pedagogy, children's and young adult literatures, and socially responsible biliteracies. Catch him virtually @escribescribe

Duane Roen is Professor of English at Arizona State University, where he serves as Dean of the College of Integrative Sciences and Arts, Dean of University College, and Vice Provost. Duane has written about writing across the curriculum; writing curricula, pedagogy, and assessment, among other topics. His books include *Views from the Center: The CCCC Chairs' Addresses, 1977–2005*; *The WPA Outcomes Statement: A Decade Later* (with Nicholas Behm, Greg Glau, Deborah Holdstein, and Edward White); and *The McGraw-Hill Guide: Writing for College, Writing for Life* (with Greg Glau and Barry Maid). He can be reached at <duane.roen@asu.edu>.

Cathy Rorai is Special Lecturer in the Department of Writing and Rhetoric at Oakland University in Rochester, Michigan, where she teaches first-year writing courses including basic writing. She began her teaching career as a high school teacher where she had a long career teaching developmental to advanced writing. Her interest in the transition that student writers make from high school to college writing led to her personal transition from high school to college writing instructor.

Ellen Shelton is Director of the University of Mississippi Writing Project and the Executive Director of Pre-College Programs for the

Division of Outreach. She teaches classes for English, Linguistics, and for Writing and Rhetoric. Her research interests include curricular support for academic writing in the secondary classroom and student transition to post-secondary education.

Martha (Marty) Townsend is Professor Emerita of English at the University of Missouri and former Director of its internationally renowned Campus Writing Program. Her publications have played a central role in the conceptualization and development of writing-across-the-curriculum programs in the United States and abroad. She is a former literacy consultant to the Ford Foundation and consults widely on WAC program implementation, development, and assessment.

Kenneth C. Walker is Assistant Professor of English: Rhetoric and Composition at the University of Texas, San Antonio. His research has been published in *Technical Communication Quarterly*, *Journal of Business and Technical Communication*, *Rhetoric Review*, *Environmental Humanities*, and *POROI*, as well as a number of edited collections. He has also worked as an assessment coordinator and writing in the disciplines specialist, and he is broadly interested in the ways writing and communication can be used to improve educational outcomes.

Index

360-degree evaluations, 99

academic discourse, 115
academic dissensus, 141
academic freedom, 136, 171, 176
accountability, 3, 5–6, 17, 140
accuracy, 65, 105
Adler-Kassner, Linda, ix, xxxii, 4–5, 18–20, 36, 95, 100, 108, 111, 116, 136, 138–139, 150, 152, 169, 182, 191, 203, 220, 262, 278
Alexander, Jonathan, xviii, xix
American Council of Research Libraries (ACRL), xii
Anson, Chris M., 144, 150, 196, 202, 278
appropriateness, 43, 65, 144
Arizona State University, 226
articulation theory, xxv, 22–23, 26, 29
assessment, xviii, xxii, xxv, 9, 14, 22, 25, 29–30, 32, 34–35, 75, 77–78, 118, 133, 139, 143, 172, 189, 237, 258, 260, 263, 268–270, 274, 275–276; writing, 5–6, 24, 141
Association of College and Research Libraries, 67
audience, 3, 71–72, 75, 78–79, 83, 102, 123, 127, 129, 130, 133–134, 162, 173–175, 180, 192, 198, 239, 245, 247–252, 265–266, 268
authority, xiv, xxiii, xxviii, 11, 65, 110, 125, 128, 146, 176, 212, 214–215, 231

Bakhtin, Mikhail, 235
Bartholomae, David, 39, 52, 239, 255, 261, 277
basic writing, xviii, xxx, 51, 257–277, 284
basic writing curriculum, xviii, 257–258, 261–262, 264–265, 276, 277
Bawarshi, Anis, 91, 101, 121, 134, 266, 278
Bazerman, Charles, 60–61, 67
Behm, Nicholas, xxi, xxiii, xxx–xxxi, 22, 35, 167, 190, 284
Beliefs about the Teaching of Writing (NCTE), 206, 211, 220
Berlin, James A., 13, 19, 276
Berthoff, Ann, 39, 42–43, 45, 52
best practices, xxix, 34, 98, 169, 171–172, 177, 196, 198, 200, 257, 260
bias, 28, 65, 70, 72–73, 75–77, 84, 205, 252
Bizzell, Patricia, 41, 52
Bourdieu, Pierre, xxvii, 119–121, 135
Broad, Bob, 31–32, 35, 182
Bruffee, Kenneth, 41, 52

293

Brunk-Chavez, Beth, xviii, xxviii, 154, 255
budget, 24
Burke, Kenneth, 247, 255

Callaway, Micheal, 156, 167
Carillo, Ellen, xiv, xxv, 38, 52, 54, 110
CCCC: Role of Reading in Composition (SIG), 55
CCCC research grant, 145
Celebration of Student Writing (CSW), 108
civic engagement, 17, 109
Clark-Oates, Angela, xvi, xxi, xxii, xxix, xxxi, 29, 86, 187, 222, 226, 236, 265
coders, 105
collaboration, xiii, xv, xvi, xxii, xxvii, xxix, 28, 71, 170, 188, 192
college and career readiness, x, xi, xxiv, 3, 9, 138, 190, 197
College Board: ACT, 55, 56, 58, 67, 266, 269; AP exams, 141; SAT, 57, 141, 149, 152
college readiness, ix, xxii, xxiii, xxviii, 3, 132, 136, 137, 138, 139, 142, 146, 147, 148, 149, 150, 189, 190, 211, 213, 257, 276
college reading, 38, 39
Common Core State Standards (CCSS), ix, x, xi, xiv, xvi, xxi, xxii, xxiii, xxviii, xxxi, xxxii, 3, 4, 9, 13, 18, 19, 38, 119, 137, 138, 140, 141, 149, 150, 151, 152, 169, 170, 171, 172, 173, 179, 182, 188, 189, 191, 192, 193, 195, 196, 203, 206, 220, 236, 283, 284
community circulation, 119
competency, xxvi, 144
competency-based programs, 141
Conference on College Composition and Communication (CCCC), ix, xix, xxi, 55, 145, 148, 151, 191
consensus, xxviii, xxix, 78, 90, 100, 139, 147, 148, 169, 270
conventions, 71, 72, 75, 76, 77, 80, 92, 162, 174, 175, 197, 210, 218, 254, 262, 266
creative writing, 25, 85, 125, 127, 130, 213
creativity, xi, xxiv, 14, 38, 45, 55, 72, 75, 77, 79, 96, 97, 119, 125, 126, 127, 143, 144, 149, 157, 174, 189, 198, 199, 224, 229, 232, 233, 235, 258, 263, 264, 267
credibility, 28, 33, 79, 244
crisis-callers, 139
critical sustained reflection, xxix, 223, 224, 225, 228, 235
critical thinking, xxii, xxvi, xxx, xxxi, 15, 61, 71, 79, 157, 159, 164, 173, 174, 197, 245, 246, 249, 251, 257, 262
Culham, Ruth, 204, 213, 220
cultural discourse, 79
currency, 4, 65
CWPA research grant, 145

decontextualized writing assignments, 261
deliberate learning, 223
Denny, Harry, 137, 151
descriptive codes, 89
Dewey, John, 207, 225, 228, 229, 236
digital environments, 48, 195
digital modes, 65
disciplinarity, 94
disciplinary consensus, 142
discursive, 22, 34
Donahue, Patricia, 39, 42, 43, 47, 53
Downs, Douglas, 16, 20, 93, 101

Driscoll, Dana, xxx, 29, 111, 120, 121, 135, 154, 257, 258, 266, 269, 274, 277, 278
dual enrollment, 170
dynamic criteria mapping, xxv, 31

education, general, 15, 32, 86, 95
Educational Testing Service, 47, 82, 138
efficacy in writing, 129
Ehman, Christa, 156, 168
Eidman-Aadahl, Elyse, ix
Elbow, Peter, 48, 52, 140, 151
English Journal, 149, 152
English Language Learning (ELL), xvi, 69, 70, 71, 72, 73, 74, 77
English Language Testing System test (IELTS), 71
English proficiency, 76
epistemology, 217
error, 72, 178, 261
ethos, 77, 79, 174, 245
Experiences with Writing, Reading, and Critical Analysis, 194

Feldman, Andrea, xvi, xxvi, 69, 218
first-year composition, xvi, xviii, xxiii, xxix, xxx, 24, 85, 86, 88, 89, 90, 91, 92, 93, 94, 95, 96, 97, 98, 99, 117, 155, 170, 171, 172, 176, 188, 191, 197, 198, 225, 226, 227, 238, 240, 241, 243, 245, 249, 252, 254, 258, 279
first-year writing, 34, 48, 58, 70, 71, 72, 73, 74, 77, 91, 101, 145, 146, 154, 171, 197, 257, 259, 262, 274, 276
first-year writing curriculum, 262
first-year writing program, 154, 259; funding, 25, 139, 170, 179, 180, 181

Fleischer, Cathy, ix, xxxii, 4, 20, 36, 116, 136, 152, 169, 182, 191, 203, 220, 262, 278
Flower, Linda, 39, 52
format, 63, 112, 193, 196, 267, 268
formation, xxvii, 10, 11, 12, 13, 17, 18, 114, 120, 126, 134, 198, 218

Gates Foundation, 180
genre, 83, 89, 91, 92, 95, 121, 123, 125, 126, 127, 173, 174, 175, 185, 200, 243, 244, 248
genre theory, 89, 92, 95
Gere, Anne Ruggles, 41, 52
goals, xv, xviii, xxiii, xxiv, 18, 22, 23, 26, 28, 29, 30, 34, 48, 55, 63, 88, 91, 92, 94, 95, 102, 113, 129, 131, 142, 155, 156, 158, 164, 167, 192, 193, 197, 199, 201, 228, 253, 257, 260, 261, 262, 264, 268, 269, 271
Google Sites, 227
grammar, 17, 76, 78, 141, 196, 260, 261
grammatical errors, 77, 80
Gunner, Jeanne, 21, 35, 37, 261, 278

habitus, xxvii, 119, 120, 121, 125, 126, 132, 133, 134
Hall, Anne Marie, ix, xxxii, 4, 20, 23, 35, 36, 116, 136, 152, 169, 182, 191, 203, 220, 262, 278
Hansen, Kristine, xvi, xix, xxiii, xxxii, 17, 19, 118, 126, 134, 135
Harvard University, 18, 236
Haswell, Richard, xvi, xix, 145, 151
heuristic, xxix, 120
Hewett, Beth, 156, 168
Hewlett Foundation, 180, 182

high school teachers, ix, 170, 190, 191, 192, 193, 253
high-stakes assessments, 137
honors composition course, xxx, 24, 30, 237, 238, 241, 243, 247, 254, 284
Horner, Bruce, 22, 36, 80, 82, 108, 116
Horning, Alice S., xiv, xxvi, 38, 39, 51, 53, 54, 60, 68, 110
Howard, Rebecca Moore, 46, 53, 58, 68, 153

ideology, 4, 6, 12, 23, 81, 148
idiomatic expressions, 75
Illinois Online Network (ION), 157
information literacy, xii, xxvi, 58, 64
Information Literacy Competency Standards for Higher Education, 65, 67
Ingraham, Lauren S., xvi, xxviii, 136, 147, 151, 169, 188, 284
inquiry, xvi, 14, 26, 31, 33, 34, 40, 71, 173, 189, 194, 195, 198, 207, 208, 219, 223, 229, 235
institutional retention data, 258
intellectual growth, 17
interactive design, 159
interactive learning environment, 164
interdisciplinary, xxvii
international students, 69, 71, 73, 75, 78, 79, 80, 81
intertextual references, 60
invention, 98, 173, 189, 198

Johnson, Kristine, ix, xiv, xxv, 3, 19, 20, 52, 104, 115, 116, 119, 135, 143, 144, 151, 154, 156, 168, 171, 172, 180, 182, 209, 221, 258, 264, 274, 276, 278, 284

Johnston Myatt, Alice, xxix, 86, 179, 187, 224

kairos, 174
Khost, Peter H., ix, xiv, xvi, xviii, xxviii, 4, 115, 136, 139, 151, 166, 171, 199, 224, 276
Kimme Hea, Amy, xv, xxv, 21, 23, 36, 154, 264
Kurtyka, Faith, xvii, xxvii, 102

Laudig, Amanda, xxx, 29, 111, 154, 257
learning narratives, 104, 105, 267
legislators, xxxi, 21, 179, 248, 253
liberal arts, 10, 12, 16, 118, 250, 264, 276
linguistics, 85, 87, 88
listen rhetorically, 244
literacy, xv, xvi, xxi, xxv, xxvii, 28, 39, 47, 48, 57, 58, 65, 93, 142, 156, 188, 204, 206, 227, 231, 260
literate practices, xxviii
literature, 25, 44, 47, 54, 63, 85, 87, 88, 177, 217, 218, 225, 231, 243
Lu, Min-Zhan, 82, 180
Lumina Foundation, 180
Lunsford, Andrea, 20, 283

Malenczyk, Rita, 138, 152
Matsuda, Paul, 69, 82
McComiskey, Bruce, xxiii, xxxii, 9, 20, 118, 135, 171, 182, 201, 202, 263, 278
meta-awareness, 86, 91
metacognitive persistence, 206, 207, 210, 212, 215, 218, 219
metacognitive spaces, 89, 91, 93
metacognitive, metacognition, xvii, xxii, 43, 49, 50, 77, 81, 86, 88, 89, 91, 93, 95, 164, 178, 204, 205, 206, 207, 210, 212, 215,

218, 219, 258, 265, 266, 268, 274
metagenre, 94
meta-moments, 92, 93
MLA (Modern Language Association), 151
Mountford, Roxanne, 108, 116
multilingual writers, 211
multimodal, 27, 28, 48, 97, 194, 200, 233, 261
multimodality, 97

Nation at Risk, A x, xix, 13, 20
National Assessment of Educational Progress (NAEP), 57, 58, 67, 68
National Association of Student Personnel Administrators (NASPA), 102
National Center for Education Statistics, 68, 140, 152
National Commission on Writing, 201, 203
National Survey on Student Engagement (NSSE), 104, 116
native-speaking students (NSS), 69
new media, 23, 224, 225, 226
new media projects, 224, 225
No Child Left Behind Act, 3, 119
Nolan, Katherine, 190
Nowacek, Rebecca, 86, 91, 101

Oakland University, xxx, 257, 258, 261, 262, 278
objectives, 26, 156, 172, 173, 194, 199, 271
Oblinger, Diane, 156, 168
online writing, xviii, xxviii, 154, 155, 156, 158, 159, 162, 163, 166, 167
Opel, Dawn, xvii, xxvi, 85
organizational identity, 107
Ostergaard, Lori, xviii, xxx, 29, 111, 154, 257

Partnership for Assessment of Readiness for College and Careers (PARCC), 137

pedagogy, xvii, xxvi, xxviii, xxix, 42, 44, 62, 70, 85, 88, 90, 99, 137, 138, 141, 142, 144, 156, 189, 194, 198, 200, 205, 206, 208, 209, 219, 222, 224, 243, 245, 257, 258, 259
peer review, 28, 70, 71, 74, 75, 76, 103, 194, 224, 234, 239, 240, 258, 268
Perelman, Les, 141, 152
persuasion, 184
Pew Research Center, 57
Phelps, Louise Wetherbee, 21, 36
Piaget, Jean, 207
placement, 137, 149, 266
Plato, 18
Porter, James, 22, 33, 35, 36, 37
portfolios, 149, 176, 269, 270, 271
Powell, Rebecca, xvi, xxvii, 118
PowerPoint, 87, 97, 123, 244
praxis, xv, xxv, xxvi, 21, 22, 23, 35, 147, 199
preservice teachers, xvii, xxix, 204, 205, 206, 207, 208, 209, 211, 212, 213, 214, 215, 216, 218
Prezi, 97, 244
Princeton Review, 6
program: agency, 23, 26, 29, 32, 33, 34
Project Information Literacy, 58, 65
purpose, xiv, xxiii, 3, 7, 9, 11, 12, 15, 30, 34, 65, 70, 102, 162, 173, 174, 184, 185, 187, 193, 198, 200, 209, 210, 238, 243, 245, 248, 251, 253, 255, 265
quality enhancement plan (QEP), 187, 189, 197

Qualley, Donna, 40, 53

Race to the Top, 179, 182, 183
Rankins-Robertson, Sherry, xxi, xxx, xxxi, 190, 284
rearticulation, 22, 23, 29, 30, 31
recursive process, 174, 222, 265
reflective habits, 223, 225
Reiff, Mary Jo, 121, 134, 266, 278
relevancy, 65
research: primary, 199
retention, 12, 260, 261, 267, 268, 270, 273
revision, curriculum, 222, 223
rhetoric and composition, xxvii, xxviii, xxix, xxxi, 3, 13, 15, 25, 85, 87, 88, 92, 96, 110, 119, 120, 137, 139, 140, 177, 218, 227, 239, 248
rhetoric, composition, 149
rhetorical awareness, xvii, 130, 219
rhetorical common denominator, xxviii, 137, 142, 148, 149
rhetorical exigence, 14
rhetorical knowledge, xxvi, xxx, 28, 61, 71, 79, 118, 174, 201, 245, 249, 257, 262, 265
rhetorical practice, 72, 174
Rhodes, Jacqueline, xviii, xix
Rockefeller Philanthropy Advisors, 170
Rodríguez, Rodrigo Joseph, xvii, xxix, 70, 204
Roen, Duane, xxi, xxiii, xxx, xxxi, xxxii, 167, 190, 226, 236, 242, 255, 284
Rorai, Cathy, xxx, 29, 111, 154, 257
Rose, Mike, 32, 36, 37, 87, 101, 241, 244, 246, 247, 256; *The Mind at Work*, 241, 244, 246
Rosenblatt, Louise, 44, 45, 53
Roth, Michael, 54, 55, 63, 68
rubric, 30, 227, 269, 270, 274, 275

Salvatori, Mariolina, 39, 42, 43, 47, 53
scaffolding, 70, 86, 116, 165, 200, 212, 234, 254, 276
second language acquisition, 61
Second-Language Writing (SLW), 71, 73
Selfe, Richard, 194, 195, 203
self-efficacy, 123, 124, 125, 145
Shaughnessy, Mina, 278
Sheffield, Jenna Pack, xv, xxv, 21, 154, 264
Shelton, Ellen, xvi, xxix, 86, 179, 187, 224
showcase, 103, 175
Smarter Balanced Assessment Consortium (SBAC), 137
social media, xi, 81, 97
social networking, 131
social sphere, 119
standardization, 5, 260
standards, xii, xviii, xxi, 3, 4, 5, 6, 29, 124, 137, 140, 141, 142, 148, 149, 169, 171, 197
standards-based education, 119, 120
strategic essentialism, 142
student learning outcomes, xv, 26, 27, 28, 29, 33
Survey of Online Learning, 155
symposium, 166, 191, 192, 193, 194, 195, 196, 201
syntactical errors, 75
systematic reflection, 222, 225, 235

teacher-action researcher, 208
technology, 28, 34, 97, 120, 156, 161, 173
Test of English as a Foreign Language (TOEFL), 71, 82
texts, multimodal, 27
The Citation Project, 46, 53, 68

The WPA Outcomes Statement: A Decade Later, 167
tone, 42, 43, 75, 174, 229
Townsend, Martha, xviii, xxx, 13, 237, 284
transfer understood as recontextualization, 91
translingual approach, 80, 81

United States of America, x, xix, 20, 68, 69, 82, 86, 101, 119, 135, 167, 183, 283
University of Arizona, 24
University of Colorado at Boulder, 70, 71, 72, 73, 74, 75
University of Illinois, 168, 240
University of Mississippi, xxix, 187, 188, 190, 197, 199, 203
University of Mississippi Writing Project, 190
University of Texas at El Paso, 183, 207
University of Washington in Seattle, 58

voice, xi, 61, 76, 79, 110, 138, 141, 143, 212, 231, 268
Vygotsky, Lev, 207

WAC (writing-across-curriculum), 67, 92, 93
Walker, Kenneth C., xv, xxv, 21, 154, 264
Wardle, Elizabeth, 16, 20, 93, 101, 115, 117, 266, 279
Warnock, Scott, 161, 163, 168
Webb-Sunderhaus, Sara, 262, 267, 279
Wenger, Etienne, ix, xix
Wenger-Trayner, Etienne, xi, xii

What Is College-Level Writing?, 140
WID (writing-in-the disciplines), 92, 93
Wilson, Maja, 148, 153
Wordpress, 227
WPA: Writing Program Administration (journal), 26, 35, 36, 37, 68, 101, 150, 151, 279
WPA Task Force, 145
writerly choices, 45
writing: family, 119
writing across the curriculum, 67, 92, 93, 237
writing centers, 188, 189, 193, 196, 197, 200, 202
writing fellows, 225, 227, 228, 230, 231, 232, 233, 235
writing preparation, 138
writing process, xxx, 45, 71, 80, 94, 97, 98, 118, 124, 133, 173, 174, 178, 196, 201, 209, 212, 214, 257, 262, 264, 265, 272, 275
writing program administration, 22, 197
Writing Program Outcomes Statement for First-Year Composition, xi, xiii, xv, xix, xxx, xxxi, 17, 19, 27, 31, 35, 55, 67, 144, 150, 156, 157, 168, 174, 182, 188, 191, 197, 199, 200, 202, 237, 238, 244, 245, 248, 254, 255, 262, 264, 276, 277
Writing Studies, xv, 28, 91, 151, 221
writing, reading, and critical analysis experiences, x, 194, 200, 258
writing-about-writing curriculum, 92, 93

www.ingramcontent.com/pod-product-compliance
Lightning Source LLC
Chambersburg PA
CBHW021647230426
43668CB00008B/545